THE NEGRO IN BRAZILIAN SOCIETY

INSTITUTE OF
LATIN AMERICAN STUDIES
Columbia University

FLORESTAN FERNANDES

The Negro
in Brazilian Society

TRANSLATED BY
Jacqueline D. Skiles, A. Brunel,
and Arthur Rothwell

EDITED BY PHYLLIS B. EVELETH

1969

Columbia University Press
New York and London

Copyright © 1969 Columbia University Press

Library of Congress Catalog Card Number: 78–76247

Printed in the United States of America

This work is dedicated to my mother, Maria Fernandes; my wife, Myrian Rodrigues Fernandes; and my children, Heloísa Rodrigues Fernandes Pinto, Noêmia Rodrigues Fernandes, Beatriz Rodrigues Fernandes, Sylvia Rodrigues Fernandes, Florestan Fernandes Junior, and Myrian Lúcia Rodrigues Fernandes.

The Institute of Latin American Studies of Columbia University was established in 1961 in response to a national, public, and educational need for a better understanding of the nations of Latin America and a more knowledgeable basis for inter-American relations. The major objectives of the Institute are to prepare a limited number of North Americans for scholarly and professorial careers in the field of Latin American studies, to advance our knowledge of Latin America through an active program of research by faculty, by graduate students, and by visiting scholars, and to improve public knowledge through publication of a series of books on Latin America. Some of these studies are the result of research by the faculty, by graduate students, and by visiting scholars. It was also decided to include in this series translations from Portuguese and Spanish of important contemporary books in the social sciences and humanities.

The Negro in Brazilian Society by Florestan Fernandes is a translation of *A Integração do Negro na Sociedade de Classes*, which was first published in Brazil in 1965 in two volumes. The English translation for the Institute series which was done by Jacqueline D. Skiles, Arianne Brunel, and Arthur Rothwell has been somewhat abridged from the Portuguese edition. Such abridgments were made by Dr. Phyllis B. Eveleth, a professional anthropologist who lived and studied in Brazil for almost ten years. We believe that the passages omitted do not in any way modify the thinking or point of view of Dr. Fernandes and make his book more easily understandable to the English-speaking public. The translation of this book was begun in 1965–1966 while Professor Fernandes was a Visiting Scholar at the Institute of Latin American Studies, but the completion of the translation and the process of editing had to be done at a distance, and by correspondence, so that Professor Fernandes has not been able to provide his constant advice on translation and editing. If we have in any way distorted his thought or omitted passages which he feels are of great importance, we apologize and take full responsibility.

The faculty and staff of the Institute feel that this is a most important and timely book. Despite its title, the book does not take all of Brazil into its scope; rather it focuses upon Brazil's richest state, namely São Paulo, and upon the dynamic metropolitan city of the same name. Why this is important is explained by Professor Fernandes in his Preface for this edition. More important, Professor Fernandes's book is made available to us in the United States when basic documents in Afro-American studies are so badly needed and we hope so much appreciated. No study of the experience of the people of African origin in the New World can ignore Brazil. We think that this book is a modern Brazilian classic.

The publication program of the Institute of Latin American Studies is made possible by the financial assistance of the Ford Foundation. The translation of this book by Professor Fernandes was financed by a grant to the Columbia University Press from the Committee on Latin American Translations of the Association of American University Presses. The Rockefeller Foundation supported the Committee's work financially.

FOREWORD

It is a rather special pleasure for me to be allowed to write a foreword to Florestan Fernandes's major book and his first full-length volume to appear in my language. He is today one of the most theoretically influential and seminal sociologists in South America. His thought is complex; thus his prose is not easy to translate into another language. And even his prose in Brazilian Portuguese is not easily understood by the poor outlander such as I, who learned that language at a late date in life. But Florestan (in Brazil one who is famous is generally referred to by his first name only) is a man of intellect whom we must know by his writings and as a personality.

I forget just when I met Florestan for the first time. It must have been between 1942 and 1944. My colleague and mentor, Herbert Baldus, had been telling of a brilliant young man who was his student at the School of Sociology and Politics in São Paulo. This young scholar was working with the historical chronicles on the Tupinambá, the coastal Indians of Brazil who are now extinct but who profoundly influenced Brazilian national culture. His first book, *The Social Organization of the Tupinambá*, which was an M.A. essay written under Baldus's supervision, won a prize for the best book on a Brazilian theme in 1948. His second book, *The Social Function of Warfare among the Tupinambá*, which was his doctoral dissertation at the University of São Paulo, established his reputation as an important ethnohistorian. Obviously, as an ethnologist studying Brazilian Indians, I had to meet the man himself—and so I did. Thus began a long and fruitful friendship which we shared with Alfred Metraux (who had written two earlier books on the Tupinambá) and with Herbert Baldus.

In Brazil, however, social science disciplines were not, at least in those days, parochial and separated. I thought of Florestan as an ethnohistorian. He thought of himself as a sociologist. Florestan studied with Roger Bastide, Fernando de Azevedo, and others at the University of São Paulo. He read widely in the sociological literature of Europe and of the United States. So, in 1953, he wrote a book entitled *An Essay on the Functionalist Interpretation of Sociology*. It was in this book that he established his theoretical position and his real field of interest. I think that he was deeply influenced by Robert Merton, but French sociology was still present in his thought. As he explains in the Preface to the present book, he is a functionalist-historian with a strong feeling of the necessity for an active participation or influence in the society in which he lives. He has written in the fields of educational sociology, the sociology of economic development, political sociology, and social stratification and race relations. He is perhaps the most prolific and imaginative writer in modern Brazilian social science.

Florestan Fernandes is also a great teacher. He began teaching at the Faculty of Philosophy of the University of São Paulo in 1945 and became a Full Professor (Profesor catedráctico) only in 1955. In 1965, he gained tenure as a "catedrático" through a defense of a thesis which is the text of this book. In these years of teaching, he has created what might be called a "São Paulo school" of sociology. Among his students have been Fernando Henrique Cardoso, Octavio Ianni, Marialice Foracchi, and a dozen other Brazilian sociologists. He has influenced and befriended innumerous graduate students from the United States doing research in Brazil—all of whom will recognize their indebtedness to Florestan when they read this foreword. Perhaps I should list some of them—Warren Dean, Robert Shirley, Robert Levine, Joseph Love, Shephard Forman, Maxine Margolis, and so many others that I have trouble remembering. He must have done as much for European students who came to Brazil to study and to do research.

Finally, I must make it clear that Florestan is thoroughly Brazilian. He never studied abroad but only in Brazil, although some of his teachers were French, North American, or German trained. He was born in 1920 in the city of São Paulo of immigrant parents from Portugal. He began his life in very modest circumstances. (He worked in a restaurant during college days just as I did.) He is married and has six children—and at an early age he in now a grandfather. He lives in a suburban district of São Paulo called "Brooklyn Paulista" in a comfortable house without ostentation. When I last saw him in 1969, he was preoccupied with the problems of São Paulo students and student movements. He was still interested more than ever in race problems in Brazil, in the United States, and in the world. It has been a pleasure to write a foreword to Florestan's book, but it has been a real reward to have shared his intellectual life and to have his personal friendship.

New York, 1969 *Charles Wagley*

PREFACE TO THE U.S. EDITION

The observation that Brazil is a melting pot of races and cultures has become a commonplace. However, the various aspects of this melting pot, whose task of fusion is far from complete and which functions differently in each region of the country, have not yet been brought into proper perspective.

This book offers the principal conclusions reached after a sociological investigation into the contact between Negroes and whites in the city of São Paulo. The city in question is important not so much because of its history under the slave system but because of its role in the emergence of urban-industrial civilization in Brazil and because of its future, for it is the only Brazilian city with an economic, social, and cultural background capable of providing the energy to develop an open-class society.

From this standpoint São Paulo is representative in the study of race relations in Brazil's industrializing society. After the breakdown of slavery the Negro and the mulatto found in this city neither the refuge provided by subsistence economy (which equalizes whites and Negroes in a rural world partially excluded from the legal and political systems of the national society) nor the ambiguities of traditional paternalism (which persist to varying degrees even in larger cities, where the legacy of the Portuguese-Brazilian colonial world still has some effect). They found themselves confronting the white man while burdened not only with the demands of a competitive society, in which they were disadvantaged by their lack of social preparation for free employment, the market economy, and the urban style of life, but also with the limitations stemming from deeply rooted restrictive or negative attitudes. These burdens created various forms of racial prejudice and discrimination (based on color) that consequently forced the Negro and the mulatto into a marginal position in the competitive social order.

Thus the reasons that make São Paulo atypical and unique on the Brazilian historical scene also make it a city in which answers can and should be sought to the question of what the present and the future offer the Negro in human and social terms in an era of urban-industrial civilization. First, São Paulo has shown, with utter harshness and clarity, that the bourgeois revolution was an upheaval that affected the economic, social, and cultural basis of the white world only. The Negro and the mulatto were left out of the historical events and social processes that brought about this revolution. Second, São Paulo has also shown that the Negro and the mulatto were considered in the political calculations of the whites only as long as slavery was a historic obstacle to the bourgeois revolution. Once slavery had been abolished and the organization of slave labor had been broken up, both the Negro and the mulatto ceased to be important as a source of labor, for the immigrant became the central element in the restructuring of the system of productive relationships. The result was a paradox. Class society inherited the patterns of race relations that had developed under slavery and maintained the principal inequities that liberated slaves faced during the time of plantations and slavery. The Negroes and mulattoes were able to do little or nothing to change the terrible course of history, since they were unprepared economically, socially, and educationally to take advantage of the period of transition. Furthermore they did not possess the cultural and political means of protecting themselves from the catastrophe that broke over the Negro milieu.

The six chapters comprising this book portray the various aspects of the sociohistoric situation created by the bourgeois revolution and by the consolidation of the competitive social order. Here we find the two extremes: on the one hand the saddest pages, describing the veritable material and moral ruin that was "the life of the Negro" in the city during the first quarter of the twentieth century; on the other hand the most hopeful pages, those describing the arduous and debatable success of small groups of black elites and the growing importance of internal migrations during recent industrial boom times. In general the book shows that the white man does not have a clear picture of the city's racial situation. He ignores reality because he does not feel threatened, directly or indirectly, by the presence of a racial group that represents less than 11 per cent of the total population of São Paulo. He continues to hold to the errors and hypocrisy of racial ideology and racial utopia that developed in the past under slavery, as if it were possible to combine "Christian spirit" with ignorance of the personality, the interests, and the values of "the other." Thus he clings to *the prejudice of having no prejudice,* limiting himself to treating the Negro with tolerance, maintaining the old ceremonial politeness in interracial relationships, and excluding from this tolerance any truly egalitarian feeling or content.

The book also suggests that there are various ways in which the Negro is led to see himself in the image of the "black man," an image which the white man creates and manipulates with the utmost skill. Some succumb to these conservative influences, while others react against the image. In any case everyone suffers, both in terms of awareness of the social situation and in terms of behavior, as a result of a negative beginning, from the hypocrisy of the white man, and from the uncertainty that frustration creates, not only in the mind of the "conformist Negro" and the "runaway Negro," but also in the mind of the "new Negro." Negro protest, which represented the height of the Negro's ability to concern himself with, and fight for, the Second Abolition, took the form of a protest within the order, as if a powerless minority could bring about a revolution by changing laws and customs. Negro protest is of enormous value, both as a historic landmark and as evidence of the larger society's power to assimilate, but it clearly shows that under present economic, social, and political conditions the altruism, nobility, and high-mindedness of social movements among Negroes do not challenge the injustices of the whites or of the existing social order. That is because protests were ultimately transformed into a value in themselves, as if the Negro were undertaking the historic task of demonstrating an integrity lacking in the whites by identifying himself with the fundamental values of the existing order.

If Brazilian society were not so indifferent to the racial question, Negro protest would have caused a profound national disturbance. The Negro, by making himself an issue and by demanding from the white his share of effective liberty and equality in the established order, took upon himself the role of champion of democracy in a country where the traditional elites and the new rising classes were striving for political or economic power, without concern for distortions in the republican regime or for creating a genuinely democratic style of life. He took the risk of formulating a counterideology that depicted him historically in terms of that which he was denying; he thus became a kind of super white, an ingenuous but upright champion of the very social order that he should have been attacking and destroying. Thus, as a victim of two cruel forms of exploitation—that of slavery itself and that resulting from the way in which slavery was abolished—the Negro neither attacks the existing order nor turns against the whites. On the contrary he tries to defend, for himself and for others, the ideal values of this social order, although these values were not applicable except to whites who belonged to dominant classes or who were rising in the socioeconomic structure.

This book is based on data patiently gathered and carefully sifted and criticized. The reports are based on conclusions founded on objective observation capable of being checked by other investigators.[1] Nevertheless, at no time during the study or when classifying and interpreting the data, or even when presenting them, does the author claim to have been "neutral." No neutrality is possible in the face of such reality. In the course of scientific training we may learn to be objective, but if science made us indifferent to the fundamental values of civilization, to violent or peaceful manifestations of ethnocentrism and racial prejudice, or to the effects of any kind of discrimination, it would not deserve to be fostered, nor could it provide the only remaining way to the reconstruction of the moral basis of human life in our time. The investigation helped us to understand the much-vaunted "Brazilian racial democracy" as part of a complicated economic and sociocultural situation, a situation which leads the white man to seek subterfuges and ways of concealing his inability to endow Brazilian society with real social equity at all levels of human relations. On the other hand the study also strengthened our conviction that the social scientist plays a highly constructive intellectual role when he raises to the realm of social conscience aspects of life in society that are inappropriately perceived and explained by the human agents involved. By thus clarifying social conscience and broadening the average intellectual horizon, the social scientist renders a great service to the national community. If he is heard, and particularly if objective awareness of the situation is accompanied by moves toward social reconstruction, the knowledge produced may become very useful in gauging those progressive social changes which are essential to the equilibrium and the transformation of the social order. In the specific case of Brazil, it is clear that sociological knowledge on matters analogous to the present topic may lead to genuine democracy, which cannot rest on myths that are believed either consciously or unconsciously. If the Brazilian—especially the white Brazilian —abandons his prejudice of not having prejudice and learns to treat the Negro, not merely as a human being in the abstract or in terms of formal contact, but as someone really equal to himself in all respects and under all circumstances, and if he learns that books like the present one can enlighten him on such matters, Brazil will rapidly become a genuine racial democracy.

Establishment of such a genuine racial democracy is probably easier in Brazil than in the United States or in South

Africa, for example. In the Brazilian racial situation there are factors favoring a peaceful and rather rapid transition in this direction. It will depend on the opportunities for economic, social, and educational equality that are made available to Negroes. However, contrary to what is usually thought, there also exist in Brazilian society factors unfavorable to this outcome, the only desirable one. These factors are manifested both in the confusion and frustration of those persons most interested—the Negro and the mulatto—and in the complete indifference and chronic neglect of the whites. These potentialities are further aggravated by two other factors which are now becoming better known. First, the class system absorbed and continues to absorb archaic social structures in the sphere of racial relations, structures which were neccessary in the old social world of slave society. Contrary to what might be presumed, the market economy, free labor, and institutional modernization did not eliminate these structures; consequently the whole range of adverse stereotypes regarding the slave or the freed slave continues in force, with explicit reference to the Negro. Thus the old traditional pattern of asymmetrical race relationships continues to blight the safety and the historical prospects of the black man. Second, under the present conditions created by competitive society the Brazilian Negro and mulatto have difficulty in forming those social movements typical of dissatisfied and restless minorities. The "new Negro" tends to make his way independently and aggressively. However, he also tends to protect himself by means of a cold and realistic individual egoism. As a result he runs the risk of combining, to an unexpected degree, "economic success" or "professional success" with moral failure, thus forcing the solution that the white man himself prefers—that of "satisfying the Negro" but keeping him out of his way. In this case, class society creates distorted channels in the relations between Negroes and whites; these distorted channels should be quickly swept away in a radical spirit. There is no other way if racial democracy is to cease being a myth and become historic reality on the Brazilian scene.

In this work importance was consciously given to macro-sociological analysis and to the possibility of obtaining knowledge through the simultaneous use of synchronic and diachronic criteria for describing and interpreting concrete data. For this reason, in view of the principal orientations of sociological investigation in the United States, it may perhaps seem that not enough attention has been given to those aspects of race relationships that would be emphasized in microsociological treatment. The phenomena that Simmel would call "microscopic" were actually not neglected, but were observed, described, and interpreted in terms of a general viewpoint that converted such aspects into mere substrata of more complex phenomena, from which the writer extracted and isolated factors or effects of heuristic significance. Broadly speaking, this general point of view corresponds to the interpretative perspective that C. Wright Mills very properly defended:

"Without use of history and without an historical sense of psychological matters, the social scientist cannot adequately state the kinds of problems that ought now to be orienting points of his studies. . . . But the view of man as a social creature enables us to go much deeper than merely the external biography as a sequence of social roles. Such a view requires us to understand the most internal and 'psychological' features of man: in particular, his self image and his conscience and indeed the very growth of his mind. It may be well that the most radical discovery within recent psychology and social science is the discovery of how so many of the most intimate features of person are socially patterned and even implanted. Within the broad limits of the glandular and nervous apparatus, the emotions of fear and hatred and love and rage, in all their varieties, must be understood in close and continual reference to the social biography and the social context in which they are experienced and expressed. . . . The biography and the character of the individual cannot be understood merely in terms of milieux, and certainly not entirely in terms of the early environments of the infant and the child. Adequate understanding requires that we grasp the interplay of these intimate settings with their larger structural framework, and that we take into account the transformations of this framework, and the consequent effects upon milieux. When we understand social structures and structural changes as they bear upon more intimate scenes and experiences, we are able to understand the causes of individual conduct and feelings of which men in specific milieux are themselves unaware." [2]

A general viewpoint of this kind permits us to understand and explain psychosocial and sociocultural processes in the context of the functioning and structural transformation of society as a whole. For the resulting theoretical knowledge is less relevant to the phychosociological aspects of the manifestations and consequences of racial prejudice and discrimination than it is to its historical-sociological and structural-functional aspects. Nevertheless, I believe that this work offers material of considerable interest for comparative investigation. Contact between the races in Brazil is important not so much because it is *neutral* with regard to both phenomena, but rather because in this contact racial prejudice and discrimination are expressed in mild, diffuse, and unsystematic forms. For this reason it is of particular comparative interest, both because it is in itself a splendid example of a typical alternative kind of racial contact and because, through comparison, it reveals the nature and structure of the motives behind racial accommodation as contrasted with racial conflict. In this sense, paradoxical as it may seem, the transition from "accommodation" to "conflict" is not a negative sign with regard to the emergence of a racial democracy. On the contrary, it appears to be an inevitable phase of transition when the rate of disintegration of the regime of estates and casts inherent in slavery is different in the Negro world, in the white world, and in the larger national society. If this interpretation is accepted as correct, then conflict and the intensification of conflict are signs of a process of progressive democratization in patterns of racial relations. On the other hand, racial accommodation in the form of passive capitulation by the Negro or acceptance on his part of extreme social, economic, and educational inequality are signs of the persistence of predemocratic and undemocratic racial stratification, whatever may be the patterns of decorum, tolerance, or affection involved in social contact between persons or groups of persons belonging to different racial categories.

Florestan Fernandes

São Paulo, Brazil

ACKNOWLEDGMENTS

A complete list of acknowledgments would be too long. In the preface of a prior work of which Roger Bastide is the co-author (Bastide and Fernandes, 1959), there is a list of acknowledgments of the principal persons and institutions that cooperated with us, thus making our project possible. We should like to add other acknowledgments to this list. First, we wish to thank Dr. Roger Bastide who led us to make a sociological study of race relations in São Paulo and who generously agreed to our making subsequent personal use of the material we gathered. Second, we wish to thank José Correia Leite, Raul Joviano do Amaral, and Henrique Cunha for their valuable help in making available to us the copies still in existence of newspapers that used to circulate or which still circulate in the Negro milieu of São Paulo. We beg leave to pay homage to Jorge Prado Teixeira, an invaluable collaborator and an untiring fighter for the Negro cause, who unfortunately has been taken from the land of the living. In preparing the original drafts we had the valuable assistance of Noemy Pinheiro Dias and José de Souza Martins, Heloísa Teixeira, Mário de Campos Pereira, Vera Mariza Miranda Tôrres Vouga, Albertina Oliveira Costa Boal, professors Marialice Mencarini Foracchi and Maria Sílvia Carvalho Franco Moreira. In performing the calculations and preparing the tables and graphs we also had special assistance from José Francisco Quirino do Santos, José Carlos Pereira, and José Barbosa. For having read the original drafts and for their attentions in commenting on them, we owe a sincere expression of gratitude to professors Renato Jardim Moreira, Luiz Pereira, and Helena Pereira de Carvalho. We also owe a great amount of gratitude to the Director of the Faculty of Philosophy, Professor Mário Guimarães Ferri, to Professor Eurípedes Simões de Paula, and to the Graphic Department of our school. We gratefully thank each of these persons for the assistance and intellectual stimulation they have given us, thanks to which we were able to gather more courage for dedicating ourselves to writing this work.

Since this book was originally written for the competition examination for the chair of Sociology I at the University of São Paulo, special thanks should be given to the members of the examining committee—Professors Evaristo Morais Filho, Thales de Azevedo, Cândido Procópio Ferreira de Camargo, Lívio Teixeira, and Sérgio Buarque de Holanda, whose critical appraisal we have tried to make use of in the best possible way.

In connection with the U. S. edition of this book I would like to express my gratitude for the efforts of several American friends and colleagues who made translation possible. I must especially mention Charles Wagley, who in various ways demonstrated his proverbial unselfishness, his intellectual generosity, and his love for Brazil. For the same reasons Richard Morse deserves equal recognition. Jacqueline D. Skiles, Ariane Brunel, and Arthur Rothwell made the English version a work having its own particular merits, in which they were helped by Phyllis B. Eveleth, who took care of the editing. I am grateful to all four for providing their constructive and creative collaboration. To Columbia University's Institute of Latin American Studies I owe more than just thanks. Without the opportunity for working and associating with others that I had as a visiting scholar, this translation would probably never have been completed in its present form. Columbia University Press, particularly through its Executive Editor, Bernard Gronert, offered genuine and stimulating encouragement, which helped me to run the risk of facing a public very different from that for which the work was originally written. I hope the book justifies the collaboration and encouragement received from these persons and institutions and helps to create better understanding and deeper intellectual relations between Brazil and the United States.

F. F.

CONTENTS

The Legacy of the White Race

On the Threshold of a New Era

THE NEGRO IN BRAZILIAN SOCIETY

THE NEGRO AND THE FORMATION OF THE CLASS SOCIETY

1880–1900

Slave - agentes do trabalho

Introduction

During the breakdown of the seignorial and slaveholding order in Brazil,* no support or social guarantees of any kind were provided for the former slaves to help them enter the free labor system following their release. Masters were exempted from any responsibility for the maintenance and protection of freedmen, while neither the state, the Church, nor any other institution took any special measures to prepare them for their new order of life and work. Suddenly and abruptly the freedman was made his own master, responsible for himself and his dependents, even though he lacked both the material and psychological equipment to handle such responsibility in a competitive economy.

These aspects of the former slave laborer's condition imparted to Abolition a quality of cruel and inordinate despoliation. Abolition became an "atrocious irony," as Ruy Barbosa stated in 1898. The prophetic words of Luiz Gama, which expressed one slave's longing for freedom, had come true on a collective scale in portentous and unforeseen fashion. "He

* *Translator's note:* This occurred during the last two decades of the nineteenth century.

lacks the freedom to be unhappy wherever and whenever he wishes." [1]

There was concern for the slave's fate as long as the future of agriculture depended upon him. This concern was expressed in the various bills which sought to legally regulate the transition from slave labor to free labor from 1823 until the signing of the *Lei Áurea* on May 13, 1888.* As an expedient to keep the slaves at work, this interest became widespread among slaveholders in the 1880s, and grew even more acute when mass escapes of slaves became impossible to control. With the advent of Abolition itself, however, slave masters turned their attention to their own special interests. The political problems which concerned them were those related to indemnities and measures to ameliorate the agricultural crisis. [2] Inevitably the position of the Negro in the labor system and his integration into the social order ceased to be matters of political concern.

On the one hand the abolitionist revolution, in spite of its humanitarian goals and content, was born, matured, and came to fruition as a historical process of condemnation of the old order in terms of the economic interests, social values, and political ideals of the dominant race. The Negroes' participation in the revolutionary process became active, intensive, and decisive, especially when the fight against slavery became specifically abolitionist in character. However, given the nature of their circumstances, their participation was no more than a sort of battering ram wielded by the whites who were fighting the old order. Even the most thoroughgoing and tenacious abolitionists could not be their legitimate spokesmen. This period of history did not respond to charges that did not consider freedom of the individual, and then went beyond that demanding it as merely a preliminary objective. Although the ex-slaves had no understanding of this fact and could not act accordingly, their own demands were of this nature.

On the other hand the structure and dynamics of the Bra-

* *Translator's note:* The *Lei Áurea* (Golden Law) was the law which abolished slavery.

zilian economy did not enjoin any other attitude on the ruling classes. In areas of waning economic prosperity, slaveholders had already disposed of excess slaves by selling out to plantation owners to the east and south. For this group, Abolition was a boon: they were freed of onerous and inconvenient obligations which tied them to the holdovers from slavery. In areas where prosperity was guaranteed by the production of coffee, there were two means of ameliorating the crisis engendered by the change in the labor system. Wherever production remained low, traditionalist patterns remained unchanged. Like the freedmen of old, ex-slaves had to choose, by and large, between reinstatement into the production system under conditions basically the same as previous ones, or a deterioration in their economic situation if they joined the masses of the unemployed and semiemployed in the subsistence economy of the same or another region. Where production was high, the patterns of economic development and the organization of work were affected, and there were real possibilities for the creation of a true labor market. In such cases, however, the former slaves had to compete with the so-called native workers who constituted a veritable reserve army that had been kept from productive work in prosperous regions because they had rejected the humiliation of slave labor. More important, they also had to compete with a labor force imported from Europe, which was frequently composed of workers more accustomed to the new labor system and its economic and social implications.

The outcome of this competition was extremely prejudicial to the former slaves who were not prepared to deal with it. Yet it accommodated the interests of the landowners and plantation owners and the normal mechanisms of the emerging economic order. As a result, to the contrary of what might be assumed, instead of favoring the Negro, the alternatives presented by the new Brazilian economic system inexorably undermined, endangered, or destroyed his position in production and as a member of the labor force. This situation explains why the clamor for compulsory measures that would compel the ex-slave to work and would protect him, by fostering his adaptation to the emerging way of life, was quieted before it could make any positive contribution. Upon losing his privileged position as the only source of labor, the ex-slave also lost all that had made him an object of interest to the ruling classes. The legislators, the governmental authorities, and the politically active circles of society remained indifferent and inactive in the face of a material and psychological drama which had been clearly recognized and foreseen all along. The former slave was left to whatever fate he could work out by and for himself. x

To the negative consequences of these sociohistorical factors, which were operative throughout Brazilian society, we must add other influences which acted against the rapid assimilation of the Negro into the competitive social order and which are peculiar to the historical circumstances of São Paulo, the city whose racial patterns we shall study in detail. If we confine ourselves to essentials, the following factors should be mentioned.

First, the expansion of São Paulo did not follow the typical pattern of those Brazilian cities which flourished in relation to the development of an agrarian civilization. São Paulo came late into the colonial export economy (as against such other cities as Recife, Salvador, or Rio de Janeiro). It did so essentially when slavery was already on the wane, owing to the suspension of slave trade and to the promulgation of laws which in various ways restricted the replacement of slave labor. Above all it must be emphasized that not until the last quarter of the nineteenth century did the city enjoy waves of economic prosperity which could make the prevailing unsophisticated way of life susceptible to change. For this reason the economic sector of free services and labor of the Brazilian slaveholding society remained restricted and largely undifferentiated until that time. In São Paulo, unlike other cities, the freedman encountered few opportunities to integrate himself remuneratively into this niche in which the competitive social order was developing. True enough, statistics indicate that in

1872 there were 5,761 free mulattoes and 2,090 free Negroes, as compared with 950 mulattoes and 2,878 Negroes who were slaves. And in 1886 there were 593 slaves, 6,450 free mulattoes, and 3,825 free Negroes. Nevertheless, the same sources that yield these data show that the employment opportunities open to freedmen were the most modest and least remunerative.

Second, we must take into account a coincidence that was disastrous for the successful competition of freedmen in the free labor market. As a rule it was the services associated with skilled labor in the cities mentioned above that gave freedmen opportunities for vertical social and economic mobility. At the time the families of plantation owners in São Paulo state began to establish residence in the city and the city's economic system became more sharply differentiated, the freedman had to face the competition of the European immigrant. The latter did not fear debasement from competing with the Negro, and thus secured the best opportunities for free and independent labor—even the most modest ones such as shining shoes, peddling newspapers or vegetables, or hauling fish and other commodities. Toward the end of the nineteenth century, when the economic growth of the city accelerated, all strategic positions in urban manufacturing and incipient commerce were held by whites. Such positions served as springboards for the abrupt changes of fortune which adorn the histories of many families of foreign origin. Relegated to the residual sectors of that economy, the Negro remained marginal to the process, deriving but personal and occasional secondary benefits from it.

Third, São Paulo at that time was one of the Brazilian cities least inclined to absorb readily the newly liberated slaves. Against the backdrop of a traditionalist conception of the world and the hereditary authority of a small number of influential families, São Paulo developed into the first specifically middle-class urban center. Not only did a markedly mercantile mentality prevail there, with its characteristic corollaries, i.e., craving for profit and for power through wealth, but it was thought that free labor, private initiative, and economic liberalism were the ingredients of Progress,* the key that would permit them to overcome the national lag and permit Brazil to acquire the prerogatives of a civilized nation. The motivations, the behavior, and the very characteristics of the economic factors were increasingly and ever more closely identified with the typical models of the entrepreneur and the free laborer of capitalist civilization.

In this context the Negro was welcome as an insubordinate slave who fled his master and rebelled against slavery in its final days. He took shelter as a protégé, unsalaried worker, or family servant under the cloak of paternalistic relations among traditional families and, to a lesser extent, among the rising new families. Above and beyond this, he stood out as a displaced and aberrant figure on the chaotic scene that was beginning to emerge as a result of the coffee fever.

Even when the Negro managed to find a place in the urban occupational system, he was not oriented toward the future and thus did not fit in. He lacked the courage to face menial jobs. He was not sufficiently industrious to develop the habit of thrift based on countless unseemly deprivations and to make it a springboard to wealth and success. He lacked the means to risk small or large speculative investments upon which banking, real estate, and industrial businesses thrived. And above all, he did not crave wealth or power. Whenever he held positions that conferred status (as an independent craftsman or vendor), whenever he secured promising employment (as a civil servant or a free laborer on a daily or permanent basis), he clung to standards which were either precapitalist or anticapitalist.

On the whole the very sociopsychological and economic conditions surrounding the emergence and consolidation of the competitive social order in the city of São Paulo made it unsuitable and even dangerous to the masses of freedmen

---

* *Translator's note:* "Order and Progress" is the Positivist-inspired motto on the Brazilian flag designed at that time.

that gathered there. The psychological distortions induced by slavery limited their ability to adjust to urban life under a capitalist system. This limitation in turn kept them as a group from reaping any important and lasting benefits from new opportunities. Since no collective movement arose to force the white population to recognize the necessity, legitimacy, and urgency of social indemnification to protect Negroes (as individuals or as a group) during this transition period, urban life was for them a condemnation to an ambiguous and marginal existence.

In short, Brazilian society left the Negro to his own fate. It laid upon his shoulders the responsibility for his own reeducation and transformation to meet the new standards and ideals created by the advent of free labor, the republican regime,* and capitalism. Under certain sociohistorical circumstances, like those that seem to have prevailed in the city of São Paulo in the period under consideration, this responsibility became even more burdensome and onerous, given the opportunities actually available to the Negro. In this chapter we shall endeavor to analyze the major features of this process: First, we shall see how the connection between urbanization and Europeanization was reflected in the morphology of the city, completely altering the former structures for the regular absorption of the Negro as a factor of production. Second, we shall show how the development of the competitive social order and the consolidation of the class system in São Paulo revolved around the dominant figures of the plantation owner and immigrant, to the almost complete exclusion of the Negro or mulatto as socially significant historical actors. Third, we shall see how urbanization enormously increased the difficulties the Negro and mulatto encountered in adapting to the new economic, social, and political patterns.

* *Translator's note:* Brazil became independent of Portugal in 1822 with the prince regent of Portugal, Dom Pedro I, as its emperor. The change to a republican form of government came in 1889 with the Proclamation of the Republic and the deposition and exile of Emperor Dom Pedro II.

Free Labor and Europeanization

Urban expansion, directly or indirectly fostered by the coffee boom, nearly turned São Paulo into a city of foreigners. Demographic data for the beginning of the nineteenth century reveal that Negroes and mulattoes—both slaves and freedmen—constituted approximately 54 per cent of the local population. The demographic situation changed to such an extent in the last quarter of the century that Negroes and mulattoes made up 37 per cent of the total population of the city according to the 1872 census, and 21.5 per cent according to the 1886 census,[3] while foreign-born persons increased from 922 (3 per cent) in 1854 to 12,085 (25 per cent) in 1886.[4] Thus at that time the immigrants residing in the city exceeded the segment of the population designated in the census as Negro and mulatto by 1,870 (3 per cent)!

It seems clear that three fundamental tendencies prevailed. First, the development of agriculture encouraged the shift of slave labor from the city of São Paulo to prosperous areas of the interior. Second, this siphoning action was compensated for by migration in the opposite direction of freed Negroes and mulattoes to the cities in search of job opportunities. As a result the Negro and mulatto population of the city remained roughly the same (11,540 persons in 1836; 11,679 in 1872; 10,275 in 1886). Third, the rapid increase in the white population was principally due to the large-scale settlement of immigrants in the city. According to the data of the censuses of 1872 and 1886, for example, 31 per cent of the increase in the white segment of the population is attributable to growth of the native stock, and 69 per cent to European immigration.

To examine the first point, we must look at the sharp contrast between the city and the state of São Paulo in the composition of the population according to color. Table 1, extracted from the 1890 census, clearly shows this contrast, which was presumably associated with the effects of economic competition and specialization on the distribution of the population.[5]

TABLE 1

The Population of the State of São Paulo and the City
of São Paulo by Color in 1890

	State		City	
Population	Number	Per cent	Number	Per cent
Whites	873,423	63.0	53,204	81.9
Blacks	179,526	12.9	4,446	6.8
Indian-white mixtures	114,199	8.1	888	1.3
Mulattoes	217,605	15.7	6,396	9.8
Total	1,384,753	100.0	64,934	100.0

The rural areas did not remain unchanged; nevertheless they did not function as favorable settings for the permanent retention and definitive reabsorption of the Negro and mulatto into the free labor system. In the interior of the state the population was nearly 30 per cent Negro and mulatto, diluting the 5.4 per cent foreign group. This contrasted little with the traditional pattern of racial composition of the Brazilian population. In the city of São Paulo, however, the 10,842 Negroes and mulattoes shrunk in contrast with the 14,303 foreigners who formed 22 per cent of the local population. The Negroes represented less than 17 per cent of a population which was becoming dissociated from the Brazilian agrarian civilization and evolving very rapidly toward an individualistic and competitive way of life. This was definitely adverse to their assimilation, even in a gradual and selective way, into the new system of production.

In terms of the organization of free labor and the consolidation of the competitive social order in the city of São Paulo, the predominant human factor became the immigrant. European immigrants constituted 62 per cent of the segment of the population designated as white, and their numbers were almost five times those of Negroes and mulattoes in the city, who totaled 14,559 persons. Since the Brazilian nationals who declared themselves whites numbered 44,258, there were more Italian immigrants than white Brazilians in the city, as shown by the following list of Toledo Piza (1894, pp. 71–72):

Italians	44,854
Portuguese	14,209
Spaniards	4,727
Germans	2,320
Frenchmen	1,107
Austrians	948

The pattern of ethnic distribution apparently has two significant ecological aspects. Wherever the concentration of immigrants was largest, the number of Negroes and mulattoes was minimal. Inversely, wherever there was a major concentration of Negroes and mulattoes, there was a minimal number of immigrants.

With regard to the occupational structure of the city, it seems clear that economic competition with the immigrant prematurely engendered a well-defined process of sheer ecological succession. The Negro and the mulatto were displaced from the positions they occupied in precapitalist urban trades, service jobs, and the peddling of odds and ends. Such a process of elimination greatly strengthened the tendency to keep them in degrading and poorly paid heavy manual labor. It should also be kept in mind that the immigrant competed on the labor and capital market even with whites of the upper classes, and that the various Brazilian groups openly fought over any and all lucrative economic opportunities.

The impact of competition with the immigrant was overwhelming to Negroes and mulattoes because they lacked the means either to defend the relatively advantageous positions they had already acquired or to compete in the successive redistributions of economic opportunities among the competing ethnic groups. This occurred in spite of the fact that such positions were at the time very accessible and elastic because of the extreme mobility that prevailed in the social and economic milieu. The white of the ruling class managed to defend and even improve his position in the economic, social, and political power structure of the city. The immigrant successively changed occupations, areas of economic specialization, and strategic positions for the conquest of wealth, social prestige, and power. But the Negro and mulatto had to contend perpetually for the remaining opportunities with the marginal components of the system—with those who *"couldn't do anything else"* or *"who were starting from the bottom of the ladder."*

The detailed table of occupations formulated by Toledo Piza (1894) clarifies the labor picture. Of 170 capitalists, 137 were Brazilians (80.5 per cent) and 33 were foreigners (19.4 per cent). Of 740 property owners, 509 were Brazilians (69 per cent) and 231 were foreigners (31 per cent). In certain important professions of public life, such as the magistracy and law, the foreigner appears infrequently. Yet in others essential to economic progress, he appears frequently and sometimes predominates. For example, there were 127 Brazilian engineers to 105 foreign; 23 Brazilian architects to 34 foreign; 10 Brazilian surveyors to 11 foreign; 274 Brazilian teachers to 129 foreign. Among industrial personnel the immigrant is the human factor *par excellence* of free, salaried labor. Except for agricultural occupations, in which 68 per cent were Brazilians and 32 per cent foreigners, the immigrant clearly predominated. He also predominated on a smaller scale in domestic services: of 14,104 workers, 5,878 were Brazilians (41.6 per cent) and 8,226 were foreigners (58.3 per cent). They predominate in a decisive and almost monopolistic way in other branches of activity linked to the dynamics of the budding economic system. In manufacturing, 21 per cent were Brazilians and 79 per cent foreigners; in lines of work performed by craftsmen, 14.4 per cent were Brazilians and 85.5 per cent were foreigners; in transport and related activities, 18.9 per cent were Brazilians and 81 per cent foreigners; in commerce, 28.3 per cent were nationals and 71.6 per cent foreigners. Of the total number of workers in the city of São Paulo, 71.2 per cent were foreigners.

In occupations essential to rapid urban expansion and industrialization, the participation of foreign workers represented 82.5 per cent of the total. Although specific data are not available, these indications are sufficient to support the conclusion that, under the conditions in which the competitive social order initially developed and consolidated in the city of São Paulo, the former slave laborer was driven to occupations that were marginal or accessory to capitalist production.

The apparent irrational behavior of the Negro and mulatto, individually and collectively, is explained by analyzing this situation during the final breakdown of the caste society and the initial development of the class society. Their rebellion in the face of the degradation and extreme humiliation resulting from slavery spurred them to appraise their situation and to develop social ambitions that were disastrous to them. Among whites, those who had favored the perpetuation of slavery became resentful at disturbances involving former slaves. On the other hand whites opposed to slavery—principally those who had been active in abolitionist campaigns—had strong reasons to denounce the government's lack of interest, the inhumanity of the powerful, and the general indifference to the material poverty and psychological tragedies suffered by freedmen.

At the base of this entire issue was the nature of the attitudes of Negroes and mulattoes toward free labor. For the white man who contracted workers on purely commercial terms, what he contracted was productivity, fulfillment of contractual obligations, and the scale of remuneration for this factor of production. For the Negro and the mulatto, all these factors were secondary; they were merely the attributes of a man who was free to sell his labor. Central to his concern were a man's integrity and his freedom to decide how, when, and where he would work. Whereas the immigrant regarded salaried work merely as a means to begin a new life in a new country, intending to leave it as soon as possible, the Negro and the mulatto made it an end in itself—as though in it and through it they might assert their dignity and freedom as human beings. Thus they introduced moral elements into the labor contract, a highly inadvisable thing to do in a social order that prided itself on purging the employer–salaried employee relationship of extra-economic duties and rights. It became difficult or impossible for the Negro and mulatto to dissociate the labor contract from transactions directly involving the individual. In contrast to the immigrant, who clearly understood that he was merely selling his work capacity under specific labor conditions, the Negro and mulatto in the contractual relationship behaved as if their basic human rights were at stake—that is to say, as if they were selling themselves, wholly or in part, upon accepting and conforming to the stipulations of the contract.

In order to protect themselves, they tried to fulfill contractual obligations according to criteria that were detrimental to the interests of the contractor because of the uncertainties and unpredictable factors which were brought into the employer–salaried worker relationship. The refusal to perform certain tasks and services; the unreliability in reporting for work; the fascination for occupations that seemingly or actually conferred status; the tendency to alternate between periods of regular work and more or less prolonged phases of idleness; the aggressive reaction to direct control and organized supervision; the lack of incentives for competition with colleagues or for making salaried work a source of economic independence—these and other "deficiencies" of the Negro and mulatto became part of the complex human situation with which they were confronted in the free labor system.

The important thing, from the sociological point of view however, is to refrain from directly attributing every negative aspect to the cultural legacy of slavery. It is true that this period limited the former factor of slave labor, conditioning him to act according to precapitalist norms. But there were other factors which induced the Negro and mulatto to confront the labor market as if the slave trade were still in operation. The swiftness with which the competitive social order developed in the city of São Paulo greatly complicated things, cutting off at the root any possibility for a gradual transition which would facilitate acquisition through experience of the behavior patterns required by their new way of life.

This frame of reference makes it possible to understand and explain the "why" of the apparent irrationality of freedmen's behavior. It also presents an irrefutable denial of malicious accusations, which gained considerable currency, that "ex-slaves ran away from work." They did try to enter the currents of the city's economic life, but they did so in their own way—because they could not proceed otherwise. And they found themselves rejected to the extent that they attempted to assume the roles of free men in too naïve a manner or with too much latitude in an environment where such attempts clashed with the general lack of tolerance.

Even in rural areas the freedman tried to maintain his position in the occupational scale and to compete with salaried workers. Paula Souza has given an incisive report in a letter to Dr. César Zama written in 1888, during the period following the mass flights of slaves.

I finally gave them a week to find whatever lodging they wanted, telling them at the same time that my house would always be open to those who wished to work and behave properly.

With the exception of three who left to seek their sisters in São Paulo and of two others—one of them born free *—who went to their father's, whom I had freed ten years earlier, they all stayed with me. They are the ones who are with me now and I am happy and content with them, as I told you before.

Now let me give you some information which should benefit the farmers up north since they will soon be facing the same social imperative—the complete and unconditional emancipation of the slaves.

Tell your fellow citizens of the province not to delude themselves by granting half-freedom, in the hope of avoiding the disorganization of work already begun. Conditional liberty will get them

---

* *Translator's note:* The "Law of the Free Womb" (*Lei do Ventre Livre*) promulgated in 1871 decreed that all children born of slave parents would thenceforth be free.

nowhere with the slaves, who want to feel free and to work only under a new system, with full responsibility.

Conditional freedom, even for a very short period, will find no response in those souls scarred by such long captivity. They suspect—and with good reason as far as some people are concerned —that such freedom is only a ruse to keep them in slavery, from which circumstances will free them. They work, but indolently and with displeasure: the body functions but not the soul.

Free of all shackles, they make a few blunders, but eventually settle in one place or another. What does it matter? What does it matter that my ex-slaves look for another employer as long as they work and others come to replace them!

Here in São Paulo we have long experience in the matter and full knowledge of all types of liberation. There is only one reasonable and beneficial kind: complete freedom—immediate and unconditional. The slaves themselves should take the responsibility for the mistake they may make in leaving the house where they were captives. Of course, there are masters who have lost all their workers and the reason must be that they didn't deserve to keep them. But the great majority of these slaves will find jobs within a month.

In my family there are good examples of what can happen. My brother freed all the slaves he owned. Some of them left and went to find work elsewhere. A week later they came to me or to my brother and settled down with us. They brought back unfavorable impressions of the vagabond life they had led during those days.

In order not to bore you any further with this, I will sum up by saying that during the month of February we passed through hours of bitterness and terror in the province, faced as we were with the most complete disorganization of work you can imagine.

The whole labor force deserted the plantations, which were almost all abandoned. I am not exaggerating when I say that 80 out of 100 were deserted while the Negroes were going to the cities or to ill-intentioned exploiters. "What will become of us?" we wondered sadly.

Little by little, they tired of their idleness, and in turn, their exploiters tired of supporting them without profit. And by now (March) everyone is pretty well taken care of. Understand that when I say "all," I am excepting a few landowners with bad reputations. These, as a matter of fact, will be eliminated and substituted by force of circumstances and they won't be missed in agriculture.

It is possible that in the present harvest there will be some loss of produce, but it is such a large harvest that it won't be an appreciable loss, and it will be largely compensated for by the beneficent effects of emancipation. There is something else which you should tell your fellow citizens of the province: that they are laboring under a great misconception if they think they will suffer great harm with the loss of slave property.

You should remember that my great argument as a slaveowner was that slave labor was the only thing we could count on for regular and indispensable work on the land, and that if we could always depend on the availability of free labor, we would willingly give up the slaves.

Anyone who argued in this fashion might have been considered pessimistic, but not obstinate.

So, your fellow countrymen should lose their fears. There is no lack of workers for those who know how to look for them. First of all, we, have the slaves themselves—who do not melt away or disappear, and who need to live and eat, therefore to work—something they soon come to understand.

Then we have an enormous labor force which we hadn't taken into consideration. I am not alluding to the immigrant who, fortunately, is abundantly available today. I'm alluding to the Brazilian who yesterday was lazy and lived off slave labor and the benevolence of the rural landowner on whom he depended as boarder, henchman, or whatever. This same Brazilian now throws himself courageously into work, either because work has gained dignity with emancipation, or because he has lost those former opportunities. This is what we are witnessing.

As for myself, I have taken in many, fearful that under the present system I might not have a sufficient supply of workers. . . .

As I told you, I have the same contract with my exslaves that I had with the settlers.

I give them nothing: I sell them everything, even down to a penny's worth of collards or milk! Understand that I do this only in order to increase the value of their work, and so they will understand that they can depend only upon themselves and will never get anything just for the asking. While the only thing I pay for is a doctor's visit, it costs me much more than all the collards I own and all the milk from my cows.

This penny's worth of collards and milk, the cattle I slaughter, the farms which I buy wholesale and retail to them by the plot— and cheaper than they can buy them in the city—all this just about pays the workers' salaries.

All of this went unnoticed under slavery!

This testimony is amply confirmed by newspapers: Even under slavery ex-slaves, freed legally or merely *de facto,* learned that they had to depend on their own labors for their own sustenance and for that of their families. They tried to get work from their former master or on some other plantation. The plantations were deserted when former masters failed to understand that they were freedmen and treated them as if they were still slaves. In short, as pointed out in an editorial of *A Província de São Paulo* (1888a): "Even when they abandon the plantations, the slaves do not abandon agriculture—they move from one plantation to another. Summing up relevant observations Evaristo de Moraes (1924, p. 308) writes:

The slave, as a rule, did not go far. Sometimes he merely left the farm where he had suffered the coercion and rigors of captivity; he fled only the slave quarters of which he held such painful memories. He would proceed to a nearby plantation and ask for employment.

Following Abolition the process continued, except that Negro and mulatto laborers had greater mobility. Data gathered directly from members of the former seignorial class and from slaves themselves reveal the following: (1) In some regions where the economy was decaying or labor was scarce, the transition took place almost without disturbance. Former slaves continued to work on plantations as salaried workers, with the exception of a few (generally artisans) who left for nearby cities, sometimes with the economic protection of their former masters. (2) Wherever there was an abundant supply of agricultural labor, especially foreign labor, freedmen who abandoned the plantations were rarely readmitted. At least one informant stated categorically that the plantation owners "sent them away, replacing them at once with Italian settlers." (3) The behavior of former slaves and freedmen was seen by plantation owners as an intolerable expression of the Negro's ingratitude, leading them to react with a thirst for revenge or to harbor unforgettable resentments.

It is important to emphasize these points. This is the only

indirect evidence we have of the assiduity with which the former factor of slave labor attempted to avoid being forced into a marginal economic existence. It shows how hard he struggled to retain even those jobs that had been most degraded by slavery. Nevertheless, he had no appreciable success, either because of his intrinsic or extrinsic deficiencies as a salaried worker, or because under the competitive system employers preferred to contract European workers. Couty (1881, pp. 48–56) observed that plantation owners had greater esteem for, and confidence in, the competence of Portuguese, German, and Italian settlers. He concluded that "under these new circumstances, the enslaved Negro cannot compete with the free laborer: all competitive production will necessarily remain in the hands of the latter."

As the free labor system came to prevail in society at large, the persistence of these notions and the increasing relative abundance of skilled labor made it possible for the settler, as a free laborer, to displace Negro and mulatto, even in jobs at which the latter were skilled and had achieved a certain reputation. From this perspective, the problem ceased to affect only freedmen and emerged as a national economic dilemma. Underlying the relation between the immigrant and the slave, or later, the freedman, was the very question of the projected future of the competitive social order and class society in Brazil. Couty (1884, p. 15) keenly understood this: "To have immigrants and not to make them into citizens—herein lies the insoluble problem to which the government continues to seek a solution." Whereas the contracting plantation owner was a citizen and voter, the contracted settler had no political rights or privileges. The equalization of the two for juridical purposes in connection with the contractual relationship was a real problem, on the solution of which would rest the development of conditions for reorganizing agriculture and adapting it to the free labor system (Couty, 1884. Cf. esp. pp. 20, 112, 125–26).

The entire process was thus directed not at the actual transformation of the slave or freedman into a free laborer, but at making changes in the labor system to warrant the substitution of the white for the Negro. The clarity with which these goals were sighted in São Paulo is amply attested to. It was known that the juxtaposition of slave labor and free labor disrupted agricultural production, fomenting the rebelliousness of the slave and the dissatisfaction of the settler.

There were also attempts to prolong the transitional period as much as possible, in order to gain enough time to reorganize the labor market. Nevertheless, no one had any illusions: the object was to derive the greatest possible benefits from the moribund system of slavery, to import large numbers of settlers as rapidly as possible, and to reorganize agriculture in order to absorb them.

Here is how *O Correio Paulistano* (11–11–1887) speaks of the economic significance of the slave and the immigrant: If the slave is useless as a factor of production, the landowner should try to substitute for him a more productive one, or at least, to use him according to the existing labor conditions (10–30–1887). There is no escaping social realities: The exploitation of our natural resources has already become the domain of the free man and not that of the slave. This is true insofar as the introduction of the immigrant as a factor of production brings us hope and heralds a new era of ever-growing prosperity. This causes us to foresee unprecedented growth, not only in the already developed agricultural sector, but also in the manufacturing and textile industry, and in every aspect of social activity."

This was also the economic policy supported by the great landowners who influenced or held posts in government. The famous motto of the Minister of Agriculture, Antônio Prado —"Free labor in a free country"—not only implied that free labor would replace slave labor, but furthermore, that in a system of free enterprise, the white man would inevitably replace the Negro as the factor of production. He proposed measures to promote the establishment of immigrants in agriculture and obstinately refused even to consider laws that would compel freedmen to do such work. It follows that neither the great landowner nor the immigrant was personally and consciously responsible for the gradual elimination of the Negro from the developing competitive social order. Forces for the reintegration of the social and economic order more or less thoroughly eliminated him from production in agriculture. The great landowners showed preference for the immigrant wherever prosperity and a relative abundance of foreign manpower prevailed. In regions where this did not occur or occurred on a smaller scale, they had to fall back upon freedmen. This gave rise to migratory movements of Negro, mulatto, and *caboclo* agricultural workers who left the areas where they suffered the intense competition of the white immigrant for areas of impoverished farms, such as the Paraíba Valley. (Taunay, 1939, p. 463.)

In short the immigrant did not replace the Negro as a mere result of physical succession, nor did the Negro simply relinquish his position in the economic structure of Brazilian society. The replacement actually proceeded on a scale and to a degree that varied in inverse relation to the degree of differentiation, the stage of integration, and the rhythm of development of the free labor system and the corresponding competitive social order in the various agricultural regions of the state of São Paulo. It so happened that the regions of greatest prosperity were also those of the largest concentrations of immigrants and the greatest outward movements of Negro labor.

It is essential, in this part of our analysis, to study the position of the Negro and mulatto in the emerging system of free labor and the competitive social order in terms of the organization of agricultural production; that is, through those elements and factors responsible for shaping the structure and dynamics of the *Paulista* rural world at the time when the Brazilian bourgeois revolution began. From a broader perspective these elements and factors reveal the nature and significance of the process of displacement of the slave and freedman within the overall economic, social, and political context of the state of São Paulo.

The Negro and the Bourgeois Revolution

The breakdown of the estate and caste society did not benefit the Negro and mulatto socially, for they rapidly became the marginal elements of the social system. The only important difference between the trends operating in the city of São Paulo and those responsible for the reorganization of the statewide rural system is that the structural and dynamic requisites of the competitive social order were more clearly present in the former from the beginning. In the rural areas the differences in prosperity brought on by coffee production led to appreciable variations in the speed with which the old order broke down and the competitive social order developed. As a result in certain rural areas where change was slower, there were opportunities which Negroes and mulattoes would not find either in São Paulo or in regions where the coffee economy showed more vitality. However, such opportunities were not properly used. On the contrary, among the chief types of adjustment, the roughest road seemed to be selected most frequently.

This raises a question which must be well understood if we are not to distort the picture. The fact that the slave and the freedman were the chief stimuli in the breakdown of the caste system does not in itself imply conscious and organized revolutionary action. Should this have happened the abolitionist movement would have given rise to a holy alliance among whites to ward off the danger of racial subversion. The caste structure implied a state of material, social, and psychological heteronomy for the slave under the prevailing circumstances of Brazilian society. He could only play the role of a catalyst in an advanced stage of the internal breakdown of the slaveholding social order or under the organized, ostensible leadership of the nonconformist faction of the dominant racial group. This was the sole ideological and political guarantee for the continuity of the established system of racial dominance and of fidelity to the underlying principles of interethnic stratification.[6]

The cooperation of the slave and the freedman was accepted as a sort of fuel indispensable to a swift breakdown of the slaveholding system. They were not regarded as, nor were they in any way encouraged to become, independent revolutionary agents capable of planning their strategy and of putting it into effect on their own. The moral of the story is simple. When the disturbances were over, the slaves and freedmen as a group were well aware of what they did not want. However, they did not have a clear idea of what they ought to want as a group or of how to act on the social scene in order to determine such a collective goal.

Slaves and freedmen became the heteronomous and alienated pole of a caste structure; and although they fought furiously against this structure, they fought as a heteronomous and alienated pole. At a time when the social reconstruction was in full swing, they were full of wild hopes but still in the same position, with another class structure considerably different in its order and potentialities. Wherever they turned, even with respect to the most modest opportunities, they came second to the settler, the immigrant industrial worker, the European artisan, or elements of the national populace who formerly had not competed for their jobs. How could they have confronted this unforeseen and onerous direct competition with the white without having any understanding as a group of what it meant and how they could use it to their advantage?

Within such an economic, sociopsychological, and sociocultural context, the humiliations, resentments, and hatreds accumulated by the slave and freedman under slavery and tremendously aggravated by recent disillusionments destructively undermined the spirit of Negroes and mulattoes. All this increased their insecurity—a natural occurrence in times of such abrupt change, and aggravated anxieties and frustrations which could not be directed outward nor constructively remedied by sociopsychological mechanisms of interaction with others and by integration into the emerging social order. The choices which had been valued socially and psychologically since the remote past directed their principal aspirations and patterns of identification toward equality with upper-class whites. The success of immigrants further strengthened these expectations.[7] However, the actual alternatives ranged from becoming *caboclos* in the country to living in poverty in the city.

Those who remained in agricultural work either sank into subsistence farming (like the *caboclos*) after wearisome migrations to other parts of the state or country—or had to be satisfied with the precarious rewards offered to the less valued elements of the native white labor force,[8] often secured only after uncertain wanderings from one nearby plantation to another in the same locality or after migration to less prosperous agricultural areas. Those who were already in the cities, with the exception of a very small number of ex-slaves and freedmen who were artisans and had the economic assistance of former masters, found themselves in worse straits. Along with the less valued and unskilled Brazilian labor force from which they emerged as the least respected economic and social group, they were able to find only irregular employment in hard labor that was poorly paid and bitterly degrading.

In short, hurled from the core of the social masses, they constituted its lowest stratum. At the same time they faced restrictions that did not affect white Brazilian workers as seriously, and they struggled with psychological inhibitions. The opportunities for employment in agricultural or urban work, poor as they might be, seemed to represent economic and social liberation to lower-class Brazilian whites—something that would propel them into the midst of the live, productive forces in the nation, yanking them out of their previous material and psychological hardships. For the Negro and the mulatto, on the other hand, such prospects represented but one more type of degradation, for they would be in practically the same conditions as before. Both consequences wounded their sensibilities and their dignity. They were just as far from being entirely free, with security, prestige, and dignity, as they had been in the recent past.

Negroes and mulattoes could have avoided such alternatives only if, in the transition to the new juridical-political and social system, they had started from a caste position that granted them economic, social, and political autonomy. This would have been the historical prerequisite for them to have been the forgers of their own destinies in the process of change. Only thus could they have imparted truly revolutionary goals and repercussions to the abolitionist movement, in the social interests and psychological needs of slaves, freedmen, and the emancipated children of slaves. Only thus would the experience gained in the revolutionary process have had real efficacy, whether in broadening the cultural horizons of the Negro and mulatto or in the development of suitable, compensatory, and strategically reliable techniques of adjustment. Only thus, too, would the Negro and mulatto have had an active influence on the juridical-political orientation of the processes of social reconstruction, defending their interests and needs during the development of the competitive social order. This did not and could not happen, however, and therefore they experienced the conquest of freedom as though it were a cataclysm descending on defenseless beings.

It should be noted that it is not a question of knowing whether the Negro and mulatto reacted passively or with indifference to these historical events. There was no passivity or apathy in their response. During the first quarter of this century probably two-thirds of the Negroes and mulattoes in the city of São Paulo, and almost half of the same groups in the rest of the state, chose the most disadvantageous of the two extreme alternatives. This self-condemnation to ostracism, dependence, and destruction can be interpreted as a mute protest or a suicidal effect of their complexes of social disillusionment. Yet it was the one and only recourse to self-affirmation open to the Negro and mulatto who had been historically deprived of the means to order their lives freely according to the ideals and requisites of their own world view.

If we were to stop here, however, the analysis would be incomplete. What, actually, was the element of rationality in the adjustment of Negroes and mulattoes who complied with general expectations? Was the Negro or mulatto who joined the competitive social order as a salaried manual laborer, factory worker, self-employed artisan, or small businessman, in the country or in the city, really adjusted to the demands of the situation? There are good examples of success on the part of Negroes and mulattoes freed before abolition: the hard shell of the slaveholding society offered them secure opportunities for free work once emancipation was achieved, and the freedmen continued to compete eagerly among themselves for jobs that were remunerative but looked upon socially as degrading. Often the white manual laborer was no more than a figurehead and supervisor. The real workman, if not a slave, was a freed Negro or mulatto. As free labor gradually undermined the slaveholding order, and especially after slavery was abolished, this protective shell lost its *raison d'être*. Yet slavery did not prepare the slave (and therefore did not prepare the freedman) to function as a free laborer or entrepreneur. Wherever economic development left no other alternative, slavery did prepare him for a whole range of occupations and services that were essential, but for which there were no white workmen available. However, wherever the latter were to be found (as in São Paulo and the extreme South) because of immigration, freedmen were gradually replaced and eliminated by their white competitors, even while slavery was still fully in force. There are two questions, then, to be asked: one regarding the skills acquired by the Negro and mulatto to face universal free labor successfully; and another concerning their sociodynamic ability to act according to the behavioral, personality, or institutional models imposed by the competitive social order.

In essence, part of the answer has already been found by students of the slaveholding society. Slavery distorted its labor factor, denying the Negro and mulatto full opportunity to reap the fruit of universal free labor under conditions of direct, strong competition with other labor factors. As Caio Prado, Jr. (1942, pp. 341–42) put it:

Truly, slavery could only foster the development of elementary and very simple relationships in the two functions it was to perform in colonial society, as the factor of production and as a sexual factor. Slave labor was never to advance beyond its starting point of forced physical labor; it was never to educate the individual, nor to prepare him for a higher plane of life. It was never to develop him morally. On the contrary, it was to debase him and rob him even of whatever culture he might have brought from his primitive state.

In short, the school of slavery hardly guided the slave laborer; it misguided him. These distortions could have been partially corrected or compensated for in those areas where the slaveholding society depended upon the freedman for the organization of slave labor. Opportunities of this type were few, however, and benefited a very small number of workers.

The observations of Couty (1881) on plantations in the western part of the state of São Paulo during slavery had already shown that all cultivation factors being equal, the productivity of free labor (i.e., immigrants) was three times greater than that of slave labor. In spite of this, overhead expenses were four times lower! These observations led him to conclude that even during slavery the slave would be displaced by the European free laborer wherever competition developed between the two. The full import of these facts is grasped when the problems they raise are examined from the standpoint of the development and consolidation of the competitive social order in São Paulo. The two human factors basic to this process, as it developed from the last decade of the nineteenth century through the first quarter of the twentieth century, were the coffee planter and the settler. The differentiation of the planters' economic and social roles, as they or agents associated with them became involved in the urban business world, served to bring about important changes in the process of capital accumulation. The links of large-scale Brazilian agriculture with the international market changed markedly during the latter half of the nineteenth century. Not only were various phases in the commercialization of relations of production assimilated by Brazilian society but some mechanisms of the flow of international capital were involved in this process, being directly related to the institutional development it engendered (growth of the banking system, proliferation of brokerages, increase in speculative investment on the part of intermediaries, etc.).

The area under agricultural development benefited doubly by this process: through differentiation in the socioeconomic sphere and through more profitable participation in the dealings of international business which had internal repercussions. These factors strongly influenced agricultural society insofar as they caused the planter to shift his center of interest from the plantation to the strictly economic or speculative processes of the coffee business, compelling him to become both producer and middleman, or to associate closely with the latter.

The gradual development and eventual universalization of the free labor system made mandatory rapid readjustments which had similar results: disengagement of the plantation from the patrimonial order, forcing the planter to develop a mentality characteristic of the capitalist entrepreneur ever concerned with production and the remuneration of the factors of production. Ultimately, through close involvement and vested interests in the most abstract commercial operations of the coffee business, the planter himself became an intermediary or a capitalist and encouraged his family to perpetuate this process.

The settler in turn entered the process of consolidation and revitalization of capitalism at three different levels: First, he was a factor of free labor who behaved as a typical salaried worker and rejected the patrimonial relationship with the planter, forcing the latter to act according to new norms and a new economic outlook. Second, the settler entered both directly and indirectly as a factor in the transplantation of new attitudes toward work and new economic methods and skills. Third, he participated as the driving force for capitalist accumulation based on savings and as the direct creator of new centers of capitalist growth, to some degree in rural areas, but mainly in the cities. In other words the settler has not only benefited from the trends related to the recent transformations in capitalism in Brazil; he has also participated to a great degree in the process itself. And, to the measure in which he managed to gain recognition as an independent entrepreneur, he has been able to act as a new and revitalizing force in the growing economic autonomy of the city vis-à-vis the rural sector. The migrant groups of the Brazilian population and the educated segments of urban populations, to a greater or lesser degree, have filled functions similar to those of the settler. The latter has been not only the numerically predominant component but also the common human factor in these economic and sociohistorical processes.

The main point in the analysis of the position of the Negro and mulatto in the emerging economic and social order is that, as a social category, they have been excluded from the modern trends of the growth of capitalism in São Paulo. The two poles of this socioeconomic process are found in the social circles of the ruling classes and in the European immigrant groups. The Negro and mulatto have actively contributed to these trends only sporadically: whenever and wherever they have been regarded as members of the important families or have been caught up, because of individual circumstances, in the waves of prosperity which have favored the middle educated groups of the society and the native-born migrant groups.

The Negro and mulatto emerged from slavery without any social models by which to order their lives and to become integrated into the prevailing social order in a normal way. Not only did they emerge from slavery materially and psychologically ravaged, but the great majority lacked the means to assert themselves as a separate social group or to integrate rapidly into those social groups that were open to them.

If we separate the human dramas from the sociohistorical processes, difficult though this may be, we shall see that these events had their positive aspect and true historical significance. The isolation of the Negro and mulatto through the economic, sociopsychological, and sociocultural forces which led to their forced or voluntary exclusion from the institutions of Brazilian society was their initial means of entry into the class system. They were but juxtaposed elements, nothing more. In this position, however, the Negro and mulatto were to be finally stripped of all that identified them as slaves. In accordance with the progressive development and strengthening of the competitive social order, they were to develop for themselves a strategy for the conquest of those positions which they would come to occupy in the structure of the class society. From this standpoint, the dispersion which the Negro populations underwent in São Paulo had productive results. On the one hand it constituted the ecological, economic, and social form taken by the incorporation of these groups into the rural and urban masses. On the other hand, it became the prerequisite for the emergence and gradual consolidation of the sociopsychological mechanisms which, in the Negro milieu itself, were later to further his assimilation into the social organization of the class society.

Urban Development and the Maladjustment of the Negro

As a rapidly growing city, São Paulo was a magnet for migrating demographic and ethnic groups. Thus it was only natural that it should become one of the urban centers that were to polarize the internal migrations of the Negro masses throughout the country soon after the collapse of the slaveholding society. This phenomenon was poorly understood at the time, and there were those who believed that the Negroes were simply collectively fleeing from the state of São Paulo. Actually, the tremendous horizontal mobility of the Negro population involved migrations to northeast Brazil and to the city of São Paulo. There are no reliable data on the proportions of such movements.

If we separate the three principal segments of the *Paulis-*

tana population of this time, it can be seen that the Negro population had the lowest rate of growth. The pertinent data are summarized in Table 2.

TABLE 2

Growth of the Negro Segments of the Population
in the City of São Paulo (1886–1893)

| | 1886 census | | 1893 census | |
Segments	Population	Base nos.	Population	Base nos.
Native-born whites	24,249	100	44,748	184
Foreign-born whites	12,085	100	70,978	587
Blacks	3,825	100	5,920	154
Mulattoes	6,450	100	8,639	134

The quantitative increase in the Negro and mulatto population in absolute numbers, during a period of intensive migration to other parts of the state and country, indicates that the number of new arrivals compensated for the departures. On the whole, however, it seems clear that it was the white contingents—with a disproportionate predominance of the foreign-born—who became concentrated in the city.

In the overall increase of 79,392 whites shown by the census of 1893 in relation to that of 1886, 58,893 (74 per cent) were foreigners and 20,499 (26 per cent) were native-born. Thus it can be seen that it was actually the European immigrants who flocked to the city to try their luck.

This trend had a moderate following among Negroes and mulattoes, even when compared with native-born whites. Various hypotheses have been proposed to explain this. Lowrie (1938a, esp. pp. 17–18) and Amaral (1961, esp. pp. 59–60), for example, emphasized the probable assimilation of the mulattoes into the white population in census reports and through miscegenation as well. There is no doubt that such hypotheses do clarify actual occurrences. However, the chief explanation for such trends is most likely to be found in the horizontal mobility of the Negro population. Everything indicates that the segment of this population that was fairly well integrated into craft occupations and urban service jobs reacted negatively to the conditions under which it had to compete with immigrants. This group moved to other cities in the state of São Paulo or to other parts of the nation where suitable work and real economic opportunities could be found. According to the census of 1872, this segment included a large group of freedmen, in which there were 2.5 mulattoes to every Negro. From these inferences the following may be presumed: First, the horizontally mobile segment of the urban Negro population leaving the city was composed of skilled or semiskilled persons who had some experience in the urban way of life and who were dissatisfied with the situation created by the strong competition with foreigners. Second, mulattoes probably formed the greater part of this migratory segment of the *Paulistano* Negro population. Such departures were compensated for quantitatively rather than qualitatively by the exodus of unskilled workers from the country to the cities, especially the cities of São Paulo and Santos. Negroes prevailed numerically over mulattoes in such groups. Cities, especially those undergoing economic and urban development, held a certain attraction for this worker because of the employment opportunities, particularly in manual labor.

The ratio of women to men in the city according to the 1893 census shows more Negro and mulatto women than men. The women had greater facility in adjusting to free labor. Domestic service under slavery, especially in urban areas, was not as degrading as hard labor in the fields. These service occupations fostered more permanent contact with whites and facilitated paternalistic relations of the traditional type. Thus various factors contributed to the stabilization of the Negro woman when employed as a domestic servant. Furthermore, competition with foreigners in this area of urban service work did not assume dramatic proportions immediately. The census of 1893 reveals that native-born whites held almost 42 per cent of domestic service jobs (out of a total of 14,104 such jobs), an exceptionally high ratio in relation to other occupations.

The important thing is to understand the socioeconomic basis of these trends. The *Paulistana* Negro population was awakened by the social and economic upheavals that shook the general pattern of relations with whites and upset the city's prevailing style of life. Previously, the Negro and the mulatto had held various occupations and services considered compensatory and even dignifying. These were gradually eliminated, and new social forms emerged from the altered economy with their own mechanisms for selecting labor. The stability or lack of stability of the various segments of the Negro population were directly related to the nature of their contact with the economic and social structure. However, the following should be remembered: First, this population was only partially composed of persons with actual experience in the urban milieu. Second, changes in this milieu were so swift and thorough that even these persons suddenly found themselves almost strangers in a foreign city. Third, the masses of people responsible for the city's continuing growth had no experience in urban services and sought peripheral jobs and a hidden marginal existence. Fourth, as a whole, only the female segment of the Negro population found conditions favorable to a fairly stable transition to the new way of life.

In order to understand the fascination which the cities held for the migrating Negro masses, it is necessary to consider the important role played by the cities in the breakdown of slavery. It was not only because the cities provided employment opportunities less degraded by slave labor and more lucrative and prestigious that they were preferred by freedmen. In São Paulo state it was in the urban centers that there first developed public opinion opposed to the excesses of slaveowners and the very principles underlying slavery. Soon after, an organized conspiracy for the freeing of slaves was initiated there, both liberation through legal action (led by Luís Gama) and direct attacks on the rights of slaveowners and uprisings in the slave quarters (led by Antônio Bento). Only in cities such as São Paulo and Santos, were there groups with sufficient economic, social, and political power to confront slaveholding interests and actively challenge them. For this reason escaped slaves and freedmen converged upon these cities, asking for hiding places, protection, or advice on how to avoid the punishment threatened by their tormentors. It was in these cities (especially in Santos), that they were able to set up their famous refuges.[9] In this sense the city became a symbol and a promise of liberty. In the eyes of those being released from captivity, the mere fact of living in the city seemed to be an ideal means of shedding quickly the ignoble connotations of being a slave or freedman.

However, in reality it was otherwise. Without being exactly hostile to the Negro, the city of São Paulo soon broke all ties with its rural past. It was not only the lower-class mores that disintegrated; something more complex occurred. At the turn of the century the city grew too large to maintain pride in traditional customs, but it was still too provincial to break with them completely in deference to an urban way of life. The Negro and the mulatto did not find there the usual advantages of a large city: specifically, the possibilities of cultural isolation, tolerance, and employment for all. Yet neither did they find the characteristics of rural Brazilian towns: social stability, the prevalence of traditional ideas, and the rewards of a subsistence economy.

This ambiguity, characteristic of the transitional phase, subjected those of rural origins to contradictory situations. Urban behavioral traits prevailed in the aims and aspirations of those bent on turning São Paulo into a cultured, modern, and civilized city. Only those who were part of the wave of progress were in tune with such a frame of mind, that is, the progressive circles of the ruling classes and the immigrants trying to get rich quick. In private life, away from economic activities, each person had to struggle in his own heart with the rough edges of some countrified background inherited in different forms by Brazilians and foreigners of all social classes. Progress, then, was quite superficial and not at all homogeneous. Too public a manifestation of behavioral traits which might arouse suspicions that the community was backward or provincial were not tolerated. But each person had to overcome these habits as best he could with the help of incentives and procedures that molded individuals in accordance with the circumstances surrounding their economic activities.

There was a surprising impact of this external situation on the Negro. He found himself frustrated in his desires to perpetuate that portion of his cultural inheritance which had survived slavery or had developed through it. At the same time he was immobilized within a rustic and ineffectual traditionalism. Both facts are structurally and dynamically related to the fate of the Negro and mulatto in that urban environment.

Measures were even taken by the police to prevent the nocturnal revival of old customs which might disturb the sleep, and perhaps the decorum, of the white population. The cultural losses resulting from this were not compensated for by the acquisition of alternate cultural values. Left out of those activities that were basic to the urbanization of ways of thinking, acting, and living, the Negro did not participate even superficially or occasionally in the progressive trends. The transformations undergone by *macumba* fully illustrate this. Lacking social autonomy to congregate on the basis of common cultural values of a truly sacred and traditional nature, the Negro population became unable to maintain the purity of its cults and finally saw *macumba* corrupted by the whites (Bastide, 1946, pp. 51–112). Consequently, the Negro ceased to reap the benefits of the constructive functions of these cults, which require a minimum number of participants and provide him with opportunities for personal and collective self-expression through organized social life.

Direct and indirect pressures dictated adjustments that made the Negro seem to be the equivalent of or substitute for the slave or freedman in the free society. Hence the positive evaluation of that portion of his cultural heritage which traditionally regulated such adjustments. In order to react against these pressures and try to shield himself from them, the Negro clung stubbornly to the opportunities for alienation and seclusion provided by urban centers. In this way he played an important role in adjustments which increased to the utmost the negative results of the Brazilian pattern of diffuse and unsystematic isolation, and at the same time fostered his perpetual subjection to a destructive cultural heritage.

Couty (1881, p. 72) wrote that ". . . the Negro in Brazil desires only one privilege, one right: that of *doing nothing*." [Couty's italics.] Nevertheless, upon becoming a freedman, he gradually assumed the duties which made him a promising economic factor. In describing this process in Rio society Rugendas (1940) pointed out that the freedman remained in the vicinity of his former work site and went into various types of activities, achieving "comfortable circumstances in a short time" and appreciable success in profitable or prestigious occupations in the cities. For this reason he even asserted: "The free Negro population is, in various ways—principally in terms of its future—one of the most important groups of the colony. This is true especially of 'creoles,' Negroes born in America." Objectionable traits were tolerated and if possible corrected as circumstances or necessity dictated. Saint-Hilaire (1851), for example, refers to a Brazilian-born Negro who had served him as a hired companion and who, "being conscious of his dignity as a free man, had the greatest contempt for tasks regarded as slave work." He would not even go to the brook to fetch water for himself because he understood this to be the responsibility of another servant.

The planters could accept neither the Negro's sense of self-determination nor the consequences of his irregular work patterns based on subsistence requirements. Here is how one planter summed up the criticisms raised against freedmen as factors of free labor: "If they are employed on a plantation as hired hands, they remain only a few days. They are too demanding, slow on the job, and stop constantly to roll a cigarette and smoke; they dawdle forever at meals and very few of them will cut a bundle of firewood, etc. They take offense at any admonishment, pull themselves up and declare that they are free men, lay down their tools and away they go." [10] The freedman, then, lacked the self-discipline and the sense of

responsibility of the free laborer, which were the only attributes that could spontaneously endow the laborer with regularity and efficiency under the new juridical-economic order.

Since the freedmen could be replaced by the numerous
immigrants who were considered strong and intelligent workers, they not only lost ground in occupational and economic
competition but also came to be seen through a distorting lens
in which the image of the slave made the freedman appear
worthless. In short, they gained a reputation which was to ban
them from the urban labor market or force them to struggle
wearily in fringe occupations that were undesirable or insignificant. Morse (1954, pp. 190–91) summarizes his conclusions by comparing the position of the Negro with that of the
immigrant as follows:

The city, however, was not always so generous to those who sought
their fortunes there. The ex-slaves who came in large numbers
from the plantations often lived in miserable hovels, and worked
for the meanest salaries at jobs such as garbage collecting which
whites considered degrading. Those who were opposed to emancipation stated that they were mainly responsible for the increase in
the numbers of alcoholics, criminals, and tramps. The champions
of liberalism, on the other hand, denied that the ex-slaves or other
Brazilians were the parasites they were rumored to be.

Data gathered directly from Negroes, mulattoes, and whites
who lived in the city during the first quarter of this century
point out the devastating consequences of these attitudes and
of the reactions they induced. According to these data young
men predominated among those coming from the interior.
Older men preferred to continue in agricultural work, often on
the same plantations where they had been slaves. The majority were not well acquainted with urban occupations and services and made their living at rough manual labor. Some were
bricklayers' assistants, but the majority did odd jobs, that is,
the jobs they chanced upon, earning by the day or by the job.
Women worked as servants since there were still those who
preferred a black nursemaid or cook. One informant was more
precise: "Now there are many blacks working as bricklayers

and even as vendors of fruit and other things. In the past, it was the Italians and Portuguese who were the vendors. Negroes are replacing them. And you didn't see many Negro craftsmen. It was the white who held these jobs." To his mind, in the line in which he worked, carpentry and cabinet-making, "the work done by Negroes was not inferior to that done by whites. The Poles were worse. "They're a worse race than Negroes. They're the ones who spoiled the trade." [11]

Judging by one of the life histories, the Negro had to be quite opportunistic, taking whatever was offered without making a fuss. He had to work as a porter, delivery boy, or housecleaner; he had to hand out pamphlets, carry posters, work in stables, be a janitor in boardinghouses, or assist bricklayers, carpenters, or house painters. One informant sold sweets made by his mother. However, it seems that Portuguese and Italian street vendors, and later the establishment of street markets, ended up by eliminating the women, children, and even in some cases adult men and old Negroes from the small trade in sweets, vegetables, ice cream, trinkets, pine nuts, cooked chestnuts, herbs, etc. Jobs with lucrative potential, even though modest ones, such as that of fishmonger, newspaper vendor, or bootblack, were the domain of the Italians. The data emphasize that Negroes were compelled to work for Italians under exploitative conditions. The latter showed interest, friendship, and charity toward the Negro, but with an eye to exploiting him, wherever and however they could, even through the ruse of drawing Negro children into their homes, treating them "like sons," and extracting free services from them.

However, Negro and mulatto informants do not try to conceal the blunders they made for lack of experience or moral support. They acknowledge irregularity in working, pleasure in changing jobs, and even the slyness with which some neglected their obligations if they were able to pocket in advance the payment for odd jobs. They made fun of the immigrants (especially of the Italians), not so much because they worked hard, but because they sacrificed every comfort—good food, decent clothing, recreation, etc.—to save money. There were frequent small clashes, which generally involved conflicts of role expectations, the protagonists being young Negroes or mulattoes and members of traditional families. Either the black maid wanted her child to be treated as "a human being" or she was offended by the ostensible lack of respect accorded her by her employers, their children, and their friends. The black worker resented the haughtiness shown by his employers, colleagues, and customers. The recurring outcome of such frictions was the prompt renunciation of the job, sometimes preceded by an emotional outburst on the part of the offended party. As Negroes and mulattoes repeatedly stated, these fits of anger were provoked by the propensity of former masters to refuse to pay for "nigger's work," or by their inclination to give it little value in flagrant contrast to their treatment of immigrants in similar situations. This gave rise, in the Negro's mind, to the conviction that whites of traditional families hated Negroes because of Abolition and took their revenge by humiliating them and intentionally replacing them with immigrants. It is probable that this did occur in numerous cases, for the statements by members of these families repeatedly refer to the Negro's ingratitude, his self-seeking attitude, etc.

Yet one of the main informants of the Negro group revealed that traditional paternalism was still of great practical importance. In explanation he distinguished between former house slaves and field slaves. The former were said to have gained considerably from their association with whites. Both men and women received a better education and had higher aspirations in life. Many of the men even knew how to read and write; all of them had better manners copied from their former masters. In addition, some had established friendships with whites, "when they weren't related through concubinage," thus making them almost certain benefactors. The women, in turn, learned much about running a household, and knew how to perform all domestic tasks, from cooking to sewing. After slavery was abolished, these groups had greater possibilities for finding better jobs than the others. Many had white benefactors who gave them used clothing to look presentable, and who opened the way to the best jobs they could obtain—in offices and especially in civil service. In reality they were no more than the humble jobs of messenger boy, servant, office boy, door attendant or, very rarely, clerk. But they provided a good salary and some prestige, in comparison with other available jobs. For this reason, around the 1920s this stratum of the Negro population became the *Paulistana* black elite, or, in the words of the informant, "drawingroom Negroes."

In contrast, those who came out of the fields suffered terribly with the advent of Abolition and settlement in the city. They could not read or write as a rule, and they had no benefactors. They suffered a great deal because they were left to their own fate. Poorly dressed, illiterate, and lacking the protection of sponsors, they settled here and there and lived by their wits. These men and women constituted the least qualified and most impoverished stratum of the Negro population. They went everywhere, even to parties, in the same worn cotton suit, and had great difficulties in finding good jobs, at least those they considered to be such. Having little knowledge of the white, they feared to express themselves to him and submitted passively to his wishes. They did not risk looking for better jobs or transgressing the role expectations which condemned the Negro to a hard, thankless, and unrewarding life. Being both timid and naïve, they preferred to suffer silently and to isolate themselves even from their more successful colleagues.

It is impossible to judge to what point the maladjustments of the Negro and mulatto were, in fact, determined by their relations with the white man's world—with its values, its way of life, and its influence on them. One thing seems certain, however: in migrating to the city, Negroes who were more familiar with and closer to former masters and their way of life had greater chances of success. Even so, paternalism could no longer fulfill the same constructive roles it had played under the old order. In the changing social context, the white man anxiously sought to free himself of all the obligations which in the past had been involved in his relations with the slave and freedman. This was the psychological significance of the abolitionist movement and its ultimate historical manifestation. The Negro became fully responsible for himself, for his own interests, and his own fate. Moral obligations were redefined and accepted only in an ultraselective way. Had it been otherwise, there would not have existed a private fortune large enough to finance a responsible humanitarianism, or prestige sufficient to arrange all the jobs solicited.

The insecurity and the dissatisfaction of the Negro and mulatto did not result merely from their material conditions and the crisis engendered by the breakdown of their integration into the social and pyschological world of whites. Occasional work and erratic earnings led the men to such a state of dependence and hardship that women became their principal resource in the struggle for existence. The data are subject to controversy, but it seems that at first the men had no intention of systematically exploiting the women. This exploitation became routine to the degree in which men experienced difficulties in finding a permanent job in accord with their ambitions. As these difficulties were perpetuated, the economic dependence on women became socially accepted. Female informants have repeatedly stressed that most of these arrangements were provisional, temporary means of cooperation among couples who lived together in free union or who were married. Nevertheless, incentives arose that fostered the institutionalization of such arrangements, and many men began to lose their interest in earning a living and became systematically dependent on women for food, lodging, and small allowances for everyday expenses. In turn, the perpetuation of this situation in a large number of cases fostered idleness in an environment where there was little of constructive value that could be done with a man's time and energies. Thus many men gave themselves up to permanent idleness and found a great pastime in spending their time in the company of other men in the same situation. The meetings of small groups on street corners, and especially gatherings in taverns, made this pastime even more attractive both from the viewpoint of friendship and from the pleasures to be derived from this practice. The psychological counterpoint of this dependent relationship developed in the increasing degradation of the Negro—first in his way of life, and eventually in the white man's judgment of him.

Immediately following Abolition, Negro gatherings of any type were not tolerated. The police broke up crowds which formed for whatever reason. There was fear for maintenance of order and public morality.[12] After a while, when it became clear that the Negroes did not constitute a particularly dangerous threat, there remained a residue of suspicion that led the police to keep them under a surveillance that always irritated law-abiding, hard-working Negroes, and that created for Negro women the additional torment of suspicion of prostitution. In this atmosphere old prejudices were revived to make the psychological drama of Negroes all the more acute. One informant pointed out how old stereotypes were revived and how new ones developed, characterizing the freedman as a Negro and the latter as a bum, drunkard, or streetwalker. The fear of the freedman and of the scope and consequences of his unrest was replaced by another kind of fear that represented literally the white's redefinition of the Negro. He was no longer seen as a threat to public order because he conspired to win his freedom, but as a threat to the propriety, property, and safety of others.

This was carried so far that true abolitionists became outraged. The following appeared in *A Redempção* (5–13–1897): "After the law of May 13 was passed, we thought that the poor Negroes would be able to settle down, raise a family, acquire property, and help increase the wealth of our country. We were wrong." In the same source there is mention of the disappearance of a Portuguese man who was the victim of violence in São Paulo. In mentioning the fact, the Portuguese consul is urged to take the proper measures, and it is noted that "if he had been a Brazilian, and especially black, it would have been a matter of shutting up and taking no interest in finding out what happened to him" (*A Redempção*, 7–18–1897). In another article under the title "Killing a Negro Is Not a Crime," the government is reproached for the "practice introduced some time ago" whereby the killing of a Negro would not be considered a crime (*A Redempção*, 289–29–1897). Whatever the motivation behind such statements, they indicate on the whole that the Negro had lost whatever material and psychological security he had gained as chattel under slavery. But he had not acquired—except in partial and inadequate terms—the material security of the free laborer, and he was far from being able to claim the psychological security of the individual guaranteed by the republican civil law and the Constitution.

Where a legitimate complaint was involved, the initiative to claim legal protection could be frustrated. *A Redempção* (5–13–1898) relates a tragic case, of which the outcome is indirect evidence of the humiliating and self-destructive violence with which the Negro reacted against his marginal and ambivalent position. A Negro worker in good economic circumstances went to the police to defend the rights of his daughter, who had been raped. Nothing whatever was done, "just because she was Negro and he was white"! The father committed suicide: "Benedito Fumaça, disillusioned with living on this Earth where Negroes have no rights in spite of being honorable men, unable to put up with this life, and seeing his daughter made into a prostitute because there is no justice to be found on this Earth, decided to kill himself."

On the other hand there were those who understood the historical origins of the injustices faced by Negroes and who lamented the accusations directed against them. The following statements in *O Diario Popular* (4–30–1898) [13] concerning the much-publicized systematic begging by Negroes is an example: "It is rare, very rare, to find Negro beggars in this city. . . . And when this occurs, there can be no doubt that they are truly unfortunates who spent their youth and their energies on work for which they were never paid, and now have no means of support. . . . [The beggars] are all foreigners, foreigners who did not become incapacitated here, but who came from their own countries at the call of our renowned generosity and who came to lend a dark note to our life with the sad spectacle of their deformities." However, the occasional goodwill and solidarity of a few did not carry enough power in themselves to save the Negro from his disorganized way of living, or from their effect on the development of stereotypes that would provide an ethnocentric basis for their exclusion from the economic, social, and political opportunities opened by the competitive social order.

The strange thing is that the reactions of whites as much as those of Negroes against this situation were of a frankly irrational character, revealing a sociopathic attachment to traditionalism. In the opinion of the aristocratic whites who were more tolerant and sympathetic to the former slaves, the latter did not have the intellectual and psychological equipment to conduct their own lives. Thus, wherever and whenever they failed to be guided by former masters, they had to pay a very high price for their freedom. The following testimony by an aged informant of an illustrious family confirms this attitude: "I think the Negroes were happier during the time of slavery, especially when they had good masters. They had housing, clothing, food, medicine, and the work wasn't that hard. In general, Negroes don't have a head for running their own lives. Look at the mess they're in! . . . I think Negroes were happier in those days; they were organized, they worked, they had housing, food, medical care—they were taken care of. On Sundays, instead of just resting and talking, they would ask to work in the fields, to earn a little money. With this money, many of them bought their freedom, but they stayed on the plantation. Others bought things in the city. Now look what they've come to, look what a situation they're in. The Negro doesn't have the head to run his own life. Some do, like Q. who educated her children, or J.B., who became principal of a primary school, but most of them don't."

This diagnosis would be complete and true if an essential element were included: Why didn't the Negro have a "head"? What he lacked was not exactly the guidance of former masters. It was experience and familiarity with the social and cultural patterns of behavior, experience with which he had always been denied as a *slave,* and from which he was excluded in the urban milieu, in spite of his freedom.

For this reason the position of whites militantly involved in the abolitionist movement was based on more realistic premises. They were opposed to this distorting interpretation of traditionalist paternalism, and demanded that Negroes be given true opportunities to be independent, to act in accord with their own interests, and to think for themselves. In short they wanted the Negro to enjoy the same privileges as whites in all spheres, from economic life to political life. Correctly, assuming that the Negro's backwardness was a socially and culturally inherited factor, they believed that it would be possible to foster their forward leap from one moment to the next, through the establishment of training programs or schools for freedmen and their children. They did not take into consideration the content and scope of the task, however. It was not sufficient to teach the Negro to read and write and to prepare him intellectually for certain trades. It was necessary to prepare him for all the institutional forms of organized social life which were essential to his competition with whites for work, prestige, and security, and to assure him, above and beyond this, of the utilization of his abilities on a regular basis and the autonomy to give practical expression to his aspirations.

In turn, Negro and mulatto informants reveal that the development of an independent and realistic awareness of their position was relatively slow. Those who had the satisfaction of success through their own efforts or with the aid of whites felt no moral obligation toward the masses of their colleagues who lived in the greatest poverty and degradation. They were continually indignant about the subservience and passivity of the latter group, and above all else sought to make clear the dividing line that was already being drawn between the emerging black elite and low-class Negroes, endeavoring to imitate as best they could the life of the white aristocracy in the days of slavery. The others, immersed in the subworld of the urban rabble, awaited the "Second Abolition." Their sole outstanding attribute was their freedom—which they did not know what to do with, although it was their all-absorbing concern.

If we duly understand this spectrum of perspectives, Negroes who had access to a class position through modest trades or jobs, and to those who were relegated to unemployment and dependency, we shall be able to discern a fundamental factor. The Negro who becomes integrated into the competitive social order, even in marginal or secondary positions, rejects anachronistic conditions of life with all their lethal consequences; the Negro who remains on the periphery of organized social life and all hope succumbs to his own inertia. As the informant relates: ". . . The Negroes who had been house slaves in a way despise other Negroes who don't have the same social ideals. They adopt the "white man's morality": they want to dress well, they want to get ahead, they want to behave like responsible persons. They are shocked and offended by the way of life and the ideas of disorderly Negroes because they're afraid that their ways will influence the white man's idea of the Negro. They see in their fellow Negroes of lower or inferior position a threat to their own social prestige, which depends on what the white man thinks of them."

This cultural gulf led to certain frictions. The Negro who is experienced and involved in the flow of social life knows when he is being belittled or hurt by the white. He is familiar with the "whites' game" and does not identify with him except to free himself of their yoke and achieve his own ends more rapidly. The others, being more timid and inexperienced, remain helpless, perceiving things too late or preferring to swallow hard. As they have maintained an exaggerated respect and fear of whites, they think it better not to protest or show their true feelings. In short a small and relatively exclusive segment of the Negro population was inclined toward constructive nonconformity and began to develop a realistic awareness of interracial relations, keeping in mind the Negro's interests in the economic, social, and political processes. Yet they withdrew from reality and from the present. They yearned for a way of life that did not even correspond to the goals of foreign whites who forged their independence without aiming for the behavior patterns of the large landowners. They refused to lend their solidarity to the members of the urban Negro lower class from which they withdrew in embarrassment, as if they did not all share a common destiny and a common cause.

Appraisals of the Negro's situation at the time were naturally formulated and disseminated by literate Negroes who belonged to the small privileged groups of the Negro population. They kept up the oral tradition but have revealed both a certain nonconformist attitude and a certain provocative tone. Like the whites, they knew and emphasized the fact that the Negroes were not ready for freedom, or for the rapid transition from slavery to being free laborers and citizens which they had to face. Yet they understood the transition problem and that which could be expected of the confrontation of the ex-slave with the white under conditions of equality: in an almost morbid way they stress that the Negro received no official or private assistance, while the foreign immigrants received all the existing attention and resources. Finally, whether or not they received clothes and financial assistance from former masters, they had a clear idea of the Negro's legacy: poverty, abandonment, and corruption, which they considered an unjust recompense to those who had been the forgers of the economic progress of Brazil as laborers during the sugar, gold, and coffee cycles.

The former masters were personally and directly blamed for the adversities suffered by the Negro population. Replaced as they were by foreigners on a collective and merciless scale, Negroes presumed that behind all this was the masters' hatred or desire for vengeance. Without a doubt the ruling circles of the dominant groups were responsible for those misfortunes. However, they were not responsible in the sense just indicated. The personal desires of the plantation owners, accented in terms of promoting or damaging the interests of their former Negro slaves, had no discernible relevant influence on the direction of historical forces. The truly important factor was the blind and exclusive egotism of those circles, that placed the solution of agricultural problems first and foremost, ignoring everything else, whether it was the fate of the freedmen or the question of indemnification.[14] In personalizing a form of social despoliation, the Negroes looked to the past for the causes as well as the solutions of their problems. They lost all possibility of understanding the present clearly, objectively, and independently, depriving themselves at the same time of the positive influence this might have on the ferment of revolutionary demands. In other words, the basic convictions that informed the critical evaluations of the more realistic, independent, and dissatisfied circles of the Negro population were not sufficient to the task of forging an independent cultural horizon for free black men. Their horizon continued to be framed in terms of the expectations of whites, in accord with the interests and values of the old strategy of ensuring the lack of leadership of the Negro masses by syphoning off the limited number of Negroes and mulattoes among those eligible for vertical social mobility.

The ultimate consequences of all this are obvious. Those who believed themselves to be part of an emerging Negro elite revealed that they were uncertain about the future and basically pessimistic in their conception of the world. The rest— the majority of the Negro population—gave in to a morbid disenchantment, for which there were not even temporary or superficial compensations. A terrible despondency took hold of these people, preventing the appearance and development of the tendencies so common among migrant and rootless populations concentrated in large cities: to overcome quickly once and for all and by whatever means an unsatisfactory, burdensome, and depressing way of life. Since they lacked the perspectives necessary to build for themselves the free man's world, nothing else mattered or had any importance.

Retrospective analyses made by informants or gleaned from documents written by Negroes well portray the persistence of these elements of the oral tradition. It is worthwhile to transcribe a few passages from these documents because they shed a great deal of light on the interpretations made and give them ample support. One informant with outstanding knowledge of the history of the Negro population of São Paulo asked:

What happened to Negro slaves? Although they had formerly accepted all the forms of oppression of which they were victims, after Abolition—freed, masters of their own persons and of their own wills—many of those who did not know where they were going or what they wanted lost their will, their initiative, their self-direction. And then, relegated to the fringes of society, with all roads blocked in many cases, they began to travel the path of vice and decadence; they became careless and gave themselves up to a disastrous and pernicious conformism. . . . Thus many Negroes met their death through excessive drinking, for lack of the most basic comforts, through hunger, and through other forms of misery originating in a poorly implemented Abolition.[15]

Another informant, on the basis of his childhood experiences and the memory of conversations with his father, alleges that he heard from Negro abolitionists themselves that the law of May 13 had been premature and that before it was passed, "the Negro should [have been] . . . taught how to live in freedom," for he "didn't know how to live in freedom, and wasn't even acquainted with money." [16] Along the same lines but with more emphasis on the legal implications is the following statement:

For all purposes, gentlemen, with the decree of May 13, 1888, tragedy began for the Negro people that remains unresolved to this day, a drama of tragicomic dimensions which has kept the Negro in the deepest pit of degradation, without light or air, although free to go wherever he wishes within the confines of the pit. They did away with corporal punishment and imposed upon him a legal equality which, even now, few manage to understand. And to repay him for the indelible scars of slavery, they openly gave him a free ticket to malnutrition and debasement by means of clever, subtle symbols, maliciously and tacitly devised by the ruling few of other pigmentation—stereotypes that haunt and beleaguer every Negro to this day, though he might have the creativity, the cultural resources, or the intellectual vigor of a Machado de Assis, a Juliano Moreira, or a Teodoro Sampaio, or be an unrecognized Bastiao dos Anzois Carapuças.[17]

There were also those who considered the economic implications of politics:

Without denying the moral responsibility of Brazilian society, the economic aspects of the problem we are analyzing here are the sole responsibility of the Government. In providing the society with a means of illicit accumulation of wealth [represented by slavery] * and leaving the persons who contributed to the accumulation of this wealth to their own fate, the Government is doubly responsible for our social and political imbalance. This responsibility becomes even more serious if we consider that after Abolition the Government, in addition to reaping benefits from slavery, sought to find the best method of recovery for the society which had also benefited from slavery—an act which is in no way in accord with the principles of legal equality inscribed in our Constitution. In fact, the measures taken to secure new laborers for agriculture—endless procedures on which fabulous amounts are spent—should have inspired the men who are responsible for the future of the country to take similar measures on behalf of the great masses of freed laborers, providing them as well with the means necessary for their rehabilitation. None of this was done, and today, 63 years later, at a time when economic stability is the basis of all social progress, there is only one thing left to us—a Second Abolition.[18]

In a document which had a restricted circulation and which was meant to serve as point of reference for the selection of a Negro political candidate and the organization of the corresponding electoral campaign, there is an overall explanation of what may be interpreted as the process of "animalization" of the Negro by slavery:

* Translator's note: Interpolation by the author.

. . . the social debasement of the freed Negro persists to this day as an almost indelible stigma which makes it impossible for him to stand on equal footing with members of the slaveholding generation. Only those branded with this indelible stigma know what it means in terms of the imbalance in the Negro's competition with the white. . . . In making this tremendous effort, the Negro became animalized. In submitting to the difficult conditions of slavery, his mind underwent a kind of atrophy, and it was to such souls that Abolition came. Men of goodwill who participated in this magnificent display of patriotism rooted out a horrible cancer from our country's organism. However, they did not concern themselves with the organ that had been affected, which in this case was the Negro; they did not subject him to a treatment that would result in a complete cure. They concerned themselves with extracting the malignant tumor, and left the wound unattended. Thus the Negro, for lack of the transitional period necessary to his complete adjustment to the condition of being a free man, was left in the most awkward situation. He assumed this new condition without plans, without objectives, without guidelines—without anything that might permit him to make a suitable adjustment. Nevertheless, in spite of the dead weight of the incompetent, the Negro managed to adjust. He won out over the law preached by the proponents of racism and racial superiority.[19]

Slavery is at the very heart of the Negro's fate in the city of São Paulo; not the slavery that was suddenly destroyed by a change in the legal order, but the slavery that endures in the hearts of men. The sociohistorical period under consideration is, first and foremost, the Negro's first crucial experience of the meaning, the uses, and the functions of freedom as a dimension of the cultural horizon and the organization of the social behavior of free men. No one can deny or even make the merciless and brutal nature of this experience seem less intense than it was. However, it did put to the test those that chose freedom by the most difficult road available in the Brazilian society of the time, without possessing the sociopsychological or moral requisites of the free man. The importance of tying together past and present in this study lies in the fact that this link shows precisely and clearly that some suffered from the terrible impact of the interaction of an inadequate sociocultural legacy and an adverse social environment, while others gained from this impact an awareness of history that makes a man the instrument of his own freedom. What might seem to be the end was a beginning, but things did not turn out as the theoreticians of Abolition had expected. Neither the most perspicacious pragmatic spirit, the most extreme democratic ardor, nor the purest idealism could give the white man the imaginative capacity to grasp the reality of the tragedy of the Brazilian Negro as it unfolded in the city that was the quickest to democratize its patterns and style of living. The idea of a Second Abolition, with the content, scope, and depth it assumed in the minds of Negroes and mulattoes in São Paulo, seemed an absurdity and an empty play on words to the white man's common sense. It was to be only through the Negro himself, in the process of transformation of his being and his mode of interaction with *Paulistana* society, that it would be possible to understand the meaning of this idea, and, consequently, the significance of the melancholy period of personal and social disorganization as a stage in the black man's arduous struggle for freedom.

It is important to note one essential fact, however. Contrary to the case of other peoples or social classes that have undergone similar historical experiences, the disorganization of the Negro's life was not a precondition or prerequisite to the change in his cultural outlook, personality, and social behavior. Nothing whatsoever bound him normatively or systematically to the sociocultural heritage which he bore against to his will. His own desires tended toward the immediate adoption of the sociocultural heritage of free and powerful men, which he valued consciously and normatively, and rapid integration into the society constituted by these men. This means that the disorganization of the Negro's life was directly related to the dual impossibility of quickly abandoning the cultural traits inherited from slavery and of rapidly adopting the behavioral patterns he valued. This can be understood in terms of two concomitant facts: first, the historical gap between the content and organization of the Negro's cultural horizon and the sociopsychological requisites of interracial relations; second, the limited possibilities at the same time of integrating into the social stream, on a large scale, individuals who were both so unsophisticated and so ambitious and conscious of their personal dignity.

In the light of these considerations, it is necessary to pose two general questions: first, whether the city really rejected the Negro as such; second, what was the nature of the sociodynamic trends inherent in the Negro's interaction with the sociopsychological and sociocultural forces in his environment.

With regard to the first question, it seems obvious that the implications of the rejection involved are truly neither racial nor antiracial. The economic, social, and cultural isolation of the Negro, with all its unquestionably harmful consequences, was a natural result of his relative incapacity to feel, think, and act in the social milieu as a free man. In rejecting him, the society was thus rejecting a human factor that bore within himself a slave or freedman. Only if there had been a gradual breakdown of the old order and a slow development of the competitive social order—along with a certain constant rate of demand for manpower—would it have been possible to assimilate the freedman immediately and would it have been necessary to prepare the slave for freedom. As noted above, however, the process was extremely rapid in the city of São Paulo. Not only did the social techniques and psychological values of the precapitalist way of life break down almost instantly; the organization of the factors of economic growth and social development began at such a level of historical integration that any creative exchange between the capitalist present and the recent rural past was ruled out. In this respect, evidence to the contrary notwithstanding, the rejection was a positive thing. It represented a demand and above all a challenge to the Negro to rid himself of the human nature he had previously acquired and to adopt the sociopsychological and moral characteristics of the head of a family, the salaried worker, the capitalist entrepreneur, the citizen, etc. It should be kept in mind that in sociological terms this rejection would be specifically racial in character only if the Negro continued to be rejected once he had acquired these characteristics. The data presented suggest the opposite. To the measure in which the Negro acquired the rudiments of these characteristics or showed some capacity to do so, he found the road open and could fit in socially. From this standpoint the Negro's vertical mobility was frustratingly unsatisfactory and slow. Nevertheless, it contributed to destroying the vestiges of the caste society, leaving no trace of their underlying sociodynamic principles,[20] and it contributed concomitantly to the integration of the Negro without the occurrence of violent conflicts with other ethnic groups. (Bastide and Fernandes, 1959, pp. 59–68.)

With respect to the second question, it seems clear that the Negro took the rejection as a humiliating affront. Although he was capable of understanding and interpreting the existing social order only in part, he had the wisdom to retain and even strengthen his identification with it and with the goals arising from his desire to find a place within it. He gradually learned to use his freedom in a less destructive manner. As late as the first quarter of the twentieth century, he learned to reconsider the nature of his aspirations and threw himself into the social stream in a more realistic spirit and with motives he had formerly considered unworthy and humiliating. His own tragedy opened his eyes to the destructive consequences of the improper use of freedom as well as to the dilemmas of social integration. He finally understood that without prior adoption of the models of social behavior he had thoughtlessly rejected as chains he would never participate in the overall prosperity. The following thoughts of one of the most lucid Negro informants make this quite clear:

Around '27 or '28 we caught on to the mistake we had made in failing to imitate the immigrant, who underwent sacrifices and hunger (in order to get ahead)—a thing the Negro used to make fun of. By this time, the Italians owned the entire Bexiga section of the city and their children, if they weren't university graduates, were bookkeepers, tailors, cabinetmakers, or owned small businesses, while the Negroes still lived in basements and suffered the pains of economic inequality. The *Clarim* called attention to this fact many times.[21]

It is not important to emphasize this point further because it will be discussed in other parts of this study. What should be remembered is a simple and almost banal truth: in order to rid himself of a harmful cultural legacy and to become a free man, the Negro had to live in freedom. If he often used this freedom against himself, it was because he did not know how to do otherwise. In the slaveholding society, he did not have the opportunity to discover that freedom as an end in itself destroys and annihilates men, making them the slaves of their own appetites and passions. Gradually he lifted himself out of his suffering and humiliation, becoming the master of his own will, increasingly able to make responsible decisions and to do something that was socially desirable rather than do nothing.

A sociological analysis of the correlation between the structure of the emerging urban society and the sociopsychological impulses of the recently freed Negro is truly important for understanding not only what the Negro's position had been, but also what it was to become in the competitive social order. On the one hand there was the rejection that was to move toward social integration through tortuous and steep paths. On the other hand there was the structural maladjustment that, by means of the gradual victory of the Negro over himself and the adversities of his environment, was to lead to the continuous improvement of his adaptive abilities, his personal stability, and his adoption of increasingly complex social forms. Without exaggeration it can be stated that this period in the social history of the Negro in the city of São Paulo should be regarded as the years of waiting. These were the years of disillusionment in which suffering and humiliation were gall, but they were also years that aroused the Negro to conquer and outstrip himself, and thus to rise to the level of his egalitarian aspirations. Finally, these were the years in which the Negro discovered on his own and at his own risk that everything had been denied to him and that man conquers only that which he is capable of building on the social level.

PAUPERISM AND SOCIAL ANOMIE

1900–1930

Introduction

The emergence of a competitive social order and the urbanization of the city of São Paulo are concomitant sociohistorical processes. However, the analysis presented in the preceding chapter suggests that this concomitance, in many of its essential aspects, was not merely sporadic. Owing to the volume of the coffee production and to its marketing patterns, the two sociohistorical processes became structurally and dynamically integrated. From a sociological point of view the correlation of the two phenomena acquired an interpretive significance at once unique and general. It was unique because São Paulo was the only Brazilian city to make a veritable leap in developing a cohesive competitive social order, thus prying itself loose from the traditional Brazilian urban patterns of organizing living space and living standards. It was typical because this correlation was duplicated in other Brazilian cities as soon as they presented the correct conditions in accelerated economic growth, demographic concentration, and the modernization of institutions. Caught at the confluence of these processes, the Negro suffered direct negative impacts which resulted from sudden changes in the relations of production in the cultural horizon, and in the organization of society, as well as from the accumulative circular reactions triggered by such impacts. Thus the effectiveness or viability of the economic and sociocultural techniques which the Negro had previously learned as slave or as freedman were lost.

The speed with which cohesion was achieved in the competitive social order almost precluded any immediate possibility of the Negro's assimilation into active and remunerative economic roles. On the other hand the trends of urbanization prevented the preservation of Afro-Brazilian mores which could have ensured the transformation of the Negro population into an integrated and autonomous racial minority. To the measure in which the competitive social order and urbanization were in full process of development, the position of each ethnic group and of each social stratum within the economic system and the society was basically dependent on its capacity to participate in economic growth and sociocultural development. The Negroes and the mulattoes remained to the side of or found themselves altogether left out of the general prosperity and cut off from political benefits, because they did not have the prerequisites for participating in the game or for abiding by its rules. As a result they lived in the city, but they did not evolve with it and through it. They constituted a social group which was scattered throughout the various neighborhoods, and all they had in common was an arduous, obscure, and often injurious way of life. Under the circumstances the condition of social anomie carried over from the days of captivity was aggravated rather than remedied.

The causes of the aggravation of this state of anomie would seem to hold the sources of inertia which slowed down Negro endeavors at social ascent. This subject has already drawn the interest of various scholars. But the great human tragedy involved obstructed their vision. The majority of them endeavored to explain the "Negro deficit," while ignoring or devoting only limited attention to its psychosocial and sociocultural causes. The present chapter aims to fill this sociological gap and to deal as a whole with the quantitative and qualitative aspects of the collapse of the Negro population in the city.

The Negro Deficit

The aforementioned trends of demographic growth continued throughout the first quarter of this century, reducing the relative importance of the Negro population of the city of São Paulo. Initial interpretations of this phenomenon were dramatic. At first it was claimed that the Negro was abandoning São Paulo. Later the idea developed that the Negro could not adapt himself to the plateau and for this reason lost out in competition with other ethnic groups. The meticulous research of S. H. Lowrie (1938a) brought such speculations to a halt by showing that it is impossible to determine objectively in our times either the selective effects of slavery on the Negro and mestizo population or the volume of the transferral of individuals formerly classified as black into the white category. Lowrie does not deny the existence of a lethal process; he merely points out, with reason, that it never assumed the alarming proportions that were at first attributed to it. In his opinion negative selection would be taking place under such difficult conditions that the mortalities still would be representative as a sampling of the total population. While immigration had reduced the percentage of the black population, in the entire state it was only a little smaller than what might be expected.

It would be of little interest to revive these debates in our times if there had been no repercussions among Negro groups, and if such debates did not refer to an intrinsic part of our analysis. Whether or not the so-called "Negro deficit" was catastrophic, it was a manifestation of the iron shackles that bound the Negro and mulatto to pauperism. Conditions of social anomie not only maintained the initial poverty level of the *Paulistana* Negro population; they also continually aggravated it, making pauperism the process by which the Negro normally adjusted to the urban world. Thus there was forged the iron chain that bound Negroes and mulattoes to the vicious circle generated by poverty and that tied him to levels of existence that were progressively degraded, whatever the voluntary efforts to the contrary.

The probable selective effects in the contact situation of southern Brazil was analyzed by Oliveira de Viana (1952) in terms of the quality of biological inheritance. It is his opinion that "the regressive influence of ethnic atavisms" was responsible for the negative filtering out of mulattoes and for the development of a clear biological predominance of whites over Negroes and mestizos. Although having declared himself to be an enemy of the doctrine of racial superiority, Ellis (1933, 1934) takes up this line of interpretation, "convinced that the Negro, even the educated one, cannot bring himself up to the same level as the white." Considering the differences between the rates of birth, of stillborn births, and general mortality from 1924 to 1927, as well as the coefficients of deaths by tuberculosis, leprosy, and syphilis in 1929, he concludes that the psychological inferiority of the Negro and mulatto will cause their disappearance from the São Paulo plateau. "Considering the total population of each public health zone in relation to the entire city I believe that melanics have an annual deficit of 4,000 to 5,000 individuals throughout the state—thus the prognosis of their extinction 40 to 50 years from now."

The data regarding the incidence of tuberculosis confirm the declarations of the chief leaders of the Negro social movements who always stressed the disastrous consequences of poor nutrition, promiscuity, and unhygienic habits. However, in order to conclusively determine the specific influence of the living conditions on the Negro and mulatto in terms of these diseases, as well as their propensity for contracting a given contagious disease, it would be necessary to make statistical surveys that would occupy long periods and would consider objectively social, cultural, and economic factors.[1] In fact, if we were to consider white, mulatto, and Negro persons of relatively homogeneous populations, we would see that there is ample margin for contrary speculations based on the resistance of the latter two to the unfavorable conditions of their environment, including resistance to the contagious diseases. The survey of Lobo da Silva (1928) presents results which, instead of nourishing catastrophic predictions with regard to the southern part of the country, suggest that the Negro and mulatto presented perfectly normal criteria of acceptance and rejection for military service during the period under consideration.[2]

Thus until more complete studies are made, it is best to put aside extreme conjectures. If one part of the city's Negro population succumbed to such severe blows, another part victoriously overcame the adversities. We ought to make an effort to retain both sides of the issue and avoid unverifiable and unscientific conjectures about the psychobiological or demographic inferiority of the Paulistana Negro and mulatto.

The trend toward lightening the city's population became even more accentuated at the beginning of the century (between 1890 and 1929, the state of São Paulo received 2,316,729 foreigner immigrants).[3] The population of the city continued to increase rapidly, owing in great part to the contingents of European immigrants. According to certain estimates, the demographic Europeanization of the city became accentuated to such a point that there were two Italians for every Brazilian in the capital in 1897 (Morse, 1954, p. 189). Internal migratory currents from the interior of the state of São Paulo to the city and from other states to São Paulo became gradually larger. The internal migratory currents that exercised the greatest influence on the reshaping in the color composition of the population in the state of São Paulo only increased in intensity after 1925. Until 1924 only 109,222 migrants had entered the state, coming from various regions of the country. It was in the three following five-year periods that this movement underwent radical change. From 1925 to 1929 there were 171,727 migrants into the state; from 1930 to 1934, 105,393 migrants; and from 1935 to 1939, 330,471 migrants.[4] In the censuses of 1910, 1920, and 1934 references to color were omitted, but it can be presumed that the movement of foreigners, now enlarged by their Brazilian descendants, was the principal factor of growth for the *Paulistana* population. Only after 1935 did this picture suffer modifications, when the city became a center of concentration for migrants coming from other regions of the country.[5]

The important thing to stress is that only at the beginning of the second quarter of the twentieth century (and especially after 1935) does a substantial change occur in the migratory currents in the state and city of São Paulo. It is evident that the divergencies in the color composition of the different migrant groups contributed to reduce the relative importance of Negroes and mulattoes. We are still far from a complete homogenization of the demographic structure of Brazilian populations with regard to color.[6] However, the decrease in the black element in the local population is above all related to the influx of migrant populations in which whites markedly prevailed.

In view of this, a sharper reduction in the proportion of Negroes and mulattoes to whites in the *Paulistana* population would be expected as normal in the period around 1930. The important question is whether there is a lethal selection of the Negro and mestizo population of the capital. Unfortunately, census data that would provide the basis for an objective and complete analysis of the matter are not available.

Lowrie (1938a) uses the death register of the Demographic Service to present a distribution of the population of the state of São Paulo by color and the Health Service for the City of São Paulo from 1921 to 1928 as shown in Table 3.

Lowrie estimates that these results are "quite reasonable" because they give a total of 16 per cent for black groups in the state. The population of the state should include 20 per cent Negroes and mulattoes considering the data of the census of 1872 and the immigratory movement. To his mind a difference of 4 per cent is admissible (Lowrie, 1938a, p. 21), given the decrease in the black population brought about by miscegenation. As the sources are reasonably reliable, such percentages would indicate the relative continuation of the demographic picture that was characteristic of the end of the

TABLE 3

Distribution of Racial Groups Based on Deaths in the
State and City of São Paulo (1920-1928)

Race	State		City	
	Number	Per cent	Number	Per cent
White	624,208	83	100,947	88
Mulatto	63,746	9	7,105	6
Negro	57,127	7	7,050	6
Mongoloid	3,991	1	296	—
Undeclared	—	—	60	—

nineteenth century before the concentration of European immigrants revolutionized the color proportions of the *Paulistana* population.

The census data of 1910, 1920, and 1934 reveal the rapid growth of the city's population, which went from 239,820 to 479,033 to 1,060,120 respectively. The growth of the Negro and mulatto population of the city during this period is not known. Lowrie (1938a, p. 27) suggests that the proportion of Negroes and mulattoes oscillated between 8 per cent, 9 per cent and 12 per cent. If we use these estimates based on the demographic growth indexes of the city of São Paulo from 1886 to 1893 and from 1940 to 1950, it would be possible to presume that Negroes and mulattoes represented at minimum 11 per cent of the total population of the capital in 1910, 9 per cent in 1920, and 8.5 per cent in 1934. Accepting these proportions merely to have points of reference that are roughly approximate, we might imagine that the Negro segment accompanied the demographic growth of the city more or less on the following scale: [7]

Census	Conjectures regarding the Number of Negroes and Mulattoes in the City of São Paulo
1910	26,380
1920	52,112
1934	90,110

None of this clarifies the existence of a selective trend in this population. The most dependable data that we have were compiled by Lowrie (1938a), who summarizes the data obtained from publications of the Health Service in Table 4.

TABLE 4

Births, Deaths, and Stillborns by Color in the City
of São Paulo (1920–1928)

Color	Births Number	Per cent	Deaths Number	Per cent	Infant deaths Number	Per cent
Whites	199,162	94	100,947	88	10,747	87
Mulattoes	7,330	4	7,105	6	1,129	9
Negroes	3,959	2	7,050	6	541	4
Mongoloids	442	—	296	—	23	—
Undeclared	—	—	60	—	2	—
Total	210,893	100	115,458	100	12,442	100

The numbers and percentages of this table indicate an alarming fact. Taken together, the deficit for births and deaths for Negroes and mulattoes would be 2,886 persons, or, the number of deaths would be nearly one-fourth larger than that of births. Considering them separately, there would be a minute credit balance of 225 persons for the mulatto and an enormous debit balance of 3,091 persons—almost the total of births!—for the Negro. In relative numbers, however, things would appear even more serious as trends connoting the rapid disappearance of Negroes and mulattoes would be revealed. Commenting on the data Lowrie (1938a, p. 23) writes:

Under such truly alarming conditions the black population would have disappeared in the course of a few decades and with the exception of the Indians and immigrants from other states of Brazil, São Paulo would have come to be composed of a race that if not totally pure would at least be white. Furthermore, these data, if true, would reveal living and health conditions—or rather lack of health—that are astonishingly precarious. Even though the living standard of the black groups is low, their greater numbers being among the lower economic groups, neither observation nor the general opinion of well-informed persons admits that the situation of these groups is so decadent that it contributes to increasing their mortality rate.

It is suggested that the way in which births and deaths are registered could possibly explain some of the discrepancies. The declarations of the father might distort the facts, with fairly dark mestizo children being registered as white. The percentage of stillborns confirms this interpretation, for it reveals that when this is eliminated the proportion of whites diminishes while that of mulattoes and Negroes doubles.* However, it seems that it is not only a matter of the father who alters his declarations in deference to the social prestige of the white race. It is probable that negligence in registering children was more frequent in the lower classes, which included a larger number of Negroes and mulattoes than the population as a whole. Furthermore, it seems that doctors also succumbed to the effects of color prejudice in an inverse way, tending to identify as Negroes persons who could be identified as mulattoes in the general census. In many social circles of São Paulo, anyone who is not white is Negro. Indulgent as they might be, many doctors are probably unconsciously influenced by this rule, at least in cases of rather dark mulattoes.

The two types of data discussed in the preceding pages make it possible to discern a trend of the Negro and mulatto population of the city to decrease. This trend seems to be the product of several factors. First, there was a rapid increase in the white racial stock that was given intermittent spurts by immigration. Second, there was racial mixture, the importance of which cannot be ignored. The lightest mulattoes try to pass as whites whenever they meet favorable economic and sociocultural conditions. There is also a reverse tendency that consists in the identification of dark mulattoes and even light mulattoes with the Negro group which leads many such persons to classify themselves purely and simply as Negroes.[8]

* Editor's note: Mulatto and Negro babies show increased pigmentation with age, causing the fathers of stillborns to register them as lighter than they would have been had they lived.

However, such cases have been neglected and there are no means for evaluating their statistical significance. Third, there was a decrease of the Negro population attributable to the differences between the birth and death rates. Although such differences are far from having the calamitous import imagined in the past, they seem to remain constant and are associated with socioeconomic conditions.

It is difficult to completely discern the nature, proportions, and consequences of the so-called "Negro deficit." The first two trends involve effects of interracial contact in São Paulo, but they cannot be given equal value quantitatively. The first can be easily perceived. The percentages provided by censuses or other sources clearly indicate how the contribution of each racial contingent to the composition of the *Paulistana* population has changed. The second trend must be approximated on the basis of clues furnished by the aforementioned percentages. Amaral (1961, pp. 70–71) calculates that the decennial average decrease in the number of mulattoes for the whole state during the period from 1836 to 1950 was 2.5 per cent, while that of the Negro during the same period was 1.55 per cent. In his conclusions he points out that:

The *pardo* group—constituted by numerous shades of pigmentation—tends to become integrated not only statistically but also *de facto* into the ruling group, the white one, robbing the black population even more. . . . The Negro group remained stationary for some time once the source of supply through the slave trade had been cut off; diseases and undernourishment—since color became identified as an index of low social and economic status—contributed mightily to reduce its proportional representation in the *Paulista* population.

For this group miscegenation is of a clearly exterminatory significance as it dilutes the group and causes it to disappear via its mulatto descendants into the mestizo contingents of the world.

The Negro and mulatto do not view miscegenation merely as a technique for achieving social goals and upward mobility; they see it as a means of racial extermination. The following

testimony, received in May, 1951, summarizes the main elements of this attitude: "We aren't against miscegenation. But
we are against the politics of forced miscegenation because
they want to make the Negro race disappear. White policy is
really to make the Negro race disappear. First through miscegenation. Second, by drowning it in a torrent of white immigrants. It's because the white doesn't want to hear anything
about us. There's the police polity to degrade the Negro in
order to see him disappear with tuberculosis, syphilis, and
prostitution. What we want is to be recognized as citizens like
everybody else and have a right to be educated. We should be
brought into society and not be voluntarily abandoned in the
hope that we'll disappear." [9]

The third trend, the decrease of the Negro population, is the
one that is of particular interest for the present analysis. In
his study of Brazilian demographic problems, Smith (1954)
includes data on the state of São Paulo from 1932 to 1941, as
shown in Table 5.

TABLE 5

Births and Deaths in the State of São Paulo (1932–1941)

Population	Births Number	Per cent	Deaths Number	Per cent
Whites	1,844,600	88.1	920,398	80.9
Mulattoes	102,860	4.9	106,977	9.4
Negroes	65,612	3.1	86,437	7.6
Mongoloids	82,332	3.9	23,564	2.1
Color unknown	—	—	205	—
Total	2,095,404	100.0	1,137,581	100.0

Thus it is verified that there was a surplus of 924,202 white
persons and that the deficit of the black population was
24,924 persons (4,117 persons for mulattoes and 20,825 for
Negroes). The number of deaths exceeded one-seventh of the
total births in this population. Smith has attempted to explain
this sociologically with two hypotheses. First, he said there is
a positive correlation between socioeconomic status and the

birth rate which explains the greater prolificacy of whites as compared with Negroes and mulattoes. Second, there is an inverse relation between socioeconomic status and the number of deaths, which would explain the mortality differential that is unfavorable to Negroes and mulattoes. Both hypotheses are consistent with the interpretations proffered by Lowrie. Since the data refer to the interior of the state of São Paulo (where the Negro population has enjoyed conditions that are apparently better) and deal with a later time span, it can be concluded that they confirm and broaden these interpretations. It is not only probable that there has been a selective trend with regard to the Negro and mulatto population of the capital, but also likely that whatever its magnitude (Lowrie supposed that it was small), this trend seems to have been persistent.

Studies published by the Statistical Laboratory of the Brazilian Institute of Geography and Statistics by Giorgio Mortara [10] emphasize that the difference in mortality rates for different racial stocks is the most weighty factor in determining the growth rate of the Brazilian population. The census makes it possible to calculate that between 1872 and 1940 Brazil had a mean annual geometric rate of natural growth of 18.68 per 1,000 white, Negro, and mulatto inhabitants, independent of immigration.

In experimenting with different combinations of rates of natural increments for whites on the one hand and for Negroes and mulattoes on the other, if all are subjected to the condition that the rate of whites exceeds that of Negroes and mulattoes, without this difference reaching an excessively high degree, however, the conclusion is drawn that an acceptable hypothesis is a rate of 22 per 1,000 whites and 16 per 1,000 Negroes and mulattoes taken together. Estimating the birth rate for all black groups at about 45 per 1,000, this hypothesis would give a mortality rate of about 23 per 1,000 Negroes and mulattoes together. . . . Estimating the average birth rate during this period at 44.5 per 1,000 inhabitants, we would have a mortality rate of 17–18 per 1,000 whites; 23 per 1,000 Negroes; 36–37 per 1,000 mulattoes; and 32 per 1,000 Negroes and mulattoes combined (Ferreira, Barros, and Etrog, 1961, pp. 28–31).

By comparing data of this nature with that pertaining to fertility and birth rates, it can be seen that female fertility is high in all racial groups in the Brazilian population, even though the differences observed in the frequency of births carry with them moderate differences in the growth rate of the various groups. Mortara (1961, p. 11) brings together the data supplied by the census of 1940 for the state of São Paulo in Table 6.

TABLE 6

Female Fertility in Various Racial Groups,
State of São Paulo 1940 Census: Average Number
of Live Children Born to 100 Women

Age (years)	Whites	Mulattoes	Negroes	Mongoloids
15 to 19	9.8	14.4	12.0	5.1
20 to 29	156.9	179.0	157.8	159.2
30 to 39	420.7	452.5	423.7	436.5
40 to 49	616.1	654.8	591.8	569.6
50 to 59	681.0	665.0	649.1	514.6
60 and over	690.5	663.2	625.9	452.6
15 and over	331.3	328.3	310.8	297.5

As Mortara points out, the fertility of white women differs little, either upward or downward, from that of mulatto women of the same age group; and the fertility of Negro women is a little less than that of the women of these two groups owing to the greater number of Negro women who did not bear children.

The important thing to emphasize is that these data show that the rate of reproduction of the different racial groups is apparently not dependent upon racial physiological factors. As Mortara stresses with regard to the prevailing trends in Brazil, "even though the studies verified that the fertility [rate] of the Negro group was a little lower than that of the white and mulatto, they showed that this inferiority is attributable chiefly to the greater proportion of Negro women who are denied reproductive function because of the disadvantage this group suffers in the choice of marriage partners. The prolificacy of Negro men is not usually inferior to that of whites or mulattoes." [11] Comparison of the results of the censuses of 1940 and 1950 made it possible to demonstrate clearly that the decrease in the average rate of female fertility is more dependent upon the decrease in prolificacy than upon the decrease in the number of prolific women in the three racial groups under consideration. Comparison of the results of the two censuses also indicates certain trends in the infant mortality of these groups. "Of the total number of live births to women 15 years and over, the highest proportion of survivors on the date of the census is found in the Mongoloid group (898.4 per 1,000); far behind follows the white group (773 per 1,000) and farther back, the mulatto group (714.6 per 1,000) and the Negro group (705.5 per 1,000) with survival rates that are only slightly different" (Mortara, 1956b, p. 11). Therefore, up until the date of the census (according to corrected proportions) the following numbers died: 104.4 per 1,000 children of Mongoloid women; 225.9 per 1,000 children of white women; 289.0 per 1,000 children of mulatto women; and 292.3 per 1,000 children of Negro women. This reveals that the differences in infant mortality increase greatly from one racial group to another.

Of particular interest for our own study is the conclusion that the progressive numerical predominance of whites has not come about as a result of the continual, inevitable decrease in nonwhites, but as a result of the differences in the rate or speed of natural growth for each racial group in the Brazilian population. In other words, all groups of the population share the tendency for rapid growth. The differences between the growth rates of Negro and mulatto groups in relation to the white group, although considerable, would be merely a matter of degree. Considered by themselves, they too are high and bear comparisons with demographic growth rates of great vitality in other countries.

Everything indicates that it would be wise to view the opinions held during the first quarter of this century regarding the widely publicized Negro deficit of the capital of São Paulo with reservations. The inconsistency of statistical data and the complexity of the demographic problems that underlie the comparisons (and which cannot be investigated or resolved objectively by means of that data) make this approach mandatory. The main factor for alarm in the face of the decrease in the population of the city was related to normal phenomena of the times. The flight from the capital by masses of ex-slaves and former freedmen was perfectly natural, whether the matter is viewed from the perspective of the redistribution of the Negro population in terms of its origins or whether the matter is viewed ecologically and socially. Some returned to their original localities, to which they remained tied for one reason or another. Others attempted through migrations to offset the disadvantages created by competition with foreign immigrants. On the other hand it is clear from the statistical data that the natural growth rates of the Negro and mulatto groups of the *Paulistana* population do reveal a certain decrease deriving from purely ecological, economic, and social circumstances. The conditions of economic and social life confronted by Negroes and mulattoes are undoubtedly responsible for the decrease in births and the increase in deaths. The circumstances are so complex and poorly understood, however, that it is not possible to say, in demographic or sociological terms, how their effects have influenced, are now influencing, and will tend to influence the growth rates of the Negro and mulatto population of the city of São Paulo. In regard to the present and future, only special demographic and ecological investigations will be able to indicate whether these phenomena are temporary or not, and principally whether or not they are normal, keeping in mind their proportions and the process of reintegration of the Negro and mulatto into the urban way of life.

Even so, the Negro "deficit" seems to have encountered a constant and compensatory corrective in the migration of Negro and mulatto groups to the city. The process, which began about 1884, developed progressively until Abolition, became intensified thereafter (as the censuses of 1886, 1890, and 1893 reveal), and continued throughout the entire period of the city's later development. As far as is known, migrations from the interior of the state to the city were uninterrupted, increasing rapidly with industrial development and the transformation of São Paulo into a metropolis whose economic influence extended over the entire regional and national economy.

Alongside this current flowing from the interior to the city there has always existed another movement to the city from the various regions of the nation. This broader current was of real importance in the slaveholding society, for it guaranteed a supply of workers in an age in which agricultural expansion was dependent on the slave and slave trading had already been prohibited. New sources of replenishment for the Negro and mulatto population of the city developed among the small segments of these migrant groups of native-born workers who felt some attraction to life in the city. This propensity appears not to have depended only upon certain emotional and psychological longings. The study by Unzer de Almeida and Mendes Sobrinho (1951) suggests the existence of a certain compatibility between the prior qualifications and aptitudes of the migrating workers and their absorption into the occupational system of the city. In other words, even though many rural workers encountered opportunities for employment in various types of urban services, there was a qualitative screening mechanism that functioned as an element of control for the process, probably restricting the rate of influx and the concentration of these workers. This reason seems to explain at least in part why, for the period up until 1935, the principal arsenal for the replenishment of the Negro and mulatto population of São Paulo was to be found in the interior of the state rather than in other regions of the country, even though the latter also contributed in an intermittent but cumulative way to increase it.

Precarious as the available information might be, it makes

it possible to verify that the comparative increase of the Negro and mulatto population of the city of São Paulo has shown great vitality. This information permits us to conclude that the basis of this increase has been the internal migrations during the period under consideration—chiefly the migrations from the interior to the capital of the state. This conclusion makes it clear that the Negro population did not tend to disappear as was supposed, but on the contrary continued to increase, yet without achieving a dynamic pattern of demographic equilibrium enmeshed to the structure of urban life. At best, the correction of the "Negro deficit" was always quantitative and external.

The effects of horizontal mobility associated with the attraction of the city and the occupational instability of the unskilled, plus the consequences of the lightening process, presuppose the influence of enduring, century-old structural factors. They could have been offset only if there had occurred profound changes in the recruitment or socialization of the human factors of the masses of migrant native-born workers, and if the influences that made identification with the dominant race imperative had ceased to operate. That aspect of the "deficit" resulting from the small margin of the death rate over the birth rate could have been corrected under one condition: that the urbanization of the standards of living of the Negro and mulatto had accompanied a rhythm that was initially rapid and constantly accelerated.

However, such did not occur in spite of the fact that the continual replenishment of the Negro and mulatto population was favorable to the persistence of demographic traits characteristic of young and migrant populations. Even though the causes of this phenomenon are poorly understood, it seems clear that in the city of São Paulo it is the result of the perpetuation of factors that hinder the rapid adjustment of the Negro and mulatto to urban life and which keep him from competing advantageously with other population groups at the biotic level.

Social Disorganization

The advantages offered by urban life to the individual and to the community did not appreciably alter the position of the Negro and mulatto in the economic and social levels. Throughout the period under consideration, they remained in the same position in which the emergence of the competitive social order and the urban revolution had found them. They were totally excluded by the new socioeconomic mechanism of occupational screening and thus totally unable to adopt the new patterns of living associated with the more promising and remunerative urban occupations. Strictly speaking, they did not simply remain on the fringes of the process of economic growth inherent in the urban revolution in São Paulo. They shared in the occupations and opportunities opened by the urban style of life in such a fashion that they perpetuated the inevitable initial maladjustments derived from the breakdown of the old order and soon were in a state of chronic social disorganization.

In order to understand this it is necessary to understand to what extent urbanization, industrialization, and immigration were dynamically intertwined with the development of the city of São Paulo from the turn of the century to 1930. As we have seen, urban development in São Paulo coincided with immigration, and in many ways was a complex product of internal economic growth induced by the capitalistic effects of the coffee business combined with the implantation of a new economic mentality introduced chiefly by immigrants. In this period continuous economic growth granted the city a true, progressive autonomy over the rural areas. Especially after the First World War, the consequences of industrialization were felt with particular force, giving rise on the Brazilian historical scene to a new pattern of urbanization that gave prominence to the economic, social, and political interests of the city itself. When this stage was reached, the plantation owner lost his importance as a dominant figure, and supremacy in the economic sphere gradually passed into the hands of the typical "big-city capitalist." This of course does not mean that coffee production lost its identity as a means of accumulating capital, or that the plantation owner suddenly became, from one moment to the next, a negligible economic agent. But it does mean that his historical role had run its course in the transition from large-scale agriculture to a differentiated capitalist economy.

Under the economic and social conditions which arose at this stage, two social groups benefited broadly from the economic, social, and political consequences of industrialization: those who retained the role of capitalist, as owners of developing industries, and those who could sell their labor as workers. Although Brazilian elements existed in both groups, participation of the Negro and mulatto was practically nil. With the exception of rare cases of racial mixture in important families, the advent of urban, industrial capitalism was prejudicial to the independent Negro and mulatto entrepreneurs, who were irremediably ousted from every favorable position they had achieved in the past. As for the free labor market, we have also seen how unfavorable it was to those who came out of slavery or from the free labor associated with slavery. Few managed to rate as skilled or semiskilled workers, because of their lack of technical training, because the foreign worker was held in higher regard, or because the Negroes and mulattoes themselves preferred to apply for more attainable work opportunities. The fact that urbanization and industrialization were to a large extent the results of immigration granted the immigrant a highly advantageous position vis-à-vis the Brazilian worker, and also practically eliminated any competitive possibilities for the Negro and mulatto, relegating them automatically to the less favored sectors of the society.

The dynamic conditions that related urbanization to immigration, and both of these to industrialization in the city of São Paulo, reveal why the Negro and mulatto were not reabsorbed into the urban occupational system. Higher and intermediary positions were out of reach, since only members of the dominant classes and vertically mobile foreigners and Brazilians of foreign descent could compete for them. Salaried positions created by urban expansion and industrialization were fiercely competed for by foreign and, in smaller numbers, national workers, who were held to be more skilled. Thus the problem of how to make a living was a serious one for the Negro and mulatto. In spite of the abolition of slavery, nothing had altered the state of affairs which had led to the inescapable maladjustment of the former slave in the competitive system. The more coveted positions remained closed. Access to open positions was selective because criteria were followed that applied only rarely to black individuals. The Negro and mulatto, who stood on the side lines during the emergence of the competitive social order, stayed in this position under later historical circumstances. The initial industrial boom engendered by previous urban development benefited chiefly the national and foreign elements who had gained strategic positions within the occupational and economic structure of the city. The others, and with them the majority of the black population, had to wait for what the future might bring, putting to use only part of their work capacity and living on a rural, precapitalist, and anti-urban level.

Unable to make a living at occupations and for salaries that were truly urban, the Negro and mulatto could not adopt the truly urban style of life. As had happened earlier, in the initial phase of development of the competitive social order and urban revolution, they lived in the city without being of it. As the powerful motivations and feelings engendered by the abolitionist struggle ceased to operate, the impact of this situation became ever more destructive and discouraging. Earlier, concealed idleness and occasional vagrancy had seemed a means of self-affirmation, a way of preserving the freedom and dignity of the individual. Now they had lost any ulterior meaning, and permanent idleness demoralizes a man and predisposes him to systematic vagrancy. The same thing occurred on other levels of human behavior, from the exploitation of women's work to specialization in the area of crime. What had seemed a dramatic and proud form of protest, for lack of anything better, was increasingly debased, leading down the path of poverty, corruption, and collective despair.

It is extraordinarily difficult to document this facet of the life of Negroes and mulattoes in the city. Travelers, historians, and essayists ceased paying attention to the Negro and focused their interest on immigrants and on the particular economic forces of industrial society. The rich and varied documentation provided by the Negro press in turn reveals the effects rather than the causes of the Negro drama in the city. It provides good clues but little conclusive data to explain what occurred.

Life stories and interviews that focus on the careers of Negroes or mulattoes show that it was impossible to earn a steady and remunerative living through specifically *urban* occupations. In fact this was at the very root of all the evils that befell the black population of the city of São Paulo. The assimilation of new behavior patterns and the urban style of life depended upon the acquisition of those ways of earning a living that were regulated by the development of the urban, industrial civilization. As long as they were excluded from such jobs, the Negro and the mulatto were deprived of participating economically, socially, and culturally in that civilization. They were condemned to a hidden form of isolation, and they did not adequately adjust to the urban world by means of the sociocultural legacy that had been passed down from the less complex past of the slave and freedman.

The evidence gathered indicates that around 1920, during the period of urban development, the position of the Negro and mulatto on the city's occupational scale was appreciably worse than before. In one of the life histories the informant told us that ". . . Negroes having a trade such as that of a stonemason, carpenter, barber, tailor, or shoemaker were rare. They were difficult trades and young Negro apprentices had a difficult time finding employment." Work opportunities rarely fell into their hands at factories unless it was "nigger's work," as the informant described it, "that the Italians wouldn't do; heavy work that involved health risks." The Negro woman, in turn, "finds it difficult even today to become an apprentice and eventually a weaver," having to content herself with jobs like domestic work, mainly for the traditional families. "There were few black persons in commerce. Only two or three haberdashers had Negro employees; as a rule they did manual labor when they worked in business establishments." Thus, Negroes and mulattoes who wanted to support themselves took menial jobs, most of which were poorly paid and required few if any qualifications. "At the beginning of my adult life (about 1920), Negroes were employed in domestic work. They did all the housework. Coachmen were usually white, but those who took care of the horses were Negroes. The coachman was an important guy who had a top hat. . . . The janitors in boardinghouses were Negroes. There were even house washers who plied their trade at certain spots. . . . Strong Negroes were well received to serve as bodyguards to protect their bosses and to show that anyone who gave them any trouble would have to deal with a Negro. . . . There were lawyers and doctors who had Negroes to take care of the office. . . . To be a private chauffeur, a low-ranking civil servant (janitor, office boy, or clerk as well as to do pick-and-shovel work or be a garbage man), or a police investigator was really something. Such jobs could only be acquired by those who had the strong backing of some white bigshot."

External aspects of dress and standard of living separated poor Negroes from elite Negroes. "Negro social life was divided between Negroes who went to the dance halls in the center of the city and who were considered to be the elite; and neighborhood-oriented Negroes who were called 'calico Negroes' because of the cloth used in the clothes they wore. The former were those who worked in public offices and chauffeurs, who earned more and were better dressed. The chauffeurs, for example, spent the most money on the buffet tables at the dance halls and wouldn't allow the others—the oppressed and more ignorant—even to get close. The other group mentioned above, although they had less money, were more independent and weren't leaning on whites, receiving their patronage and buttering them up."

By using the data of Lobo da Silva (1928) given in Table 7,

TABLE 7

Occupations of Military Draftees, State of São Paulo (1922–1923)
(*Figures in italics represent respective percentages*)

Total population		Whites	Mestizos	Negroes	Indian-white mixtures
	5,364	4,380	657	314	13
	100.00	*82.01*	*12.00*	*6.00*	*0.20*
Agricultural workers	2,560	1,999	377	173	11
	100.00	*78.00*	*14.70*	*6.70*	*0.40*
Factory workers	1,499	1,202	184	112	1
	100.00	*80.19*	*12.20*	*7.40*	*0.06*
Artisans	28	27		1	
	100.00	*96.40*		*3.50*	
Business employees	761	691	56	14	
	100.00	*90.80*	*7.80*	*1.80*	
Civil servants	165	145	16	4	
	100.00	*87.80*	*9.60*	*2.40*	
Professionals	72	70	1	1	
	100.00	*97.20*	*1.30*	*1.30*	
Students	165	156	9		
	100.00	*94.50*	*5.40*		
Sailors	7	3	4		
	100.00	*42.80*	*57.00*		
Soldiers	52	42	3	6	1
	100.00	*80.70*	*5.70*	*11.5*	*1.90*
Not declared	55	45	7	3	
	100.00	*81.80*	*12.70*	*5.40*	

it is possible to get a more complete picture of the occupational distribution among the various groups of the population in the state of São Paulo. The sampling is from persons drafted for military service and includes groups that tended toward low or intermediate positions in the occupational structure.

The fact is that there was great uncertainty in securing and maintaining a steady source of earnings. The majority had to live off odd jobs involving no prospective for salaried work. Having professional qualifications was no guarantee that one would get a job. The following example illustrates this: "A good stonemason who had come from Bahia where he had learned the trade as a child had to work for a week's tryout because the foreman didn't believe that he was capable of doing such work." But even after getting employment they were always susceptible to setbacks. One informant managed to become employed as an office worker in a bank. After a certain period, when he thought that everything was going well in his life, the manager of the bank was replaced by another. The new boss "tells me to shine his shoes. I told him angrily that I had taken care of his lodging accommodations because I had been given this task, but that I was an office employee and it wasn't fitting that I should do what he had asked. 'That's what a nigger's for,' he retorted. I grabbed him by the collar! The intervention of fellow workers kept me from smashing his face."

Chance decided the occupational opportunity of the Negro and mulatto, and nothing restricted their great mobility— which led them to flit like butterflies from one job to the next, looking for one good opportunity, better pay, and humane treatment. Both men and women began to work at a very early age, in barbershops, firewood stores, workshops, and homes. They worked hard until the end of their lives, earning barely enough to support themselves and feed their children. Several informants indicated that unmarried mothers worked wherever they could, and when they were unable to find work, they had to resort to begging and occasional prostitution. The children helped out with the family budget as best they could; "we pickaninnies were all called 'street urchins.' Families liked to have us around for messages and errands." In short, by performing small services they learned in the street how to live off odd jobs earning a few pennies with which they could help support the household.

The tramp, the thief, and the prostitute ran much smaller

risks and built themselves a comparatively better future. In a certain sense they were the only successful ones, and they could flaunt the marks of their triumphs in the style of life they led, in the clothes they wore, and in the fascination that they eventually induced in the minds of the others. A prostitute who visited her goddaughter in a slum or took her mother a monthly allowance carried herself as if she were a great lady and was certainly looked upon as such, even by those who pretended to look down upon her. The professional thief or the habitual loiterer who exploited one, two, or more women and stole occasionally led "a he-man's life," always had money, and by luck managed to get what his friends who were well behaved but fools were unable to earn by years of humiliating labor and often not even after a lifetime of privations.

However, the commercialization of vice was not an unavoidable and spurious consequence of the slums and the streets. Naturally the disorganization prevailing in the immediate social environment encouraged learning about vice and crime, but it did not impose it as the desired and preferred adjustment pattern. This occurred because the roads of self-assertion were blocked. The braver, the more impatient, and the more apt, physically and intellectually, often opted for crime or vice to avoid the slow torture and humiliation of "nigger work." Obvious and recognized success, comfort, and respect could hardly be won by any means that did not involve vice and crime. This occurred on a scale that revealed beyond a shadow of a doubt that it was in crime that the best prospectives for a career could be found by younger Negro talents. In the Negro milieu the differentiation of behavior and personality in ways that were disapproved of socially constituted a "normal" phenomenon.

In time there developed a whole mythology about the poverty, promiscuity, and destitution in which about three-fifths of the Negro population of the city normally lived at this time. This mythology circulated among whites as much as among Negroes and mulattoes. Nonetheless it did only partial justice to reality. The images that we have been able to gather reveal turbid and shocking scenes that are almost inconceivable in the Brazilian historical setting.

Habitation was one of the basic problems of the struggle for survival. Much has been said about the living conditions in the slum and the consequences of the close crowding of persons in a single-room occupancy. However, those who lived in these conditions already had acquired something, for they had a roof over their heads. One of the most reliable sources of information tells that "many had no place to live: my mother had to sleep with me and my sister in an outhouse for lack of any other place." In describing the room which he shared with both he says: "there wasn't any bed, or mattress. The floor was pounded earth. The bed was an old straw mat. There were no blankets nor sheets." Being able to rent a slum room already represented some success, for it was necessary to have money to pay for it and to eliminate the resistance of the landlord. The Negro applicant might be turned down, sometimes because of color but also because the landlord had misgivings about the regularity of payment. Only when good references could be obtained did he agree to rent.

One informant tells that "in slums where there was a mixture of Italians, Spaniards, and Negroes, the latter had to ingratiate themselves. They had to keep on the good side of the landlords because they were always in economic difficulties. The Negro's lot was that of subservience. Many fed on the leftovers that the cooks brought home at night from the houses of their employers. But ill-disposed Negroes who called the Italians "peddlers," "dirty," and "onion-eaters" were rejected. This was a cause for fights in the tenements and led to the investigation of a Negro's past every time he asked for a room." Another informant points out that at this time the Negro and mulatto developed "the ideal of living in a slum," which to this person's mind became deeply rooted in Negro people. They did not know what decency and comfort were, preferring to live in this way in collective habitations, in close quarters with numerous families of strangers. Even after ac-

quiring enough to rent a house, they liked a basement or
tenement better, the informant said, and cited the case of his
own brother-in-law who paid more for lodging in a tenement
than he would spend in rent for a good house by itself on the
outskirts.

The usual lessee of one, two, or three rooms with a separate
or a shared kitchen was the head of the family—an unwed
mother, a father, a mother's lover, or a stepfather. But even
though they had only one room, there was no certain or fixed
limit to the number of persons who shared the room. There
might be the father, the mother, and her children from two to
six or more; at other times in place of the father there might
be a stepfather or the mother's lover or, vice versa, the stepmother or the father's mistress. In addition a relative (mother
or sister of the wife or husband, a cousin or a brother- or
sister-in-law, etc.), an acquaintance, or a friend might share
the same room. Whenever a son or daughter married and
could not set up housekeeping, the couple also could come to
live in the household for an indefinite period of time, along
with any children they might have. And there was nothing to
keep a son, a brother, or any other relative or friend who was
suffering a setback in life from coming to live under the same
roof as long as the need lasted. Consequently, some dwellings,
such as those described by the informants, had a large number of occupants.

The most well-known tenements were constructed for commercial, not residential, ends: with unhygienic conditions,
poor ventilation, bad lighting, and little useful space. It is easy
to imagine what happened—the dwellings forced people out
into the street. Those who worked away from home often left
in the morning and returned at night. But those who were
unemployed or semiemployed spent more time in intimate
contact with others in the room. Nothing was hidden from the
others, from gossip which the minors had inklings about or
witnessed to the adults' sexual relations. And since the walls
were often but partitions or were falling down, the stage was
even larger. Things that went on in neighbors' rooms could

also be heard and seen. One of the informants recalled the following incident from childhood: "I witnessed some armed Negro men assault a Negro woman who lived next door and grab her by force, one from the front and the other from behind."

The information gathered implies that living in crowded conditions directly influenced the disorganization of sex life. Children learned the secrets of life precociously, and knew how adults proceeded to achieve sexual pleasure, how the species is reproduced and how birth occurs, when they were going to have a new baby brother, etc. In cases in which the husband or lover did not leave for work at the same time as the woman, because they were accustomed to doing odd jobs, loafing or drinking, they ended up staying in the house a good part of the day and inviting their friends in. From this resulted not only associations that were dangerous for minors but also various kinds of incentives for practicing vice. The stepfather or lover tended to take advantage of such opportunities for seducing his companion's daughter and entertaining himself sexually with boys and youths of his own sex. The opposite could also occur: the stepmother or mistress seduce her companion's son. We can register a certain amount of data confirming both. Ultimately the children themselves began to find sexual activity attractive: they already used each other at five and six years of age according to informants, although the adolescent boys and girls were the most likely to take advantage of this source of pleasure. Thus there occurred heterosexual relations among brothers and sisters and among cousins as much as there developed homosexual pairs and groups in which neighborhood friends might participate. The violation of thirteen- and fourteen-year-old minors was quite common, with even the mother's brother and a girl's father among the violators. During this period sexual relations promoted the contamination of minors with venereal diseases. There was no barrier erected to the propagation of these diseases and many thought it natural that things should happen this way, giving little importance to incidents in the sex life of children, youth, and adults. After all, it was said, "Negroes were made for just that!"

The streets eventually produced similar results. Girls and boys were attracted to adventures of this variety by friends or adults, at times in return for small favors. One informant told of a typical case of a fifteen- or sixteen-year-old girl. The parents normally went to work and the girl was left alone. She fell into bad company and ended up being violated. When the father found out about it he was furious: he beat her and threw her out of the house as his shame and dishonor. In such cases the mothers attempted to smooth things over and prepare the way for their daughters' return. After a few days they returned to the family if they had not fallen into the life of a streetwalker. The neighbors talked a bit, but it didn't go beyond this:

"You know, so-and-so is already lost!"

"Already? With who, huh?"

"With so-and-so," or, "She won't tell."

The boys, in turn, did not escape untouched. Here is what one informant tells about his experiences in the street. "It was common for those Negroes to grab one of the street urchins and take him into the woods. Those who were sorry, if indeed they were, only made the boy play with them. I saw a big Negro fellow grab a boy and stick him. There was a fuss. Those Negroes wanted to catch a guy and they invited us to go to the woods with them. . . . They grabbed the more naïve boys. The innocent-type kids went through that as if it were natural. Some, like F., went after the men. I was full of the devil. I grew up in the street. I always got away."

This brief sketch sets forth the details of living conditions of the Negro and mulatto groups in the city. Deprived of the social guarantees which they deserved and urgently needed and driven away from the centers of interests that were vital to economic growth and sociocultural development, they discovered in the human body an undestructible source of self-assertion, compensation for prestige, and self-realization. The idea of the animal in man cannot be applied to their erotic trade. The cultural tradition of the Negro milieu has focused on the significance of erotic excesses—a pastime and a source of pure pleasure. It has only erred in attributing this propensity to the supposed human nature of the Negro and mulatto.

Thus the dramatic aspect of the situation is not to be found in the area in which the self-assertion of the Negro and mulatto were realized, but in the pure erotic explosion that characterized this self-assertion. No internal or external discipline sublimated the emotional nature or the psychological meaning of sexual pleasure. This did not occur in the last African tribal traditions: in those traditions the vitality, joy, and purity of sexual pleasure were expressed according to certain norms, which included self-respect and respect for one's partner in erotic activity.[12] It was slavery that broke down these barriers and all the naïve but refined delicacy that crowns the relation between man and woman in African models. In preventing the selection of mates and even the times for amorous encounters, forcing a woman to serve several men, and encouraging coitus as a mere means of carnal relief, slavery degraded the slave's body and soul, his erotic activity, and his techniques of lovemaking.

Sex came to be the source, par excellence, of the intensification and revitalization of the factors of social anomie among Negroes and mulattoes. It has hindered, undermined, and at times even distorted the assimilation of new patterns of behavior, blocking or retarding the full development of the stable and integrated family in the Negro group. Students of the *Paulistana* black population have generally placed more emphasis on other factors of the social disorganization of the Negro milieu. Unemployment, alcoholism, abandoned children, elderly persons and dependents, begging, vagrancy, prostitution, disease, and criminal behavior undoubtedly do constitute social problems of undeniable importance in the cultural history of this group. Their influence still can be felt today, in a structural as well as dynamic way, in the factors that contribute to the disorganization of the social life of the Negro and mulatto. However, it seems to us that these things have flourished and have been perpetuated owing to certain *impedimenta* of a sociopyschological and sociocultural nature that have turned the erotic explosion into a condition highly unfavorable to the consolidation of the family in the Negro milieu.

The relation between sexual obsession, as some informants have preferred to call it, and disorganization as an actual way of life among large sectors of the black population of the city of São Paulo, developed at this point. The manner in which sex became the topic center of interest for individuals and dominated their social relationships, becoming a sphere of artistic expression, competition for prestige, and congeniality (and thus of community association), clearly indicates the lack of certain socializing influences that originate in and are controlled by the family. It was not the family that broke down as a social institution; but the family failed to set itself up and did not have a sociopsychological and sociocultural effect on the development of basic personality, the control of ego centric and antisocial behavior, and the development of bonds of solidarity. This can be historically confirmed by a simple reference to the main policy of the seignorial and slaveholding society of Brazil, which always sought to hinder the organized social life of the family among slaves.

From the sociological viewpoint the central issues are the nonexistence of the family as an integrated social institution, or its erratic functioning owing to its development under extremely adverse conditions. This does not mean that unemployment, alcoholism, abandoned children, aged persons and dependents, begging, vagrancy, prostitution, disease, and criminal behavior should be ignored or underestimated. But they should not be considered the causes of the social disorganization that prevailed among Negroes, nor should they be looked upon as isolated phenomena.

More attention should be given to the mechanisms of integration and the functioning of the Negro family, around which other negative and disturbing influences of the environment revolved. In view of this, in the following pages we will merely outline some of the more significant aspects of these social problems, and then concentrate on the description and analysis of the institutional deficiencies of the socializing functions of the family. However, in the final discussion—of a more general and systematic interpretative nature—we will attempt to discuss as a whole all the structural and dynamic effects of all the sociopsychological and sociocultural factors that should be considered in a sociological description. At this point, in an effort to achieve a balanced approach and an overall understanding of the situation, we will discuss the structural and functional interrelationships that explain the extreme apathy of the black population to the perpetual disorganization of its material and psychological conditions of social life.

The problem of unemployment has special features. Although white, Negro, and mulatto informants have invariably emphasized that unemployment was rampant throughout the black population of the city (especially among males), it looks as though the proportion of those who were unemployed in the strict sense of the word was minimal. In order to understand the position of the Negro and mulatto in the *Paulistana* society during this period, it is necessary to approach the matter in a way that will permit us to study their forms of occupation as if they participated in a subsistence economy that was more or less blocked by the surrounding urban area. Several types of economic adjustment can be discerned, from occasional or regular parasitical dependence on the female companion, to performing paid work that appeared by chance or permanent, salaried work.

As long as the Negro and mulatto were not incorporated into the emerging class system or were only partially integrated into it, they remained in an ambiguous position in relation to native-born and foreign whites. The majority of the latter moved into social roles which made them into salaried workers or "entrepreneurs," whether they desired it or not. Negroes and mulattoes enjoyed this status only when they could find a place in the network of institutionalized urban occupations—that is, only a minority of the black population could confront unemployment as a social problem. As a whole the various forms of adjustment and the criteria of evaluation that were part of the sociocultural heritage of the rural past still prevailed in this group. These forms and criteria involved the tolerance and even the approval of various modes of unstable employment, underemployment, and even permanent unemployment of men. They did not see themselves as salaried workers at all, and many preferred to earn a living by means that excluded permanent positions involving obligations and responsibilities.

The system of occupations and services of the city was in a state of transition, there being a relative abundance of service jobs that would guarantee only the semiemployment or partial occupation of the labor force. Most of these jobs were related to the survival of archaic economic structures, but a few were the products of urban growth itself. The truth is that the majority of the opportunities for earnings open to Negro labor fell into this category of service jobs, bringing dire consequences for Negro and mulatto workers. Such activities kept them out of occupations in which they would have improved their skills and effected their socialization for permanent salaried work and the type of social organization that such work presupposes. In addition, such activities fostered extreme occupational instability which was attributed to the Negro by would-be employers who characterized him as an "unsteady worker," one who "flits" from one job to the next, and one "you can't depend on," as if the "liking for odd jobs" were the product of unchangeable predilections of the Negro worker's personality. On the other hand there was marked resistance to employing Negroes and mulattoes in jobs that required difficult training and demanded a minimum amount of initiative, discipline, and responsibility. It was said that the Negro "wasn't cut out for this" or "wasn't made for such things" because he was "unstable," "undisciplined," and, in addition, "that he didn't have ambition as the Italian did."

Thus Negroes and mulattoes faced a typical situation of

involuntary, hidden unemployment, in spite of the fact that the general economic situation was one of full employment. In order to circumvent this situation they had to depend upon economic arrangements that inevitably led to precarious, unsatisfactory, and socially undesirable adjustments. Exploitation of the female companion, occasional remunerative work, and preference for the commercialization of crime appeared the rule for achieving the easiest and most marked success. If this did not happen, they transferred the centers of interests of professional life to other things. Instead of being prepared to compete with whites in industrial civilization, the Negro and mulatto were turned into deformed economic factors. With the exception of a small group of those who held stable and conspicuous positions in the occupational structure, the large majority of the black population lacked opportunities for reeducation for the kind of work, the ethics, and the way of life of the free laborer. Lacking the capacity to discern the social consequences of their behavioral practices, Negroes and mulattoes came to cultivate those attributes which made them unstable workers with a propensity to interrupt their employment for most any reason, change jobs frequently, and leave a job as soon as they had made a certain amount of money in order to live as they wanted, working as little as they could.

Second, the degradation resulting from the available occupations, together with the detrimental effects of a deficient diet, the unhygienic conditions of their dwellings, negligence with personal hygiene, promiscuity in the basements and tenements, sexual excesses, and disease, made them lack the spirit to work. Not only did they receive limited material and psychological compensation as salaried workers; they had no reason to share the convictions that led the salaried worker to consider organized, disciplined, and permanent work as something necessary, useful, and ennobling.

Third, their first concern was what could be called the final product: the living standard that is associated with well-paying, prestigious employment. Conspicuous consumption, especially in dress and food, became the characteristic mark of the city Negro's interests. A carpenter whose earnings were insufficient to support his family and who needed the financial help of his wife liked to dress formally for the parties at his club. He used a large part of his own and his wife's earnings for this purpose. The same happened with regard to women, who made hard sacrifices—sometimes for a whole year—in order to be able to make an impression at a certain party or during Carnival * with beautiful and expensive costumes. The goal in question was described by a figure in one of the life histories as being the ideal—to distinguish oneself as a "big handsome Negro." The desire to have plenty of food all the time (and not only on Sunday "like the Italians") was also irrepressible. Whoever "had the dough" ate meat every day ("to stuff oneself," if possible) and liked to see two or three "side dishes" on the table. The moderate eating habits of foreigners that made them "impose sacrifices on the stomach" or "save money through the mouth," were severely criticized. The prolonged associations with friends in bars and taverns gave rise to a third contradictory tendency among men. They liked to have money to spend on their drinking bouts and to have plenty of time to spend entertaining themselves with friends as well.

This list of examples reveals the nature of the sociopsychological tendencies that relegated work to a place of secondary importance and made it a necessary evil. It is undeniable that some implications of these tendencies were compensatory and constructive, such as the propensity to want "to look like a big handsome Negro" and the desire to "have plenty of food." Nonetheless, such tendencies hampered the effective adjustment of the Negro and mulatto to the ordinary cultural outlook of the salaried worker. In the light of the slim household budgets of Negro families, the aspirations described here produced harmful results that only contributed to "gild the prevailing poverty" without eliminating it. The worst is that such aspirations impeded ideals which would have contributed to professional advancement and vertical mobility. Conse-

* *Editor's note:* Four-day pre-Lenten celebration consisting of street dancing and parades; Mardi Gras.

quently, the negative interests contributed to aggravation of the Negro's maladjustment to the urban way of life and encouraged the propagation in society at large of conceptions that were unfavorable to the Negro.

In addition to these points, it is necessary to consider other factors in the situation. There existed extremely low-paid employment (part time or full time) along with the hidden unemployment. It is impossible today to say which of the two weighed most heavily as a dynamic factor in the economic maladjustment of the Negro and mulatto. It seems undeniable that a large number of adults rejected and refused regular work because it looked like an unacknowledged form of slavery. The resultant adjustments perniciously and persistently underscored the reluctance of the Negro to throw himself enthusiastically into the existing opportunities for salaried work. The mechanisms of slow but gradual assimilation of Negro labor into the system of free labor, the capitalist economy, and the democratic social order were continually undermined. As we are dealing with a group that was emerging from a state of social anomie and had to face various types of objective and subjective resistance to its efforts to become classified socially, this factor becomes especially important.

It is appropriate to consider three more problems that are barely perceived or ignored. First, the truly marginal weakness of the Negro nuclei of the manpower reserve of the urban centers. Any disequilibrium in the economic system affected them catastrophically. Thus the informants remark that the effects of the crisis of 1929 were highly prejudicial to the city's black population. The paralyzation of work left them disoriented, with no way to make a living and with not knowing what to do. The increase in dependency and begging and the return to other geographic centers underscored their reaction to the crisis, which was weathered with relative stability by other sectors of the city's population. The lowering of salary levels of the Negro worker, for example, continued for manual labor until the minimum salary was legally instituted, and continues to this day for occupations that exceed this salary ceiling.

The situation of the poor, well-behaved Negro, the type that rejects vagrancy and attempts to live on the fringe of conventional society is still another case. His convictions and behavior are overly strict for the world in which he lives and cause him to be an easy target for the Negro operator and to make decisions that involve risks for himself and his loved ones. He considers it degrading for his wife or children to work, but he allows both of them to do work that can be done at home or work that is usually considered to be that of children. Thus, instead of allowing full collaboration of his family to bring in money that could permit savings, the acquisition of his own home, or the education of his children, he accepts their assistance only to the point that it serves to preserve an appearance of dignity. After some years, any incident (such as an illness, aid to some needy relative, unemployment) can break down this artificial stability. In summary, an inflexible, preurban ethic has caused the "poor, well-behaved" Negro to act in a self-defeating manner, exposing his family to a kind of insecurity and poverty that is worse because it has been accompanied by anxiety and perplexity. The negative character of his behavior is revealed even more clearly in his obligations to third parties (relatives, friends, and acquaintances in need). As soon as his hard work begins to show results, the marks of his prosperity are noticed by all, and no one has any doubt that "so-and-so is well off" or "rich." At this point relatives (his own or his wife's) and even friends or acquaintances begin asking for help. The traditional patterns, which are still being followed, compel him to help this one and that one: to house, feed, and at times to pay the expenses of one, two, or three persons for a limited or indefinite period of time. Owing to a long tradition of disorganized social life, it has not been unusual for the dependent to be one of the "Negro operators." If accepted, the newcomer to the household begins to live off the relative, friend, or acquaintance and to fleece him through an extremely destructive and ruthless parasitism.

This concept of duty, according to which those who are well off have a responsibility to take care of the rest, has conflicted with the individualism of the urban environment and has functioned as a definite sociopathic influence. Although the immigrant has been able to depend upon domestic solidarity in order to overcome economic adversities and to rise, exactly the opposite has occurred in the case of the Negro. Domestic solidarity has taken the best fruits of his labor, thereby preventing an increase in the standard of living.

Third, the economic weakness of the head of the family became the material foundation for the insecurity of all its members and the source of the perpetuation of the state of dependency from one generation to another. Nearly all the informants pointed out that the low salary level had been both the cause and effect of a low educational level. It was imperative that a radical change be made in the degree to which the Negro shared in the city's income so that parallel changes in the degree to which they shared in social rights and guarantees could be made possible. But this occurred too late and in an extremely relaxed fashion. The slowness and the selectivity with which the Negro was accepted for positions that guaranteed an increase in income caused his place in the occupational structure of the city to remain unimportant for a long time in relation to his competition with the white and his social classification and vertical mobility. Thus the paradox that many well-behaved Negroes frankly admitted that "it didn't pay to be honest," "to go straight," and "to be a hard worker." The sacrifices they made resulted only in subjective compensations of highly questionable value, which did not protect them from the direct or indirect effects of the disorganization that prevailed in the Negro milieu, or increase their ability to take advantage of new opportunities.

Alcoholism is another social problem in the Negro community that has been exaggerated and poorly understood. The data collected support the conclusion that the ostensive and intensive consumption of alcoholic beverages did in fact reach alarming proportions among the Negro population of the capital. However, this was not due as much to the number of drunkards as to the institutional deficiencies of the Negro milieu which lacked appropriate mechanisms in society for the control of the effects of alcoholism. In quantitative terms, it seems that the number of actual alcoholics was small in relation to the high number of groups that habitually frequented bars and taverns. It is evident that the constant gathering of certain individuals in public places eventually gave rise to the general conviction—among whites as much as among Negroes—that "alcoholism was rampant on every side, leading the Negro to perdition" (as one of the informants of the Negro group emphatically put it). The overtness of the behavior patterns in question thus contributed to the exaggeration of conceptions and judgments that were partially unfounded or improbable.

A comparison of the situation of the Negro at present and that which prevailed from 1900 to 1930 immediately suggests that the gathering of Negroes and mulattoes on street corners, empty lots, and especially in bars or taverns was a direct product of the form of adjustment to urban social life. Involuntary, hidden unemployment was responsible for the great number of persons who had "almost all of their time free" or at least "a lot of time" to devote to leisure and to the type of entertainment that was accessible to anybody's pocket. Since there were no other obvious ways to use leisure time constructively, the habit of such gathering soon became a veritable cultural pattern. There were strong sociopsychological motivations that imparted special significance to these groups. First, they had been continually forbidden in the past under slavery, and they were discouraged by the police during the years immediately following Abolition. Holding such meetings thus took on the character of defiance and group self-affirmation. Second, the Negro had always been deprived of the liberty of fraternization and communication within his group. These gatherings allowed him to explore a new area of human experience, of participating in group life and in the pleasures of conversation.

These two motivations imply that the consumption of alcoholic beverages did not constitute the main objective of such gatherings. They primarily represented a self-protective mechanism for the realization of desirable adjustments independent of and above alcohol. These interests gradually took second place and other subjects became the main attractions—such as gambling or the criminal plotting of "Negro operators." Yet even in this context, alcohol was not the axis around which such meetings revolved. Fellowship, conversation, storytelling, and the sentiment of participation were the chief goals. The consumption of alcohol—although constant and relevant—came about as a natural development, a supplementary source of pleasure and stimulation. It was essentially a matter of meeting the basic desires of the human personality that motivated individuals to want to be recognized for their value and to feel part of the group. It was because such desires could not normally be satisfied by the family, by the group one worked with, or by other institutionalized groupings that these cliques were formed—in which exhibitionism, congenial relations, and group rapport were encouraged by alcoholic libations.

What interests us much more than the dissemination of patterns of the habitual consumption of alcoholic beverages are the sociopsychological and sociocultural drives that made such patterns necessary. Such activities represented an accepted way to "pass the time" and attracted bohemians or the residents of a specific neighborhood. The strictness of law-abiding Negroes protected them from the risks that such company involved. Even so, many of them succumbed to the seduction of the bohemian life, and several dutiful workers fell into the pattern almost without realizing it. On his way home from work a fellow would stop for a drink. He would run into a neighbor or an acquaintance he knew by sight in the group gathered in the bar or tavern. The other would greet him and they would strike up a conversation. Everyone would be introduced and the fellow would be offered a drink— usually to toast to the friendship. Unless he were very snobbish, a trait that was censored by the cultural tradition, he accepted and reciprocated the toast. He would converse a little and leave. On the days that followed, the scene would be repeated and the man would tarry longer in the company of his new friends. Finally, he would come to stay as long as he could, and the family would know where to find him if anyone came looking for him. From then on he was part of the clique, dividing his interests among his friends, his family, and work. Little by little he succumbed to the vice and gave more time to fraternizing with his friends and to drinking cane liquor than to other activities. After that, the family would go through new hardships, especially if he became an alcoholic. In that case, his way of life changed completely. The person began to drink excessively, leaving home already drunk, and was no longer esteemed by his friends in the clique. They did not reject him with hostility, but if he lacked enough money to offer a few rounds and if he were prone to pick fights, they openly manifested their dissatisfaction with his presence. A fellow had to have a strong character in order to stand up to the situation without becoming a dead weight to the others.

The drinking cliques did not exercise a destructive influence only. They were of a certain dynamic import as an arena for the self-realization of the Negro and mulatto, especially those who had difficulty fitting into society. Because of these cliques the social disillusionment of the Negro and mulatto went beyond the level of concrete experience to that of verbalization. Wherever intellectual groups became involved in them, they created a certain amount of social unrest and were responsible for the first widespread demonstrations of dissatisfaction that later emerged as the social movements of the Negro milieu. On the other hand, it was in these groups that the only hostile attempt at independent self-assertion on the part of the Negro and mulatto took place. The cliques were unable to promote the establishment of a dynamic link between the Afro-Brazilian cultural tradition and the sociocultural conditions then prevailing. Yet their members did not hesitate to develop autonomous sociocultural interests that revolved around the samba, gambling, vagrancy, and sex. Through these activities they provided channels for the expression of Negroes' needs that had been suffocated by society. Finally, the internal reactions of the black population itself emphasized what was destructive and pernicious in cliques. It is evident that these reactions served to cohere the societal condemnations of alcoholism, gambling, sexual incontinence, and vagrancy among Negroes.

The abandonment of minors, the aged, and dependents was generally the result of a combination of three basic factors: First, the disorganization of the Negro family, invariably intensified and made worse by the spurious sexual relations among Negroes, whites, and mulattoes; second, the economic and institutional weakness of the Negro group, which made the traditional mechanisms of solidarity (of domestic, community, or neighborhood origin) inoperative and hindered the development of indigenous institutions for material and psychological assistance; third, the indifference of a society that remained practically blind to the gravity of the Negro's social problems and reacted to them with mechanisms of control, repression, and assistance that were sometimes ineffectual, corruptible, and degrading. Despite the continual interest in the subject, Negro informants provide very little clarification about these subjects for sociological study and show greater interest in expressing their criticisms of the government, the police, and public welfare agencies. This reveals that there are deep resentments produced by the disdain attributed to whites —who sit in judgment on the Negro's misery.

The disorganization of the family was the chief factor in the abandonment of children and adolescents. They were left to their own devices with no one to care for them. If an unwed mother kept her child and raised it, she had to leave it in the slum. Some female relative or friend took care of the child. A married mother or a mistress with a child who lived with the father of the child or another man often worked away from home and left early for work. If a grandmother, aunt, or older sister lived with them, there was someone to assume certain responsibility for the child. If not, the situation was identical to the one just mentioned. The child was left to himself since the neighbors' way of taking care of a child involved two negative aspects. The adult responsible thought that "you can't tell other people's kids what to do"; and in turn, if the child were older, he thought that only his father or mother had the "right to hit him and tell him what to do." As a matter of fact, even in the mother's presence he had plenty of liberty.

The situation of the elderly and those having chronic or incurable illness was delicate and most difficult, especially when they were unable to work. The disturbing idea that they were a burden for the family prevailed in the minds of everyone, including those in need. This feeling was softened by the notion that it was necessary to "be patient" and "accept the will of God." Nonetheless, there was little to share in the majority of homes, and one more mouth often unavoidably broke down the barrier that separated poverty from destitution. It is clear that those persons were no worse or better off than the rest. The same sacrifices were made by all. Children, old persons, and the sick could never get the right food, adequate treatment, or basic hygienic care. One charitable neighbor or another did occasionally help them to better their diet or treatment, but the temporary character of these gestures prejudiced their efficacy. They merely increased the psychological sense of well-being of the persons involved by making them feel that they were of significance in the lives of others. In turn, to the degree that they were able, the dependents—especially the aged and the ill who could do something, but minors as well—sought to take the responsibility for small chores. They tried not to weigh too heavily and some actually became a blessing to the families because their contributions were so important. An old woman, even a senile one, could keep the house clean, prepare the meals, wash and iron clothes, care for the children of the family and those of the neighbors, and secure small sporadic contributions from ex-employers or relatives. In the end it was thanks to her that the conditions developed for the existence of an integrated family.

If there were strong ties between the dependent and the person responsible for his support, the sacrifices of both were sometimes touching. One case known to us will illustrate the point. The youngest son of an elderly lady lived alone with her. His earnings were only sufficient to support the two of them. They lived comfortably. She had her tiny room and he slept in the dining room. Even though it was a basement, the dwelling had its own kitchen and bathroom, and was comfortable and very clean. Early in the morning she prepared a meal in a lunch pail that the boy ate at work; at night he played the banjo while she sat in a rocking chair, listening to the music and smoking a clay pipe. They hardly spoke to the neighbors and lived in a state of semireclusion. Similar sacrifices, or even harder ones, were made by the unwed mother who wished to keep her child. Many found themselves forced to occasional begging and chance prostitution in order to feed and dress the child and to have a place to live.

Adolescents were the principal problem. There was no one to supervise their actions and prepare them for adulthood. Even relatives and neighborhood friends paid little attention to the issues involved in raising teen-agers. The accepted principle was that "each one is responsible for his own children." If a puberty-aged girl began to "wander from bedroom to bedroom" where boys of the same age or dissolute adults lived, someone soon made remarks about the matter and someone warned the mother and chastised the girl. If she persisted in spite of everything—and this was the rule—everyone washed his hands. They waited, then, for what would probably happen and got ready for the wise counsel that would be given when the thing exploded. This weakness had its roots in the system of domestic and neighborhood solidarity.

Much worse things could happen in the contacts between Negroes and mulattoes with whites, however. Young girls who were employed in homes, for example, ran the risk of being seduced by the sons of their employers or by the latter themselves. Various cases revealed the white's lack of sensibility with regard to the dramas that ensued. There were families who thought it better that the boy be adventurous in this way rather than to catch some disease outside, and as a rule, they only interfered to protect their children's futures. (If the seduced girl's family went to the police, it was necessary to quiet the case down. If these adventures bore fruit, the girl had to be removed from the scene to avoid complications.) At this level, it is clear that the institutional weakness of the Negro group left adolescents at the mercy of all types of dangers, whether they originated in the environment itself or whether they were the result of the disorganized pressures bearing on their relations with whites.

This weakness was also reflected in the Negro's inability to establish an autonomous welfare network. Clubs and associations that proposed to fulfill philanthropic as well as recreational and cultural goals were founded in various neighborhoods and in the center of the city. But the financial support of members turned such objectives into mere fantasies.

This combination of circumstances heaped obvious additonal duties on public authorities. The urban system of welfare services was organized according to obsolete models, and there prevailed an atmosphere of total neglect of the material and psychological dilemmas of the Negro. Even if there had been the intention to help the Negro, the precarious state of public welfare services would not have permitted them to go as far as was necessary. Even today the city lacks a modernized welfare system that can meet the needs of urban social life. The lack of interest in the Negro and, above all, certain prejudices inherited from the slavery of the past and reformulated in contemporary times have dictated another course of action, adverse to the Negro and mulatto.

Two examples will adequately illustrate this. At first, there existed a certain provincial zeal in repressing the courting of white adolescent girls. The Juvenile Court actively intervened in recurring cases, calling the attention of the parents to their responsibility and forcing families to watch out for their daughters. It seems that the same did not occur with regard to young Negro girls. Their presence in bars and dance halls and their walking through the streets were tolerated at late hours, and no one cared about the bad company that led them to vice

cf Rhodesia, S.A.

and prostitution. Several dependable informants have stated that the police themselves openly tolerated these occurrences because "they were waiting for their chance to take advantage of the girls' downfall." Therefore, even today the opinion in Negro groups is that the police and the Juvenile Court have followed a dubious policy and that color has interfered with supervision and repression. Presumptions of the type "he's (she's) a real Negro," "Negroes like to live like that," and "that's in the very blood of the Negro" contributed to develop this atmosphere of neglect and disrespect. However, there have also been those who have informed us that "the authorities were forever warning Negro adolescents and their families" but went unheeded. After several unsuccessful experiences, many decided it was better to leave them to their fate since this was the way they wanted it. Regarding the abuse of Negro and mulatto minors by the police, there is no doubt that such occurrences were frequent.

The other example deals with the treatment of Negroes by the police. The repressive mechanisms often functioned backwards. The evaluation of the slaveholding society that the Negro represented a public danger persisted. The black man or woman who wandered through the streets at night aroused distrust and risked being "picked up by the paddy wagon" or even "locked up in the clink." The general suspicion that the man was a thief and the woman a whore fostered such behavior. There hovered over Negroes, therefore, the fear of being undone. The women found themselves forced not to go out unless they were accompanied, and the men were always on the alert, ready to flee or to respond with violence to the ill-timed approaches of policemen. One informant left it clear that he had become a policeman at this time in order to escape these offenses and stressed that the Negro wanted to be a policeman "to keep from being a prisoner."

Prostitution does not seem to have been an important economic specialty of the Negro woman. Men who were attracted to Negro women could satisfy their desires without resorting to prostitutes. Colored maids, neighbors, or acquaintances would respond to courting—knowing, of course, what was involved. In addition Negro and mulatto men had meager finances to frequent the houses of prostitution regularly. They have always shown a certain reluctance to pay for love, by cultural tradition, and prefer nocturnal affairs or concubinage. In short the prostitution of the Negro or mulatto woman never reached the proportions commensurate with the disorganization of their sexual behavior. Those who accepted prostitution on a regular basis as a rule fell into the hands of the old brothels of low-class prostitution. They generally went into the ranks of the so-called hags and soldiers' whores. However, in the extreme degradation to which they found themselves exposed, they maintained certain standards of dignity. Many of those who frequented brothels had perverted sexual desires and tried to "get a mulatto by the tail" to "get rid of their jinx" (it was said that this brought luck). White prostitutes, even high-class ones, acquiesced to these desires without protest. The Negro and mulatto women revolted against this if it was not to their liking. Even on the streets they shouted at their propositioners: "I'm not a Pole, you S.O.B!" or "I'm not French!"

Not all Negro women who received money for sexual intercourse considered this monetary compensation as payment. It was considered to be a retribution, a generous gesture, and an amorous expression of recognition. If there was need to, some hinted that they wanted this or that before or after the amorous act, but excluded the petition from the context of sexual favors. They received money with naturalness and felt that they were not selling themselves. If in fact they received propositions in this sense, they would become offended. Since they had various boyfriends or lovers (depending on the nature of the relationship), such compensations came to represent a regular supplement to normal earnings through work. As a rule occasional prostitution was an expedient with which to meet hardships or necessities that were insurmountable by any other method. The unwed mother returned to it in times of adversity. The same behavior could be put into practice for other reasons, including that of pressure by a lover if he were a pimp. The woman who decided to become a professional prostitute gave preference to disguised prostitution.

It is difficult to make a retrospective analysis of the personality of the Negro or mulatto prostitute. The data collected do not permit us to discern how the frustrations associated with the socioeconomic situation and color led to the acceptance of this condition. It looks as though after a certain period of time they got tired of living like maids, having several successive or simultaneous sexual affairs, and having to put up with the demands of their lovers. The latter generally behaved like the professional seducer typical of the Negro milieu. He slipped into his girl's bedroom on the sly while her employers slept. Without realizing it, she became everybody's woman without getting any direct benefit from the small sex business that developed out of it. By herself or in discussing it with some friend she eventually discovered that she was a fool. At this point she left the job, left her Negro or mulatto lover, and disappeared. No one would know her whereabouts until it was discovered through the gossip of friends that so-and-so had decided to go to the streets.

Certain scattered but concordant information indicates that skin color was an important factor in the development of the process. Many brothels refused to accept the Negro prostitute and when they made exceptions to this policy, accepted only light, pretty mulatto women. The Negro and dark mulatto girls had to be content with less demanding brothels or regular but clandestine prostitution that was carried on in the streets and bars. One of the informants, speaking about more recent times, stated that even in prostitution color influenced the assessment of a woman's value. She said that at best a dark mulatto woman could command only one-fifth the price of a white woman. For this reason, she explained, the former lost interest in prostitution and preferred to work, occasionally exploiting covert prostitution as a means of income.

Vagrancy and loafing were closely connected to each other and to criminal behavior, according to Negro and mulatto informants. To the contrary of what many people think, vagrancy and loafing have never been considered ennobling nor have they been valued socially among Negro groups. Both were rejected as despicable in the cultural tradition inherited from a rural society; and later on when they became widespread and what might be called well rooted, they were considered by serious and law-abiding persons to be a condition that affected those having weak wills and no character. Involuntary unemployment and the symbiosis of the sexes that nourished the disguised exploitation of women by men were accepted as an unavoidable contingency But the same was not true for the perversion of this relationship of solidarity. Whenever vagrancy became a regular behavioral pattern and along with it the Negro idler appeared, formal, violent condemnation was heard that remains prevalent to this day. It would appear to have been a police matter but the police remained indifferent merely for the sake of "further debasing the Negro." Around 1920 the black elites did not want to have any connection with this spurious group of *Paulistana* society. If it had been up to them, such characters would have been imprisoned and deported to the interior of the state or subjected to programs of correction under police supervision.

The professional seducer then makes his entrance, a typical variant of the mulatto or Negro vagrant: sharp, unscrupulous with a clever tongue, the raw material from which were drawn the carousers, the ruffians, and the thieves that infested the disorganized Negro milieu. This type, which has its mythology in the city's folklore, represented the final product of a process of sociopathic differentiation of the Negro personality. According to the data collected, this type was not the fruit of what might be called inevitably bad or corrupt tendencies or inclinations in the Negro or mulatto youth. A large number (the majority, according to dependable information) ended up there after having taken other paths that were approved by the Negro milieu and accepted as normal by the larger society. The sociopsychological and socioeconomic conditions to keep them on these paths were inadequate and fostered the devel-

opment of progressive maladjustments, to which the figure of
the professional seducer appeared as the first answer. If the
youth were successful in his life of a delinquent, other successive stages indicated to him the new steps he would have to
climb in order to raise himself from inveterate vagrancy to
organized crime.

It is well known that life in the tenement houses and
chance or steady participation in groups of unemployed men
fostered the development of the ideal of becoming a delinquent among youth. However this ideal crumbled in the face
of necessity. Between the ages of ten and fifteen, a minor had
to find some means of earning a living and helping out at
home. Thus the normal thing was not to begin one's career as
a delinquent, but as a worker in the marginal sectors of service
jobs. Even at the outset of this adventure in the realm of free
labor a youth suffered setbacks and humiliation. He had to be
content with manual labor tasks and cleaning jobs in which
he had to work very hard to earn a few miserable pennies. If
he belonged to an integrated family, relatives encouraged him
to be patient and taught him that there was no other solution.
If he was pretty much on his own, he moved rapidly from one
job to the next. He often left his parents to live by himself and
under the influence of friends acquire certain illusions.

The critical point in the process of differentiation arose
when the youth began to share the conviction that he needed
to dress well because his appearance and way of presenting
himself would be decisive in his obtaining good positions and
moving up in his job. At this point he earnestly dedicated
himself to the goal of saving money. He did everything he
possibly could to increase his income and build a small savings. Upon reaching his goal, he bought one or two pairs of
shoes, silk shirts, two or three suits, some ties—all in the
latest style.

Once he was well dressed and had money in his pocket, he
left the job. It seemed to him that a person in his position had
a right to hope for better things and should therefore not
dedicate himself to menial work. He set out simultaneously to

find a new job and make an amorous conquest. He soon found himself hopelessly defeated in the first goal. He suffered harsh disillusionments; he felt that someone should have taught him that appearance is not everything. In the second goal, however, he was always successful. With money, a dapper appearance, and a "line," he could always get as many women as he wanted, Negro or mulatto. Once he had made his choice, he deceived the girl by taking her to restaurants and other places and then ended up taking her for all she was worth. Meanwhile he captivated her. If she was a virgin, he deflowered her. On the sly he began to spend the nights where she worked. Little by little he came to feed himself and supply himself with cash through his mistress. After a certain length of time he actually lived at her expense and continued to do so as long as she would allow it. In the process his personality also changed. He learned how to please the woman, how to make himself an indispensable sexual partner, and simultaneously how to frighten her with the fear of losing him or with violence. In other words the woman became his source of income. He became well versed in the techniques of using it to his advantage and never released his prey without reluctance.

We have only sketched the characteristic outlines of the process. Even so, it can be discerned that it initially took place and developed in the context of normal adjustments. The inevitable frustrations of the conditions of interracial contact described above fostered behavior that transferred the individual from one pole of society to the other. It is clear that the external environment provided certain basic incentives, either by examples that were considered worthy of imitating or through concrete opportunities to imitate them. The essential thing, however, we have already stressed in several ways: the individual had not been socialized to behave as a worker and to fulfill himself through the careers open to him as a salaried worker. Thus he became maladjusted for lack of skills and attitudes that should have been acquired beforehand or that could be assimilated through learning on the job. On the whole the Negro youth became a worker without having received any basic training in order to be able to accept, tolerate, and value the relation involved in salaried work; and he was given opportunities of a marginal character that neither gratified his pride nor opened real prospectives for gradual assimilation of the cultural outlook of the salaried worker. His personality was easily influenced by contradictory motivations that aggravated the disillusionments and the frustrations. They turned open maladjustment (which was at times conscious) into the only effective alternative for actively overcoming the conflicts. Thus the tendency to seek adjustments to the external world on the basis of fictitious status and the simultaneous tendency to evade the roles inherent in real status can be sociologically explained.

There were certain basic dispositions to normal adjustment that were of considerable dynamic importance in the organization and development of the process that has been analyzed. Sociopathic outcomes arose from two fundamental circumstances (and from varying combinations of the two): either the individuals were not socially capable of putting them into practice (by virtue of the inconsistencies in the mechanisms of socialization or social solidarity of the Negro groups or of the society as a whole); or the conditions of adjustment that they confronted on the different levels of organized social interaction (of the Negro groups to society), inexorably rejected them, partially or completely. All this shows that it is essential to understand the channels whereby the Negro and mulatto could avail themselves of these mechanisms of adjustment as well as why they found it so difficult to control them socially.

Of the socializing influences that shaped the personality of the Negro and mulatto the family was unquestionably the only institution that functioned universally among Negro groups and had the prerequisites to organize and control the manifestation of these influences. In turn, the functioning of broader socializing influences that were organized and controlled by society (such as schools) depended strictly on the degree of integration and stability of the domestic group.

Wherever minimum unity and durability were not achieved in the latter, the Negro child had no possibility of being touched by those influences; inversely, wherever the domestic group achieved minimum integration and stability, the assimilation of society's mechanisms of socialization became more rapid and more effective. For this reason the Negro family actively influenced the process referred to above, even though the quality of this influence oscillated in an irregular way from a highly unfavorable extreme to one that was relatively favorable, passing through a medium point of near neutrality. Nevertheless, through participation in various life situations the child and the young person broadened and reinforced what had been learned from this process, gradually assimilating in an inevitable way the adjustment mechanisms by which they became men of their society and of their times.

However, as we have noted above, the Negro and mulatto came out of the slaveholding and seignorial society lacking a broad, complete command of the institutional forms of the white man's social patterns of living. Their experiences with integrated family life in terms of the way of life and organization models sanctioned by the culture were new, superficial, and contradictory. This limitation did not become a hindrance in the rural areas, where the subsistence economy and rural patterns of living simplified the structural and functional requirements which the pattern of family integration had to meet. Yet considering the economic, cultural, and sociohistorical background of the city of São Paulo, this limitation was without exaggeration a veritable catastrophe. In a developing class society, the family was the chief and sometimes the only form of support to which individuals had recourse. Without a minimum amount of domestic cooperation and solidarity, no one could be successful in that wilderness. Restrained or unrestrained individualistic competition demanded a complex institutional substratum for which the integrated family was the foundation. The examples of immigrants are conclusive because for them the family always functioned directly or indirectly as the foundation for rapid vertical economic, social, and political mobility. Even though the integrated family could not by itself either create or develop opportunities for professional and economic classification, it undoubtedly functioned as a kind of determinant for the optimum exploitation of such opportunities.

The fact is that resettlement severely affected the Negro family's course of development. But it must not be assumed that this happened because the change was excessively sudden and rapid; there are more profound reasons. It must be remembered that the assimilation of Brazilian institutional models of family organization had barely begun. The economic and social instability of the black population in the urban setting hampered this process in various ways, seriously retarding, undermining, and perverting it. Yet even those who brought with them greater autonomous experience of the free man's mode of living were also hopelessly bound to the unsophisticated character of the rural past. Whether they came from the country or the city, the common stamp of the various segments of the black population was lack of sophistication. Consequently those that managed to protect themselves by carrying out certain minimal functions of the integrated family were not any better prepared to become a part of the developing urban, industrial society. Because of its rigidity, relocation maintained the orderly pattern of living, but at the expense of increased isolation of the Negro and mulatto groups. It was poorly tuned to the environment and failed to become differentiated during its process of transformation. Clearly, resettlement brought adverse influences to bear upon the consolidation of the family in the Negro groups, while it simultaneously limited the adaptive potentials of the family organization inherited from the rural past.

We are not interested at this point in every aspect of the events that marked the development of the Negro family during the period under consideration. The objectives of the present analysis demand only that we examine the inconsistencies of this institution that had a sociopathic influence on the ordering of relations between the sexes and the socialization and control of adolescents by adult generations. Since the preceding exposition includes ample documentation of instances of efficient and poor functioning of family ties, there is no drawback to making the condensation of this analysis more abstract.

The Negro family as it was constituted in São Paulo during the first three decades of this century could be defined as an *incomplete family*. It is impossible today to determine the frequency with which the different structural arrangements appeared, but it seems that without question the most frequent pattern was the pair consisting of an unwed mother or her substitute—usually a grandmother—and the mother's child or children. In second place were couples who lived together, along with the child or children of both (from their own union or from previous affairs). Finally there were couples whose union was established according to legally sanctioned matrimonial arrangements. Thus the family might tend toward a high degree of integration and stability (as usually occurred among law-abiding Negroes, who were also called Negroes of the elite in the cultural tradition) as much as it might show various degrees of disintegration and instability. However, it should be pointed out that common-law marriages did not in themselves represent obstacles to structural stability and functional normalcy. Several known cases reveal that some moral and well-behaved Negroes who tenaciously clung to the traditionalist code with its rigorous etiquette conspicuously practiced this type of matrimonial arrangement. In such cases it was only the legal statute that imparted a certain characteristic difference to the truly integrated family that was constituted according to the prevailing patterns of society. On the contrary families organized according to the legal norms might manifest a degree of instability and disintegration comparable only to that of couples living together in what was considered debauchery. It can be seen that sensibility to external pressures that demanded the progressive assimilation of marriage as a basic social value—in the Ibero-Brazilian Catholic cultural tradition and in accord with the republican civil code—was far from having any common denominator and average result.

With respect to its morphological composition, this family might mean a pair (constituted by the mother and her child or by the couple) or it might mean a much larger number of persons. The most common alternatives were related to what might be called a trend toward the modern conjugal family pattern (families that include the couple and their children) and to what might properly be called a *composite family* (a term dealing with the effect of overcrowding and promiscuity in habitations on the composition of the family). The statements of informants refer to this type of family and common-law marriages in which the husband or companion was a habitual vagrant as disorganized families. Nevertheless, overcrowding and promiscuity were not always associated with riotous living and sexual incontinence. The term also referred to couples that were blood relatives on the paternal side (only occasionally on the maternal side), especially in cases in which the composite family was correlated with extreme poverty and the rural pattern of living of the law-abiding Negro, in which all lived together very correctly.

Some informants stressed that the past of the Negro and mulatto had much to do with their attitudes toward marriage and family organization. The so-called field Negroes were thus considered to be the most primitive. They were barely aware of permanent mating, and neither the man nor the woman really knew what a home was. Meanwhile the Negro from the big house who had more intimate contact with the master's family was better acquainted with the subject. The latter not only valued marriage as a social distinction, but they had also acquired certain basic notions concerning the mutual obligations and rights of the marriage partners. The woman learned at minimum how to keep the house in order, cook well, and live with the amount of comfort that her level of poverty would permit. In turn, the man knew better how to deal with his wife and children, was accustomed to inviting selected friends into his home, and was concerned about the future of his family. These ideas could also be applied to the differences between Negroes and mulattoes because many families recruited the slaves that would be in more intimate contact with them from the lightest and most intelligent ones. This means that such ideas were related to the experience accumulated socially by freedmen since the number of free mulattoes in the capital was always larger than that of Negroes.

Although evidence shows that the type of integration to the domestic environment of the white family was indeed important, it does not seem that the relation between past and present in the sense stressed above was so relevant for the integration or disintegration of the Negro family. The reason is simple. The extreme mobility of the capital's black population caused its oldest groups to become dispersed extensively during the breakdown of slavery and the development of the competitive society. The results of our inquiries suggest that two other factors should be considered more relevant. The first was the time of residence in the rural area and the concomitant opportunities for family life. Negroes and mulattoes who had this opportunity and moved to São Paulo already married (or living with someone) shared certain convictions (like the obligation to support a wife, live with her, care for the children, and carry on domestic life in a decent manner), and they were more inclined to confront the sacrifices that maintaining a family demanded. The second factor was the vague, mute influence of the immigrant, especially the Italian. Through fraternization and observation of the Italian's life, the Negro and mulatto discovered the importance of the family. Economic insecurity and the weakness of certain social bonds hindered rapid, constructive imitation of the immigrant's behavior, but it shed great light on the deep roots of the disorganization prevailing in Negro groups and on what should be done in order to really correct them. It was only a small minority of the Negro population that considered marriage to be a social value and strictly followed a pattern of living that was compatible with the stability of the integrated family. The majority rejected both and the resulting separation was so marked that the individual who left one milieu for the other suffered a kind of shock.

The norm served to disguise men's continual evasion of the obligations derived from premarital affairs. From this came the symptomatic linking of courtship with physical seduction and the rejection of marriage. Various cases reveal that the youth preferred to take a jail sentence to marriage; and that often he lacked the economic conditions to support a household even with the collaboration of the woman. The informants used the term "irresponsible" to designate the behavioral patterns described above. The term is justified if it is understood that the lack of ego involvement and identification with the social values in question would redound in the continual evasion of the expected behavior patterns.

On the whole the situation sanctioned extremely fickle sexual behavior for the man. The interesting thing is that the counterpart permitted the equivalent right for women, and there were no repressive mechanisms for correcting its harmful effects. With regard to the first point, the case of a young woman who fell in love with a youth who did not return her affections is illustrative. She had no qualms about taking the initiative necessary for achieving her goals. The youth, in turn, told her openly that he loved another woman and was going to marry her. This was no stumbling block. The girl, even though she was a virgin, surrendered herself without hoping for anything. According to the informant, she was happy to have this opportunity to belong to the man she loved. With regard to the second point, legal mechanisms were forgotten or they failed to function in any effective way, and the individual reserved the right to act as he pleased. One example deserves to be mentioned. The youth undid the girl and as usual refused to marry her. But she became pregnant with his child, and he married her against his will. After marriage he lived with his wife, but carried on his usual life. That is, he spent all the money he earned himself, used his time as he willed, frequented bars and taverns, and had his sprees just as before. The woman had to work to support the household and the child.

With regard to women, it is of interest that the unwed mother sought to be free of her children, abandoning them in charity institutions and giving or surrending them to third persons in order not to lose her freedom. Several informants made it clear that in many cases employers consented that their maids raise their children in the homes where they worked and lived. But the maids refused to do so because they would be tied down taking care of the child at night. On the other hand, like the man, the woman partially or completely evaded her domestic obligations. Her desire for dances, fancy Carnival costumes, or stylish clothes might involve expenditures which affected the family budget. If things failed to go her way, she sulked until her whims were satisfied. One case reveals that one unwed mother imposed no limitations upon herself when she was in the mood for drinking and having a good time (for example, she neglected her youngest daughter's welfare to such a degree that she was seduced and led into prostitution). The most interesting thing, however, is that just as she did not want to tie a man to her against his will—even if she were his sexual partner or the mother of his children—neither did she tie herself to any man against her own will. Whether she were married or just living with the man she abandoned him if she took a notion—taking any children with her, abandoning them to him, or giving them to some relative to raise.

The instability and weakness of marital bonds were directly related to the person's lack of socialization. Since the family was still in the process of development, individuals failed to acquire the attitudes and behavioral patterns that would have given rise to relatively strong identifications and loyalties for the values held by society at large. For the same reason, the mere living together of two persons in marriage, cohabitation, or some relationship to see what might come of it was not adequate in itself to correct and supplement the lapses in socialization prior to this period. Unless there were other in-intervening factors, the stability of the union, mutual devotion, and predisposition for giving came to depend largely on bonds of friendship. "I liked him (or her)" or "I stopped liking him (or her)" functioned as the indisputable, irrevocable basis for making decisions that led a man and a woman to live together or to go separate ways.

The structural composition of the Negro family also contributed to precipitate and sustain certain anomalies. The most frequent sociopathic influences were those associated with the perpetual impoverishment of the family nucleus. The absence of the father not only hindered the normal functioning of the institution that was deprived of the masculine roles of husband, father, and head of the household; it irreparably impaired the basic stability (both structural and functional) of the group, thereby causing distortions in the concrete expressions of all other roles; the accumulation of the obligations of the adult member of the family who was present and responsible for the children (the unwed mother or her substitute, usually the maternal grandmother); and the prevalence of a moral climate that was as impoverished for the resocialization of this member of the family as it was for the socialization of minors. The result of all this was a union of forces and influences that worked together to perpetuate this extreme state of disintegration for an indefinite period instead of contributing to its rapid and definitive defeat.

The excess of the woman's responsibilities, her permanent incapacity to fulfill all the social roles (both masculine and feminine) as an unwed mother, and the lack of solidarity to compensate for the difficult life that became her lot imperceptibly identified her with the personality status that she acquired and encouraged her to look in this direction for whatever sources of compensation that were available. This explains the existing conformist attitudes in relation to this type of structural arrangement, its wide dissemination, and the very tendency of women to preserve the resulting patterns. Many unwed mothers had and supported children from two, three, or more successive affairs. Yet the Negro milieu lacked the mechanisms of solidarity and understanding to be able to correct, compensate for, or at least render adequate assistance to the mother and her children, materially and psychologically. Loneliness, destitution, and humiliation plagued the path of the woman who had the indomitable courage to keep the fruit of her mistakes and struggle for existence. Her own relatives might or might not help her with some money or spiritual comfort. Even during her greatest adversities when she might be in despair at seeing her own fate relived in the life of a daughter led astray by some white man or some boy friend of her own color, these relatives would only condemn her for not watching out for the girl. During her greatest need she might not even be able to appeal to the child's natural father, either because she did not know who he was or because she took it as a matter of honor not to tell anyone who he was (not even the child itself). Only by chance, through the indiscretion of some relative or acquaintance, did the child come to know who his father was.

Thus the child's state of deprivation was even more complex, pernicious, and irreparable. The child was forced to grow up at the hand of fate and in the school of the streets, for the mother left early for work, casting on his small shoulders the responsibility of looking after the house and himself as well as to discern which of his older companions and adults would be true friends and which would like to take advantage of his naïveté. If luck was with him, he might learn something or at a tender age find a charitable benefactor. Yet none of this could make up for the lack of paternal care, the vulnerability of his relations with his mother, and the total ignorance of what the normal condition of being a son was. It is clear that he would be ignorant of the existence and usefulness of certain social roles in which adults and minors confront each other as "father," "wife-mother," "son," and "daughter." But this was not the worst. In the street in which he grew up he rarely had the opportunity to learn to respect and obey others out of love. A crudely egotistic and individualistic code prevailed: the individual had to be smart even in his relations with his mother and brothers.

Overcrowding caused pathological consequences in the morphology of the Negro family. Many persons living in a small space could cause, but did not necessarily cause, a sociopathic differentiation in living conditions or in human behavior. What we have been able to learn in this regard reveals that it did in fact occur. The sociopathological influences of the congestion of the Negro family were related to lapses in the mechanisms of socialization and control. Either the parents were unaware that they could not maintain an aura of complete secrecy around their activities in sexual intercourse, or adolescents and especially adults allowed themselves liberties that should have been proscribed (through the initiative of the individuals themselves or the control of others). In any case, the greatest victims were adolescents who were initiated to the secrets of sex through the wrong doors or who served as prey for the sexual appetites of older friends or adults. We have already described these occurrences in the proper place. The surrounding environment did not provide the necessary institutional support. In order to function normally, the Negro family had to be self-sufficient. No one would prevent a young woman from taking a false step or an adolescent from satiating the sexual appetite of his oldest brother, stepfather, or another adult. But gossip was rampant afterwards, branding the persons deeply, especially the victim.

The Negro woman—and not the man—was the dominant figure wherever any kind of disintegration affected family or conjugal bonds. Whatever the seeming depravity of her acts or her prevailing material and psychological impoverishment, the Negro woman loomed as the means of survival for her children and even for her husband or companion. Without her cooperation and her earning power provided by domestic work, a large part of the black population would have succumbed or would have returned to other areas. A mute and patient heroine, she could do no more than preserve the fruit of her womb: sustain the life of those to whom she had given it! No one can look back at this era without sensing the immense human stature of the humble black maids, the instruments at one and the same time of the propagation and the salvation of their people.

Alongside the incomplete or disintegrated family there was also the integrated Negro family. As a rule it tended to be of the conjugal type: zeal to maintain the appearance of a good standard of living with a fairly low salary presupposed a decided rejection of collective solidarity. In fact, in the circles in which this family appeared—those of the Negro elite—the promiscuity of the tenements was already being condemned along with its cause, overcrowding, and with its effects: the physical and psychological abandonment of children, the precocity of sexual initiation, the contamination of diseases, etc.

The manifestation of the family among Negro groups interests us for several reasons. First of all, it reveals a state of structural and functional consolidation of the institution that was uncommon. How can this phenomenon be explained? We have already pointed out that more or less prolonged permanence in rural areas (the equivalent of the participation of the free Negro or mulatto in the rural past of the city of São Paulo) facilitated the acquisition of the family organization patterns that prevailed in our agrarian society. Those segments of the migrant groups who had the prerequisites and found opportunities to secure a permanent and satisfactory source of income thus also acquired favorable circumstances for the preservation and consolidation of the cultural legacy handed down from rural society. According to the information gathered, these persons had the protection of important white families. They generally knew how to read and write. They moved freely among whites. They were not intimidated by the presence of whites and were capable of performing their duties. The majority worked as trashmen, office boys, and custodians in public offices. Others were chauffeurs or workers (fewer in number). Their salaries were no larger than those of whites employed in the same occupations, according to what is said (and Negro and mulatto informants even imply that they were smaller). Even so, they were able to build the physical structure that would sustain organized family life. Whether we like it or not, this underlines the conclusion that the exclusion from the urban occupation scale was a basic factor in the deterioration in the patterns of living (including the disorganization of the family) of the Negro and mulatto in São Paulo.

The complete and integrated family better reveals the nature of the adjustments employed by the Negro and mulatto to maintain a high level of family morality and the social-dynamic inconsistencies that they presuppose. The sociopathic aspect of the integrated Negro family is not to be found in its structure and functioning but rather in the pattern of its dynamic integration into the social order of society. The conclusions of the preceding analysis point out the degree to which the surroundings actively contributed to the corruption of domestic life.

Although the data gathered does not provide the basis for a thorough study, it seems unquestionable that at its level of structural-functional development the Negro family could not maintain its stability and integration without isolating itself from the influence of neighborhood gossip. It lacked the mechanisms to deal with it and to correct it in a constructive manner. Thus normality was achieved at the cost of abnormal isolation. Leaving aside what this in itself represented and keeping in mind the integration of the Negro and mulatto into society, this situation caused the complete, integrated Negro family to separate itself to a large degree from a changing society. This family remained a kind of relic of the polished segment of rural society encrusted upon a city in the throes of urbanization and the industrial revolution. They were perpetuating and refining conventions that whites had already completely abandoned and which made little sense in the context of the emerging urban-industrial civilization. No one questions the importance of conspicuous patterns of living, polished formalism, and seemingly aristocratic exclusivism and refinements for the self-affirmation of the Negro and mulatto, in their relations with whites as much as in the distinctions and divisions that were established between the Negro elite and Negro idlers. But it is clear that the integration of the family involved the risk of an undesirable separation. In isolating himself in order to ward off certain dangers, the Negro created others that were just as serious, among which loomed the very paralyzation of the development of the integrated Negro family.

Second, there were certain weaknesses in the capacity of this family to organize itself, all of which were more or less related to the precarious bases of its pattern of internal equilibrium. The rigidity with which the attachment to traditional norms was manifested is the most serious. Rich or poor, the well-behaved Negro or mulatto man stubbornly opposed certain inevitable compromises as a matter of honor. If the family was in need of the woman's financial contribution, he only accepted it when it was too late; if a daughter succumbed to the uncontrollable dangers of the environment and went astray, he took refuge from his shame by driving her out of the house and thus exposing her to even greater dangers; if a friend or relative went to live with his sexual partner or committed a socially disapproved act, he severed relations, and so on. All this, naturally, created an atmosphere of hidden insecurity and obsessive concern for social position, prestige, and the opinion of others which ultimately undermined relations between the marriage partners, those between parents and children, and those among the latter. At the same time it accentuated the transformation of the head of the family into a little domestic despot who made decisions about what was good and evil, what one should and should not do.

On the other hand any setback—such as involuntary, prolonged unemployment; the death of one of the marriage partners (especially the husband); a false step (chiefly on the part of the woman)—undermined the whole structure as if it were a castle of sand. Since everyone was apprehensive of this possibility, no one wanted to hear anything about it or prepare to face it. The result was that when misfortune struck no one was in a position to stand up to it.

Last was the difficulty in finding a suitable social group outside the home. Communication with the neighbors and with other Negro families was subjected to a distrustful and rigorous surveillance. If a daughter or son wished to form relationships with young persons of their own age or the woman were prone to seek entertainment, complications arose. Only those who had a little more experience and income were able to resolve these problems to their satisfaction by participating in the respectable, exclusive clubs of the Negro milieu.

Alongside these organizational debilities of a more or less general nature, two kinds of highly sociopathic consequences could result. Most of the information about domestic frictions associated with the preferences concerning the color of the children was related to these families. The lighter marriage partner did not hide his anxiety (sometimes ambivalently shared by the darker partner) that his son or daughter might be born dark or later become so. Such preferences engendered tensions in the relations between the marriage partners or between them and the children and among the children themselves. There are also references to educated parents who entertained great ambitions in relation to their children's future but who lacked the courage to stimulate them. They knew through their own experience the subtlety and force of the social barriers against improvement in the social status of Negroes. Therefore, at the same time that they encouraged their children to live an orderly life, to behave themselves, to marry, and to be respectable, they dared not inspire high ambitions in their children, or did so in fear. Some informants even gave examples of parents who convinced their children to give up their studies in the fear that their children would come to suffer incurable disillusionment. Last, the appearance (or the pathological strengthening) of irrational preferences regarding the sex of children should be mentioned. The fear that daughters could go astray tied to the belief that it would be easier to raise a son and that he could better take care of himself made fathers and mothers predisposed to have hopes that led to disillusionments, frustrations, and sometimes animosities and tensions within the home.

Thus the important thing about the integrated Negro family was to show that the Negro and mulatto could develop patterns of conjugal life that were highly respectable. In an era in which few had overcome the selective barrier imposed by whites to ward off the upward mobility of Negroes, the integrated Negro family was proof that the Negro was just as capable as the white of achieving respectable patterns of living. Everything depended upon economic and social opportunities. The level of assimilation of the patterns and institutions of the larger society revealed deficiencies and disturbing oscillations because of the exclusion of the Negro and mulatto —not because they were inadequate to the task. Nevertheless, even when they were not relegated to the sideline, they were able to take advantage of such opportunities only in such a way that they found themselves forced to make compromises and to accept adjustments that redounded in a second kind of exclusion: that of voluntary isolation, chosen as a path to purity and self-affirmation through morality.

If we compared the integrated Negro family with the disintegrated one, we would see that the former was more effective in the three areas studied—the ordering of relations between the sexes, the socialization of adolescents, and the control of youth by adults. It constantly employed a greater number of mechanisms operative in society and the results of its socialization and control reached farther. Not only did it foster greater identification with and loyalty to the explicit values underlying the attitudes and motivations for social action, but it better protected the Negro and mulatto from conformist behavior, social discouragement, and disillusionment arising from the pernicious but general conviction that "the Negro's life is just that way," "the Negro was born to suffer," and "the Negro's no good for anything else" that became prevalent among the disorganized social groups. However, these differences were only a matter of degree; that is, on the average, the integrated family preserved the accepted norms of family life better than did the disintegrated family. Nonetheless, it was far from producing the results of integration, socialization, and control demanded by society at large, which can be easily verified by comparing it with either the immigrant family or the traditional Brazilian family of the ruling groups. Even the disorganized Italian family, for example, had decided advantages over the Negro family in this respect.

There was another, more serious problem. Neither the integrated nor the disintegrated Negro family prepared minors, especially youths, to confront the risks which they would have to face in the Negro milieu as well as in their relations with whites. The tendency to seek pleasure might have been severely attacked and reprimanded; but nothing was done to enable the young man or woman to deal effectively with sexual adjustments, which were so difficult and serious in an atmosphere of such opportunities, seductions, and temptations. The same thing occurred in relation to economic and social adjustments: the fear of disillusionment led to a philosophy of just keeping things from happening, when the mandatory orientation for parents was to prepare their children to become aware of dissimulated manifestations of color prejudice and discrimination and to teach them how to defend themselves against its insidious consequences.

In the light of these considerations it seems clear that even where the Negro family was the most protective and effective as an instrument of socialization, integration, and control, it manifested serious social-dynamic deficiencies. It kept the younger generations more or less devoid of the mechanisms of essential competitive adjustment and drastically diminished constructive action on the part of the adults.

The problems of schooling reveal a difficult situation. Parents were unaware of the existence and utility of schools. The abandoned child was forced to go to work prematurely and so came into contact with vice at an early age. Someone might advise a friend to enroll his child in a school or encourage the child himself to attend. This was a difficult matter. Going to school demanded an organized life and the availability of resources, and the two were rarely found together. Often the unwed mother or backward parents were fearful of their child's studying, thinking that later on he might become ashamed of them. And in law-abiding families, parents having some schooling at most allowed their children to go to primary school. They believed that in proceeding in this way, they would avoid future disillusionments for themselves; nonetheless, they would have loved for their children to have become educated. They behaved in this way because they knew that they would find all the doors closed. Thus the Negro and mulatto children were kept out of school and in ignorance because this source of instruction was not substituted by any alternative education.

As a matter of fact, the dominant tendencies of the process of assimilation of Negro men and women into the occupational structure of the city did not develop an understanding of the importance of education in relation to the new way of social life. In general their occupations demanded manual skills that could easily be acquired on the job. On the other hand the most sought-after jobs were not obtained through competition and on the basis of the intellectual qualifications of black applicants, but through the patronage of whites. Once employment was secured, learning would always take place on the job. This situation maintained among Negroes the undefined lack of interest in literacy that was prevalent in Brazilian rural society.

The experiences acquired through living with adults were not totally useless in spite of the sociopathic influences of their disorganized social life. The early age at which the Negro child was introduced to various practical subjects of interest, besides sexual ones, was responsible for his being more mature than the white child of the same sex at the corresponding age. He knew better how to take care of himself and was more clever and sometimes was better trained for earning money through expediency or work. It behooves us to point out that owing to the insistence of adults he was also able to learn something about the importance of good manners, affability, and proper dress—things that were often neglected in white families of the same economic level.

Nevertheless, informal education seldom opened the door to learning a profession or trade, as generally occurred among immigrant families. When a Negro child perchance went to work and lived in the home of one of these families, the quality of his experiences improved and he was able to learn a trade or even be guided toward serious studies. We observed in two of the life histories that such circumstances enabled one person to go to junior high school and the other to college. Sometimes the child discovered the existence of the school by himself, but was unable to finish the course. Here is what one of the reports relates: "I lived in the streets where I was raised, learning to read a little here and there. I even tried to attend school. I saw many of the boys I played with going to school. After hanging around one of them (a private school) for some time (I went many times to wait for friends to be dismissed), I presented myself to the teacher. I told her that I wanted to go to school but that I didn't have any money to pay her, and then I proposed that I work in exchange for her teaching. Three months later the teacher, who had come from the interior because of her fiancé and had started the school in order to support herself here, closed the school and returned to the interior because she had broken the engagement. In bidding us farewell during the last class, she gave me some books, advised me to keep trying to read, and said that one of the things she was most sorry about was having to leave me. She held me up before the class as an example. That was the most wonderful thing that happened to me during this period."

Finally it should be mentioned that the elite Negroes nourished ambitions that they were unable to fulfill. By virtue of their relations with whites of the ruling groups, they were guided by the traditionalist conception of the world and believed that the important thing was to study for a degree.

Since they found this road blocked, they took little interest in the sacrifices demanded for other types of study.

Thus the Negro child had few possibilities for taking advantage of the educational opportunities of his environment. Even though such opportunities were potentially open to them, the form of organization of the Negro family—the integrated one as much as the disintegrated one (and the latter on a much larger scale)—did not include this function among the normal relations of adults with minors. Consequently one factor that could have speeded up the change in the cultural outlook inherited from the rural world was not employed in a productive way. The Negro family remained neutral to constructive social influences that should have improved the position of the younger generations in the competitive social order and provided them with better opportunities for fuller and more advantageous participation in urban development. In compromising the position of the child and youth by denying them the steady assimilation of a normal prerequisite for competition with whites and integration into the urban social environment, the Negro family exercised a disturbing, negative influence that eventually irreparably prejudiced the future of the Negro and mulatto in the city.

To sum up, the social disorganization of the Negro population may be seen as a factor of a historical situation that serves no constructive social purpose. It could not become a source of motivation for change because all the sociopsychological and sociocultural conditions of the immediate environment and the society as a whole contributed to make it a dynamic factor of confusion, disorientation, and inertia. Instead of acting as a bridge between the past and the future, fostering the changes that were essential to the incorporation of the Negro and mulatto into the competitive social order and the class system, it functioned in the opposite sense. It tied them to a patrimony of contradictory cultural patterns and social techniques that were often obsolete and incoherent in the face of the demands of the sociohistorical context. It kept them from becoming aware of their real situation and from formulating a strategy that would correspond to these exigencies, thus cutting them off from the historical course of the processes of social reconstruction. In short, it isolated them in a restricted and suffocating material and psychological atmosphere which gave them neither security nor satisfactory social compensations, and in addition failed to encourage the acquisition of these things in a coherent way. In seeing the adjustment efforts of the black population from this point of view, it becomes clear that the conformism it manifested was passive in nature. As a by-product of total impotence, it did not originate in concurrence and consent or in identification with the social values upheld by the dominant race. This adjustment bore the mark of the vicious circle created by the continual harnessing of social anomie with poverty. This adjustment was only made possible and had full historical meaning because the debasement of the man who asserted himself in this fashion engendered individual resentments and social disillusionment without bringing about racial unrest. It is evident that if the situation had been otherwise and the Negro and mulatto had had integrated forms of social intercourse and solidarity adequate to the situation as well as sufficient social autonomy to employ them freely, the tensions would have been revealed in that historical context and could have fostered coherent manifestations of active adjustment to the class system.

All this indicates that the black population's apathy toward a humiliating social existence served a certain historical function. There are no words that can disguise this truth, nor do we pretend to do so, out of love for the oft-sung praises of Brazilian racial democracy or a liking for the Negro people. Yet even though we frankly admit the facts presented and what they signify for sociological analysis, it is undeniable that the black population's apathy goes beyond mere historical fatalism. In spite of its origins and the undisguisable sociopathic consequences, this extreme apathy represented one of the following alternatives: to continue to live in the city or to move to the interior of the country. From this viewpoint, apathy may be seen as a potentially dynamic condition, as a choice that involved the predisposition to use the limp-body technique to the end. In other words, this meant deliberately using the only form of resistance and voluntary adaptive behavior that the Negro and mulatto had at their disposal. To leave the city for the rural areas would have been equivalent to admitting defeat, which in the slang of that period presupposed open admission of a certain vexing weakness: "to show that he hadn't much backbone." In this complex sociopsychological context, purely and simply remaining in the city had in itself a positive and ennobling connotation—similar to that accorded to the freedman in the same situation in the past. It should be noted, however, that these more deeply rooted semiconscious preferences were not associated with any dream of a better future; they were directly associated with the immediate present and the value of the persons involved in it. Thus it was a matter of a clearly defined resistance. It is true that it was indirectly reinforced by the foresight of what would happen to those who returned to the interior. It was known that there would be no perceptible improvement in the economic and social conditions of such persons, and if there would be any at all, it would not be sufficiently compensatory to make it worth seeking. The attraction of the city was thus the positive pole in the choice to be made, and this implied the greatest self-affirmation that a black man could make in practice. To remain was to resist, to protect oneself from a defeat that was even worse and more humiliating than that of surrendering to poverty and social debasement.

From this state of affairs a paradoxical conclusion can be drawn. The extreme apathy of the Negro and mulatto revealed itself to be a method of personal self-assertion while it hid its significance as a means of collective resistance. No one blamed himself for his poverty and its pernicious effects. They all knew that if they were able to choose, they would live like the rich and powerful whites. Yet fate seemed to be adverse and man is not always able to change it, they thought. But for a man not to know how to bear this fate, to not be able to face it with dignity and courage, would be proof of his weakness. This is why the adjustments that would turn inertia and passivity into mechanisms of adaptation to the urban agglomeration were centered around apathy. Perhaps this is the only positive and constructive element that had influence which both permeated and originated in the chronic social disorganization. It was due to this apathy that the Negro and mulatto were able to blaze a path that was beset with difficulties and to turn living in the city into living like human beings.

The important thing is that apathy functioned as an effective form of adjustment to the urban way of life. It protected the Negro and mulatto, keeping them from risking even more serious and dangerous frustrations. What would have happened if, under the economic and sociohistorical conditions described above, they had adopted behavioral patterns of aggression and conflict? It can be seen that apathy was a kind of launching pad, the elementary and simple starting point from which the black man was lifted in the gradual transition from naïve passivity to a conformism of which he was fairly aware, and with the passage of time, to a consciously considered and declared dissatisfaction. As it will be seen in Chapter 4, by the time this dissatisfaction had become manifested there had arisen dynamic structural conditions which were favorable to the manifestation of nonconformist attitudes and their development as constructive social forces in the Negro milieu, and these conditions were being taken advantage of. Apathy had borne its fruit, making it possible for the black man to get that far; it had served as a protective shell that dulled his sensibilities and at least reduced the physical, mental, and moral wear to which he had been unmercifully submitted.

In conclusion, permanent social disorganization functioned as a factor of apathy, forcing the Negro and mulatto to accept the anomic conditions of life that prevailed in the Negro milieu as normal. The internal tendencies for the spontaneous correction of this situation were sufficiently efficacious to foster integrated social intercourse on certain restricted levels. Nonetheless, such trends were incapable of incorporating and controlling the factors that functioned above and beyond the primary groups of black persons in the differentiation and integration of the social order itself. Since integrated social intercourse could be carried on simultaneously with the stratification in the class system and vertical social mobility, it was often accompanied by sociopathic manifestations that were especially damaging to the stability of personality. Considering the situation as a whole, it can be seen that chronic social disorganization as much as integrated social intercourse fostered the perpetuation of archaic structural constellations and drove the Negro and mulatto to apathy (the dominant trend in the disorganized segment of the Negro milieu) and extremely passive, conformist adjustments (the prevailing tendency in the integrated segment of the Negro milieu). Considered in terms of the structural and dynamic exigencies of the established social order of society as a whole, both trends were sociopathic and functioned to hinder its normal development.

On the other hand the standard of differentiation and integration reached at this time by the competitive social order and the social class system in the city of São Paulo revealed well-known structural and dynamic weaknesses. Therein seems to be found the explanation for the very inertia of society at large in the face of the material and psychological dilemmas that plagued the black population. This inertia was ambiguously bound up with survivals of archaic social structures that perpetuated the old order in the heart of the competitive social order and the class system. This trend was in itself strongly anomalous for it meant the preservation of patterns of sociopsychological and sociocultural isolation that came into open conflict with the legal foundations of the new social order. Owing to these historical circumstances, however, the maladjustments and disequilibriums that undermined the Negro community could be ignored or resolved according to routine and ineffective procedures that failed to restrict either their propagation or their continual aggravation. The truth is that the real correction of such maladjustments and disequilibriums was only of direct interest to the persons and social groups affected by them, for they never came to threaten in any way the prerogatives granted to the white race by that social order.

The class system presented the black population with very difficult options. Its members had to assimilate the cultural techniques, the patterns of living, and the social values on which such patterns were based, thus overcoming through their own efforts the negative aspects of anomie, pauperism, and sociocultural inertia, or they were fated to forever perpetuate the latter state of affairs and become identified as a social entity through the stigmatizing sociopathic characteristics of the way of living that corresponded to that state. By employing a euphemism, it could be said that the class society opened its doors to black people on the condition that they prove their capacity to confront and solve their problems in accord with the ethical-juridical code established by this society. But in reality what it did was to cast upon their shoulders the burdensome task of working out the salvation of the Negro race by themselves.

RACIAL HETERONOMY IN A CLASS

SOCIETY

1900–1930

Introduction

In the last two chapters two essential points have been established. First, the competitive social order and the social class
system did not develop in a rapid and homogeneous manner
in the city of São Paulo. In spite of the strong initial impulse
given by the commercialization of the coffee enterprise and
the increasing acceleration of the bourgeois economic revolution, it has been an extremely slow and discontinuous sociohistorical process. Although it has undoubtedly been accumulative, its structural development over a period of time indicates
that every decisive phase of differentiation and progress has
occurred between relatively prolonged phases of commitment
to the past and even selective resistance to urgent sociocultural innovations. It also remained attached to the past and to
archaic structures that fostered the reconstruction of the old
order at various levels of human life. The most marked examples of this occurred at the two extremes: the social circles
constituted by the elites of the ruling groups and the dependent segments of the lower classes.

The second point is that which can be called "the capacity
for change" which had less to do with the content and organization of the cultural horizon of people and groups than with

their position in the economic and power structure of the city. The interrelationship between economic activities and the resulting profits and impositions are what governed the degree of identification, neutrality, or rejection for innovations. For this reason the rustic attitude that prevailed among the various ethnic groups was subject to fluctuating corrective influences. They who became part of the business world either voluntarily or under the pressure of inescapable exigencies tended more than others to take open stands regarding modernization.

The historical trends toward differentiation and reintegration of the social order did not in themselves favor any special ethnic or racial groupings. Yet this came to be the ultimate result. Direct participation in the processes of economic growth and sociocultural development required material and psychological resources. In other words, it required economic resources, technology, and administrative capacities. As the former factors of slave labor and the kind of free manual labor practiced under the caste society, the Negro and mulatto entered into this process with insuperable disadvantages. The sociopathic consequences of the social disorganization that prevailed in the Negro's milieu and those of his incomplete integration into urban life helped increase the destructive power of these disadvantages, which eliminated or undermined even the strongest and most sincere individual intentions to help the black man get ahead.

From this perspective, it can easily be seen how debasement by slavery, social anomie, pauperization, and incomplete social integration worked together to foster the development of a pattern of economic and sociocultural isolation by the Negro and mulatto that was aberrant in a competitive, open, and democratic society. These forces were appropriate for fostering adjustments that maintained the maximum social distance between the white and the Negro as if the latter were still under the yoke of the slaveholder. It is clear that the sociohistorical position of the Negro and mulatto during the period of development of the class society in São Paulo may be considered sociologically to be a problem of cultural lag.

The implications of all this are that special attention should be focused on certain sociocultural influences that fostered a kind of synthesis between the present and the past, between the caste society and that of social classes. The extinct order did not disappear completely following Abolition. It persisted in the mentality, behavior, and even in the structure of social relations of men—even among those who should have had an interest in the total destruction of the old order. At the very time when the competitive social order and the class system were being consolidated, the black population remained in an ambiguous position that was confusedly represented as constituting a state equivalent to that occupied by freedmen in the former social structure. This strange situation is highly illuminating, however, for it brings to light the historical origin of the Negro's social debasement at the heart of the new socioeconomic system: the endless perpetuation of patterns of racial adjustment that took for granted the anachronic criteria of attributing status and social roles to the Negro and mulatto.

If we take the network of race relations of our times as a frame of reference, it might appear that the economic, social, and political inequality existing between the Negro and the white were the fruit of color prejudice and racial discrimination. However, historical-sociological analysis makes it clear that these mechanisms have another function: that of maintaining social distance between these races and the corresponding pattern of sociocultural isolation of the Negro, which are preserved together as a whole by the mere unrestricted perpetuation of archaic segmental structures. Therefore, whatever dynamic importance color prejudice and racial discrimination might have had later, they were not responsible for the poignant reality that concerns us here. Owing to this fact, since the advent of Abolition neither color prejudice nor racial discrimination was intended to institute economic and social privileges for the benefit of the white race. Their function was to defend the barriers that structurally and dynamically protected the established privileges and the very position of the white as the dominant race. In the preceding chapter we attempted to explain why the Negro and mulatto remained apathetic in the face of the sociohistorical process and the inequitable consequences. In this chapter we shall turn our attention to the opposite side of the picture: how and within what limits the white man continued to be the captive of a system of social values and racial domination that carried with it the prevalence of a pattern of intersocial adjustment similar to that which prevailed in the society of estate and caste.

The Racial Democracy Myth

It is very difficult in our times to reconstruct and interpret objectively the white man's motivations orienting his racial adjustments during the period of the development of the competitive social order in the city of São Paulo. However, two things seem to be clear: First, the perpetuation of the total set of patterns of race relations that developed under slavery and were so damaging to the black man occurred without the whites having had any fear of the probable economic, social, and political consequences of racial equality and open competition with Negroes. For this reason at the root of this phenomenon there can be found no kind of anxiety or restlessness and no sort of intolerance or racial hatred which these two consequences brought to life in the historical stage of action. Therefore, barriers designed to block the vertical mobility of the Negro were never erected, nor were measures taken to avert the risks which competition with this racial group might have incurred for the white.

As paradoxical as it may seem, it was the white man's omission rather than his action that redounded in the perpetuation of the *status quo ante*. It seems that the white man put into practice a limited number of the techniques, institutions, and social values inherent in the competitive social order in fairly restricted and confined sectors (in certain kinds of economic activities, legal relationships, and political privileges of the members of the "upper" class). Thus, the field remained open for the survival *en masse* of patterns of social behavior that were often archaic. Along with these patterns there were passed along the norms of the old pattern of race relations, as well as certain social distinctions and prerogatives, the rights and social guarantees, the stereotypes that served to justify such distinctions and prerogatives racially as well as materially and psychologically. From this perspective the historical weaknesses that surrounded the formation and initial development of the class system were much more decisive for the preservation of a great part of the old order of race relations than the white's tendency to be on guard against the free Negro. The white purely and simply did not confront this kind of historical alternative—as did occur, for example, in a similar situation in the United States.

Second, these circumstances multiplied the dynamic power of the factors of sociocultural inertia. While at the same time that the white did not feel that he had to compete, contend, and struggle against the Negro, the latter tended to passively accept the continuation of old patterns of racial adjustment. Owing to the sociopathic effects of the permanent social disorganization and deficient social integration, whenever the black man managed to overcome his apathy regarding his own fate, he did so only to become attached to a timid and confused conformism. It was inevitable that orientations that were already established and fairly well rooted in conventional behavior should prevail. During the final breakdown of the old order, the ideological and utopian conceptions of the nucleus of landowners almost imperceptibly governed the readjustment of Negroes and whites among themselves and to the new sociohistorical situation.

In this context only one group manifested specific tenacity: the elites. Accustomed to dealing with racial tensions in a social milieu in which they had an explosive power to be reckoned with and thus had to be repressed without a second thought, the elites tended to maintain rigid, incomprehensible, and authoritarian attitudes regarding the problems of the black population. They acted as if they still lived in the past and exaggerated the potential risks of an open liberalization of the social guarantees for Negroes. They especially abhorred the agitation related to the Negro problem that erupted in sparse and disorderly ways here and there, bearing the germs of a social restlessness that was in time susceptible to become racial conflict. On the other hand they were opposed to manifestations of solidarity with the Negro which went beyond the traditionalist paternalism that protected individuals or select groups and preserved the white's superiority.

Distrust hindered the modernization of attitudes and behavior in both racial groups, on the presumption that the discussion of certain issues would only prejudice the Negro and destroy the social peace. Thus the attitudes that were manifested socially as a substitute for a conscious collective will represented a veiled rejection and condemnation of the black man. He was not openly rejected, but neither was he openly accepted without restrictions, in accord with the social prerogatives that derived from his new juridical-political position. There persisted an ambivalent attitude of rejection of trends to treat the Negro as an equal coupled with apparent acceptance of the exigencies of the new democratic order. In practice this ambivalence was of no help to the Negro and mulatto. Wherever paternalism prevailed, it facilitated economic and social classification by means of intermittent personal interference. However, the result was that the Negro failed to prepare himself adequately for free competition and suffered the harmful effects of the unavoidable siphoning off of its leadership that this process of vertical socioeconomic mobility engendered.

It should be understood that none of this was born of or happened because of any intention (open or covert) to harm the Negro. In the purest Brazilian tradition such an attitude was not raised to the level of social consciousness; and wherever an attitude of this type was discovered (in the attitudes or behavior of certain immigrants and in anachronistic discrimination in certain institutions), these same social groups sent up the cry of alarm and categorical reproval.

The political philosophy of the solution to the Negro problem was based on the old pattern of gradual absorption of black people through the selection and assimilation of those who showed themselves to identify most with the ruling circles of the dominant race and manifest complete loyalty to their interests and social values. Expectations and conceptions of this nature were in unavoidable conflict with the existing social order and could never function as a bridge of understanding between the races in the new socioeconomic and juridical-political context. Nevertheless, these expectations and conceptions prevailed in that historical setting and nourished the illusion that in this way the social peace could be consolidated and the defense of the Negro's interests could be promoted. In the zeal to avoid hypothetical racial tensions and to ensure an effective means of gradually integrating the black population, all doors were closed that could have permitted the Negro and mulatto to receive the direct benefits of the process of democratization of social rights and guarantees. The logic underlying this historical standard of social justice is clear: In the name of a perfect equality of the future, the black man was chained to the invisible fetters of his past, a subhuman existence and a disguised form of perpetual enslavement.

As could not help but occur, this attitude brought forth a spurious fruit: the idea that the Brazilian pattern of relations between whites and Negroes was in accord with the ethical-juridical principles of the republican regime that was in force. And thus was born one of the great myths of our times: the myth of Brazilian racial democracy. It should be said in passing that this myth was not born from one moment to the next. It underwent long gestation and gradually emerged as the judgment that slavery contained "very little gall" and was Christian and humane. Furthermore, at present, the contrast between the law and the true situation of the black population does not tarnish the illusion that the city of São Paulo is the paradigm of racial democracy. At that time the actual situation which has been described in the first two chapters did not hinder the formulation of this image to dress up the white race's self-glorification. Unfortunately, as equality before God in the past did not eliminate slavery, equality before the law at this time only helped strengthen the white man's hegemony.

Seignorial hypocrisy was easily unmasked; it was a matter of convention. But the same was not true for the myth of racial democracy. Since the opportunities for competition remained potentially open to the Negro, it seemed that the continuation of the parallelism between the social and racial structures of Brazilian society represented a clear expression of the relative possibilities of the various racial groups in our population. No one considered the fact that the true test of a democratic racial philosophy would be its manner of dealing with the problems raised by the displacement of the slave, by the disintegration of the forms of labor associated with slavery, and mainly, by the systematic assistance given to the black population in general. The myth was imposed as something necessary to the Brazilian's respectability, to the normal functioning of institutions, and to the stability of public order in the nation. Ultimately it came to be known as the "Brazilian racial ideology."

The myth served some practical purpose at three different levels even at the time of its historical development. First, it engendered a widespread attitude which attributed the problems of the urban black population to the Negro's incapacity and irresponsibility, although they were actually unquestionable evidences of economic, social, and political inequality in the structure of race relations. Second, the myth exempted the white from moral obligation, responsibility, or solidarity of social import in relation to the progressive deterioration of the socioeconomic situation of the Negro and mulatto. Third, it strengthened the technique of judging the relations between Negroes and whites by means of external appearances of racial adjustments, thus fostering a false concept of the reality of Brazilian race relations. This technique became so deeply entrenched that it became the veritable link between the two successive periods of the cultural history of the relations between Negroes and whites in the city.[1] Consequently it also contributed to the dissemination of a false concept of race relations, giving rise to a whole panorama of ethnocentric convictions: the ideas that "the Negro has no problems in Brazil"; that because of the very nature of the Brazilian people, "there is no racial discrimination among us"; that the opportunities for the accumulation of wealth, social prestige, and power were open to all on a nondiscriminatory and equal basis during the period of urban and industrial development of the city of São Paulo; that the Negro is satisfied with his social situation and way of life in São Paulo; that there does not now, never did, and never will exist any problem of social justice in relation to the Negro except the one that was resolved by the repeal of the slave law and the granting of citizenship to all—which assumes the corollary by which poverty, prostitution, vagrancy, and family disintegration among the black population would be but transitory consequences that could be handled with traditional resources and overcome by spontaneous qualitative changes.

The descriptions of Everardo Dias (1955) of the formation of the proletariat and the development of worker's struggles in São Paulo are particularly illuminating at this point. He points out how the prevalent mentality viewed the social issue as a police matter and broke up manifestations of grievances of the most pacific nature through the use of violence. Such demonstrations

alarmed the conservatives and other authorities who held the reins of government in the country and filled them with panic. . . . Brazil had just left the slaveholding order behind—and a generation had not yet passed since this important event. With the exception of a reduced number of progressive republicans who were more theoretical than objective, the people active in politics desired a work system that differed little from the slave system that had been abolished. All of these individuals were former slaveowners and the word "worker" was still a pejorative expression that belittled the person. . . ." (Dias, 1955, p. 71.)

At that time it would have been unadvisable to publicly debate with frankness subjects of the sort that could be raised by the situation of the black population in São Paulo, even though the intention might be to defend ideas that were traditionalistic and paternalistic. If the debate became centered on the interests of the Negro or if it began immediately with the Negro's way of seeing things, there was tremendous opposition—an opposition that was the child not only of misunderstanding but also of egotism and fear. It was tacitly preferred that the black population never come out of its apathy and passivity.

Two examples will be sufficient to prove this hypothesis: In 1927, a young mulatto who was the illegitimate son of a white man belonging to an important family and who was anxious to start a newspaper and dedicate it to increasing the Negro's awareness of his own situation in the city sought out his father to ask him for help in acquiring a typewriter. He asked him for only three hundred thousand *réis*. "I told him about our group and our intentions. He then forbade participation in movements of this nature, saying there was no need for them in Brazil." The second case is related to a similar experience in which the Negro leader Vicente Ferreira confronted a well-known conservative politician of a traditional and important *Paulista* family:

At the Easter mass for workers (1929) at the Pari Church, at which M.S. and the abbot F. were present, Vicente Ferreira, who was there with Carlos Cavaco, made a long speech which as usual touched upon the unfortunate situation of the Negroes. After the speech, the abbot kissed Vicente Ferreira on the forehead before the large crowd in order to show that the Catholic Church had no prejudice against Negroes. Coming back from the church, Vicente Ferreira, who was always poorly dressed, was invited to ride back to the city with Dr. M.S. Carlos Cavaco rode in front with the chauffeur and Vincente Ferreira behind, with M.S. and the abbot on either side of him. Upon arriving in the city, M.S. insisted upon taking him to his residence. He had no fixed residence: he slept in an inn that used to be on Piques Square whenever he could get two thousand *réis* to pay for a bed. M.S., seeing Vicente Ferreira's situation, invited him to pass by his house the next day to have some coffee and told him that he could ask for whatever he wanted because M.S. was interested in helping him. Before going to M.S.'s house, Vicente Ferreira stopped by the office of the editor of the [newspaper] *Clarim* and told his friends that he was going to teach that important *Paulista* a lesson; he told them that he wasn't going to ask for anything for himself but that he would ask for the favor of a loan of the amount necessary for the *Clarim* to be able to set up a small printing shop. He did, in fact, just that, but M.S. was surprised by the request and asked for the back issues of the newspaper in order that he might study the matter. Later on he returned them, saying that he could not help the Negroes publish a newspaper like that. M.S. proposed that the *Clarim* be changed to an illustrated magazine, promising to arrange for the magazine to be printed for a reasonable price.[2]

Both examples above reveal the white's accessibility, his propensity to help the Negro, and his horror of the black population's demonstrations that he could not guide correctly and discreetly.

Although the juridical-political order of the total society underwent a true revolution, its racial order remained almost identical to that which existed under the caste system; and the Negro never found in the white man any real support for his attempts to develop his self-awareness and to improve his sociohistorical situation. Instead of being democratic, the *Paulistana* society was extremely rigid in this sphere, and it banned and repressed black persons' demonstrations of social autonomy. Considered in terms of this historical context, the conviction that the relations between Negroes and whites corresponded to the requisites of a racial democracy was no more than a myth. As a myth, it was connected to the social interests of the ruling circles of the dominant race and had nothing to do with the interests of the Negro and mulatto. For this reason the myth failed to function as a constructive social force for the democratization of social rights and guarantees among the black population. Instead of being an element in the modernizing of race relations, it was a source of obstruction and stagnation that undermined or destroyed the trends of innovation and democracy in social relations.

In considering race relations according to the interests of the power elites, we have left aside the role of the lower and middle classes of the dominant race. Yet as we saw in the first chapter, these groups represented one of the human poles of dynamization of the development of the competitive social order. Composed of European immigrants and the Brazilian groups that competed with them, these groups supplied most of the individuals that were engaged in active economic pursuits. It would be interesting to know why there were indifferent both to the perpetuation of the traditional techniques of social domination and to the fate of the black population in the city. It seems obvious that from these groups there could have arisen a determined opposition to the domination of the traditional elites and that such an opposition would have changed the racial situation described here.

Limiting the explanations to the essential, we would say that the capacity for political action by these groups was canceled. It is easy to explain this unusual situation if the sociohistorical conditions of the development of the competitive social order in São Paulo are taken into account. During the final breakdown of the slaveholding order, the ruling circles took the direction of the revolutionary process into their own hands. It fell to them to make the decisions concerning all aspects of the policy of replacing the slave population, which would solve the economic problems created by the elimination of slave labor. The most important fact, from the sociological point of view, concerns the preservation of the political roles of the traditional elites. They directed the overall process in such a way as to safeguard and preserve all their basic prerogatives in the power structure of the society. The immigrant and the member of the national labor force who had just arrived on the historical stage were manipulated by these elites. They did not appear as equals or persons who might have an autonomous political orientation. As was the case of all other economic interests of commerce, and importing and exporting, they were subordinated directly to the interests of large-scale agriculture; in general, the dictates of the latter prevailed.

There was a sort of mechanical adjustment of parallel interests. The dominant groups coming out of the seignorial and slaveholding past maintained themselves in the seat of power that was politically, economically, and socially structured. The remaining social groups concentrated their energies on seeking their fortune. The important thing is that nearly three generations passed before they entered the arena as competitors and even adversaries of those elites. In the interim power remained one of the undisputed prerogatives of the traditional families (although others could exercise power by explicit delegation). For many immigrants the dream of returning to their country of origin was more important than gaining social prestige and respect. For Brazilian groups the traditional mechanisms of the organization of power enmeshed everyone in the web of paternalism and loyalty to its interests. In summary, it was only during the period under consideration here (1924 to 1930) that the first integrated attempts were made to break with the adjustments and their psychological and political consequences.

Therefore the lower and middle groups of the community became very poorly engaged—nearly always in a tangential or superficial way—in activities that were of no immediate economic significance for them. The traditional elites had had the time span of almost three generations of absolute rule in the old order, and only at this time began to suffer the direct or indirect effects of the presence of other organized interests in the struggle for power and ideological control.

The results of this brief retrospective analysis show that the conditions for partial perpetuation of traditional forms of patrimonialist domination were at the very roots of the disequilibrium that arose (and became progressively more pronounced soon after) between the racial order and the social order of the class society. Democracy developed in a timid and weak manner. Since its normal development depended upon the relative power of the social groups that competed with each other in an ideological and utopian way [3] at the social level, democracy provided an exclusive historical stage for the few social groups that were organized, possessed the proper techniques for exercising domination and authority, and fought without wavering for the monopoly of power (under the cover of "democratic ideals," if necessary). The lag in the development of the racial order was like a vestige of the old order and can be eliminated in the future only by the indirect effects of the progressive normalization of the democratic way of life and the corresponding democratic social order. As long as this does not happen, there is no possibility of synchronizing the existing racial and social orders. The whites will constitute the dominant race and the Negroes the subservient one.

As long as the "racial democracy" myth cannot be openly used by Negroes and mulattoes as an instrument to control their desire for social classification and upward mobility, it will be innocuous in terms of the very democratization of the prevailing racial order. The dynamization of the racial order in the democratic and egalitarian sense must come from the black segment, even though it should be tolerated, welcomed, and accepted by whites in general. If this myth is constructed and used to reduce such dynamization to the minimum, however, it becomes a formidable barrier to the black man's progress and autonomy—that is, to the advent of racial democracy in Brazil.

The Traditionalistic Patterns of Race Relations

The picture presented above suggests that the patterns of race relations which had developed in São Paulo in the past remained almost intact during the breakdown of the caste society and the initial phases of development of the class society. In other words, the sociopsychological and sociocultural conditions which supported the traditional forms of race relations structurally and functionally were constantly renewed in spite of the changes incurred in other spheres of human life. As a result the traditional forms of racial interaction remained in full force. Concomitantly there was a perpetuation of the conceptions of status and social role which regulated the manner in which individuals identified with each racial group "must" (or "could") share in the rights and duties inherent in the prevailing social order. The tenacity and inner vitality of those structures was such that the historical pattern of prejudice and racial discrimination did not undergo appreciable change, even though it was no longer necessary to recur to it for moral justification of the enslavement of one human being by another, or to impose the monolithic supremacy of the white race. It would be possible even today to describe such racial structures as they persist in actuality. They survived with such tenacity that it would be perfectly possible to study the past through the present. The past is not preserved solely in documents and in the memories of men: it is also revealed in their psychology, in their behavior, and in the functioning of institutions. We shall not systematically explore the possibility of historical reconstruction only because we have sufficient data to draw our examples from the period involved.

In this brief survey we find it advisable to restrict our analysis to three central points: first, the expectations which fostered racial adjustments; second, the traditionalistic patterns of race relations, which made asymmetry a basic feature of adjustment between whites and Negroes; third, the chief sociological characteristics of the racial ideology of the ruling whites.

Those expectations which determined the reciprocal adjustments in the interactions of Negro and white individuals will be better understood and interpreted through the description of concrete situations. Therefore we have selected data pertaining to ten different case histories which effectively illustrate the sociopsychological tendencies that determined the behavior of the protagonists.

J. lived on friendly terms with the children of his master, a man of Italian extraction in whose home he lived, and with other white children in the neighborhood. They formed a harmonious group, in which he was accepted and happy. One day a new focus of interest arose which brought out the color factor. "At that time I used to go out to watch the antics of the clowns. I volunteered to hand out posters in exchange for a ticket to the show. When the idea came up of our setting up a circus that would give performances and charge admission from the neighborhood children, I was the logical choice for the clown. A ring was built in the yard of one of the children's homes. When the time came to assign roles, there was a big fuss about the assignment of the clown's role. Some thought that it really should be me. Others, among them those who lived in the house where the ring was built, claimed that my color was an obstacle: 'What will people say of a circus with a black clown?' The first group won out. In the first place 'I was the funny one'; and then someone recalled that 'He will paint his face and no one will know what his color is!' I should add that on that occasion, as on others, the children of the Italian were on my side."

The same informant was confronted with similar situations, where color was raised as a barrier to friendly relations. "As long as the group was interested chiefly in soccer, there were no serious clashes with the other boys, because I was a good player and they needed me. It is true that sometimes out of anger, sometimes as a joke, they called me *minelite* [4] and *negro* and I couldn't help being hurt." However, as they grew older, the boys were drawn to new interests which involved association with girls and reintroduced the color problem into their relationships. "At one point I became aware of subterfuges to keep me from going to certain places. This went on until the day when one of the boys, who was very fond of me, said: 'We are joining a dance club and I have already spoken to the directors who agreed that you could apply, but on the condition that you attend only the men's rehearsals.' I could not attend meetings in which the ladies participated, but I accepted the condition in a moment of weakness." It seems that "to dance with a black man" was something degrading.

The third case shows even more dramatically how a graduation sponsor belonging to a traditional São Paulo family did not attend the party in order to avoid such a risk. G. writes in an autobiographical sketch: "Upon graduating from high school I asked one of the daughters of the man who raised me to be my sponsor. I am regarded as her *irmão de criacão* (foster brother). She accepted, and we all got ready for the day. I went to the party, and everything went as usual until the dance began. Since I was chairman of the graduation committee, I went to the ballroom ahead of time to make some last-minute arrangements, and shortly before midnight, when the members of the graduating class were to dance the special waltz, I got a message from her saying that she was not going to leave home because she was not feeling well. I pretended to believe it, because having lived with them for many years I knew them well and knew that she was excusing herself merely to avoid dancing the waltz with me. On the following day, I found out that she had spent most of the evening playing cards."

The same informant shrewdly enumerates the tricks used by white friends either to exclude him unfeelingly from situations which would prove embarrassing to them, or at the same time to shield him from overly painful experiences. "To help me adapt to the group, my fellow students gave me the prerogatives of political leader of the school and always selected me as head of socials and outings for our club. During my five years in office I managed to plan the biggest socials and outings in the history of that school. Nevertheless, since at our socials the selection of participants was strict, I sometimes felt out of place. But it was precisely to avoid my having any feelings of inferiority (a fact which I understood only much later) that my fellow students placed me in that position, because at the socials (dances, literary meetings, theater parties, picnics, etc.) I would always be busy directing things and would not participate in the activities, and on outings I would always be attending to accommodations for my fellow students and to their behavior. Sometimes my responsibility increased when parents permitted their daughters to join our outings only on the condition that I should look after them. They trusted no one but me, and I was expected to act as a baby sitter. I believe such parents behaved in this way assuming they had no reason to fear that I would flirt with their daughters, since I was a Negro and the girls could not possibly be interested in me. They were completely wrong, and in revenge I took good advantage of the situation. . . . Yet, frequently, my responsibilities ended before the party was over. On such occasions my fellow students would send a few girls who knew me better over as a delegation so that I could select one to dance with. I found this untactful and silly, since as a man it was my business to ask them to dance and not vice versa. My excuse was that I did not know how to dance. And I really did not know and had no interest in learning, to be honest with myself. . . . Frequently, the six boys who were my closest friends would notice the embarrassing situation in which I found myself, unable to share in the gaiety of the parties which I had organized, and would leave their dates and girl friends and come to me. We would sit around a table and drink as much as we could. In the end, we would all be taken home quite drunk." [5]

The fourth and fifth cases revolve around courtship: the passing romance of an adolescent and the serious courtship of a young man. The first case is again that of G.: "None of the white girls I went out with told their parents about it, because in some cases my very life might have been in danger. Most of the parents believed that my relationship with their daughters was nothing more than a simple friendship. They never suspected the truth. There was only one exception, which is worth mentioning: I was in my third year in high school, and in my class there was a brunette, the prettiest girl in the class and the daughter of an important coffee planter. Right from the start there was much competing for her approval. As would happen I did not join in the competition. But I worked hard at my studies until I was at the top of the class. Since she was not a very good student, she had to ask me for help once in a while in order to keep up with her courses. This contact led to friendship. We met every night, and she grew increasingly fond of me. We signed up for a review course and were together even more often. We exchanged photographs, and after she had given me more than half a dozen of her, I agreed with many misgivings to give her one of me. One day, the director of the school where the review course was given called me in and told me that she could not allow me to continue. I pressed her to tell me why, but she would not tell me anything. A few days later I was called in unexpectedly by the principal of the high school. I went to his office, and he told me that he would not expel me from the school because it was a public school, and also in deference to the family that was raising me, but that he would shift me to another class section —which he did. I was furious and tried hard to find out the reason, but without success. I had a slight inkling, because I had no further contact with the girl, and she was picked up every day by her father's husky chauffeur. I found out everything some days later through a girl who worked in my girl friend's home: The girl's mother, while going through her daughter's things, came across my picture tucked away in a silver box in her closet. She called the girl and questioned her about the picture which, in view of the inscription, she suspected to be a token of more than mere friendship even though it was just of a Negro kid. The girl told her that she was fond of me in spite of my being a Negro, and that she thought that she was old enough at fifteen to make her own judgments. Result: She got a dreadful beating and was forbidden to go out alone for a long time. The mother, in her implacable anger, went to the school where the review course was given and asked for my dismissal. The director found it expedient to agree. Then the mother went to the high school principal and asked him to expel me, for she could not abide my impudence in betraying the trust of her daughter, who was only a child. I, too, was fifteen years old. So this romance almost came to ruin my life."

The other case was J.'s. Contrary to G., he was a light mulatto and good-looking—one of those whose color alone is different. When his friends and acquaintances began to court girls, he found himself involved in the marriage plans—but in a different way which he just could not accept. "About that time, the Italians kept telling me that they would find me a woman to marry. I noted that whenever the subject was brought up, the girls who were suggested to me as good prospects were not members of the family but mulatto girls. Among the Italian's relatives there was a niece that I liked; but my interest for her was cut short when she said to me: 'What spoils you is that you're too dark.' That was when I began to notice that color was a stumbling block.

The sixth and seventh cases relate to F., a dark mulatto, and to how he was treated at the home of a rich and traditional family where his grandmother had worked and where he had been raised. "When I was a student, I once found myself in serious difficulty. The only way out was to ask a friend for help; but my friends could not help me. Then I remembered Mrs. M. T. I went there and asked to speak to her. She received me and I explained what I wanted. I told her that I was studying and that I was in terrible difficulty because I had to buy certain (dental) books and did not have the money. I had remembered her and thought that perhaps, for my grandmother's sake and because she had known me since I was a child, she might help me out. Mrs. M. T. listened to me, said yes, and went into another room. She came back with thirty *milréis* and handed them to me. I refused and left." The informant regarded her behaviour as a serious insult. Nevertheless, as time went by he forgot this bitter experience and visited her once more. "When I had graduated and had a practice, I went one day to visit this family. This happened by chance. I was in the vicinity around 11:30, and decided to look up my childhood companions. They (the young men) received me in a friendly way. We talked for a while. I told them that I had graduated and was practicing in my own dental office. Soon the maid came to say that lunch was ready.

Then I prepared to leave. I explained that I had been in the vicinity by accident and that I had not planned on eating out. The boys insisted that I should eat there until they persuaded me and I stayed. The maid soon came to say that she had my place ready. And she took me to the kitchen. Half the table had been set up for me. When I accepted the invitation I did not expect this. I thought that we would all eat together and talk. I immediately understood why they had done this to me, and did not accept the lunch. I asked the maid to tell them after I had gone, that I would not eat in the kitchen. I never set foot in that house again."

The eighth case relates to the same kind of difficulty. But the person involved, J. [an illegitimate child], called on his father for help. Once, when he was twenty-two, he sought him out in his law office. "Not having found him there, I left my name and address at the insistence of the people in the office. A month later my father came to look for me, also failed to find me, and left his card. I went back to the office. He [the father] said that it was not his fault—my mother was proud and had disappeared, taking me with her. He spoke very close to my mouth to see if I had alcohol on my breath. . . . He gave me a hundred *milréis*. . . . And afterward it was always like this. My problem was the pregnancy of the woman with whom I was living. I never had much contact with him [the father] because he was a man of experience, and I knew that he had misgivings and fears because he felt that Negroes tend to 'sponge off' people."

It is hard to say whether the *filhos de criação* and "protégés" were better off when it came to the selection or pursuance of a career. In his autobiography G. points out the psychological dilemmas which arose when his friend selected a profession which he himself would have liked to pursue if he could have. "Once, as I talked to one of my friends, he told me that he dreamed of a diplomatic career. He already visualized himself as ambassador to London or Paris with all the customary ritual. He thought that I too should enter the Foreign Service, because there was no better profession in Brazil. I told him that it wasn't my vocation and that my plans for the future were quite different. But he argued with me so much that he ended up convincing me a diplomatic career was the best thing for me. So, relying on the fact that he had a cousin who was at the time secretary-general of the Department of Foreign Affairs and also an uncle who was an ambassador, I began the basic study program along with him. I already knew some English, which I perfected, and I also learned French. After two years of study I was familiar with all the subject matter required for the examinations. . . . I was well upon the requirements in international law, etc. Nevertheless as I prepared for the exams I became aware that a Negro could not enter the Foreign Service and I decided not to risk a formal rejection in Rio de Janeiro. Just before the exams were to be given, my friend came to my home to see if I was ready to go with him. I told him that I was no longer interested in taking the exams because I had come to the conclusion that this was not the career for me. He insisted I tell him the real reason why I had given up at the last minute after studying so hard. I finally told him I had found out that Negroes could not enter the Foreign Service. He laughed and said that in Brazil there were no such barriers, that all this was a figment of my imagination, and ended up offering to pay for my trip and other expenses in Rio, since we would be staying at his grandmother's house. I stuck to my own opinion, asked him not to insist since I had decided not to continue, and requested him to wait until the next exams which would be held in January. In the meantime he could find out whether I could enter the Foreign Service. I agreed to go with him but not to take the exams at this time. While he was there, he discovered the truth: a Negro could not enter the Foreign Service Institute even if the President of the Republic were to order it.* My friend was terribly disappointed and decided not to enter the Foreign Service (although he passed the examination with flying colors) but to study law and go into politics in order to combat this heinous prejudice which hinders the advance-

* *Translator's note:* This is no longer true.

ment of the Brazilian Negro. He is now a lawyer and an official in the cabinet of the Minister of Agriculture, and it won't be long until he is a candidate for some elective post. Another friend wanted me to go with him . . ." [he related the problems involved in other careers, just as closed to the Negro].

The tenth case refers to the experiences of a matron from an important and traditional family in her relations with former domestic servants. Once she met a very old Negro woman whom she had not seen for some time. She called her *Dona* * and got the following report: "What did you say, Missus? Not *Dona* to be sure! You can't make a *Dona* out of this stuff!" and she beat her breast. The same lady was sometimes visited by a woman who had been raised by her family and who had been their cook. She came with her daughter. "The daughter would come in, sit down, and chat without further ado, but the mother would not sit down: 'she couldn't sit in the presence of the lady.' It was only at the insistence of the grandmother of the house and because of her daughter's impatience—'Sit down, Mother!'—that she finally did sit down, on the edge of the chair."

These cases, selected in order to emphasize the significance of the actions which led individuals to behave as Negroes, whites, or mulattos, clearly show that black people were not freed—either objectively or subjectively—from the heteronomous condition inherent in the former positions of slave, freedman, *filho de criação* etc. The Negro became on the social scene the substitute for and equivalent of the slave, freedman, or *filho de criação,* and thus had to be regarded and treated as such. Resistance to change in these expectations of behavior came from both whites and Negroes, although here and there among the latter there were nonconformists who openly rebelled against such patterns. The informants themselves, of both racial stocks, were fully aware of these facts.

* *Translator's note:* The polite form used before the Christian name— e.g., Dona Maria—in addressing social superiors or equals, but not normally social inferiors.

They openly acknowledged the Negro's subservience and the white's supercilious pride. Yet they also pointed out that things were changing. A lady from a traditional family gave vent to her feelings: "Today Negroes no longer know their place. They are ill bred, impertinent, and sometimes even dishonest. A., a cook I had, left here being cheeky, saying that Negroes are better than whites, that Negroes know how to bring up their children, that Negroes are not loafers, and a lot of other things I can't even remember! A. was a mulatto girl, she had an education, and she seemed to have some polish; but she resented her color. When she first worked for me, she said she had left her former employer because the lady was too proud, she thought Negroes were not human, and she did not permit A.'s son to come into the house to talk to his mother. He had to remain at the gate. I told her that I thought this wasn't right, that here she could receive her son in her own room, give him a snack or even lunch once in a while. Do you know what happened? Once I came down to look for a sewing basket and do you know what I saw? A.'s little mulatto boy, sprawling in the armchair in the living room, reading the magazines, with his feet on the coffee table. Not even my children and my guests take such liberties! When I told A. that she must receive her son only in her room and not allow him to sit in the living room, she was furious: 'That's how it goes! She says she's not like the others, just in order to look good, but in the end they're all the same, they always think Negroes are not human!' Such impudence! So a teacher is going to sit in the principal's chair? A nurse will take over the doctor's office as though it were hers? To each his own place, his own job. Don't take over what isn't yours. But when you treat black people well, they think they are equals, that they can do whatever they like!" As she elaborated on such incidents, this matron stated that the Negroes' insolence had grown slowly and had become habitual and intolerable only after the enactment of Getulio Vargas's labor laws. "The result is this total lack of awareness of their own place which is so noticeable nowadays," and she went on to say that this was the case with the masses as a whole, including the poor whites.

The Negro, in turn, might not like the servile position to which he was relegated. But he had to submit passively to the whites' expectations regarding his behavior. As J. points out in connection with his own case, "I put up with it, because it was the Negro's lot at the time." On the other hand, the white pulled as best he could the strings of the Negro's conformism and passive submission. The following passage from G.'s autobiographical statement vividly illustrates this: "Once I was sitting in a beautiful armchair on the porch of the house of that friend who wanted me to enter the Foreign Service. His family is extremely wealthy; they are important coffee planters. His mother was also there knitting. And I was downcast, thinking about my situation at the time. I was welcome in most of the homes in the city, both rich and poor; I had a very good reputation; I was a "pet" to all these people. And yet, I thought, if I were one day to marry and have children, would my wife and children enjoy the same privileges? My common sense said no. And I grew increasingly lost in thought and melancholy. At a certain point the lady broke the silence, and as though almost guessing what was going through my mind, she asked me why I seemed so sad and whether I did not enjoy the life I was leading, for she could not imagine that I could already have problems. I told her that indeed I had, that they were quite serious, and that I didn't know how to solve them. I told her what I had been thinking. She said that I was too young to think about all this and that I must struggle to hold on to the position I enjoyed at the time as a friend of the best families in the city and living in an environment that was truly aristocratic, for as far as she knew I had the privilege of being on familiar terms with all these people who treated me as one of the family, etc. Then I told her that I just couldn't accept this situation, because the position I enjoyed in society was a false one, and I couldn't hold on to it permanently. One proof of this was that in spite of all the privileges I enjoyed, those friends indirectly kept me from dancing in their social clubs unless my school held a party there, from swimming in their pool, or from playing tennis or basketball on their courts. I concluded by saying that if I enjoyed this position of relative friendship, with its limitations, it was because I was the adopted son of one of the richest and most highly esteemed men in the city, and that I actually believed that the day I should have to get along without that family's support the entire situation would change. The lady didn't know how to answer me; she couldn't contradict me. She merely advised me not to struggle too hard against things as they were, for otherwise I would end up badly."

These cases are sufficient to underline the point at issue. Negroes, whites, and mulattoes have interacted as though they were still separated or united by the traditional patterns of race relations that prevailed under the seignorial, slave-holding order. In any situation where social rights and duties depended on racial affiliation, an individual has been expected not only to know his place but also to act accordingly and abide by the consequent etiquette, obligations, and impositions. In short, to know your place and to honor and exalt it are still the same thing in spite of the black man's ever more apparent, unpredictable, and uncontrollable dissatisfaction. Color served as a brand that identified the black man, and along with him, those of the masses who came from the slave quarters and from work in the fields—from the ignominious and unending subordination of slavery. Within that sociopsy-chological and sociocultural context, the slave and the freed-man did not vanish: they survived in the Negro as both a racial and a social category. And if the white man should ever forget this, it was the job of the Negro himself to proclaim his position and to protest that from this "stuff" there could emerge neither a person nor the equal of the master.

All this shows that special attention must be given to the *egalitarian patterning of race relations*. This did not immediately arise or prevail as a typical element of the class society. It was corrupted and assimilated by traditionalist patterns of race relations, thus achieving the appearance of a democratic social order while stubbornly retaining the substance of the old order. While full equality has apparently prevailed in racial adjustments, the traditional heteronomous relationship that separated whites from Negroes and masters from slaves and freedmen has actually survived almost intact. The sociohistorical conditions for shaping and developing the class structure in the city of São Paulo were such that this fate of the Negro became inevitable. Class structure becomes a reality only when a given social group attains the economic, social, and cultural requisites of a class (or subclass). In racial terms only the white elements of the São Paulo population achieved from the start the sociopsychological and sociocultural characteristics that are typical of class formation. The Negro and the mulatto remained outside this process to varying degrees, along with those segments of the white element that also encountered difficulty in becoming part of the new social forms, and made up the "riffraff," a survival of the old order. As long as he remained in this position, the Negro lived in a class society without being part of it. The term "black" permitted the selection of color as a racial mark in order to single out both a racial grouping and a social category that occupied an ambiguous, not to say altogether marginal, position in society.

This leads us naturally to the second point of the present discussion. The Negroes and mulattoes slowly and belatedly joined the emerging social classes, but did not identify with any of the existing classes. Their relations with the whites were not, typically speaking, class relations. The patterning of racial relations proceeded according to avowedly aberrant models, closer to the traditionalistic and patrimonialistic heteronomous relations than to those inherent in the competitive social order. The whites zealously and stubbornly held on to the active and dominant position of the seignior, while the Negroes remained in the corresponding subordinate position, as though they were still stripped of legal status. Therefore, what must be emphasized is not properly speaking the exist-

ence of relations of dominance (in every class society there
are legitimate forms for the exercise of dominance, leadership, and authority), but the interpenetration of the class
system and of archaic forms of racial dominance. If the Negroes and mulattoes had attained at an early stage a social
classification within the emerging class structure, their relations with the whites would have changed at once. A new
parallelism would have been established between the social
structure and the racial stratification of the whole society.
Since this was not the case, there was double corruption: On
the one hand the class society was openly undermined by
social distinctions based on racial privileges incompatible with
the structure and dynamics of a democratic society. On the
other hand the traditional patterns of dominance of the white
race persisted above and beyond their juridical and historical
sources of legitimacy. Thus they took on the nature of an
irreparable violation of the basic rights of black people, and
lost any and all ethical-juridical basis. Lost in the class society
without enjoying any of the established social guarantees, the
black man was at the mercy of a tutelage that lacked moral
sense and that acknowledged no limitations, whether based on
material interest, decorum, or subjective obligations. The final
paradox resides in the tendency to imagine that the race
relations have evolved historically, based on valid models of
social structure. Such models have applied to the interrelations of whites among themselves, with notorious inconsistencies in relation to the democratization of power and to the
social intercourse between the elite and the masses. Only
occasionally, however, have these models been applied to the
interrelations of whites and Negroes. Nevertheless, it has
been implicitly agreed that democratic principles prevail in
interracial relations and that the predominant form of racial
adjustment is egalitarian.

We are not interested here in the sociopathic aspects of
such a manifestation of ethnocentrism. We merely intend to
make a sociographic analysis of the egalitarian patterning of
race relations in order to show its characteristic structural and

functional components.[6] Basically, if we disregard the misleading new name, the form of adjustment that was instituted and which has been perpetuated almost to this day (though with some attenuation and substantial changes in the Negro's social prospects) has come down from the traditionalistic and patrimonialistic past as though the whites intended to retain paternalism in their relations with black people. Yet the economic, social, and political conditions for the survival of paternalism had ceased to exist, as already noted. Paternalism could be practiced on a small scale, in conjunction with the persistence of some of the social and political traits of the old order imbedded in the life of important families; and in more fortuitous fashion, in the protection of one or another more intimately known black person. The paternalistic relationship became a severe and gratuitous burden for the protector, not only unsatisfactory but degrading for the protégé. In short, once the social world created by slavery had vanished, the material and psychological foundations of the old models for association between whites and Negroes and mulattoes disappeared—especially the models that connected the two extremes of society. The continuance of such models in itself became an anomaly, and wherever it became associated with practical interests there was nearly always an element of perversion in the motives of whites or Negroes or both.

The research reveals the breakdown of traditional relationships in interracial relations. The legal suppression of the caste system and the unavoidable but slow disintegration of the old order gradually eroded the material and psychological foundations of those relationships, so that the direction taken by race relations was not favored historically. The sociopsychological and sociocultural requisites of the archaic forms of racial adjustment were irrevocably condemned, and the directions for reintegration of the racial order would have to be supplied by the class system. Nevertheless, the various factors of inertia analyzed in the preceding chapter operated simultaneously in the Negro milieu and in the ruling circles of the "dominant race." There arose a sort of tacit understanding that granted the white man the right to decide how the Negro should be treated in concrete situations, instilling in the latter a tendency to abide passively by the patterns of behavior expected by the former. Such an outcome would have been inconceivable if the Negro's conformism had not been forged by the school of slavery and if, in spite of being a slave, he had been the historical instrument of his liberation.

Two of our women researchers were interested in the traditional influences that nurtured the extreme conformism of older Negroes. Here is how one of them freely summarizes the philosophy of life of a woman informant: "The hardships she went through made her fatalistic. Fate decreed that she should marry and be widowed three times. She does not blame her parents for not sending her to school, but fate which so decreed it. Her poverty, too, was predetermined. She accepts all vicissitudes with a slave's submissiveness, without rebellion, without desire to interfere. The mere fact of being black is a warning to her to remain submissive." The other researcher, in talking to the members of the family she was studying, found out that the father was a spiritualist * and that the mother had no specific religion. "Sometimes I follow this one, sometimes that one." From the head of the family she got the following explanation about curing diseases: " 'Faith in God is what counts; without faith the doctor isn't any use!' 'Then why do you go to the doctor?' I asked. 'Well, it helps!' he answered." The researcher was confused by what she saw and heard, and let off steam in her working diary: "All the members of the family are conformists to a revolting degree. Although it seems impossible, they are relatively satisfied with their lot. . . . 'If it's the will of God, what can we do?' . . . They do not blame color or the lack of opportunities for the situation." The truth is that is was easier for the Negro to struggle against the material trappings of slavery than to fight its hidden ideological foundation, the traditionalist conception of the world. A slow reeducation through experience

* Translator's note: He participated in macumba, an Afro-Brazilian religion. See the glossary for further details.

would be necessary to make him aware that he must achieve through his own efforts a Second Abolition which would be egalitarian and represent his definitive redemption. In short, everyone has spontaneously agreed to perpetuate the traditional external forms of racial relations.

The asymmetric pattern of race relations centers around the idea of whites and Negroes seen as "guardians" and "wards" respectively. The foundations of this are clearly evident in the following testimony, which summarizes the basic elements of the relation: ". . . the Negro knows that he is inferior and acknowledges that the white man is more intelligent and must have authority over him. For this reason, he is meek and respectful and keeps his place. He will never be able to attain the same position as the white, no matter what he may do." Black people themselves have developed a sharp awareness of this attitude, which they point to as the cause of color prejudice and racial discrimination: "Under the circumstances, what we ordinarily experience in the street is not only the result of prejudice but in this case the cause of such results as well. Prejudice is this concept of inferiority which is held about the Negro, and as a result of this inferiority the behavior of superior to inferior arises."

Beliefs of this sort were firmly held and deeply rooted. As late as 1952 we had the opportunity to note the indignation of a Brazilian of Portuguese descent when L., a great mulatto soccer player, was promoted to coach in his club. The informant was an ardent fan of that club and felt that its team was doing poorly as a result. "L. is still a great player. But it was a mistake to make him a coach. Negroes are no good at that. They're no good at giving orders to anyone, much less to white people. . . . Like every black man, L. is disorganized and insubordinate. How can he be top man and give orders? No one wants to obey him; they follow his own example of insubordination. . . . Besides, there are white fellows on the team with good educations, even lawyers. How can they be bossed around by a Negro and take orders from him?"

Just as he cannot "give orders to a white man," a Negro

cannot be received in a home or treated as an equal. Former domestic servants or *filhos de criação* are received in the pantry, at the kitchen door, or on the porch. Various sources show that the reciprocal placing of the parties in this regard has been strict and tacitly acknowledged. This is not meant to hurt anyone's feelings since it is felt that such procedures are not directed at the individual but only at his inferior social position. The same sources reveal that the main thing has been for everyone to know his place and faithfully obey the hierarchical tradition. A lawyer and plantation owner had two Negro servants. He explained the reasons for this preference as follows: "I am the one who chooses the servants in our home. We now have two wonderful Negro boys: they're smart and excellent workers. In any case, I prefer Negroes for the job. . . . As long as we're going to help someone, we might as well pick Negroes since they need help more. I'd rather help a Negro than some pushy little Italian who wants to get ahead in this world. The Negro is different; he associates the desire to get ahead with a hierarchical tradition: he is respectful and well behaved; the Italian is ill bred and impertinent." There have been complaints against mulattoes for the same reason. As one informant put it: "Now, I don't know if you've noticed that mulattoes are worse than blacks. I, for one, have nothing against Negroes. I think they're good people and I get along with them. But I don't want to have anything to do with mulattoes. Mulattoes think they're white and stick their noses in where they don't belong. I prefer blacks, because they know their place and keep their distance. Not so the mulattoes. They're obnoxious and think they can act like whites at all times." In interracial contact, social distance and the "hierarchical tradition" were emphasized by social etiquette. A Negro was not to be addressed as *Senhor* or *Dona,* and a white person would not remove his hat before him or shake his hand. Some people went as far as to deny Negroes the use of such formalities among themselves. "I am familiar with one case that now comes to mind. In the home of a well-to-do family that still had aristocratic airs, Negro servant girls were not permitted to address the older ones as *Senhora* * because the word was reserved for the white ladies of the house."

To the measure in which he has identified certain habits and forms of behavior with aristocratic status, the Negro himself, whenever possible, has tended to absorb the behavior patterns of the white elite and imitate them to differentiate and separate himself from the "poor Negroes" or "Negroes in work clothes." The well-regarded Negro clubs are known for the formalism that rules the social life of their members, by the decorum of their social activities, and by the zeal shown for strict formalities of behavior between the sexes at dances. In relations with the white man, however, such symbols of prestige and power might be negatively interpreted and greeted with hostility. In the face of such a situation white people will often say: "It seems like Negroes are trying to be somebody"; "This rabble can't see what it looks like"; "Negroes seem to think they're people"; etc. Not long ago, we encountered a taxi driver who was very much upset: "Today I'm jinxed. The first customer who showed up was a woman. She signaled me to stop. When I did, three fellows pushed into the car right in front of her. [It was raining and cabs were in great demand.] I didn't like it. I said that it was the girl's turn. Two of the fellows were white and the other was Negro. The Negro said he didn't care. 'All I want is for you to get me to the Praça Clóvis Bevilaqua in a hurry!' I was furious. I told them they couldn't boss me around and their shouting wouldn't get them anywhere. If they wanted to boss someone, they should buy a car." As a result he decided not to work for anybody and he parked the taxi. "Now you can shout as much as you want. I won't move even if you call the police." This was his final comment: "Hell, it would have to be the black fellow who spoke up! If I liked coal, I'd buy a kiln. If it had been one of the white fellows, it wouldn't have been so bad. But a Negro! Let them boss the whore who bore them!"

Taken as a whole, this material shows how asymmetrical

* *Translator's note:* The formal form of "you," used with all except intimates, children, and animals.

patterns of race relations have become embodied in social behavior and what happens when they fail to be observed. As a rule, if the Negro attempts to thwart expectations of submissive behavior on his part by failing to keep his place, and, especially, if he tries to act as an equal or superior, the white man will react negatively, sometimes with uncontrollable violence, and the course of action and its outcome on both sides are impossible to foresee.

Thus, friendliness toward Negroes does not necessarily imply the total absence of social distance or racial intolerance, but something much more complex: the operation of a pattern of interracial behavior that regulates extensively and strictly the attitudes and actions appropriate to every situation. By stipulating how each person ought to behave in routine types of racial contact, this pattern of behavior has controlled the feelings and emotions of the individuals by structuring their actions in accordance with social conventions. At the same time this pattern of behavior has outlawed or condemned systematic resort to violence, labeling as unseemly actions that would imply a loss of self-control in dealing with persons of "inferior" social position. If the Negro fails to meet conventional expectations of his own accord, this calls for giving him a "lesson"—serving him his lunch in the kitchen or openly refusing to go along with his pretensions. When the traditional system of interracial behavior has broken down and the Negro has rebelled against the discrimination that ensues from respecting it, ambiguous situations have arisen, rife with resentments and tensions which have tended to lead to conflict.

Various examples allow us to elaborate on this aspect and show how far matters have gone since the dawn of true democratic conditions in the appraisal and acceptance of the Negro. It would seem that aside from deliberate instances of discourtesy work situations have provided the chief sources of friction. In one of the life histories we find the following incident: "In 1917 they got him a position as consumer tax inspector. He couldn't take it because he lacked the qualifications. Then they found him a clerk's job. Everything was going well until the day when the boss ordered him to wash out the spittoons and he rebelled. In an outburst of temper the man reminded him that he was black and almost illiterate. He resisted. He did not wash out the spittoons and he never showed up on the job again."

It seems that black women also react similarly when provoked. E.N. was a seamstress in a dress shop in the elegant part of town. "One day the lady who owned the shop wanted me to take her daughter home. I said, 'I won't. I'm not a nursemaid.' The lady retorted: 'You nigger! Are you going or aren't you?' 'I'm not.' 'Then you can leave!' I left right then and there." Another interesting example is that of the temporary promotion of a young man who worked as a clerk in a government office. The section head had to leave for a few days. He made the necessary arrangements and gave the young man responsibility for the office while he was away. "My white fellow workers were furious. Some could not contain themselves and even told me that they didn't want to work for a Negro. 'Who's ever heard of a Negro giving orders to *us*?' I was upset at first, then I didn't let it bother me. I was the boss and they had to obey me. They could complain all they wanted. They had to take orders from me!" Experiences of this type have naturally left their mark on the white as well as the Negro.

In the course of our survey we came across various types of complaints on the part of whites who could no longer understand Negroes and their behavior. Many had become very much aware that the Negro "sought out the white out of interest rather than friendship" and were shocked by independent attitudes which they tended to label as "ingratitude" or "rebellion." One informant, who stated that he was "sympathetic to the Negro" and that "he tried to help them out whenever he could," gave a bitter account of his disappointments. The two Negroes he had tried to help "gave him a headache" and led him to undergo "very sad experiences." To his mind "they are very rebellious and turn violently against those who help them." He mentioned as an example that his two protégés treated him rudely and gave coarse answers to some ticklish remarks he was forced to make. "Negroes take offense too easily, and the more they depend upon you the more arrogant they become. White people are different. They don't forget a favor and always show gratitude for those they receive." For this reason he had become convinced that "Negroes are ungrateful" and that "they soon forget their obligations toward other people." The Negro, in turn, is faced with a dilemma. It is his behavior toward whites that determines whether or not he gets a chance to make use of his abilities and not, as he would like, his worth as a human being. This comes through in the following statement by J.L.: "There are possibilities to fulfill my wishes by means incompatible with my principles and my character—fawning on politicians and begging for a right which I have won through my own efforts and my own work."

The asymmetric pattern of race relations naturally had some normal sociopsychological results. Keeping to fundamentals, we shall discuss five basic points: the dynamic consequences of adherence to the traditional patterns of racial adjustment; influences that distort the asymmetric patterns of racial behavior in the personality configuration of whites; influences that distort the asymmetric patterns of racial behavior in the personality configuration of Negroes; trends to differential identification associated with the asymmetric patterns of race relations; and specific consequences of the absence of reciprocity in the perspectives of race relations.

It seems obvious that continued adherence to the traditional patterns of race relations was the sociopsychological requisite for the perpetuation of many aspects of the old order in the area of contact among Negroes, whites, and mulattoes. This adherence was thus at the root of the slowness with which the racial order legated by the late nineteenth century has changed. Yet it was not this general issue we wished to emphasize, but the real motive behind the underlying conservative attitudes and behavior of whites and Negroes. Continued

adherence to this pattern of race relations has not only preserved but revitalized the white's image of the Negro, and vice
versa, and made them relevant in society. Furthermore, it has
perpetuated these images as though the abolitionist revolution
and the advent of the Republic had been of no account in the
area of racial accommodation.

In short, the image of the "good Negro" is associated with
well-defined expectations of submission, loyalty, and conformism to the interests of the dominant race. The more the
Negro and mulatto identify with the democratic ideals of
personality linked to the image of the citizen and to the basic
rights of the individual, the more they are misunderstood,
judged ethnocentrically, and deprecated. Inversely, the closer
they adhere to the model of the faithful and devoted servant
or strive for the related attributes, even if they are not servants or dependents, the more they evoke affection, understanding, and esteem in the heart of the white.

About Negro servants an informant relates:

What a good woman Joaquina was! She personified the devoted
affection that Africans usually feel for children. When the kids
were sick, she would take them food and the medicine their
mother ordered; when they went to sleep, she would sit on the
floor by the bed, guarding their slumbers; when they were well,
she would tell them stories. . . . It was wonderful to hear the
African legends about little girls who were stolen and trussed up
in bags, and sang in the streets. Or about horsemen in headlong
flight from the enemy who would toss a pin behind them and see it
turn into a thorny forest.[7]

They were almost part of the family, enjoying its company
and protection, as is shown in the two excerpts that follow:

We would never allow anyone to say that Malva was black. Malva
was "colored," she was "a dark brunette." One of the tricks my
uncles used to annoy us and make us terribly angry (we ended up
shedding tears of rage, time and time again!) was to repeat:
"Malva? She's a piece of burnt wood. She's blacker than coal dust.
She's so black that she doesn't show in the dark. She's the black
mummy to you kids." Such comments aroused furious retorts,
such as this one, which was used as the supreme argument:

"Malva is black on the outside, but her soul is whiter than all of yours put together!" In spite of the devotion of Nhá Benta,* of Rosa the cook, and of Malva, Mother has always said that she prefers white servants to Negroes and mulattoes. She thinks that Negroes and mulattoes are sluggish, lazy, idle, and care little about work and cleanliness. Yet we usually had black servants, and there never grew between us and the white women the same affection that often developed between us and the black ones.

This image of the "good Negro" was later to be sharply repudiated by Negroes and mulattoes involved in social movements for the "redemption of the Negro race." They set forth counterimages that mercilessly exposed it, such as that of the disloyal Negro. At the same time, they presented their own interpretations with which to debunk the white man's sentimental stereotypes.

This pattern of racial behavior naturally and inevitably brought about certain well-known distortions in the personality structures of whites and Negroes. It seems obvious that the former developed a peculiar type of authoritarianism which falls into the categories of despotism and paternalism. The slaveholding tradition associated color with social position to such an extent that the white who had just come out of the caste system still behaved as though he were the master and was extremely intransigent toward any apparent break in the traditional, acceptable pattern of race relations. For this reason intolerant evaluations, attitudes, and behavior were more prevalent in racial adjustments involving the reciprocal positions of the two races in the power structure of the society. As had been the case in the past, the vertical mobility of a Negro did not alter those relative positions but operated through mechanisms that individualized the procedure and made him a sort of exception that proves the rule. The Negro leaders of São Paulo had a clear and profound understanding of the nature of this process. "When a Negro attracts attention through his own worth, white people grant him respect born

---

* Translator's note: Nhá was a familiar term in the days of slavery, used as the equivalent of "missy."

of admiration—it's as if he were a prodigy of some sort," one of them told us. As a result, paradoxical as this may seem, changes of status for black people did not affect the reciprocal positions of the two races in the power structure of the society.[8] Nevertheless, white people kept a sharp and watchful eye on the psychological attitudes and behavior of such black people. Anything the latter did that was at variance with conventional expectations was used to demonstrate the incapacity of the Negro to fulfill social roles regarded as natural prerogatives of the whites. If the Negro or mulatto policeman, army sergeant, or office supervisor achieved something worthwhile, he was not likely to benefit the racial group to which he belonged. On the other hand if he ran counter to norms and customs or made a false step, he was pointed out as a prototype and presented as conclusive evidence of the limitations of the Negro race.

This mechanism of perception and identification provided the white with effective means to defend the ruling position of his race, while at the same time making him impervious to the causes and consequences of the Negro's resentments. In short, the vertically mobile Negro did not open a path for others, nor did he contribute to a liberalization of the white's cultural horizon. On the contrary, he made it clear to everyone, vividly and publicly, why under conditions of equality he would be unable to assume certain duties and responsibilities in society. Thus the intolerance that lay concealed behind the asymmetric patterns of racial behavior was immensely subtle and complex. Without directly and frankly aiming at or bringing into question the innate characteristics of the Negro, it achieved the same result through indirect and disguised means.

None of this stands counter to the fact that the white neither annoyed nor attacked the Negro. He only protected his own social position with its corresponding appearances and attributes. While he did not accept him as an equal and rejected him as a superior, he did so in the name of the past experiences which clearly showed the impossibility of ex-

changing places—since one had been born to exercise authority, while the other had been born to obedience and subordination. The traditional conception of the world thus provided the
frame of reference for an understanding of human nature, of
the symmetric positions of whites and Negroes in the social
structure, and of the normal relations that were expected to
prevail in encounters between the two races. The fact that this
social world was in upheaval sharpened rather than blunted
the white's aggression. If someone offered lunch in the
kitchen to a vertically mobile Negro, the latter would not
return to that house, and so forth. Since the attitudes and
tendencies of the whites remained constant, they thought it
was the blacks who were changing—and changing for the
worse, acquiring vices that were incurable and prejudicial in a
system of freedom and irresponsibility. Thus did the belief
first arise that the Negro problem was originating through the
agency of the Negro himself. In his anxiety to become equal
and superior to the white, the Negro was said to be engendering prejudices that did not formerly exist and to be forging an
inverse prejudice against the white.

This rapid sketch covers a broad gamut of individual relationships. Some whites belonging to various social classes
subscribed fanatically to the democratic conception of the
world and put into practice a philosophy of loyal competition
with the Negro. Others were indifferent to problems of this
sort. Between the two extremes there were those who clung to
the traditionalist conception of the world and who set the
norm for the way in which Negroes should be treated. But
even within this group there were obvious gradations. According to the data gathered it would seem that two types of
reactions prevailed. One was based on the fear of being ordered about by a Negro. In a testimony which he wrote himself, one informant asserted that he would dread such a relationship because "the trouble with Negroes is that they have a
color complex, and when they climb they want to step on
whites." As another informant wrote, it was conceivable that
the Negro should mix "with backward whites who are on his

moral and intellectual level," but never with "the cream of society." The other chief reaction was related to signs of strict adherence to established conventions. It was understood that good relations between whites and blacks should be maintained through all available means. Yet the only relations presented in this light were those that were faithful to the old concept of hierarchy. They excluded contact with black persons who departed from the norm (such as "modernized" servants who wore makeup and silk clothing and stockings, who answered back to their mistresses, etc.) as much as with impudent Negroes (who spoke loudly to their white interlocutor, expressing antagonistic opinions of their own, interrupting or changing the subject without the slightest consideration, etc.). The past still weighed upon them so oppressively that the democratization of certain forms of behavior was not considered natural. It did not seem merely improper that a Negro should speak or act like a white person. It was also regarded as unseemly to show familarity with a Negro, especially in public. One informant told us a very curious story in this connection. He was somewhere on the coast with his father-in-law. They wanted to have a drink before lunch, but there were no bars in the locality. They noticed that a mulatto peasant and his wife had a bottle of *pinga*. The younger man brought up the possibility of asking them for some. The old man replied: "Are you mad? That would be the last straw, for me to ask a Negro for a drink!" If resistance to the democratization of behavior and of ways of speaking and acting was so great, resistance to a leveling of social rights was bound to be far more drastic. The most striking example relates to the revocation of a law that prohibited the admission of Negroes to the Civil Guard. When he received the order, the head of the Guard acidly commented in the presence of witnesses: "Since we're going to admit Negroes, we might as well take lepers and physical misfits."

Ultimately, however, active shows of solidarity among Negroes ceased to be regarded with the dread panic of the past. Yet they continued to be disapproved of and misunderstood.

T.G. related a striking incident that reveals how the white man interfered negatively in such movements by attempting to "divide and conquer." As an army sergeant, he had been in charge of the soldiers' classes of instruction. "There were things which the whites, because of mutual contact and communication and previous education, did not have to learn because they already knew them. This was not the case with Negroes. To help out my black brothers, I tried to teach them separately what they had to know, or else dwell at length on certain points to make them more understandable. When the class was over, I would dismiss the white soldiers and tell the Negro ones to remain, calling them by name. Then I would do whatever was necessary, making it a longer class and going into further explanations, etc. The black soldiers indicated that they understood why I did this. To everything I said, they would retort at once that they understood, that everything was clear, etc. Then I would send them off, after ten or fifteen minutes. This was of no value to me—I was the instructor. It could only be of benefit to them. But the white soldiers would wait for them and surround them:

" 'What did he want from you?'

" 'Nothing! It was just to explain things better.'

" 'Explain things, my foot! Can't you see he doesn't like blacks? He does this to punish you!'

"The whites schemed to destroy what I tried to achieve, arousing suspicion in the minds of my black subordinates."

The distortion of the Negro's personality followed the same path, but in the opposite direction. The data collected imply what the whites hoped to make of him: a flesh-and-blood automaton, without moral pretensions, or dilemmas, always submissive, respectfully conscious of his place, devoted, hard working, and servile. Under all circumstances he was expected to prove spontaneously to himself and to the whites, through word and action, the symmetric nature of his relations, annihilating himself as an *individual*—as though he were not and never could be a real person. The data cited amply prove this inference. The Negro was well regarded, understood, rewarded, and loved only when he acted as if he were the white man's possession and remained in his place. The data given above suffice to prove this. Yet we should like to add a characteristic illustration—that of the *filha de criação*. Lea, "black as coal," lived in the home of Dona E. She had been raised as a "daughter" and was treated as an "equal" by relatives and friends of the family. She sacrificed everything to that lady: her youth and her maturity. She dedicated herself to the lady's interests and comfort with the greatest diligence and devotion. She never considered marriage or a career, for this would have taken her away from Dona E. In her report the woman researcher points out: "She wants to live with Dona E., to look after Dona E.'s home, to cook and sew for Dona E. She says this is her happiness." When there were family parties or reunions, in spite of her status as *filha de criação* and of the fact that she would be meeting former childhood playmates, she merely sent greetings through Dona E. "If she visits close family members, she insists on remaining in the kitchen, saying that this is her place. She seems to feel no constraint, no resentment, no maladjustment, in spite of her rather ambiguous situation." The vertically mobile Negro who rises through his own efforts represents the other extreme of the racial scale. How does he assert himself in relation to whites? The following quotation regarding the personal experiences of a Negro dentist makes it quite clear: "When I went to take over the position to which I had been assigned, the head of the center thought that I was another janitor, as she confessed to me much later. This type of reception did not bother me, and I tried to build cordial relationships. A black man in my position has to be much more pleasant than a white person to achieve the same goals. I think this is the best attitude to take, because, by being friendly to everyone, I put them at ease about the color problem. (There are Negroes who won't talk about color, and this alienates them from people.) People can then speak freely about the subject, and no one is ill at ease." In short, as in the case of T.G., he attempted to win over his white interlocutors, obtaining their goodwill by means of specific techniques. Those who are unable to make one adjustment or the other must take the painful path of voluntary isolation.

They found that withdrawal, isolation, and apparent sub-servience were adaptive mechanisms. From this standpoint, as publicly stated by Jorge Prado Teixeira, "The Negro is compelled to adopt an element of defensiveness, an area of defense reactions, a defense mechanism, and this has its expression in an inferiority complex." When he submits pas-sively or voluntarily withdraws and isolates himself, he is putting into practice the best mechanisms of adjustment, those that reduce the sphere of friction with the whites or lessen the inner drama induced by his frustrations. On the other hand they found that in reality Negroes are prejudiced, but although this prejudice is useful to the Negro, it is not deleterious to the white. As Francisco Morais publicly stated, ". . . Negroes are also prejudiced toward whites. But the Negro's prejudice toward the white is humiliating for him and flattering to the white, because it means that he too holds the idea that the white person is superior." This awareness of reality fosters the ambition to imitate the words, gestures, actions, and personality configurations of the whites. In short, it engenders the urge to overcome the causes and effects of color prejudice through the progressive elimination of the social distance between the two races. Here is how Dr. Arlindo Veiga dos Santos, one of the architects of the social move-ments that grew out of the contradictions of this racial situa-tion, has spoken of the matter in public:

The Negro needs a separate education in order to acquire self-re-spect, to face up to the inferiority complex that was instilled into him from childhood. This is what must be done. This is what I did. This was my role: to educate the Negro to speak up, not to stand with his head lowered, hat in hand, while his own personality is crumbling. As I said, we didn't offend anyone. As long as Negroes stand hat in hand they will have an inferiority complex, and it is Brazil that suffers from this complex. It remains a subservient, inferior country, lacking character on the international scene. The way things are with us, we're bound to be a weak country at the mercy of all the world powers.

Nevertheless, the situation did not change so quickly. Even persons who had been very active members of the Negro Front acknowledged in interviews that "the Negro is timid and fearful. If a white person with a certain air of self-confidence does something, he [the Negro] falters and becomes intimidated." And worse still the personality distortions induced in Negroes by authoritarianism left deep scars. Alongside the basic principle of racial coexistence in the traditionalist world, there persisted vigorously, even in the midst of the Negro population, and in fact chiefly there, the idea that "the Negro needs to be curbed."

In an interview with a figure who is representative of vertically mobile Negroes, we heard views which are widely shared and which show the continuance of this cultural pathos among Negroes: "Democracy is a senseless word. Brazil is in the adolescent stage. It needs a strong government for the good of the country. Freedom is impossible. In every home there is always a head: the father. No democracy there. It is no place for everyone to do as he pleases. They do what they can, what they must do, or what it is right to do. It is the father who gives orders, supported by his wife. If it were otherwise, the eight-year-old son would demand to have the house key. And the daughter would do the same. This wouldn't be freedom, it would be anarchy. Well, the Negro requires subjection, far more than the white. He requires discipline, someone who will give him orders, someone who will compel him to do this and not to do that. Like a child or an adolescent, he doesn't know yet how to set his own course. He hasn't come of age. So the government should discipline the Negro in order to compel him to improve his economic situation and his way of life, to educate his children. If not, he should be put in jail. He should be forced to have a regular trade, to work in an organized way; forced to give up certain bad habits and practices. Those without a trade and without work after a while should be put to building roads and working in agriculture. Each man should support himself through his work and have enough to live on. Jail and forced labor would be the therapy for those who refused to comply. The Negro needs discipline, and a government that tried to do them good would not be violating freedom, even though it used methods that were violent and against their will." In spite of the progress shown by this statement in terms of the absorption of the ideas, cultural techniques, and values of the competitive social order, it clearly suggests that the bitter experiences the speaker has undergone in the area of freedom have led the Negro to ambiguous positions in society and to a sort of exhaustion. Previously he had chosen poverty and freedom. In the period we are analyzing, freedom was no longer worth much. It was merely a condition of the inevitable abasement of the disorganized Negro population. For this reason it seemed preferable to many to sacrifice it in exchange for a secure, respectable, and prosperous way of life. Contrary to the poor Negroes who stoically accepted the destructive and demoralizing impact of social disorganization, the small Negro elites did not fear the dangers of an authoritarian social order based on the principles of seignorial domination.

We gathered large quantities of data, which unfortunately could not be listed here, on the new stereotypes which refer in a derogatory way to a Negro's color. In these stereotypes the Negro associated with the personality status which can be inferred from the crudest manual labor, but classification of the Negro's characteristics suddenly points in a different direction. His disorganized social life has provided the point of reference for this process of reevaluation. The word *Negro* becomes interchangeable with words such as "drunkard" or "boozer," "bum," "carouser," and "thief"; and *Negro woman* with "street-walker." At the same time the psychological characteristics attributed to the Negro have been drastically reinterpreted. Favorable characterizations survive, born of the experiences of slaveholders and of associations on the same social levels. On the other hand certain beliefs have become quite strong, such as "You can't (or you shouldn't) trust a Negro." Positive qualities are also mentioned in interviews, but in not too favorable a context in the class society. Such qualities are fidelity, devotion to the white, and capacity for hard physical labor. More frequently emphasized are potential disloyalty, envy, timidity, falsity, insecurity, and hatred of whites or of "all that is good," in connection with capacity for manual labor and limited intelligence. Even children were raised in an atmosphere of fear and timidity toward Negroes. Not only were bogeymen and hobgoblins represented as Negroes, but there was a song:

> *Look at the old Negro*
> *On top of the roof;*
> *Leave my poor child*
> *To sleep in peace.*

Misbehaving children were told: "Watch out or I'll call that black man to come and get you!" or "Watch out or the bogeyman will get you!" Negroid facial features were also ridiculed and their bearers stigmatized: "Negro hair" or "kinky hair," "thick lips," "big-lipped Negro," "Negro smell," "dirty as a Negro," "filthy Negro," "to stink like a Negro," "to scratch behind the ear," or "I think that so-and-so scratches behind the ear just like a he-goat." [9]

Two essential things out of all this material are of importance to us. First, negative stereotypes led to a redefinition of the Negro's personality that was highly adverse to his being freely accepted as an equal. Second, Negroid physical features inevitably brought humiliation to the person considered to be Negro, granting the white person the permission (and sometimes the duty) to treat him accordingly. If a black person applied for a job, he was offered manual labor; if he took over a new position, even though he was a professional, he was mistaken for a servant or janitor; if he worked, whatever his job (as tailor, beadle, or clerk), it was considered legitimate to take him from his tack at any time and order him to do "nigger work"; if he visited an acquaintance, friend, or patron, it was considered awkward to receive him in the living room, to treat him as a friend or simply as an equal, and censurable to treat other visitors with the "lack of consideration" of being placed "on the same footing as a Negro." Other material indicates that they declared (and thus shied away from) a public show of friendship with Negroes and admitted liberties in dealing with them. There was greater tolerance in relationships with former house servants, *filhos de criação,* or sons. But even these had to be dignified, that is maintained according to custom, with each person keeping his place.

This distorted image of black people was used to justify various types of interracial adjustments that were degrading or offensive to the individuals concerned. Among the data gathered in connection with the period under consideration, there are several significant cases. One man recommended a protégé of his to a friend without mentioning that he was black. The protégé was accepted sight unseen. When it was discovered that he was a Negro, he was rejected because "customers would not want to be waited on by a Negro salesman." Another job was offered to the candidate, who was told that unfortunately the vacancy anticipated had not materialized. He accepted, only to find out that it was "to wield a broom." He left in a huff. The two friends later met and commented on "the ingratitude of Negroes." In certain bars black persons were not served. In others, where there were no such restrictions, Negroes were discriminated against. Attempts were made to serve them only at the far end of the bar, away from the white customers. Or else, and this sometimes infuriated Negroes, they would be served *pinga,* the cheap rum of the poor, without being asked.

This extensive presentation of data on the various structural and functional aspects of the traditional and asymmetric pattern of racial interaction was necessary in order to draw certain general conclusions. In the first place it makes clear that the egalitarian patterning of race relations is that in name only. The existence, intensity, and closeness of the contact between whites and Negroes were not, in themselves, indisputable evidence of racial equality. All such contact developed within the most thorough, rigid, and unsurmountable racial inequality. Such inequality can exist in a climate of mutual tolerance, and the peaceful coexistence of different racial groups with divergent or antagonistic social interests can be attained through a persistent control of the potential causes and results of racial tensions and conflicts.

Second, the traditional pattern of asymmetric race relations presupposes the identification of a certain racial identity and a specific social status. The pattern was ambiguous as far as the dominant racial group was concerned: it merely worked out in detail, structurally and functionally, the position and social roles of the segment of that group which monopolized wealth, power, and authority. But it was clear and explicit in regard to the subordinate racial group, which was associated in close and almost monolithic fashion, through racial attributes such as skin color and other somatic characteristics, with inferior social status. Nevertheless, in spite of these contradictions, the pattern did not prohibit or preclude but rather encouraged other members of the dominant racial group to identify themselves, in all that pertained to racial coexistence, with the ruling segment of their own group. At the same time the pattern did not proscribe vertical mobility on the part of members of the subordinate racial group or their material and psychological identification with the interests, ideals, and social values of the dominant group. Nevertheless, it restricted opportunities for vertical mobility to the capacity for the absorption of such elements into the organized social existence of that racial group. Furthermore, it did not in any way imply procedures that would lead to the automatic readjustment of social relations to changes in the social position of vertically mobile members of the subordinate racial group, but allowed for much confusion between the social status attributed to the group as a whole and that acquired individually by some of its members. This means that in actuality the Negro's social, economic, and political vertical mobility, aside from being restricted, was continually disguised and undermined. Since there did not exist a pattern of systematic racial segregation that was at the same time institutionalized and selective, vertically mobile Negroes did not form an upper social segment within their own racial group, but blended in various ways into the various levels of the lower and middle classes of the dominant racial group. Their undisguishable racial characteristics placed them in a position in which they could be regarded and treated by members of the dominant group both in terms of the inferior social status attributed to the subordinate racial group and in terms of the social status acquired by the individuals in question. It all depended on the social position, the psychological makeup, and the material or moral interests of the members of the dominant racial group with whom they came into contact. A similar confusion of alternative forms of behavior and treatment in race relations led to widespread belief in the existence of a racial democracy in São Paulo (as, incidentally, in Brazilian society as a whole). Actually, however, this confusion merely points to the nonexistence of racial equality and to the impracticability of an authentic racial democracy.

Third, the link referred to between race (in terms expressly of skin color) and social position excluded individuals who bore the physical characteristics of the subordinate racial group from the social rights and safeguards granted to the elite (and, by extension, to the masses) of the dominant racial group, making such rights and social safeguards into prerogatives and privileges of this group.[10] Racial discrimination arose as the result of those societal mechanisms which fostered the distribution of individuals within a social space by regulating their rights and the distance to be held between them as *socii;* and racial prejudice appeared as the very source of material and moral justification for the differences established in this way, on which the differentiation between inferior and superior racial groups was based.

Fourth, the preservation of the existing social distance between the two racial groups was effected primarily through spontaneous behavioral mechanisms. Whites, Negroes, and mulattoes knew how to act in each routine situation. Nevertheless, the breakdown of the old order gave rise to increasing numbers of anomalous situations where certain black individuals adjudged themselves the right (and sometimes even the duty) to demand for themselves social treatment and safeguards identical to those granted to members of the dominant race of equivalent social standing. Such incidents were in the nature of disguised or open endeavors to undermine the non-egalitarian racial stratification and the resulting patterns of asymmetric race relations. For this very reason they met with strong resistance among the various strata of the white population, and they were the first historical indices of the existence of racial prejudice and discrimination in São Paulo. The reason for this is simple. Where the Negro and mulatto arose, at least in an economic and social sense, as the white's equal, the parallelism between color and social position was broken. The persistence of certain forms of asymmetric racial behavior was thus fully exposed.

Fifth, expressions of dissatisfaction and nonconformism on the part of the vertically mobile members of the subordinate racial group could not be developed as a constructive and autonomous social force. On the one hand the dominant racial ideology prevailed over both racial groups, governing their perception of reality as they confronted one another. On the other hand the vertical mobility of the subordinate racial group proved insufficient to make the inevitable racial contradictions and tensions collectively meaningful. Thus, on the whole, the vertical mobility of a small portion of the black population merely intensified the confusion that prevailed in racial matters. But this is were we find, from a sociological standpoint, the explanation for the indefinite perpetuation of the *status quo* in racial relations. The positions of the two racial groups in the power structure of the society did not alter sufficiently to impose radical changes on the racial order inherited from the slaveholding past.

Sixth, the almost unalterable persistence of the traditional pattern of asymmetric race relations conditioned and governed the process of redefining the Negro's image. If this pattern had been quickly and profoundly altered, replaced by the alternative and exclusive pattern of democratic and egalitarian race relations, there would have been no reason to perpetuate discriminatory practices or to retain prejudiced racial concepts. Since this did not occur, owing to the slow, discontinuous development of the competitive social order in the local society, the traditional patterns of asymmetric race relations prevailed and served as the focal point in the reconstruction of the Negro's image. From this standpoint the transformation of slaves and freedmen into "Negroes" answered to the social necessity to limit the democratization of the citizen's universal social rights and safeguards in the racial sphere. Thus, it was not the negative and restrictive image of the Negro that gave rise to racial discrimination and prejudice, but the opposite process. It was the existence and persistence of both which led to the development of this image, which was to serve as a catalyst for those processes which have prevented the rapid absorption of the Negro into the structure of the developing class society.

We must nevertheless point out some sociologically crucial facts. The complex mechanism of racial accommodation inherent in the overall interests of the ruling circles of the white race did not arise from any stubborn hostility against the Negro, or from segregationist aims. Classification as a black person implied two distinct factors: a certain racial ancestry and a certain social position. These two factors, from the time the African slave was introduced, remained conveniently paired. Color became, at one and the same time, a racial mark and the undisguisable symbol of social position. Intolerance toward the Negro, in the sociohistorical context we have described, was not aimed at individuals because they belonged to a certain racial group, but arose as they proved nonconformist and rebellious toward that rigid linkage of racial position and social position. In such cases racial marks served as points of reference. They served to identify one segment of the local population, which must hold itself and be held in an inferior social position. Thus, although the fact of belonging to a certain racial group was not the motive for exclusion, the social position of black individuals could be identified through certain physical characteristics, and this identification led to social barriers which were raised clearly and incontrovertibly only against such individuals. It should be noted that this method of social discrimination did not operate with the same efficiency and persistence in relation to "poor whites" of native or foreign stock. The democratization of attitudes and forms of behavior was more rapid, and the consequences of economic and social vertical mobility contributed to an attenuation of differences and a strengthening of egalitarian attitudes, contrary to what occurred (and still occurs) in relation to individuals characterized in stereotyped fashion as Negroes.

Prohibitions of a social character which were imposed on the Negro and mulatto because of their inferior social position also affected the "poor white" and the lower-class immigrant. They all made up the undifferentiated masses of the working classes, kept strictly in their place in spite of all the expressions of courtesy, friendship, and familiarity on the part of privileged people. During the · period under consideration, while these prohibitions were gradually toned down or slowly vanished with reference to whites, the opposite occurred in respect to Negroes. In some social circles they were intensified while in others they began to be held with obvious stubbornness. It is true that above and beyond individual fluctuations in the tolerance or intolerance shown to Negroes, there prevailed certain universal tendencies of adjustment which excluded the Negro and mulatto from close contact in the home, from certain social services and positions, from marriage—in short, from a position of unrestricted equality with the white. There was open and shocking resistance, as shown by incidents described earlier, even against the democratization of ways of being, thinking, and behaving. This resistance became stronger and more aggressive when the Negro's claims hit the core of white dominance: the personality ideals, prestige positions, and authority roles which involved the whites' position in the power structure of the society. Hence the opposition to intermarriage on that social level.

Prescriptions and prohibitions which affected racial and social status at the same time continued to be carried out after the breakdown of the slaveholding and caste systems. According to our theories, this happened because race relations did not change at the same pace as the social structure of the larger society. The prevailing pattern of patrimonial rule was retained after the disappearance of the sociohistorical context which had engendered it. But why did this occur in a city like São Paulo, where the development of the competitive social order was so rapid and where the "poor whites" so soon evaded the inconveniences of old-style despotism? The answer seems to be obvious. Resistance to democratization in the racial sphere of the forms of behavior, prerogatives, and social rights and safeguards of the traditional elites resulted from the color lines. Where the latter did not interfere with the process, vertical social mobility was a gentler, faster, and more thoroughgoing process. The sociohistorical situation described above thus throws light on the nature of the sources of opposition to the socioeconomic rise of the Negro and mulatto. Behind the sociodynamic assimilationist forces, there lurked tendencies clearly favorable to a nonegalitarian racial order that would preserve the *status quo* in the racial sphere, or at least would hinder the free play of certain integrationist tendencies of an inevitably egalitarian character.

In closing, it should be determined in what ways the changing sociohistorical situation influenced the reelaboration of this racial ideology as a whole. Several informants stated that family pride and racial pride had gradually subsided. Some even said that the revolutions of 1924, 1930, and 1932 * had

* *Translator's note:* In July, 1924, a few thousand *Paulistas*, soldiers and civilians, rose in unsuccessful rebellion against the federal government in protest against its traditional bureaucracy and conservative oligarchy. In October, 1930, Getúlio Vargas seized control of the government and inaugurated the Second Republic. In July, 1932, *Paulistas* rose against the government for the restoration of constitutional rule, but were defeated by governmental forces.

contributed to this. Others pointed to the behavior of the Negroes themselves as the decisive factor: in rejecting certain antiquated forms of treatment, they had compelled the whites to review their old prejudices. Explanations of this type are not very enlightening, because they do not make clear which were the sources of liberalization of the whites' behavior and which were its actual fruits. It would seem that the consolidation of the competitive social order gradually led to a great broadening in the cultural horizon of the ruling classes, thus softening the psychological atmosphere of race relations. Actually, at the end of the period under consideration there no longer was a consensus in those social circles about "how the Negro should be treated." There were those who clung to an intransigent exclusivism and who continued to regard the Negro strictly in the light of the old seignorial code. This was at the root of intolerant tendencies in the observance of the traditional racial ideology. Those were the people who stuck up their noses at everything that seemed to indicate that "Negroes were becoming people." Here is how such individuals conceptualized the contact situation: "Negroes, because they are black, don't seem to care about life. They are careless; many become thieves, criminals, etc.; and their sexual morality is dubious." In the informant's mind, this arose "far more from color than from the social and economic situation." He stressed that he "would not accept under any circumstances a Negro boss or master," and that in the "higher professions" (executive positions, technical work, teaching) "there must be color segregation." He believed that "we must give greater opportunities to Negroes to make up for their color." On the other hand, a large number of persons were beginning to share the democratic creed and to bring a new outlook to race relations. There still existed distorted perceptions of the nature and social sources of equality among men. But they already accepted a method of fighting color prejudice and racial discrimination which was in accord with the incipient demands of the democratization of race relations.

We are still within the boundaries of the old racial ideology for two reasons. First, the problems of the Negro are regarded through the perspective of an erroneous understanding of the situation of racial contact. Second, practical opinions are based on a fundamental assumption: the unequal position of the Negro race, the material and moral foundation for the traditional pattern of asymmetric race relations. Because of the first reason, even whites who were democratically oriented could not attain a realistic vision of the racial situation, clinging as they did to ideas soon condemned as "romantic" and "unworkable" by the leaders of social movements among the Negro groups. Because of the second reason, identification with the Negro and mulatto was more emotional than considered and rational, greatly fostering both ignorance of the real problems of the city's black population and indifference toward the special measures demanded for the control of these problems.

Even at the end of the period under consideration, truly democratic and egalitarian measures and reactions were undermined and offset by the prevailing racial ideology. Even when he endeavored to act as an equal, the white could not break down the barriers of sociocultural isolation, could not make contact with the Negro, and could not understand his basic needs. Even so, the trends favorable to greater racial understanding and tolerance were of tremendous sociodynamic importance on the historical scene. They destroyed irremediably the monolithic consenses of the white race that authoritarian racial domination was legitimate and defensible. They also created an atmosphere less hostile to free discussion and to the fight, started by the Negroes themselves through their social movements, against the more blatant inequities of this form of racial domination. Finally, if the competitive social order did not have sufficient vitality to absorb the old seignorial patterns of relations between whites and Negroes, it succeeded at least in broadening the cultural horizon and in opening new perspectives for the democratization of social rights and safeguards in the community.

SOCIAL MOVEMENTS IN THE NEGRO

MILIEU

1925–1948

Introduction

From 1925 to 1930 the bitterness and dissatisfaction of the black population built up to such a degree that there developed spontaneously several movements representing the Negro's growing awareness of his situation and his criticism and rejection of the difficult destiny to which black men were relegated. By virtue of the very historical situation of the Negro and mulatto, the rebellion did not take on the character of a revolt against the established social order. It was a matter of a deaf and irrepressible insubordination to the greatest shortcomings of the system of race relations that were linked more to the disguised continuation of the old order than to the flagrant injustices of the present order. Thus the Negroes did not pit themselves against the latter. On the contrary, they openly confessed that it satisfied their desires for social security, dignity, and equality and they pleaded only that it be open to them also.

From this perspective the episodes related to these social movements mark the return of the Negro and mulatto to the historical stage of action. Now they begin to appear as a kind of intransigent and puritan vanguard of liberal radicalism, demanding complete consolidation of the competitive social order and the corresponding model for the democratic organization of human relations. They rebel literally against the historical inequities and impurities of the regime, fighting in order that the open society not be closed to anyone, much less a racial group. Consequently the movements that are organized affirm themselves historically, politically, and psychologically as the first great collective attempts to remove the contradictions existing between the legal substratum and the social reality implanted through abolitionism and experience with the republican form of government. In arrogating to themselves the solution of problems ignored or disregarded by the elites in power, the Negro and mulatto delegated to themselves two historical tasks: to begin the modernization of the system of race relations in Brazil; and to prove in a practical way that men must totally and consciously identify with the values that express the chosen legal order.

Things being what they were, this revolution within the order and for the purity and normalcy of the order was destined to failure. Even though he was satisfied to remain within the limits of the established social order and intended only to purge it of elements or influences that could be condemned in the light of the prevailing mores, the Negro could never be successful without the understanding, cooperation, and solidarity of the white. For this reason such movements developed and disappeared or became dissipated in certain institutions before achieving their ultimate ends and fulfilling the sociohistorical revolutionary functions to which they were dedicated. Even so, it is imperative to study them on one hand because they represent the only mechanisms of consistent societal reaction to the social dilemmas created by racial contact in the city of São Paulo; on the other because they constitute an impressive historical feat in the struggle for the modernization of Brazilian society in contemporary times. In this chapter we shall enumerate the principal factors correlated with the manifestation of these movements. We will then focus on their contribution to the perception and condemnation of the racial situation in São Paulo and in Brazil.

Manifestation and Objectives of the Social Movements

The unrest which began to develop toward the end of World War I and the social movements that began to appear during the second decade of this century mark the beginning of participation by the Negro and mulatto in the modern history of the city. Little by little poverty, discriminatory treatment, and isolation begin to engender protests that put the black man on the historical stage in the action against his own economic, social, and political grievances. The meaning of these grievances is well known. Anxiously corresponding to the assimilationist expectations of society, the unrest and the social movements seek cover under the name of a moral revolution. They do not struggle against the established economic, social, and political order, but against a kind of racial despoliation that it has harbored owing to the prevailing relationship between Negroes and whites. Contrary to what was thought by the ruling circles of the dominant groups, the rebellion had a clearly and expressly integrationalist stamp.[1]

Negroes and mulattoes did not threaten the social order instituted by Abolition and the Republic because they never questioned the material and psychological bases on which it rested. They began with two presuppositions: that this matter be resolved in the context of the constellation of interests and values of the dominant race; and that such a disorganized and impotent minority as the black population ought to concentrate its efforts on the struggle for the real conquest of the opportunities and social guarantees legally authorized by the prevailing order. Thus it endeavored to abolish social distinctions that were automatically transformed into racial privileges and to achieve within a short time economic, social, and political equality with whites.

The revolutionary nature of this unrest was manifested in opposing the indefinite continuation of the old order on the level of race relations. The economic, juridical, and political ideology of the ruling circles of the dominant race were acknowledged and accepted. It was desired that this ideology be impartially and wholly applied in order to check the distortions as well as the inconsistencies of the competitive social order. In short the Negro and mulatto emerged as the champions of the revolution within the order. They demanded the concrete manifestation and full authority of the principles and values on which the equilibrium of the established social order was legally based. For this reason they became historical actors and they reveal how the lower strata, kept at the margins of the political process in the society of estate and caste, emerged in the struggles related to the institution and consolidation, of the democratic style of life. In search of a class position, that is of a status involving certain social autonomy, they came to be active elements in the development of the class society.

We are not interested here in proceeding with an exhaustive survey of the historical circumstances that surround this sociocultural process. It is sufficient for us to deal with that which is at the same time essential and specific in the manifestation and development of the Negro protest, in itself a historically frustrated attempt to consummate the heralded Second Abolition. From this perspective it is important to analyze: the sociohistorical incentives and the sociopsychological or sociocultural prerequisites that make it possible for us to understand how and why such movements became viable; the principal historic events that mark and limit the modernization of these movements; the situation of Negro groups that account for the discontinuity, inconsistency, and ultimate frustration of the movements in question; and the constructive social functions in terms of the integration of the Negro and mulatto in the class society as it developed and tends to develop in the city of São Paulo.

Several factors that were analyzed in the preceding chapters contributed simultaneously to keep the capital's black population from developing any type of united, conscious reaction to the social problems that afflicted it. On one hand pauperism and social anomie led to collective disillusionment and chronic discouragement. On the other the preponderance of the white race functioned in such a way as to maintain the archaic models of racial adjustment with all the onus involved for the Negro, from passivity to the distorted perception of reality. Nonetheless, intensive and rapid urbanization would come to promote profound changes in the style of social life, human relations, and the mentality of men, making the city of São Paulo the main center of technological and institutional modernization, worldly thought, propagation of new ideologies, social agitation, and gradual democratization of the patterns of political behavior. For this reason, when the first surge of industrial growth associated with the first decade of this century occurred, there emerged along with it important and irreversible social trends. As a result of proletarianization the populace was transformed in disorderly fashion into the worker, and models of social adjustment typical of mass societies were gradually established. Meanwhile the ruling circles of the dominant strata gradually lost the capacity to act according to authoritarian and arbitrary patterns in matters of collective interest as they were increasingly forced to consider the opinions and pressures of groups deprived of any expression in the old power structure. Conflict then came to be used regularly by these groups: first in a timid and vacillating way; later with a certain boldness, as witnessed in the grievances and strikes by workers.

In this context the sociohistorical situation was propitious for the open and continual undermining of the traditional form of racial adjustment and domination. The Negro milieu was not immune or indifferent to such occurrences. It became related in whatever ways possible to the general atmosphere of the ferment of ideas, social upheaval, and political reform. Since about the end of World War I and the beginning of the second decade of the century, small nuclei developed at the heart of this milieu making autonomous and critical formulations of the Negro's problem. A handful of pioneers managed to break down the apathy of the Negro milieu in spite of the limitations of permanent social disorganization, their incapacity for cooperation among themselves for their own collective objectives, and their almost total lack of political experience. They endeavored to involve the Negro and mulatto in these general trends and were successful in three ways. They fostered a new attitude that oriented integrationalist and assimilationalist aspirations in the directions of egalitarian demands. They awakened interest in the objective understanding of Brazilian race reality as a condition for the enlightenment of the black population and its conscious action in the historical setting. They mobilized the Negro group and attempted to involve it directly in the discussion and solution of Brazilian racial problems—which was in itself a revolutionary occurrence. At last there was heard the clamor of the Negro people sounding the clarion that called all men to live up to the ideals of human fraternity and racial democracy. This was the image that the Negroes themselves developed for the situation as witnessed by the title of their main publication of the movement, the *Clarim da Alvorada* (Clarion of Dawn).

It is possible to discern certain specific sociohistorical incentives that were of topical, dynamic importance or were active locally in the fomentation of the social movements of the Negro milieu. Among these incentives the most significant is the reaction of the Negro and mulatto to the situation in which they found themselves confined by society. The majority of the black population came up against successive obstacles to their aspirations for social classification; it was almost as impossible to secure, maintain, and improve a respectable source of income as it was impracticable, once secured, to make it yield the same material, psychological, and political fruits that such sources provided for whites. On the other hand the elite of this population had to avail itself of a degrading isolation if it wished to enjoy the style of life it was in condition to achieve, and it had to practice a humiliating self-discipline to conceal the frustrations that weighed upon the adult generations that were continually disappointed or to block the free manifestation of the legitimate desires of younger generations for vertical mobility.

Another psychological incentive derived from indirect emulation, stimulated by the economic and social success of immigrants, especially the Italians. We have already mentioned how preference for the foreigner and his rapid climb disturbed the free Negro and mulatto. Barred from the system of salaried labor and artisan trades by the competition of the white European, they viewed the almost magical changes that were occurring to their former tenement neighbors with anxiety and resentment. Gradually, however, negative emotions and feelings were overcome and sublimated, and there emerged a state of perplexity that soon gave place to constructive assessments. Owing to the neighborhood, and chiefly to the intimate familiarity with certain families that took in black children, a mature understanding of the reasons for the success of the Italian developed. Thus importance gradually ceased to be given to the preference of white Brazilians for men of their race, to the favoritism of the government, and to the assistance of the consuls to the subjects of their countries. A perception of the more important factors developed and comparison was drawn between the way of life of the Italian and that of the Negro people. In this way the black population of the capital achieved a realistic view of things and began to absorb the attitudes and behavioral patterns typical of the immigrant populations. Not only did it do justice to the Italian, attributing wealth to hard work, extreme frugality, and the desire to get ahead in life; it went to the root of the problem and related his patterns of success with the forms of organized social life that prevailed among Italians and other immigrants.

This understanding, arrived at more or less when the social movements began to germinate, was of enormous dynamic significance. It concentrated the attention of the leaders of these movements on that which was essential: the acquisition by the Negro and mulatto of new social techniques and institutions. They finally understood that classification in the competitive social order depended on certain sociopsychological prerequisites, integrated family life, domestic solidarity, respect for women, the importance of the education of children.

Furthermore, the model of the Italian was in itself stimulating. It was a matter of people who had begun from apparently the same starting point: despicable manual labor, the hardship of living in basements and tenements. The fact that the Italians had lifted themselves above this social level and had equaled or surpassed the important families of the city rocked the black man in new dreams. The hope or certainty arose that if he carefully tread a similar path, he could also lift himself out of the mud and build for himself and for his children a worthy, secure, and respectable future.

A third incentive was engendered by the disappearance of the slaveholding and seignorial order, which destroyed the material and psychological bases for the perpetuation of the traditionalistic pattern of human relations. It was maintained in the relations between whites and Negroes for a longer period of time. Owing to the general predominance of salaried labor, the consolidation of the competitive social order, and industrialization, irrational veneration for the white continued only in certain pockets; and the white had neither the interest nor the means to revive paternalism. Internal migrations and the high degree of horizontal mobility of the Negro and mulatto population contributed to this trend. Eventually the majority of this population came to be unacquainted with and lacked access to the traditional white families. Thus the number of those who did not expect nor seek to find a solution to their problems in "my white man" steadily increased. The latter proudly stated that they "wouldn't wear anyone's halter" and were prepared to live as best they could following a primitive code of independence in relation to the white.

Meanwhile the city's power structure itself was undergoing thorough transformations. In the third or fourth generations the wealthy families of foreign origin radically changed their strategy of accommodation. The final return to ancestral communities revealed itself to be a truly unattainable mirage. Economic and social upward mobility gave rise to new types of cultural participation and specialization. Grandfathers, fathers, and uncles needed men to replace them or assistants with a different kind of preparation, with the capacity to deal with administrative and political problems and to have direct influence in the power structure of the larger society. Therefore they encouraged and compelled the youth to enter careers in the liberal professions and, using their fortunes as a base, gave them a start in careers in politics or public administration. Since they no longer owed anything to or feared the powerful traditional families, they began to compete with them for political power.

These overall changes were closely followed in what might be called their external aspects by the black population. In many of their circles a secret joy was felt at the overthrow of these families. As one of the informants told us: "It was only after World War I with the industrialization boom an established fact that more astute Negroes noticed that the appearance of the *petite bourgeoisie* of immigrants was causing a change in the ruling strata because the immigrants began to replace the supposed rural aristocracy that had no interests in industry and commerce, which remained in the hands of Italians and Turks." Even the revolution of 1930 * was looked upon and greeted by the black population as a death blow and "the destruction of the oligarchy that ruled the country."

The predisposition to be open to involvement in collective acts of nonconformity was born of the incipient unrest that was widespread in the Negro milieu owing to the undesirable consequences of poverty, chronic disorganization, and general discontent. Traditionalist fatalism and apathy made possible the passive absorption of bitter deceptions and disappointments, but they were unable to prevent the dangerous accumulation of resentments and extended tensions that turned persons into sticks of dynamite ready to explode at the smallest spark. The repressed revolt worked on their spirits in a latent fashion, forming a natural base for the development of solidarity, consensus, and collective nonconformist behavior at any opportunity for the sociohistorical formulation of the

* *Editor's note:* The bloodless coup d'état in which Gétulio Vargas made himself president.

Negro problem. The transition from what this revolt represented in terms of personal despair, embarrassment, or humiliation to socially integrated and conscious types of rebellion depended merely on the existence of sociopsychological catalysts. For this reason the revolt was expressed for some time in a negative way: by the avoidance of work, the transgression of the expectations of behavior held by society, or the deviant adjustments of the delinquent, the prostitute, and the professional criminal. Then it found channels of verbalized free expression in the cliques of friends that met in bars, on street corners, and in empty lots. These cliques provided the stage on which the material and psychological dissatisfactions could be presented to the collectivity. Gradually, however, these two types of incipient unrest developed in another direction, encountering dynamic orientations that guided nonconformity in the direction of broader collective goals requiring awareness of the environmental reality and organized social action.

The situation is well-defined by the newspaper, O Clarim da Alvorada, that appeared in January, 1924, with purely literary purposes but a year later by virtue of the contributions it received, became a doctrinaire journal dedicated to the struggle. The original orientation was to establish closer relations with whites and to regenerate the Negro in addition to the idea of the necessity for class unity. . . . Alongside this situation by which it was perceived that Negroes were beginning to become aware of their existence as a group with special problems in our society, the situation of the past yet remained and in fact prevailed.[2]

The receptivity of the Negro milieu to these purposes was so great that the success achieved came to surprise and disorient the very agitators and leaders of such initiatives. They thought that the various obstacles inherent in the state of the Negro milieu and in society would make the recruitment, retention, and encouragement of proselytes difficult. Yet when the Frente Negra (Negro Front) was organized, for example, another reality was manifested with the influx of enthusiastic supporters en masse. "Its extraordinary success left those responsible for its direction disoriented and without knowing which direction to take" (Moreira and Leite, n.d., 16).

On considering the vertical mobility of immigrants and their descendants and the circulation of elites in the socioeconomic structure, the Negro and mulatto attempted to discover why they were excluded from the general prosperity as well as what would be necessary to correct this situation. Because of this, contrary to what happened in the case of the white, open tension and conflict (confined to assimilationalist demands) became arms for the struggle and techniques of a socially constructive nature. The black population of the city underwent a true learning process and along with other segments of the lower strata became involved in the process of political mobilization that made them into direct instruments of the democratization of the rights and social guarantees established by the prevailing legal order.

Various episodes mark the way in which the decision to fight grew with relative rapidity. Descriptions of these episodes reveal how the transition was made from discreet, veiled opposition to firm, decided attitudes of opposition to color prejudice. At first, they supported the manifestations of democratic solidarity of the white more than anything else. The following case clearly suggests this:

In 1926, a Negro—the son of a well-known Negro Latin teacher—wanted to join a sports club. He was barred. The columnist Carlos de Campos Sobrinho began a campaign against this action in the *Diário da Noite*. As a result of the columnist's position, the newspaper received a large number of letters supporting the action of the club's directorate. The argument made then to justify the club's position invoked the backwardness of Cuba and other countries governed by Negroes and the majority of the population of which was constituted by Negroes. On this occasion the columnist was approached by a group of Negroes who in greeting him offered him an armful of flowers. Nonetheless, the general feeling in favor of the club led him to give up the campaign [Moreira and Leite, n.d., 6].

At the same time it was necessary to develop channels of communication that could lend viability and continuity to the efforts to promote understanding and criticism of the Brazilian racial situation. Thus the Negro press linked with goals of proselytizing took on the appearance of a press involved in specific problems of the Brazilian Negro. It synthesized and disseminated nonconformist interpretations of the Brazilian racial situation. It contributed to the transformation of mechanical consensus based on shared frustrations into conscious, organic solidarity. Finally it aroused assimilationist tendencies among the black population. At the same time there was a constant exploitation of means that could contribute toward bringing Negroes and mulattoes together for common goals. In addition to taking advantage of the establishment of newspapers, clubs, and libraries for this purpose, the most varied attempts were made to achieve this end. During the period from 1926 to 1929 it was wisely attempted to involve Negroes and mulattoes in activities that made it possible to unite them around common interests which did not conflict with those of the white population. To the degree that incipient discontent served as a mere point of reference and the objectives envisioned were clearly of nonconformist nature, the ground was being prepared for a greater psychological and intellectual autonomy of the black population. Finally even the fear of identification through use of the term "Negro" was overcome.[3] It became increasingly clear that the essential thing was complete liberation from the past and the development of a new style of life in the present that would prepare the Negro to compete with the white wherever possible in progressively broader ways in all spheres of society.

The development of an active and respected elite was essential in this regard. What was at stake was the Negro's pattern of reaction to the prevailing racial order. It would be impossible to achieve success without compelling the black middle classes to come out of their splendid egotistical isolation into the mainstream of the movements. Although the results did not always correspond to the efforts, the fact is that as long as these movements maintained some vitality, they managed to draw into them at least a small number of those elites, principally from among individuals or groups that had not yet become lost in the mass of the white population.

The social movements of the black population were able to emerge and to be successful without becoming a concern to the police. Among considerable numbers of the other ethnic and racial groups the legitimacy of these movements was already recognized, and there was a minimum of tolerance for them as long as they restricted themselves to their stated goals: improvement in the standard of living, and the reeducation, and upward socioeconomic mobility of the Negro in the social order. All this was far from signifying understanding and solidarity on the part of the white population, but it was an advance in the democratization of the average cultural outlook. And to the degree that it granted the liberty to take risks, it assumed the character of an indirect incentive to go ever further and to affirm itself with increasing autonomy. The fact is that the Negro eagerly used this freedom. His position would be much different today if he had stayed on the path that opened during the decisive decade from 1927 to 1937.

The data gathered make it possible to study the sociopsychological and sociocultural requisites of the social movements of the Negro milieu in terms of the resocialization of the Negro and mulatto; the understanding that racial prejudice and discrimination are social problems and ought to be treated as such; the development of urban-industrial forms of society that would serve as a basis for the organization and growth of the movements; the sociodynamic orientations such as the so-called prejudice of the Negro; the radicalism of the mulatto; the constructive influence of the social movements as instruments of the differentiation of social roles and social control. Other aspects of marginal or secondary importance will not be discussed.

In synthesis, by virtue of the mere fact of living in the city and having passed the stiff test of staying in it, the Negro revolutionized his cultural outlook. We might say that he polished up his primitiveness and harbored a strong desire to advance even further. Many attitudes and patterns of behavior that made the Negro and mulatto distrustful of their fellow men gradually disappeared as they became urbanized. On the other hand living conditions in the urban milieu opened many channels of communication with the local community, the rest of the country, and other countries. This not only broadened the content but also changed the very quality of the Negro's social outlook. There emerged a kind of secular radicalism that exercised the functions of a regulatory mechanism in the substitution of former categories of thought and action by new ways of perceiving and judging situations and persons.

Owing to this radicalism, three behavioral orientations were strengthened. In the first place, clearly defined tendencies of criticism, consideration, and rejection of the conservativist influences of traditionalism emerged. By separating the traditions from the context in which they were manifested through the patrimonial domination of the white race, that which should be preserved was distinguished from that which was rejected. In addition to this, it was seen that loyalty to the interests of the Negro groups was not rooted in the style of life (or degree of povery) or in the condition of isolation. A person established in the white milieu yet identified with the interests of the Negro people could be much more useful than indifferent or cowed black brothers. In the third place it began to be understood that it is in the political sphere that the practical problems of the modern man are decided. This discovery aroused not only indignant accusations against the political henchmen, the election bosses of whites, and the Negro vote traders; it aroused an opposite trend to organize the Negro for his own ends, in the electoral sphere as well as in a broader sense as an integrated, autonomous social group capable of freely managing his portion of political power for his own ends.

This motivation was revealed in the manifesto of the *Frente Negra Brasileira* as follows:

Let us unite, Countryman! Let us unite, Negro Associations, as a social force, as a moral force, as an economic force, as a Political

Force to help the Brazilian Powers be Brazilian and to solve our problem that is within their sphere and to become ourselves radically nationalistic and a part of the Public Power, championing all causes that are in the interest of the Negro and Brazil (as the nationalization of commerce); meaning the destruction of the foreign political influences found in some associations; meaning a halt to the gross failures that a policy that does not serve national ends (but international and cosmopolitan), that a policy that is crassly materialistic and amoral is causing for this Nation created by Our Dead, by our ancestors, whose mighty and tragic Blood is fighting still, working still, producing still without restraint and without local pride for Our Country.[4]

Thus it seems obvious that secular radicalism was specifically directed against passive accommodation and its effects on the perpetuation of the old pattern of racial domination and the socioeconomic dependence of the Negro. There was a concern for preserving certain values as long as they were dissociated from the functions that they performed as techniques of domestication and subjugation. The following quotation is illustrative:

Thus, defining the problem as we have already had an occasion to do in the "Message to Brazilian Negroes" on 8–6–29 [see the *Clarim da Alvorada*], we establish that—THE PROBLEM OF THE BRAZILIAN NEGRO IS THAT OF DEFINITIVE, TOTAL INTEGRATION OF THE NEGRO IN ALL OF BRAZILIAN LIFE (POLITICAL, SOCIAL, RELIGIOUS, ECONOMIC, LABOR, MILITARY, DIPLOMATIC, ETC.); THE BRAZILIAN NEGRO SHOULD RECEIVE COMPLETE EDUCATION AND ACCEPTANCE IN EVERYTHING AND EVERYWHERE, GIVEN THE COMPETENT PHYSICAL, TECHNICAL, INTELLECTUAL AND PSYCHOLOGICAL QUALIFICATIONS (which should be encouraged) REQUIRED FOR "EQUALITY BEFORE THE LAW." Brazil must absolutely cease to be ashamed of its Race both here and outside the country in international life. . . . Therefore we repeat that we should fight for a Negro Association, however—pay close attention —one that is radically Brazilian and which affirms the Tradition and which extends to wherever the problem might exist [A. V. dos Santos, 1931b, 3–6].

These clues suggest that urbanization of the style of life and the secularization of attitudes and behavioral patterns were dynamically related to the yearnings for classification and vertical mobility in the structure of society at large. The Negro tried to change himself in order to become materially and psychologically integrated into the social order. Yet at the same time he demanded for himself the opportunities for sharing in the wealth, culture, and power which were enjoyed by whites. Such sociodynamic impulses rested on the progressive assimilation of the ideals of what it meant to be somebody as established by society. For this reason, profound, revolutionary sociopsychological changes occurred at this level. The Negro changed his self-concepts regarding status and social roles and made efforts to assimilate the personality-status models prevalent among whites. Yet these changes were not conceived as ends in themselves, as a kind of ideal means of self-improvement. They were seen and practiced as a means for achieving desirable goals (the complete integration of the Negro on equal terms with the white in the social order). Consequently they were motivated by a spirit of protest, the minimum demand of which was the expectation of similar behavior on the part of whites. It was expected that they, in turn, would modify the conceptions of status and social roles and the stereotypes they held with regard to the Negro.

A psychological condition necessary for the Negro to be able to judge himself equal to the white was to have the courage to demand from him the respect he deserved and to decide to become active socially without any subjective barrier. According to the statements of one of the informants, it was the element that would make it possible for him to control his resentments and to act as a *man* rather than as a *Negro*. This involved overcoming the passivity and conformity that made him servile, timid, and fearful in face of the white; and victory over the hatreds, resentments, and frustrations that made him a distrustful, rebellious, and violent person.

A new kind of Negro began to emerge, one who revealed himself to be a son of his times and a man of his era. This man hoped to gain a rational understanding of his situation and knew that he had to fight with the support only of those who found themselves in the same sociohistorical circumstances. "We shall see, then, *who shall solve our problem and how it shall be solved. Only we can solve Our Problem in the context of the National Order, through Organization and Education*" (A. V. dos Santos, 1931b, 4—5, emphasis added). For this reason he had to begin to learn how to use the social techniques that had formerly been denied to him. He had to learn how to deal in an organized way with voluntary, conscious, intelligent behavior on a collective scale.

The "Frente Negra Brasileira" taught its adepts to break the taboos—for example, to invade the forbidden public promenades and skating rinks, to stand up to rude mistresses, etc. The watchword of the Frente Negra was "separate now to unite later." The Negro had to join forces with the white, but he needed to be educated for this in order not to be accepted according to the old traditionalist code. "Separation was a necessary contingency." The Negro was not prepared technologically, psychologically, or spiritually for freedom. This was the reason for what had happened in Brazil. The Frente Negra proposed to fight against this: the strategy was to bring the Negroes together in order to train them, to destroy their fear and cowardliness before the white man, and to instill into them courage and daring in economic competition and in the defense of their rights. But the Frente Negra fought against every attempt or tendency to achieve racial separation. Thus the political motto was: "Brazil belongs to Brazilians. What should be done is to make true Brazilians of Negroes. . . . Our watchword was conceived so that Negroes everywhere would take a position. It would be that of separation. We separate in order to unite." [5]

Thus in order to "fight" for his integration, the Negro had to learn new skills at three levels of organized behavior. First, he had to learn to identify himself with his Negro brothers, uniting amongst themselves and mutually supporting each other. Second, he had to develop new patterns of cooperation in order to achieve this end and to put organized, conscious group behavior at his service. This was difficult because such social techniques did not form part of the traditional social legacy. The recent past had made predatory individualism and blind egotism the only effective arms in the struggle for survival. Therefore, it was necessary to develop mechanisms of repression and control over egotistical behavior and to make way for the rapid assimilation of alternative forms of intraracial cooperation and solidarity. Third, he had to develop integrationalist motivations that were strong enough to function independently of psychological motivations and social controls either of the Negro milieu or of white society.

Potentially dangerous difficulties arose with regard to relations with whites and in part to adjustment with nonparticipating groups of the black population. It is clear that the bulk of the white population could have become hostile to these movements, especially if they manifested an openly racist character and appeared to be revolutionary in social terms (that is, if it were possible to link them with the intention of changing the prevailing social order). On the other hand Negroes and mulattoes who remained apathetic to civil rights drives and those who were against them owing to their identification with the dominant race did not understand the causes for such movements, feared their campaign strategy, and tended to censure the deliberate use of conflict.

For this reason the prior development of certain thoughts and actions whose function it was to give a moral stamp to the grievances, demonstrate their conformity to the existing social order, and subject their concrete manifestations to conscious restraint became essential. Conflict was seen as an arm to combat diffuse isolation; the intention was to limit it and keep it from engendering something worse, such as systematic segregation. What was at stake was making the class society a system that was at least open to Negroes who were in condition to compete with whites—not turn it into a system that was closed to all Negroes and mulattoes. Not only was avoidance of a regression sought, but there were great efforts made to the end that it would be understood that the civil rights movements constituted an extreme, unavoidable, and temporary recourse of social justice.

As it can be seen, the resocialization of the Negro affected all areas of the perceptual and cognitive bases of his behavior, personality, and cultural outlook. He not only gained new possibilities for understanding his situation as a black man; he achieved a new capacity for confronting this situation, in terms of individual adjustments calculated to serve self-interest as much as in terms of nonconformist collective adjustments. He raised to the level of the social conscience many of his conditions for existence and some of his ideals for changing the existing relationship between the races. The chief consequence of these sociopsychological and sociocultural changes appears in the understanding and interpretation that the Negro soon achieved regarding his position in the racial order of society. He discovered that he was not rejected purely and simply for being a Negro. Rather, he learned that color and other racial characteristics formed a reference system that kept him in an inferior social stratum which lacked access to the standards of living and social safeguards enjoyed by other national groups of ethnic or racial character. The notion of color prejudice thus arose as an inclusive category of thought. It was formulated to designate structurally, emotionally, and cognitively all the aspects involved by the asymmetrical and traditionalist pattern of race relations. For this reason when the Negro and mulatto speak of "color prejudice," they do not distinguish "prejudice" per se from "discrimination." Both are based upon the same conceptual representation.

The social movements sought to consolidate and spread a given type of awareness of the Brazilian racial situation; to bring together those interested in discussing it and combating it; to reeducate them; and ultimately, to turn them into an indomitable force that was capable of changing this situation. One of the most significant documents of this era of the Frente Negra Brasileira is the result of the understanding of Brazil's younger generation as developed through the study of the national situation.

The world is going through a critical period, impregnated by new ideas and demands that are almost always just and necessary ones, which requires of all racial groups a harmonious outlook with regard to crucial problems. . . . In Brazil, more than in other countries, the Negro man suffers the consequences of his captivity of almost four centuries, during which he made effective contributions to the development of public and private wealth and has been an ethnic factor in the mixing of races to fuse together a more uniform type, suitable to the tropical environment. . . . Cast at the margins of Brazilian life—whose organization he has sustained on his shoulders throughout the passing centuries, lacking economic resources, lacking education and health—the Negro has suffered the terrible effects of the Machiavellian campaign of color prejudice which only he feels and is aware of, because at every moment it is a fact. . . . Various attempts at organizing Negroes for other purposes than that of simple recreation have failed. *Reaction*—this is the exact meaning of this organization. The last attempt was that of the Centro Cívico de Palmares some ten years ago with its less developed program which, however, had the same objectives. . . . It was then that in understanding and feeling the immediate necessity that circumstances of life demanded the organization which took the name of "Frente Negra Brasileira" was formed with more enthusiasm and experience.

And later on it asserts in the same tone:

it is an irresponsible if not malicious statement to say that there is no color prejudice in Brazil. We have already inscribed on our standard: "Only we Negroes can feel the color prejudice that exists in Brazil." This is because the campaign against the Negro is deceptive and dissimulated; it is not carried out as in the United States, in particular, where the materialistic mentality has imposed the standard that: "A man is worth what he is capable of doing." It is not an open conflict of values. On the contrary, he is promised much more but given nothing. And the prevailing mentality is to always make the Negro a servile element, denying him all the rights that the law, ironically, grants him. . . . The Negro has been laboring under this malicious infiltration and Machiavellian insinuation; and wherever he goes he is looked upon only as a Negro and with an undisguisable touch of irony, as if the color of one's skin could affect his intellectual capacity! [R. J. do Amaral, *ca.* 1936, 1, 3–4.]

The progress made in the resocialization of the Negro, in turn, corresponded or followed the appearance of new social forms. The proliferation of recreational, cultural, and benefi-

cent associations was of well-defined importance in the resocialization of the black man. These associations not only
broadened the area of internal contacts in the Negro milieu;
they disseminated and consolidated new patterns of living
that contributed to increase the Negro's self-respect, his bonds
of solidarity, and especially his dissatisfaction with being left
at the sidelines.

It seems that these associations were rarely able to perform
their stated functions:

Since 1915 organizations of Negroes have been founded which
ended up turning from their purpose and becoming social parties.
It is a fact, however, that the objectives of these societies were not
those of organizing the race, but rather cultural and beneficent
ones. For these purposes the Sociedade Beneficente 13 de Maio,
the Grêmio Recreativo e Cultural, and others were founded between 1918 and 1924. The Grêmio Recreativo Kosmos that carried
out an educational program during this period constitutes an exception: It had a drama group and a newspaper that published
social news and literary essays. Some, however, in addition to full-
filling these functions, attuned themselves to the prevailing atmosphere of social ferment. Such was the case of the Centro Cívico
Palmares founded in 1927 for educational purposes and which
soon became a nucleus for the organization of the Negro and an
active center of the struggle against the manifestations of color
prejudice [Moreira and Leite, n.d., 4].

It is necessary to keep in mind that these associations did
not serve only as the indirect sources of the beginnings of the
rights movements. First, they concentrated the manifestation
and channeled the otherwise diffused opinions concerning the
fundamental importance of education for the Negro and mulatto. Education was made the first condition for the Negro's
struggle against poverty, color prejudice, and social disorganization. It was given even higher value than conflict,
which was regarded as a recourse whose effectiveness depended directly on the prior success in reeducating the Negro.
Second, these associations functioned as the first types of
pressure collectively exercised by the Negro. All of the agitation during the turbulent period from 1927 to 1931 against

the concrete manifestations of color prejudice or for the repeal of discriminatory regulations in public offices was begun
and directed through these associations. Third, they provided
the psychological environment that counterbalanced the cen-
tripetal tendencies of the black elites—little inclined to identify themselves with humble or poor Negroes—and raised the
first objections to the identification of the vertically mobile Negro with the interests and values of whites. In this sense they
helped offset various effects of the technique of draining off
the leadership of racial minorities practiced by society and to
increase the loyalty of nonconformist groups to the interests
of the Negro people.

Another issue deals with what some white intellectuals
have called "Negro prejudice against the white." It seems clear
that as long as the Negro saw himself through the negative
images formulated by the white man he would never be able
to represent himself autonomously as a person and have an
independent vision of his destiny in society. For this reason
the awareness that color prejudice existed and the direct or
indirect opposition to its manifestations were in themselves of
considerable dynamic importance for the Negro psychologically as well as sociologically. In one life history the man (a
dark mulatto) spontaneously revealed his subscribing to the
motto that "anyone who isn't white is Negro" in classifying
himself as a Negro. In two other cases light mulattoes (one of
whom would be considered white by Brazilian racial criteria)
identified themselves racially and psychologically as Negroes,
emphasizing that only the social situation of a person is of
importance. This engendered a kind of racial pride of a compensatory nature that then served as a standard for the rights
movements. "We protest when we are rejected 'only' because
we are Negroes, which we are with pride today" (A. V. dos
Santos, 1931b, 3). From this perspective it is possible to see
how the "Negro's prejudice" might seem objectionable and
even intolerable to the larger society. But it constituted a truly
important sociopsychological condition for the formation and
development of attitudes of psychological independence and

social nonconformity at the heart of the black population.

The last two points—the radicalism of the mulatto and the constructive influence of the social movements—should only be mentioned in passing. Observations suggest that the participation of mulattoes in the leadership of rights movements was especially intense. These were mulattoes who considered themselves Negroes and declared their loyalty to the Negro people. One of the informants who was particularly active in those activities asserted the following: "The Negro is subservient, a flatterer; the mulatto is not; he is rebellious, unsubmissive. I'm agraid to try to explain this fact because I'm almost illiterate. But I think it can be explained through atavism. After all, three centuries of slavery ought to weigh. Even the educated Negro is humble. Look at Dr. S. and his ideas that the Negroes ought to look for white leaders." Nonetheless, it seems that the mulatto had greater chances by virtue of his own experience and the prestige gained beforehand. Many of them better understood the social techniques to be employed, and the rest placed the tasks of greater complexity or importance in their hands. In any case the fact is that the mulatto's dissatisfaction made his reactions radical and led him to a definite involvement on the side of the Negro people.

Ultimately, to the degree that the rights movements asserted themselves and developed, they created new models for behavior and social aspirations. Social roles emerged that were linked specifically to the roles of the participants in campaigns carried out or in the associations that sponsored them. On the other hand a new routine was established in daily life with its own centers of interest. Individuals could cooperate and compete with each other by means of this participation. The objectives of the demands imposed obligations that were altruistic and truly burdensome. Yet, depending on the way in which they fulfilled them, individuals could fortify their self-esteem and gain social prestige in the Negro milieu. Active militants ended up occupied with regular, integrative tasks, forming a circle that was highly subject to the influence of group morale. In this case the tendencies that dynamized their attitudes and behavior took on another quality and intensity. They were subject to external, personal, and direct controls which exposed their activities to constant supervision. These influences were of a conditioning importance since they determined the degree of loyalty, perseverance, and dedication with which each person would devote himself to the objectives collectively envisioned.

The conclusions of this discussion concerning the sociopsychological and sociocultural conditions of the Negro milieu reveal the reactions to the sociohistorical incentives described above. The city's black population had elements for attuning itself to the processes that were making an impact on the structure of Brazilian society. It could synchronize itself with other social groups that were projecting themselves at this time on the historical stage of action, demanding for itself the sum of power and self-determination that it should possess in an open, competitive, and democratic society. Having recovered from their scars, the Negroes prepared themselves to vie with whites for the rights and duties of the citizen.

Having seen this, we will discuss the main events that mark historically the manifestations of the civil rights movements in the Negro milieu. In the period from 1927 to 1945, various beneficent, cultural, and recreational associations came into being and many of them sponsored campaigns or activities with practical objectives.[6] The majority of these associations had a short or even ephemeral life. Some succumbed to the designs of unscrupulous directors and found themselves involved in lamentable affairs. Others managed to give certain continuity and creative spirit to their work. For the purposes of our study, however, it is deemed advisable to restrict the analysis to the what might be called the "pioneer" phase, the first organized manifestations of the Negro's struggle for his social integration. For this reason, we have chosen the Frente Negra Brasileira as the unit of investigation, which limits our discussion to the time period between 1931 and 1937. This limitation, however, has the considerable advantage of situating the sociological analysis of the connections between meaning, structure, and function to be raised in the study of the factors and conditions that explain both the failure of the rights movements and their constructive influences on the Negro's behavior, his conception of the world, and the orientation of his social aspirations.

The Frente Negra Brasileira was founded on September 16, 1931. It emerged in an atmosphere of unrest and anxiety because since 1927 various groups, with the *Clarim da Alvorada* at the fore, had been preparing the ground for an organization of this type. For this reason it was received with rejoicing, and at the beginning it brought together all the groups existing in the Negro milieu. The immediate success was amazing. In a short time it had thousands of members with a powerful directorate in São Paulo and various supporting groups throughout the interior and in other states. Moreover, beginning on March 18, 1933, it had its own newspaper, *A Voz da Raça*, and put into action a program of proselytism that was never paralleled in later attempts. Some members became a kind of group of professional agitators. "Their assignment was to go out into the neighborhoods in search of supporters" (Moreira and Leite, n.d., 13–14).

The Frente Negra was recognized through its bylaws as having the purpose of fostering the "political and social unity of the Negro People on a national scale for the affirmation of the historical rights of the same by virtue of their material and psychological activities of the past, and for demanding their present social and political rights in the Brazilian Communion." It was directed by a Grand Council that was "sovereign and responsible, having twenty members and having established in it the Chief and the Secretary, all other necessary offices being filled by the President." The Grand Council was "assisted in its function by the Auxiliary Council formed by the district subchiefs of the capital." This organ became the center for the development of the Negro Front militia which had paramilitary organization. Its members wore white shirts; were subject to rigid discipline; received military training; and were headed by Raul Joviano do Amaral, who held the post of captain. (The other posts of major and colonel were honorific and fell to the members of the Grand Council and to the President of the F.N.B.)

Moved perhaps by the success achieved, perhaps because they thought that in this way they could better serve the purposes of the organization, its mentors transformed it into a political party in 1936.

The Frente Negra finally registered as a political party. The petition to register caused discussions in the court about its constitutionality, but it was finally accepted. Negroes in general were not greatly interested in the fact, but those closest tied to the Negro movements were surprised. The coup d'état of 1937 found the Frente Negra registered as a political party, and the government outlawed it. It immediately became the União Negra Brasileira under the presidency of Raul Joviano do Amaral, who worked to continue its activity until May, 1938, the date of the celebration of the fiftieth anniversary of Abolition [Moreira and Leite, n.d., 27].

The sociopsychological context described above involved tendencies that structurally and dynamically presupposed certain ideological orientations. The repudiation of the traditionalist and asymmetrical pattern of racial domination and the aspirations for rapid social integration on a collective scale irrevocably turned the Frente Negra into an assimilationist type of rights movement. At the core it functioned as a mechanism of the societal reaction of the Negro milieu. It purported to consolidate and disseminate an autonomous understanding of its own regarding the Brazilian racial situation, to develop the tendencies in the black population that would organize it into an integrated racial minority, and to encourage patterns of behavior that would speed up the integration of the Negro into the class society. In order to achieve this end it functioned on three distinct levels: in the undermining of traditionalist racial domination by means of open combat against the manifestations of color prejudice and the debasement of the values or social techniques on which it rested; in the reeducation of the Negro through encouraging him to compete with the white in all spheres of life, even psychologically, in order to confront the color barrier; in the development of organizational forms that extended and strengthened cooperation and solidarity at the heart of the black population. In addition it made a conscious effort to foster the historical image that the Negro constructed of himself and left him to understand the role that the Negro race had played as "the most important one in the stability of national life for almost four hundred years" (R. J. Amaral, n.d., 2). It also hoped to extend its socializing influence to the reeducation of whites, for it was recognized that a new attitude toward Negroes' rights and toward living together on an equal footing was necessary for the stability and progress of the national social order.

However, the specifically political emphasis coincided with immediate and basic social interests as witnessed by the following quotation written under the title *Our Necessities and Demands:*

This association (that the F.N.B. hopes to become) should deal with the total Negro problem—with education and assistance in general (assistance that today would look out especially for the elderly men and women who are former slaves and the invalid or helpless Negro veterans of imperial wars and republican seditions). It should deal with the Uniting of Negroes in homogeneous professional groups, the only ones possible within the terrible cosmopolitanism of São Paulo, which put an end to the situation of poverty and unlimited exploitation in which Negro workers perpetually live—rejected here, mistreated there, humiliated elsewhere; working more and earning less in addition to being poorly paid or not paid at all. It ought to extract them from the exploitative clutches of landlords who are nearly always usurious and coarse foreigners, the owners of the holes and cellars that go by the name of houses in which people live without light or hygenic conditions. . . . It should teach them economic habits and care in investing their income in real estate converted into unmortgageable "family property" as established by Article 70 of the Brazilian Civil Law. It should take measures to ensure access to craft and technical vocations from which Negroes have been systematically excluded by the policy favoring only or principally foreigners that has marked the rule of the P.R.P.* [A.V. dos Santos, 1931b, 6].

* *Translator's note:* The P.R.P was the Partido Republicano Paulista (Paulista Republican Party).

The possibility of turning it into an instrument of political influence to be autonomously controlled by the Negro was foreseen from the time of its founding. At least this is what is inferred by Article 4 of its bylaws: "As an organized political force the FRENTE NEGRA BRASILEIRA, in order to more perfectly achieve its social objectives, will contest the elective posts for representation of the Brazilian Negro People according to the legal order instituted in Brazil, carrying out its political-social action in strictly Brazilian terms."

It is necessary to note that there was a remarkable congruency between the formalization of the objectives and the ways of putting them into practice. In spite of the insuperable limitations born of the poverty of the black population and the difficulty in raising funds, the Frente Negra Brasileira strove hard to achieve its ends. For this reason it did in fact correspond to the principal expectations and made an important contribution to creating the moral climate that was to produce the "new Negro." In these aspects it was chiefly the expression of deep-flowing currents in the Negro milieu that demanded basic, long-term changes in the behavior, personality, and life style of the Negro people. In other words it served as a point of reference for the initial forms of social manifestation of these currents in a moment in which the Negro was not yet able to formulate them in a more ordered, serene way and in one that was in accord with the possibilities of existing interracial relations. The fact is that the Frente Negra Brasileira placed the black population of São Paulo before the behavioral alternatives and collective options represented by those currents, thus opening new possibilities for the ideological influence of the rights movements and fostering advances that would not otherwise have been made except under the emotional and moral pressure of action itself for the redress of grievances.

A brief survey will justify these interpretations. Much was done in the period from 1927 to 1931. Incipient agitation was rapidly transformed into social unrest and this was expressed in several ways through ordered, nonconformist action. After the establishment of key ideals that contained real objectives of dynamic import (such as the rehabilitation of the Negro, racial unity, and close relations with the white on the basis of complete equality) came the undermining of traditionalist racial domination. This was accomplished through fighting against the concrete manifestations of color prejudice and the organization of Negroes for the realization of activities of their own (such as veneration of the "Negro Mother," the creation of cultural associations and the Negro press, etc.). Activities of this nature took new vigor with the founding of the Frente Negra Brasileira. It had to coordinate the various ideological motivations existing in the Negro milieu, reduce them to practical formulas, and at the same time elevate them to the level of practical application or manifestation. What is important to point out is that a strategy was formulated that was direct and crude, that the masses could understand and follow. The grand objectives whose realization depended on changing the structure of the total society were not put aside, however. They continued to be pursued, at least at the level of verbalization and idealization. The goal of making the Negro a "good citizen," an "honest man," and a personality respected and accepted in the bourgeois society never ceased to be pursued. The same might be said of other more or less complex ideals.

Any academism or intellectualism was deliberately avoided. It was not intended that the Negro should first understand these basic objectives and then act. On the contrary, action was encouraged as the first step, leaving it up to supporters to understand as they could, during the action or after it, the true meaning of those basic objectives. Thus the essential fact was that activism constituted the real link between the leaders and the masses as well as among propaganda, the development of a common ideology, and the transformation of leaders or supporters.

This shows that the Frente Negra Brasileira functioned realistically within a narrow range. This was the price of an efficacious performance which did not hinder the expectation for a radical change in the strategy followed whenever the

Negro might have a chance to put into practice political plans of action of greater scope. In the interim action was directed toward immediate ends that could be collectively enjoyed. There are five points that deserve special consideration here. First, inspired by prior directives derived principally from the group publishing the *Clarim da Alvorada,* they insisted on assimilation of the behavior models existing in the larger society. But the demands were oriented strictly toward the immediate present, be it the indoctrination of persons in the advantages of maintaining an organized family life and child care; or be it the fostering of ambition for stable employment, the acquisition of land, and the construction of one's own home. The attacks in this field were intrinsically direct. Criticism of the present situation slipped to a secondary and subsidiary level. What was of real importance was the tendency to assimilate the living patterns of whites and through them redefine the position of the Negro in the social structure as well as the negative images of him that were circulating.

Second, the Frente Negra Brasileira tenaciously endeavored to modify the Negro's pattern of adjustment and societal reaction. On one hand it fostered the ostensive and even angry repudiation of passive capitulation. On the other it encouraged behavioral patterns that were consciously demanding: to receive or to obtain their "due respect" and to do things with "the maximum perfection." If a female employer were to act disrespectfully, servants were prepared to reject the insults. There resulted frictions and conflicts that did not previously occur, at least not on the same scale. The servants would say: "Now we have somebody to defend us. We have the Frente Negra looking out for our interests." The result was that many mistresses began to avoid the "Frente Negra girls." In compensation, others preferred them because "they knew they could trust them, that they were upright people." Similar things occurred on other occupational levels and in other spheres of life. The Negro was not being prepared to await the dawning of the Second Abolition patiently, but encouraged to bring it about through his own efforts—with violent methods, if necessary.

Third, the Frente Negra Brasileira followed a definite policy toward the manifestations and consequences of color prejudice. There was always a certain ambivalence in the Negro milieu with regard to this matter. The more the Negro or mulatto identified with the constellation of interests and the values of the dominant race, the more confused he was and inclined to claim that "this problem doesn't exist in Brazil." The indoctrination program of the Frente Negra combatted these ambiguous reactions, unmasking them by means of explanations of the interests, concessions, or confusions behind them. But principally it instilled in its followers a belligerent spirit, causing them to rise up against whites with color prejudice and encouraging them to struggle bravely for the redress of the injustices directed at them.

At the time when we were militants in the Frente Negra Brasileira, these issues always came to the fore. While traveling through the interior on business we encountered cases of prejudice like this. Once the group was formed in the city [the nucleus of the F.N.B.], the order was to break the taboos. In various cities this custom existed: Negroes would wander through the garden [while whites promenaded there]. Then someone would say, "They're in the garden." And when we did this, [that custom] was broken and ended. There . . . was a skating fad. Owing to the flexibility of their bodies—perhaps because they really know how to do the samba—Negroes soon became the best skaters. Then Negroes weren't permitted to enter the rink. They did not allow a Negro to enter. The Frente Negra sounded the alarm. It went to the newspapers. They took no action. The order of the Frente Negra: go, skate carefully; enter with respect. Don't destroy anything and skate. The Negroes went and no one broke anything. . . . It's the same thing that always happens. Wherever the Frente Negra gets involved, these things are ended. It even seems that the whites thought it was good, because after all, there wasn't any reason [they shouldn't]. There are also some different cases in which it's the Negroes who think they can't enter, that their place is outside. If they wish to enter, go ahead and they'll enter also. . . .[7]

The endeavor to force the Negro to have courage to live among whites and to face them firmly was put in first place.

Fourth, the Frente Negra Brasileira sought to prepare the

Negro subjectively and materially to withstand the tensions
and conflicts that could result from the adjustments advocated. The data given here illustrate the nature of the orientation given. Dr. Arlindo Veiga dos Santos explained that the
existing situation was the consequence of the Negro's lack of
preparation for collective integration. Thus "the strategy of
the Frente Negra was to bring the Negroes together in order to
prepare them, to destroy their fear and cowardice in the face
of the white man, and to give them courage and daring in
economic competition and in the defense of their rights."
Nonetheless, they did not accept concessions compensated for
by exclusions. Such an alternative would have introduced into
Brazil a systematic segregation that was arduously combatted
by the Frente Negra.

Fifth, there prevailed a clear understanding that the Negro
by himself would never be able to change the white's nature.
Consequently, the Frente Negra Brasileira hoped to reeducate
the white in only a limited sphere: that of his expectations of
adjustments to the Negro. In long-range terms it hoped that
new forms of living together would contribute toward broadening minds so that the irrationality of color prejudice would
become evident. However, the F.N.B. never took a dogmatic
and utopian position in regard to this social dilemma. Thus it
limited itself to disseminating the awareness that prejudice
existed and that it blocked the Negro in society; and it propagated societal mechanisms for active reaction against the
manifestations and consequences of color prejudice that were
harmful to the Negro people. It never imposed upon itself the
aspiration of eliminating it forever. This is a truly important
point. By acting in this manner, it could limit tensions and
conflicts with whites to concrete situations, but it could not be
accused of preparing something like a sedition by the Negro
race.

The techniques of manipulation of the violence it advocated
found moral justification in the very facts that it was directed
against. Society had to tolerate these techniques and to admit
that the Negro sought to defend legitimate rights through

them. On the other hand this procedure gave a small strategic advantage to the Negro. The tensions and conflicts that were provoked by concrete cases of color prejudice could be resolved independently of any more profound change in the personality of the white or in the social order. It was enough that the grievances be redressed, with the merited and respectable treatment being dispensed to the individual or a certain safeguard to which he was socially entitled being granted to him in order that the reasons for dissension might disappear. Just as they did not wish to change the social order, neither did they see why they should be interested in changing the white man beyond the limits involved in egalitarian acceptance. To judge by the statements gathered, they even viewed this issue as a secondary one.

What took first place was the correction of the social injustice of which the Negro had become *victim* and the conquest of a socioeconomic position that would serve as a guidepost for his normal integration into the existing social order. Beyond that, many thought that color prejudice was a matter of human misfortune; and they were not sure that it would disappear with the achievement of economic, social, and political equality in relation to whites. The more sensitive tormented themselves with this. The majority were interested only in the practical problems related to the economic, social, and cultural betterment of the Negro people.

This does not mean that the Frente Negra Brasileira was a perfect organization. It paid a high price for its lack of political experience and for other adverse influences of the Negro milieu or of the larger society.

Harassed by some who were not aware of its high, salutary, and beneficial goals; combated by others who looked upon it with the poorly disguised eyes of spite and ire; and, finally, warred upon by those who preached inhuman and petty prejudice, the Frente Negra Brasileira proceeded fearlessly with its task of organizing, unfurling its flag of race and nationalism to the four winds and sounding its clarion to rally [the black population]—the echo of which resounded in most inhospitable corners of the nation [R. J. Amaral, n.d., 2].

The truth is that the factors mentioned here, added to the deficiencies of internal organization and the advent of the Estado Nôvo,* completely destroyed it, never more to rise again. We are not interested in examining all the aspects of this woeful outcome. However, we must list at least certain essential points so that it may be understood how difficult it is for the Negro to react to the drama in which he lives by means of collective movements for protests, the redress of grievances, and combat.

The first divergencies were caused by the authoritarian methods of the organization of power within the movements adopted by the first group of top leaders of the Frente Negra Brasileira.

At the time of the founding of the Frente Negra about the middle of 1931, São Paulo witnessed the enthusiasm with which the Italian colony embraced the new political ideas that had arisen in Italy with the advent of Fascism. . . . The first divergencies arose right away in the formulation of the bylaws that gave the organization a clearly Fascist character. Certain persons withdrew on this occasion [Moreira and Leite, n.d., 16–18].

The sudden initial success of the Frente Negra left the leadership disoriented and forced it to cling to authoritarian methods of organization. The leadership became impermeable to communication with the rest, and new, discouraging frictions developed. "At the first meeting of the Frente Negra held in the halls of the *Classes Laboriosas* [Laboring Classes]— which were completely filled—the group related to the *Clarim* had its first conflict with the leadership of the Frente." (Moreira and Leite, n.d., 18.) Discussions followed which created factions and later brought on the abandonment of the Frente Negra by the group related to the *Clarim da Alvorada*. Internal conflicts in the Negro milieu then began.

Once the opposite positions of the Frente Negra and the group related to the *Clarim* were defined, a violent struggle developed between them. In the Frente it was said that the group related to

* *Translator's note:* The *Estado Nôvo* (*New State*) was the name given by Getulío Vargas to his regime after 1937.

the *Clarim* and others considered to be enemies were the "Judases of the Race." The group linked to the *Clarim* was accused of not taking action, never having done anything for Negroes and of knowing only how to talk and criticize. [The Frente declared] . . . "our followers do not need intellectuals; we need more action and fewer words." On the other hand the group related to the *Clarim* continued to criticize the orientation followed by the leadership of the Frente through its newspaper [Moreira and Leite, n.d., 20].

Tempers became so incited that the inside of the building where the newspaper was published was even plundered. "After this shocking event there was a time of confusion and contradictory judgments in the Negro milieu. An attitude of reproval could be noted and a few dissimulated protests were heard by means of expressions such as these: "The heroism of Cain"; "Can it be that the Negro's enemy is the Negro himself?"; and someone said in jest: "I won't go in the Front, I'll go behind." (Moreira and Leite, n.d., 21.)

Finally, after the revolution of 1932, the idea arose to register the Frente as a political party. The idea was accepted, but the ultimate result was tragic. With the advent of the *Estado Nôvo* in 1937 its activities were closed down. Under the name of *União Negra Brasileira* [Brazilian Negro Union], there were unsuccessful efforts to save it. (Moreira and Leite, n.d., 27.) Never again was it possible to raise up an organization of such proportions in the *Paulistana* Negro milieu.

We shall recall certain painful events—only the essential ones—in order to cast some light on the nature of the difficulties that blocked the normal development of the Frente Negra Brasileira internally. First, there was the development of insuperable divergencies on basic issues. These divergencies can apparently be attributed to the unstable social position of the Negro and mulatto. The variety of interests, conceptions, and experiences born of the various possible forms of racial adjustment made impracticable the objectification of one racial policy that was acceptable to all. Furthermore, the Negro milieu lacked the appropriate mechanisms of coercion and control.

Second, the selection of leaders caused serious maladjustments. Leaders were not the product of a spontaneous and prolonged screening process carried on among the mass of militants. They were recruited among persons with sufficient fame and prestige to attract followers. As this mechanism was not counterbalanced by the degree of political awareness and the capacity for self-defense or moral pressure on the part of the mass, the result was that the leaders exercised the functions of leadership with a flexible autonomy. They even came to hold an amount of authority that was potentially dangerous for the stability of their action and their relations with the mass and the organizations.

Third, the developmental process of the factions reveal notorious anomalies. Even in the absence of external mechanisms for conciliation of the divergencies, the devotion to a sacred cause or the mere consciousness of sharing very strong common interests should have kept the division from developing into a suicidal struggle. The persons and groups involved in those struggles are known for their exemplary dedication to the cause of the Negro and mulatto. But why, then, did things go so far? It looks like a fortuitous but crucial condition was added to their lack of political experience: for the first time the possibility arose in the Negro milieu for competing for prestige and power in the political arena. After a certain moment the divergencies represent interests and motivations that were as strong (or even stronger) than the common cause for the persons and groups involved.

Taking into account what is to be learned from these three factors, it is easy to conclude that the Frente Negra Brasileira was already destined to failure at its inception. It provided magnificent proof of the capacity for organization and virile struggle by the Negro and mulatto. However, it also simultaneously showed that it was still early to go very far in the struggle against the current. It remained in the political annals as a kind of historical landmark of the first demonstration of rebellion and force by the Negro people. It was a test that served to provide better understanding of the means and ends that the Negro will have to employ if he wishes to change the prevailing racial order abruptly.

In order to understand the deepest sources of the failure of these movements, we would have to take into account how the Negro milieu reacted to them and especially to their innovational goals. The idealistic pioneers of the movements were victims of an illusion that has blinded the majority of social reformers. They thought that it was enough to sow the seed of reason for it to flourish. It happens, however, that before men throw themselves into a struggle for some social cause—however important or vital it may be—they must be convinced that it is socially imperative and that it ought to be attempted. The leaders failed to instill a goal and a vision in the Negro's understanding of the world and in his capacity for collective action. Involvement with the modern way of life contributed in shaping the cultural outlook of the average black man, but not enough to make a July Fourteenth for the Brazilian Negro.[8]

In order to accomplish this deed the Negro would first have had to assimilate social techniques whose existence he hardly suspected. By virtue of living in a world created by and for white men, he confronted many social forces that he was unaware of and could not submit to some kind of social control of his own. While it was not difficult to adopt the categories of thought that made it possible to verbalize these social forces, the same did not occur at the level of conscious social behavior. Here success came to depend on the mastery achieved over the techniques of organizing collective behavior that corresponded to those categories of thought. The last word would not be given by the man and his wishes, but by his culture; that is, by man as a bearer of culture, viewed within the historical context of his social wishes and action.[9]

There are those who believe that the function of the social movements consists in formulating the ideologies and techniques of action demanded by circumstances. If we believed the same, we would make a severe but unilateral criticism of the rights movements described above. The truth is that if the analysis made is correct, they did not meet the requirements of the sociohistorical situation. However, even so, they went beyond the average possibilities of the black population. In the second place, the initial limitations and the chronic inconsistencies of the movements were never corrected and overcome because of these same possibilities. Here is the crux of the problem. The conditions of social living of that population have contributed directly and indirectly to undermine and even destroy the dynamic factors on which the development of such movements could be based. The following explanation summarizes the ten principal aspects of this situation.

1. The breakdown of traditionalist patterns of racial domination is far from having completed its course. The racial ideology that still prevails is the one that was formulated to legitimate the extreme social heteronomy of the Negro race. The invisible psychological barrier that incessantly assimilated and counteracted the autonomist *élan* of the rights movements derived from the social images through which considerable numbers of the black population conceived their social status and roles. Such images were constructed by whites and introduced into the Negro subculture, engendering humble adjustments and a distorted understanding of reality. They not only inhibited or absorbed the egalitarian tendencies of the environment; they fostered highly passive identifications and expectations of behavior.

Since the beginning of the rights movements, all attempts to corner the Negro vote have always failed irremediably. Some have explained such an outcome (a shocking one in some cases because the Frente Negra Brasileira had thousands of followers but the chosen candidate received an insignificant number of votes) through the Negro's illiteracy, which excluded him en masse from the voting body.* Yet the Negro voter seldom pays heed to arguments in favor of a racial concentration of votes despite the obstinacy of those who advocate this policy. As can be inferred from a statement of an advocate of this line, they do not become discouraged:

* *Editor's note:* Literacy is a requirement for voting in Brazil.

We need to have representatives in the assemblies because if we don't have them, we won't have resources to maintain organizations that strive for the economic and cultural betterment of the Negro because our folks are all poor and those who do improve their life no longer want to maintain relations with Negroes. We must educate the Negro to vote for Negroes because only a Negro himself knows what our problems are. In the election for the Legislative Assembly we weren't able to elect R., but this time he'll win. Once we have someone inside there, the rest will be easy. There will be money for us to use for organizing ourselves and in future elections we'll elect others. That's the road to improving the Negro's living conditions.

This shows that the perpetuation of the traditionalist pattern of racial domination has roots in the conformity prevailing in large segments of the black population. Those inclined to compete in an open and systematic way with whites, although they be numerous, constitute a minority. The majority, even when it comes to reject color prejudice and its pernicious or humiliating consequences, is incapable of denying its identification with the dominant race or of overcoming its ambivalent attitudes, both engendered by the overwhelming influence of the whites' racial ideology.

2. In spite of the demands made by the social movements, the Negro was not able to break the pattern of diffuse isolation. He was not even able to achieve a kind of direct control over effects known to be disastrous. For him to have achieved this goal it would have been necessary for his means of integration into the society to have undergone radical change, including the incorporation of the black population en masse into the different strata of the competitive social order. But the structural changes that occurred were not of such magnitude. Owing to proletarianization, thrift, and vertical social mobility, the number of black persons who infiltrated the highest levels of the lower class and the middle class has progressively increased. These processes contributed very little, however, to create conditions of communication between the Negro and the rest of society that were truly open and dynamic.

3. The internal social differentiation of the Negro milieu was sufficient to engender certain perplexities and apprehensions at the time of the initial transition which led to the organization of the rights movements. Yet it is clear that it was not sufficiently widespread and thorough to provide those movements with the material, institutional, and psychological base that they lacked. In this aspect the inconsistencies of the movements reflected the precariousness of the associations on which they were based and which were as a rule ephemeral and lacking in solid ideological underpinnings. As the fruits of the goodwill and dedication of a small number, the majority were destined to failure from their inception, as they evoked little response in the Negro milieu as a whole and no solidarity on the part of whites. After making touching sacrifices, they stopped their activities without achieving their basic goals or else they resisted stubbornly for years on end with their congenital limitations. Some, in spite of their humanitarian goals, were never even useful to the rights movements because of their conservative nature. For this reason these movements suffered deeply from the lack of motivation based on stable and constantly growing institutionalized groups.

4. Difficulties continue to cause complications in the sphere of socialization. The emotional and psychological bonds that unite individuals socially are created, governed, and structured through their forms of association. The inconsistencies and limitations of the latter were bound to engender quite serious psychodynamic and sociodynamic consequences. Predatory individualism and lack of consensus were the two specters that hovered continually over the rights movements. Attention was given to the character of the leader who took over the movements and made them into a platform for his self-glorification or source of income, a base for bargaining with whites, etc. There was also discussion about the insoluble dilemmas brought on by the masses that were no more than aggregations of individuals, for each one entered and left with intransigent personal opinions.

The solidarity that linked black individuals who had just

come out of the slaveholding society was not even a tribal solidarity of a mechanical nature. Yet the economic, political, and social problems that the Negro faced demanded the patterns of organic solidarity that were typical of the class society.[10] The Negro could not perform any miracle that could help him make this enormous historical leap. It is not surprising that the norms and forces of social cooperation that would make the uniting of forces possible did not exist. Nor is it surprising that the forces acting in the opposite direction of disunity and disintegration were so brutal and hostile.

The basic, irremediable weaknesses were a result of the Negro's attitude toward himself as a Negro. "They would be incapable of uniting to elect a Negro deputy." "He even resents seeing another Negro get ahead. He won't vote for him." "They prefer to vote for a white." "It's impossible to think about Negro politics." "It's no use for a person to want to fight against color prejudice and to improve the Negro's situation. There is no unity among Negroes. In order to get anything there'd have to be unity." "One Negro won't help another. On the contrary, they're more likely to fight each other than to help each other." "They don't act cooperatively nor do they encourage each other. There is no single opinion. Each one has his own and defends it as if it were the best." "The problem is that there's a lot of confusion among Negroes. This is really a crazy thing. It's not very simple. If you want to study the Negro you should come with me. I'll show you how everything that looks simple is complicated." These affirmations are symptomatic. Against this background, the amazing thing is that the rights movements came to the fore and flourished, surviving until today.

Yet one thing must be recognized. Where cooperation is so difficult to achieve, how can a pressure group or a conflict group be organized? In order to employ nonconformity and conflict as constructive cultural techniques, it is imperative that behind the men involved there be patterns of social solidarity that are sufficiently integrated for the purposes envisioned. From this perspective it seems evident that this was the principal factor of the weaknesses and inconsistencies of the rights movements of the black population. The discontinuity and especially the historical neutralization of such movements resulted to great degree from this factor. The behavior attributed to the leaders or the masses merely expresses this factor in concrete, visible manifestations.

Factors that are not as common and without the dynamic influence of the previous four should at least be mentioned in an overall survey.

5. The effects of individual vertical social mobility led to the permanent loss of leadership for the Negro masses.

6. The black population's lack of political experience was in great part responsible for the lack of skill and maturity perchance revealed in the inept employment of certain social techniques (even in the assimilation of ideological affiliations that conflicted with the very nature and objectives of the rights movements.

7. Historical events had a destructive repercussion in the Negro milieu. The latter did not reveal the same flexibility and vitality as the rest of society in assimilating these events. The revolution of 1932, for example, temporarily paralyzed the Frente Negra Brasileira.

8. The opportunism and swindling practices, dissimulated or overt, contributed to demoralize the rights movements in the Negro milieu as much as in society at large.

9. The rights movements did not influence the black population to increase the degree of identification (individual and collective) with the objectives they espoused.

10. They did not come to assimilate the organizational patterns typical of an open, competitive, class society. They fostered tendencies of turning the black population into a monolithic racial minority, though with communication with society. This orientation had two negative effects. On the one hand it did not introduce the rights movements as a force into the structure and dynamics of the class society. On the other it was responsible for the black population's maladjustment to the existing reality in their very population that was undergoing internal differentiation.

The evidence presented here suggests how varied and complex has been the relation of the rights movements to the more or less adverse conditions and factors of the Negro milieu. The resulting limitations have influenced the structure, content, and internal dynamics of those movements. Their shortcomings (of organizational or durational order) can be explained in terms of the deficiencies of the material and psychological supports on which they depended. The other side of the coin, however, reveals that the weaknesses referred to have interfered with their constructive social functions. To the degree to which this has occurred, they have ceased to continually achieve their conscious, formal goals. The consequences of this are irremediable in terms of destroying the influence they might have either in the development of new models of solidarity among Negroes or in fostering new types of social adjustment of the Negro to society. In other words it is in the material and psychological foundations of the rights movements themselves that we encounter the explanation for the extremely limited influence they have had in changing the system of race relations.

The next issue is the constructive social function of the rights movements in integrating the Negro into the class society. In view of the wall of indifference and silence with which society surrounded those manifestations of nonconformity and revolt of the black population, it would be useless to formulate any frame of reference that involved whites in such processes. The useful effects of the movements have been limited to the participants and those who have fallen into their circle of reactive or indirect influence—that is, the segments of the black population that have shown themselves to be susceptible to the racial ideology that these movements have helped formulate.

The chief contribution of the rights movements was related to the immediate social context in which they themselves developed and operated. Resentments, frustrations, and hopes fostered a certain basic enthusiasm so that initiatives like the Frente Negra Brasileira could within a short space of time point to thousands of followers. However, it was an unsophisticated mass of unpolished and uneducated individuals in the majority without the minimal social techniques needed. The first task to give continuity to the movements consisted of reeducating the mass, in preparing it emotionally, intellectually, and psychologically for the state of being an active, responsible, and functioning group. As one of the former leaders of the Frente Negra Brasileira pointed out in his life history: "One Negro never judges another to be superior to him. At most he considers him his equal. For this reason he doesn't help other Negroes. The Negro who gets rich, for example, avoids Negroes: he never helps them or lends them money." For this reason it was necessary to encourage feelings, emotions, and psychological bonds that redounded to the increase in the sociodynamic potentials required by organizations of that type, which demanded tenacity, a sacrificing spirit, and a great sense of responsibility.

The struggle for social classification and upward mobility had to be necessarily also a struggle against color prejudice. This involved developing certain attitudes regarding the white man which were often repressed or undermined in various ways. As a primary source pointed out:

Various attempts in the direction of organizing Negroes for ends other than those of simple recreation have failed. *Reaction: this is the true meaning of this organization.* The new organization established the bases of its activities [with consideration for the fact that] it harbored in its breast Negroes of all social conditions, dealing with all aspects of the problem of living. Everything was examined in the cold light of impartiality, from the economic aspect, be it individual or collective, to political activities. In the process, the injustices and more than this, the persecutions and Machiavellianisms suffered by the Negro were focalized [R. J. Amaral, n.d., 1, italics added].

Thus it was a matter of preparing the Negro to live in society as a condition for his even becoming a productive element within the movements he joined.

Orientation became the nucleus of the formative influences of the movements. From this perspective:

The problems faced by the Negro are multiple and varied in the social aspect as well as in the psychological, intellectual, and economic ones. . . . In the first case we have the exemplification of the exclusion from societies and public places or those open to the public pending payment of admission, keeping Negroes out of civil service jobs of importance even though he doesn't lack the ability and giving him the assistance he needs in order to help him meet the situation. In the matter of psychological pressures there is this pressure that the Negro continually suffers from all sides which attempts to diminish him even in the eyes of foreigners and denies him the newly designated place to which he has a right. In the intellectual field they continually close the doors of schools on him, from primary schools to universities, denying him any kind of assistance while the government frequently gives considerable help to newcomer racial groups that undermine our social organisms. It might be said that there secretly exists a general pact against the Negro to keep him from becoming educated and rather continue out there unorganized without a roof over his head, subject to political roguery and the deceiving dangers of Carnival sambas [R. J. Amaral, n.d., 6].

Once established this base of civic education as it were, the Negro could enter the rights movements and in them learn the social roles that he would have to play in the organizations. Even though as a whole the movements failed to develop permanent cadres, it seems beyond doubt that they achieved considerable success on a more general educational level. What was understood by "organization for the sake of reacting" and "orientation" produced long-range benefits that can be perceived in our times. They not only channeled and strengthened amorphic and diffuse tendencies; they impelled vague, preexisting tendencies in new, constructive directions, imparting to them vigor and the mark of something that is irreversible for its being collective, imperative, and capable of being realized.

At the same time the rights movements governed the gradual emergence of unique psychosocial and sociocultural identification. Slavery had led to the total destruction of identification with the symbols or values of the Negro sociocultural heritage. The resulting cultural loss was never compensated

—because the forced assimilation of social techniques and patterns of behavior imposed by the dominant race could not be understood as such. The vacuum that was formed can be assessed by the gratitude with which free Negroes took to historical-sociological interpretations that "recognized the value of the Negro's historical contribution." Such interpretations opened new prospectives for the self-assessment and self-gratification of the Negro race. The axis of such interpretations, however, continued to turn around the range of interests and the social values of the white race. They did not and could not take into consideration the interests and values of the enslaved, oppressed race.

The rights movements were built around this latter axis. Consequently, the conception of the world and of the history they propagated carried with it the mark of *negritude*—that is, an understanding of the past, present, and future that was consistent with the social perspective and longings for justice of the Negro people. They began a process that is still going on and which can produce other fruits. Without rejecting solidarity with the white, the Negro has discovered that there are various ways of writing history and plotting the future. In this way he made an attempt to find his place in the historical process. It can be seen that this original contribution of the rights movements has led to unforeseeable and unfathomable consequences. It has provided a social perspective which the Negro had lacked before and from which it will be possible for him to identify with society in an autonomous way. Thus the Negroes have come to participate in the sociohistorical processes as Brazilians while retaining their own distinctive kind of "Brazilianness" deriving from specific material and psychological interests.

The Negro rediscovered his place in society owing to the violent break with the past and a fate of unalterable submission that was propagated by the rights movements on the ideological level. The fear of coming out of isolation and competing with others constituted a great obstacle. There was nothing Negroes as isolated individuals or as an independent race could do to overcome it. The source of support for over-coming this obstacle had to come from the Negro, if not as a race, at least as a collective unit. In spite of the discontinuity, fluidity, and deficiencies of the rights movements, they pro-vided this indispensable source of support both structurally and dynamically. They helped decisively to dispel fear of the white man; more important, they instilled in its place the courage to confront the white man in all spheres.

The social rights movements performed a historical task of undeniable magnitude. They broadened the cultural outlook of the Negro and better adjusted it to the nature of the class society in addition to encouraging him to depend on himself in the struggle for life through trusting in his own material and psychological resources. Above all, they taught him that "the Negro is not inferior to the white" and that his place in society will depend on what he knows he must do to use his capacities to his own advantage. All this underlines the fact that the movements constituted a force for adjustment in an era of transition. With regard to the present and the immedi-ate future, various predictions are possible. If the egalitarian tendencies of the black population reveal themselves to be timid and weak or if they are strong but the class society reveals itself to be open enough to accommodate them, the social movements will remain stagnant or will only develop their resocializing activities unilaterally. Yet they may be able to manifest themselves again with a vitality and force they did not possess in the past. Such a thing might happen if the Negro's desires for social classification and vertical mobility become too intense to be absorbed with relative speed by the class society. In such case the dynamic elements of the black population linked with the racial protest could acquire unpar-alleled importance, for its thirst for social justice continues to be unquenchable. The essential thing is that the final answer is not exclusively in the hands of the Negro. It depends on the relations that are established between his social necessities and the dynamics of the total social order.

THE EGALITARIAN FORCES OF SOCIAL

INTEGRATION

1940–1960

Introduction

It seems undeniable, from a historical and social viewpoint, that the rights movements of Negro groups were a response to the situation of racial contact which had taken shape during the establishment of the competitive social order. The imbalance existing between the economic, social, and political bases of this order and the prevailing system of race relations gave rise to the need for the Negro protest. However, that same imbalance contributed heavily to keeping the larger society indifferent to the yearnings of the black population for social integration. Society not only failed to react to the moral and political pressures of the rights movements but increased the economic, political, and social criteria for selection confronting the Negro and the mulatto with inevitable choices. Negroes either adjusted individually to the requirements of the competitive social order or were left out of the dynamics of economic growth and sociocultural development, regardless of their common desires for cultural participation.

In short, the collective hopes of the Negroes came crashing to earth. It was impossible for them to break the racial order inherited from the past by suddenly introducing into the organization of the larger society progressive tendencies to make racial relations more democratic. Nevertheless, the very consolidation of the competitive social order eventually modified the social panorama. From 1937, when the Frente Negra Brasileira closed down, to 1948, when *Alvorada* ceased publication—and simultaneously destroyed the ideal of founding the Associaçãs dos Negros Brasileinos (Association of Brazilian Negroes)—the larger society had changed to such an extent that it affected the spontaneous adherence of the Negro population to the strategy the movements had recommended. The Second World War greatly favored industrial expansion, with its effects on the differentiation of the economic system and on the pace (not to mention the method) of urbanization. Up to that time it had been urbanization that had fostered and guided industrialization. Now the situation was reversed and industrialization would determine the recrudescence of urban expansion. More than simply an industrial community, the city has become, day by day, a powerful financial center dominating economic activities. For this reason it will experience a new type of industrial growth, which will make the region known as Greater São Paulo the symbol of modern Brazil and which will govern, directly or indirectly, the vast number of undertakings involved in the transplanting of industrial civilization to the nation.

Our interest centers on the fact that these transformations were associated with the changing of the demographic, economic, and social structure of the city, to better adapt it to the normal requirements of the competitive social order. Above all, these transformations tended to correct the negative effects of the original Brazilian population by the introduction of an immigrant population in the late nineteenth and early twentieth centuries. Furthermore, the very style of life underwent drastic modification. The economic growth and sociocultural development made "Europeanization" a historical accident of the past. Tendencies developed in spatial distribution in social intercourse, and in the cultural horizon which were typical of mass society (similar, therefore, to those of the American metropolitan community).

In conjunction with the emergence of the metropolitan way of life the competitive social order is redefined both structurally and dynamically. It becomes more open, to the extent that it offers unsuspected opportunities to the speculator and the daring risk-taker, regardless of his social or ethnic origin. However, it becomes noticeably more closed insofar as opportunities are concentrated in groups which either have solid positions in the power structure or are suited to attain such positions as a starting point. Under these circumstances a sort of purge takes place in the competitive social order, whose obligations to the old agrarian and property-holding structure suffer their first collapse. From one moment to the next the past takes on the appearance of something obsolete, a harmful burden endangering the present and the future of the community. New myths begin to be developed, glorifying boldness, the mystique of strokes of luck and rational organization. In the light of these myths, both the daring planter and the ingenious and successful immigrant become examples of a petty spirit representing a bygone age.

These developments mean that purification of the competitive social order favors modern industrial capitalism and that the hiring of wage earners abides by the orders of a large-scale economy. It is at this point that the overall transformations we have described will tend to impinge on the urban populace and hence on the social situation of the black population in the city. This populace finally encounters, with an average delay of half a century (in relation to the universalization of free labor), wider means of proletarization or entry into the middle classes. It was through these means, owing to coincidences totally unrelated to racial agitation, that the Negro and the mulatto in São Paulo found themselves suddenly caught up and carried forward in the social torrent. The city, which had not heard the noise of their protest and had remained indifferent to their dreams of racial equality, opened some paths which simplified and satisfied their desires for membership in the nucleus of the legitimate social order. Thus the Negro penetrated, not as a group or as a racial category, but as individuals among the multitude of wage-earners in almost all kinds of work. This alone was not enough to put an end to resistance, ambiguities, and reservations; however, they became attenuated, blurred, or variable, depending on differences in the demand for labor.

Thus we arrive at a point where the internal tendencies for development of the competitive social order begin to undermine the material and moral bases of the traditional standard of racial relations. The whites do not try to discredit and break down the hidden perversion of racial inequality, as the Negro did through his movements. Nevertheless, whites are increasingly obliged to abandon their former conventions and expectations of behavior which denied the Negro his standing as a worthwhile, respected, and reliable partner. Let it be said, in passing, that matters are proceeding extremely slowly and with discouraging delay in the eyes of the black population. The bulk of the opportunities appeared in the areas of manual, unskilled, or semiskilled labor. From that starting point, the Negro and the mulatto began to find a response to their desires. They can already start to follow in the footsteps of the old immigrants. They know that under present circumstances things are harder. No one fills his stocking with savings, nor would that be enough to start him in profitable enterprises. Nonetheless, and this is what matters, they manage to put into practice their cherished ideals of a social life which is orderly, decent, and dignified.

In general, similar prospects divide the past and the present of the Negro in the city. The contrast should be understood more in terms of appearances, symbols, and external compensations. However, it contains some significant implications, for now some simple hopes can be realized and the future ceases to be a threat as an ignominious but inevitable reality. The feeling of being somebody can be spread and shared with a minimum of security, offering a new basis for the age-old desires for autonomy, for competition with the whites, and for social ascension. Poverty and social disorganization still prevail among the Negro population. The *favelas* (shanty slums) have replaced, and are even worse than, the sufferings of the basements and tenements. However, such living conditions affect a considerably smaller proportion of the black population. On the other hand, improvements have stifled the interest of Negroes and mulattoes in affirming themselves as a racial category. Caring little for collective movements, they try harder and harder as individuals to benefit from the existing situation. They concern themselves with race prejudice, its pernicious effects, and its eradication from Brazilian society. However, they do not immediately express this concern through collective nonconformist attitudes or behavior, nor do they believe that it would be feasible to eliminate prejudice by unilateral action on the part of black people. In short, instead of coming together to uncover and combat racial concentration of income, social prestige, and power, they prefer to compete as best they can for the opportunities that come to the poor Brazilian along the road of progress.

It is impossible to foresee how long and to what point this type of adjustment will continue. The fact is that it dominates the present scene. The Negro and the mulatto become more and more indistinct, abandoning, restraining, or remaining unaware of the goals of self-identification as part of a racial category. The counterideology, developed and disseminated by the rights movements, still germinates and bears fruit, but in silence, as if it were submerged in the deepest and most unplumbed part of the psyche. What appears on the surface is the desire to flee from the past, from the uncertainties arising from poverty and social disorganization, just as soon as each one can manage. Disappointed with the futility of collective efforts, individuals try to build, with their own resources and without depending on others, their own niches in class society. When they seek out others, they do so less in a desire for companions than out of the need for association with friends and colleagues in order to show in public the fruits of the success they have achieved. If these friends and colleagues are of the same color or face the same problems, these are eventualities that no one wants to discuss and face directly. Like the immigrants in the past, each one carries with him his own fantasies. The only difference is that the Negro is a late guest at the table and only dreams of "improving his lot," "having an opportunity," or purely and simply "living like a human being." He does not aspire to tremendous feats, for he knows that this is beyond his reach. It hurts him to see the setbacks suffered by his friends or colleagues because of their color, but this pain is alleviated by means of two rationalizations—confidence in the many opportunities for fortuitous correction of the injustices and the strong hope, which each one embraces individually, that his time will come.

Against this backdrop we must pursue our inquiries in other directions. First, we shall establish how the new trends affected the racial composition and the socioeconomic stratification of the *Paulistana* population. Second, we shall go into the process and effects of vertical social mobility among the Negro population. Third, we shall analyze the social nature and function of egalitarian forces which lead to the adjustment of the Negro and the mulatto to existing living conditions. In the following chapter we shall describe how racial pressures still weigh heavily on the behavior and the vision of the Negroes and the mulattoes of our age.

Color and Socioeconomic Stratification

The trends of economic and population growth in the city of São Paulo during the last thirty years have been reflected in several ways, both in the racial composition of the population and in the form of Negro and mulatto participation in the system of urban work. Space does not permit us here to give these questions the extensive treatment they deserve. Nevertheless, mention of some socioeconomic aspects is essential for an understanding of the problems of sociocultural dynamics to be taken up in this chapter.

The occupations pursued by the black population according to the 1940 census [1] are summarized in Figure 1 and Table 8. In Figure 1 two things stand out clearly. First, only as employ-

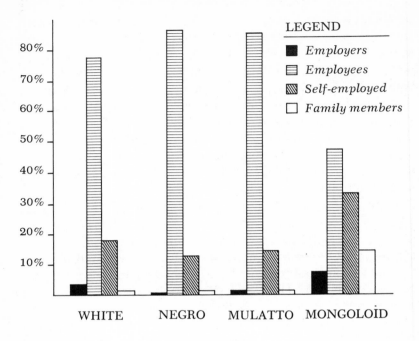

FIGURE 1

Distribution of Persons Aged 10 and over by Color and
Occupational Position, City of São Paulo, 1940

ees do the Negro and mulatto participate in the occupational
system to an extent in keeping with the proportion they represent of the population over ten years old. Second, their participation as employers is very small (indeed, almost zero), and
in the other two roles, as self-employed and members of the
employer's family, it is very low. In fact, these data suggest
that the Negro and the mulatto are still on the fringe of the
working class. On the whole the standard observed for the
white population and the Mongoloids is still inaccessible to the
Negro and the mulatto. Not only is the position of employer
almost closed off to these latter, but they are markedly concen-

TABLE 8

Distribution of Negroes and Mulattoes Aged 10 and over in Some Fields of Nondomestic Activity—City of São Paulo, 1940

(Figures in italics represent respective percentages)

Activity	Employer	Employee	Self-employed	Family member	Occupational position not known	Total
Agriculture, Stockraising, and Forestry	8 / 6.45	1,033 / 3.96	243 / 6.66	37 / 27.20	14 / 2.05	1,335 / 4.35
Extractive Industries		330 / 1.26	29 / 0.79	7 / 5.14		336 / 1.19
Manufacturing	32 / 26.01	15,279 / 58.67	492 / 13.49	25 / 18.38	64 / 9.39	15,892 / 51.89
Business	39 / 31.70	2,266 / 8.70	426 / 11.67	35 / 25.73	14 / 2.05	2,780 / 9.09
Real Estate, Credit, Insurance, and Finance		195 / 0.74	33 / 0.90			228 / 0.74
Transportation, Communications, and Warehousing	4 / 3.25	2,946 / 11.31	172 / 4.71	4 / 2.94	16 / 2.34	3,142 / 10.25
Services and Social Activities	35 / 28.45	3,633 / 13.95	2,159 / 59.21	27 / 19.85	529 / 77.67	6,383 / 20.84
Liberal Professions and Private Education	5 / 4.06	357 / 1.37	92 / 2.52	1 / 0.73	44 / 6.46	499 / 1.62
Total	123 / 100.00	26,039 / 100.00	3,646 / 100.00	136 / 100.00	681 / 100.00	30,625 / 100.00

trated in the least favorable position, with insignificant participation in the other two positions.

Table 8 enables us to view this drama in another dimension. An approximate idea of the social utilization and the
working capacity of the Negro and the mulatto may be gathered from their occupational position in different fields of
economic activity. There is a distinct concentration of the
position of employer in three main fields—in order of importance, business, services, and social activities, and manufacturing industries. More than half of those occupying the position of employee are linked to manufacturing industries and
more than a quarter are distributed among three areas: services and social activities; transportation, communications,
and warehousing; and business. Similarly, more than half of
the self-employed are engaged in one field of activity (services
and social activities) and another third are engaged in either
of two areas (manufacturing and business). Those who occupy positions as members of a family are distributed among
four main activities: agriculture, livestock raising, and forestry; business; services and social activities; and manufacturing.

The proportion of Negroes and mulattoes of both sexes
engaged in domestic services is high. This is particularly noticeable among women, however; the numbers of domestics
out of 100 women of each color group are as follows: 4.53
white, 35.44 Negroes, 23.61 mulattoes, and 3.99 Mongoloids.
It seems obvious that the participation of the black population
in the city's occupational system follows heterogeneous tendencies. An apparently small portion of this population finds
itself in occupations and secondary positions characteristic of
the occupational structure of the class system. Another portion, apparently considerable,[2] remains linked to occupations
and secondary positions typical of preindustrialism and precapitalism. In the absence of other indicators we should pay
careful attention to this historic fact, which is not only the
result of an unfavorable heritage but also a condition providing a fundamental explanation for the integrative weaknesses

of the black population. There is difference between living in, and belonging to, a class society. Only the Negroes and the mulattoes who comprise the first portion really enjoy, partially or totally, class situations (as entrepreneurs, skilled or semi-skilled workers, etc.). The remainder find themselves in peripheral or marginal situations which do not lead to professionalization, or to proletarianization, or to the accumulation of capital. For these the occupational drama has somber overtones, for it takes place on the boundary which effectively separates the Negro from the white population.

From this angle, the standard of occupational distribution attained by the white population defines a minimum that the black population must achieve in order to break down the material disparities existing between the two racial strains. Since analogous data are not available for the censuses of 1950 and 1960, we cannot say categorically in which direction matters have evolved. Apparently, as in the past, the changes have been more quantitative than qualitative. In other words, data from 1940 show that there has been a remarkable increase in the number of Negroes who have become free workers. At the same time it can be seen that their incorporation into the regime of free workers does not, in itself, constitute inclusion in the class system. The numbers of those who have proletarianized themselves and those who have entered the middle classes seem to be notoriously smaller. These two orientations seem to continue to be present, although the growing opportunities to become free workers have, in turn, continuously increased the opportunities for real classification of the Negro and the mulatto under the class system.

The total of 381 men and women [3] were grouped according to occupation in 1951: artisans, 29.39 per cent; domestic services, 20.76 per cent; government employees, 9.18 per cent; skilled or semiskilled industrial workers, 8.13 per cent; office workers, 7.08 per cent; sales workers, 4.46 per cent; variable or occasional work, 3.93 per cent; horticulture and gardening, 2.33 per cent; and in other occupations, 14.69 per cent. These data reinforce the hypotheses we have expressed.

Apparently regular employment of the Negro and the mulatto is greatest in the area of activities most affected by rapid urban growth, where there is a relative shortage of skilled, semiskilled, or unskilled workers. This explains why the greatest opportunities for professional work exist in the artisan trades. It seems clear that in at least two ways traditional tendencies prevail, as shown by the data for the employment of Negroes and mulattoes in domestic services and by the government. As for the trends toward professionalization initiated by industrialization, the expansion of administrative services, and the growth in trade, it seems obvious that the opportunities are still limited. Finally, the situation of the independent artisan and of those who live by odd jobs does not come up to expectation (not even to the expectations of Negro respondents who are well informed and knowledgeable regarding the "métier"). This situation is expressed by a percentage that is apparently too low.[4]

In general, therefore, the important difference with regard to the recent past concerns the acquisition of a steady source of income. In other words the Negro and the mulatto have obtained ways of earning a living which give them regular (and sometimes permanent) positions among the free workers. Nevertheless, these positions do not always assure them of classification in the capitalist system of productive relationships. For this reason they are connected in various ways with occupations that are poorly paid and represent rather precarious forms of participation in the power structure of the larger society. From these standpoints there is a considerable difference from the past, especially considering the situations described in Chapters 1 and 2. But this difference is merely one of degree. Negroes and mulattoes are still blindly struggling to convert their work as free men into a means of socioeconomic classification and vertical social mobility.

In view of this, it is not surprising that the black man continues to be inwardly dissatisfied with his occupational situation and its social consequences. The results of our questionnaire show that the occupational specialization of the

Negro and the mulatto is still largely a matter of chance. Thus, to the question, "Do you have any profession?" we obtained the following replies:

	Men	Women	Total
Yes	250	119	369
No	11	11	22

Combining these data with those provided in answer to later questions we can draw some interesting conclusions. Thus, to the question, "How did you learn it?" they replied as follows:

	Men	Women	Total
At home	2	20	22
At school	37	19	56
On the job	217	82	299

To another question, "Can you engage in other work?" they replied:

	Men	Women	Total
Yes	231	112	343
No	30	14	44

These data not only show the role played by chance in the adoption of occupations and professions but also make it clear that the choice is made on an opportunistic basis depending on offers or opportunities arising around them. The extent to which this causes marked dissatisfaction among the respondents is expressed openly in the replies to the question, "In what profession would you like to work?"

	Men	Women	Total
The same one	60	18	78
A different one	184	101	285

It is noteworthy that this fluctuation is not due to a warped or perverted view of reality. Only one man and one woman replied no to the question, "Do you think one should have a profession?" The remainder (252 men and 125 women) replied yes. On the other hand, two questions permit us an indirect evaluation of the kind of perception that the Negro and the mulatto have acquired with regard to occupational competition:

1. "Do you think one should go to school to become better acquainted with one's own specialty?" [5]

	Men	Women	Total
Yes	206	101	317
No	9	5	14
"It's better"	16	16	32
"Not always"	16	8	24

2. "Do you think a good specialist always finds work in his field?"

	Men	Women	Total
Yes	206	105	311
No	11	3	14
Sometimes	39	22	61

The replies make it clear that the Negro and the mulatto have full rational awareness of the qualifications demanded by occupational competition. The fact that 19.5 per cent of the men and 19.2 per cent of the women chose the negative alternatives presupposed by the last question even expresses the degree of consensus existing with regard to the effects of "race prejudice." In fact, we received the following answers to the question:

"Do you think that being black limits one's opportunities?"

	Men	Women	Total
Yes	149	77	226
No	86	40	126
Sometimes	8	8	16
Partially	10	3	13

Therefore 66 per cent of the men and 68 per cent of the women in the group under consideration definitely hold the point of view that race prejudice is a negative factor in occupational competition, while 59 per cent of the men and 60 per cent of the women express this opinion categorically, as indicated by their preference for the first alternative. Despite this conviction, they realize objectively that intellectual and technical qualifications are of primordial importance for occupational competition.[6] This fact shows, in our opinion, that the dissatisfaction in question is directly linked to repeated and general frustration of desires on the part of the black population for occupational adjustment.

In order to understand this frustration it is necessary to have clearly in mind what work represents to the Negro in the competitive social order. Because of his origin he has no other way of redeeming his past and establishing himself socially. In other words, work becomes the only link capable of joining his destiny, for the time being, to the formula that inspired and guided our bourgeois revolution—"free work in a free country." In short, he depends on work to establish a socioeconomic foundation and to build on this the material or moral bases of his standing as a human being. For this reason, what he does and how much he earns become matters of little importance in his immediate calculations, which revolve, literally, around sociocultural objectives combining the acquisition of a steady source of income with regular participation in a regular standard and style of life. Consequently the Negro refuses to compete for mere survival. He desires the kinds of work that qualify a man, not only economically but socially and politically. In other words, he wants to compete for types of work that produce social benefits, giving people social classification and introducing them into the spirals of vertical social mobility. Such reasons really interest him in the alternatives offered by professionalization and in the paths open to him in the competitive social order.

From this social perspective it is difficult to reconcile the most realistic and modest ambitions with the potentialities of the existing situation. Analysis of the ideal occupations indicated by both men and women reveals three constant features. First, with some variations, they are, as a rule, real occupations which have been achieved by Negro workers who have managed to become classified through them. Second, they are also, with some exceptions (which even seem reasonable in the light of personal possibilities), highly accessible occupations in an expanding urban society like São Paulo. Third, they are strongly concentrated in the age group from 16 to 35 for men, particularly between 21 and 30, and in a variable way between 16 and 40 for women. Everything indicates, therefore, that the crucial points are the level of the job, the steadiness of income, and the total social prestige—elements which go to make up the social aspects of the occupations. As a result, in expressing his plans for a career, the Negro inevitably focuses on certain occupations with well-defined intentions of social classification and ascension.[7] Looking at himself in such a frame of mind he often has ample reason to feel pessimistic and frustrated in view of the chances offered to him by current occupational opportunities.

Accordingly, when collecting personal data we have paid careful attention to the existing opportunities for work. Starting from the premise that change in the economic and social position of the Negro and the mulatto is a function of structural changes in their position in the occupational system, we have tried to examine as closely as possible the negative and positive aspects of current trends.

With regard to the negative aspects one thing is obvious: there are still structural obstacles to the constructive adjustment of the Negro to the free work system and, what is more important, to his movement from the fringe to the heart of the relationship system of capitalist production. Limiting ourselves to the essential, we can discern five active sources of structural difficulties: the interference of negative stereotyping in the social definition of the Negro worker by limiting his working opportunities; the uneven previous socialization of the Negro worker; the harmful effects of his present way of life; the compulsive effects of his complex; and conformity. As a rule several obstructive factors operate simultaneously to make the most modest occupational successes into real feats. The following condensed description merely attempts to convey a general idea of the influences which contribute to make the Negro worker a case apart.

Without doubt, negative stereotyping interferes in two important respects: First, it establishes the pattern for social definition of the Negro and hence the desirable or undesirable characteristics of the Negro worker. Second, it regulates the manner in which the white man applies a code of appraisal and recognition of worth which is wholly unfavorable to the Negro and consequently to his occupational aspirations. In fact, the free work regime grew and consolidated itself in São Paulo under a monopoly of all basic positions by the white man. This practically excluded the Negro from the white man's cultural horizon, not just as a legitimate competitor but even as someone who should be considered in matters of any importance. As a result a paradoxical situation arose. From the beginning, and even today, the Negro worker needs considerate understanding and constant protection, whether he is beginning a career or continuing in one, in order to use his capacity for work to the maximum, for himself, for his employers, and for the community. Negative stereotyping not only kept the white man from discovering this aspect of reality but also produced something worse: a universal, invisible barrier preventing any rapid redefinition of the Negro's image that might have facilitated the transition from slavery to free work and at least accelerated the proletarianization of the black man. In this way there was created and maintained a climate of moral appraisal of the Negro which inevitably instilled a residual distortion into the attitude of employers, supervisors, colleagues, subordinates, and clients. Instead of considerate understanding and constant protection the Negro finds a mechanism of appraisal which strongly contributes to his maladjustment and to his elimination from the competitive arena.

Leaving aside those who judge that "the Negro is really inferior" and exclude him systematically and totally from their firms and organizations,[8] we shall give here some restrictive appraisals consciously made in firms which accept or tolerate the hiring of Negroes. In general such appraisals are consistent with stereotypes that convert the Negro into the opposite of the white man or into the very image of the "anti-white" man. These are appraisals of the type already described in Chapters 2 and 3, representing the Negro as "shiftless," "irresponsible," "cheeky," "lacking in character," "inefficient," "careless," "of doubtful morals," and so on; they are sometimes less strong with regard to the mulatto who, however, is rejected even more insistently when he is classified as "a typical Carioca mulatto" or a "lazy, cheeky fellow." As a result of such premises the white men fall into the traps prepared by their own statements. The heads of personnel sections in large firms show us how frequent this is and how it almost follows a standard pattern, of which the following statement is characteristic: "In reality the mental level of the Negro is inferior to that of the white man. They don't seem to have the same intelligence or the same capacity for work and for organization." This context for appraisal gives rise to a policy of cold animosity toward the Negro worker. There is no systematic discrimination against him, but he is not judged impartially. He goes from one place to another at the whim of circumstances which considerably hinder his illusions and his hopes of getting a good job. We give below a small collection of statements showing the tenor and the nature of the restrictive and ethnocentric appraisals made of the Negro worker: [9]

In the construction industry: "They are very rough and ready. They only work when they need money. Then they stop. In time they learn, but they don't like to work regular hours every day. . . . They are very touchy. You can't shout at them or criticize them."

In a large commercial firm: "They have no capacity for organized work. They like their freedom more than white men. That is why you cannot count on them for work. . . . They work one or two days, but when they have the money they need they stay away for another two days. That is no good for a business firm in which everything is regulated.

Now white people are not like that. They don't want to be so independent."

In a commercial organization with various branches, the head of the personnel section frankly informed us that he did not hire black persons, even when they were well recommended. We asked, "Why don't you hire black employees? Because of the public?" The reply was: "Not so much because of the public. In our business that would not be very important. It is because of the work itself. I need people who have certain qualities. First of all, it must be someone honest in whom I can have confidence. The majority of the Negroes have no sense of responsibility and may take what is not theirs. Then again, in a firm dealing in parts for automobiles, one must be careful. The parts cannot be taken out of their place and then left just anywhere. They must go back to their place. Order is essential in a firm like this. That is something impossible to get with Negroes, who are very sloppy. Another important thing is cleanliness. A person must be very clean, not only because of the customers, but because of the work itself. A great deal of care is necessary in working with parts. Negroes are nearly always very dirty. The fourth quality is education. To do my work, a person must be able to read, write, and make calculations. Without that, he cannot make out the sales tickets. It is hard to find Negroes with enough education."

In a small store the manager alleged that he did not accept black girls in the shop as a result of unfortunate experiences: "They are rude and easily irritated. They quarrel with their supervisors."

In a banking establishment: "All our work requires contact with the public and under our policy of pleasing and favorably impressing the client in the smallest details, we demand that our employees be persons intellectually qualified and of good appearance. Just the fact of being colored spoils the appearance."

In a large office: [10] "It is wise not to educate a Negro and for this reason I don't make it a practice to help them. They have a precarious way of life, they grow up in poverty, and they don't know how to behave themselves. A candidate for office boy comes swaggering up like a little tough guy, leans on your desk and says: 'I am going to work here. Do you have anything for me to do?' They are very forward and you always have to be careful to see that they don't start running you." In other respects, the same personnel officer said: "Negroes show no mental agility. They are routine employees and do not adapt themselves to new work. We have a draughtsman whose section was eliminated, and we have had a lot of difficulty with him because he cannot adapt himself to the new work. . . . It seems to me that they don't worry about making a career. They get to be clerks and stay at that level. No Negro has yet appeared with ability to occupy higher positions." Most of the firm's employees begin work as office boys. However, he explained candidly: "For these jobs I don't accept Negroes and I have no trouble rejecting them because they are still children and don't guess the reason for their rejection."

In a large factory the head of the personnel section said that "the Negro is not a good worker," and he avoided hiring Negroes. And then as a summary of his justifications: "In the case of a man, lack of sexual morality, which is very serious in factories where almost all the workers are women. . . . In the case of women, the reason is their extreme mobility. They don't stay in any job." The head of the placement section of a large employment agency explained that the restrictions are so severe in some factories that even to place Negroes in just simple jobs, such as driver, bag-filler, and sweeper, there were insuperable objections: "It is particularly difficult to place Negroes as night watchmen because they are thought not to do the job properly. They sleep, drink, things like that."

In a large private firm, a public utility: "We have both white persons and Negroes in all kinds of work, but the latter are few in number. Hiring is done by rational selection. We place no obstacle in the way of Negroes because, if we did, we would be going against our own past. In order not to create problems for the Negroes themselves we avoid placing them in jobs requiring contact with the public. The situation in which the company says no to everybody could lead someone to react against the employee and to insult him because of his color. A situation like this [could lead to well-known ways of redressing an insult]: 'I could go out there and sock him in the jaw.' Indeed, it seems that the Negroes themselves understand the situation and do not apply for jobs requiring contact with the public."

These examples are enough to illustrate the most dramatic aspect of the occupational situation of the Negro. He is viewed in a system of reference that distorts his person and his capacity for human achievement. For this reason he is not always able to prove, by means of concrete experience, what he is capable of doing and how far he can go. It is irrelevant whether he has professional aspirations or not, since they come up against such varied and tenacious resistance that they wither or cool before they can produce results. No doubt we are faced with attitudes and appraisals that reveal the past in the present and that are fated to disappear gradually. But they persist tenaciously and continuously reshape the present and the future of the Negro in accordance with his past. We must therefore examine the social functions that such attitudes and appraisals perform as long as they remain on the historical scene.

It seems clear that the stereotyping described above would be normal in a caste society. On the other hand we obviously receive it as an inevitable inheritance from the master and slave system. To the extent that stereotyping persists and multiplies today, this is an indication that there are social conditions and needs that maintain and renew it. Specifically, in the professional sphere, it serves to keep in force differential criteria for the social appraisal, encouragement, and recognition of work. It confers on the white man the right, the power, and even the duty to resist redefinition of the occupational roles of the Negro and therefore to limit the egalitarian effects of professional democratization. In short, if stereotyping does not legitimate the double standard of occupational appraisal, it at least justifies it as the result of chance. Thus the white man does not exactly try to protect himself from professional competition with the Negro, he simply makes it impossible. As a result, the way is open to keep "the Negro in his place," in this case doing "Negro's work," and the white man himself maintains a whole rich arsenal of rationalizations to justify and make sense of his exclusivist attitudes or behavior. Thanks to these rationalizations he wields a dangerous two-edged weapon, the principal effects of which are well known. It permits the application of open favoritism for the white worker and his professional aspirations or achievements. At the same time it fosters a kind of inverted realism toward the Negro worker and his professional aspirations or achievements.

There are four frequent negative applications of this realism. First, it nourishes a fierce rejection of the Negro worker in general through impersonal justifications. In these cases the white agent blames the rural system from which the Negro comes as the cause of his professional inexperience and inability. Second, it prompts resistance, which is relatively strong and generalized, against the utilization of the Negro and the mulatto in important positions or in jobs requiring supervision, administration, and leadership. Third, in various ways it encourages the policy of letting the Negro go just so far. As a result, those who manage to carry out their occupational aspirations come up against limitations of another kind which inevitably limit their area of professional competition. This policy is so well known that the Negro himself knows beforehand how far he can go. For example, a Negro clerk who was about to be promoted to chief storeman, said to the interviewer: "I know, however, that I will not rise above this position. To do better I will have to change my employer." Fourth, in situations where competition between the Negro and the white man tends to favor the plans of the former, it makes it possible to resort tacitly to procedures outside the rules of the game. Usually the practices employed consist in spreading rumors, slandering the person in question and showing his hand, thus allowing the latent hostility to appear. This kind of behavior is not considered unfair by white people, and is only called dirty and deprecated when the agents do not moderate it and keep it on apparently impersonal grounds. In this way the white man refuses to share with the Negro the socioeconomic security conferred by professionalization and by free occupational competition and does not risk involving himself in economic conflicts based on race, which would inevitably be devastating.

The other three dynamic sources of structural difficulties place the Negro himself in the center of the stage and lead him to provide ammunition for the white man, as the Negro is somewhat inclined to take advantage of the evidence that justifies his negative stereotypes and the corresponding rationalizations. Negroes and white alike are subjected to the economic mechanisms and the competitive processes of the capitalist organization of productive relationships. Since the black population is continuously enlarged and renewed by internal migration, its dilemmas in this respect are like the heads of Medusa. Scarcely have certain segments of a generation begun to adjust themselves to the adaptive and integrative mechanisms of a capitalist economy in society when other segments of the same generation or of other generations come to the surface, with the same sociocultural inconsistencies and inadequacies. The dilemmas are renewed in concentric circles, constantly returning to their starting point. This does not prevent growing portions of the black population from creating their niche in the great metropolis. But the problem of maladjustment to work is kept alive as a permanent reality.

The effects of the limitations resulting from insufficient previous socialization are well known and have been examined in the last chapter in connection with the mechanisms of societal reaction among Negro groups. Without question they reduce the opportunities available to the majority of Negro workers, preventing them from rising above Negro's work and causing inadequate adjustment to the capitalist economy and to an urban society. Of course feelings of security and stable competitive attitudes require involvement in the occupational structure and socialization by experience, that is, by work. The Negro has only had late and incomplete access to this opportunity. For this reason he does not always master the social techniques of free labor and those required by the modern company (and rarely becomes skillful in them) because he is incapable of adjusting himself fully to the social roles of the laborer, the entrepreneur, the member of a liberal profession, the buyer and seller, the administrator. He is notably lacking in qualifications for occupations which were or still are monopolized by the white man. These circumstances have given rise to a very general tendency to build up an artificial cultural horizon and a distorted view of apprenticeship. A man says he is qualified to work as a carpenter or bricklayer because he thinks it is simple to handle a saw, a hammer and nails, a shovel, a pick, a trowel, and a wood float; another time, after a short apprenticeship, he already considers himself a tradesman, a competent specialist, able to do any work in the occupation; again with poor training and limited experience, he tackles jobs which he thinks are "up to his level." These false notions on the part of the free worker and this simplification of the mechanisms of economic competition do not affect only the Negro. They affect to some extent all those waves of workers who are under the burden of a primitive sociocultural heritage. But the Negro and the mulatto are particular victims. Insofar as their color compels them to anxiously scrutinize the external signs and the moral or material compensations of their social position, they are more likely to persist in this obstacle race where the rule is "to put the cart before the horse." This results in systematic occupational maladjustment and repeated disillusionment which, in time, corrode and tear apart his constructive inclination for work and occupational competition. Besides this general propensity there are other frequent negative manifestations, frequent but circumscribed, of his lack of previous socialization. The most obvious one concerns occupational and competitive inequality with regard to the white man. The so-called "lack of minimum qualification for the job" functions at this level, mowing down wholesale those who try to pass from Negro's work to a better job. For example, the manager of a store told the interviewer: "When hiring we give an arithmetic test and this fact eliminates them [the black candidates]. The majority of those who come to us are domestic servants, who do not know how to add." Another frequent manifestation is related to the way they persist in unsuitable adjustment to salaried work. The following illustration is typical. A carpenter was approached by a young Negro. He needed an assistant and tried to use the young man. "I asked him if he knew how to hold a hammer and drive nails. He said yes. He began to work the same day. But the next morning he arrived at 7:30 [half an hour late] and went slowly up the ladder. The following day he was even later. I criticized him: 'Here, boy, if you want to learn and to work you won't go very far that way!' He replied immediately: 'If you want, that's how it is! I am nobody's slave! If you ain't satisfied, pay me off.'" The informant fired him immediately.

Finally, we must consider a whole series of manifestations related to the content of the rural cultural outlook and to the traditional pattern of relations with the white man. As to the content of the rural cultural outlook three effects warrant consideration. First, it fosters a partial or total lack of ability to observe and take advantage of work opportunities existing in a growing urban environment; second, a tendency to cling to levels of occupational aspiration which are too narrow and unrewarding, seriously restricting the competitive potentiality of the Negro worker; and third, a tendency for parents to encourage their children to have modest aspirations and to make occupational choices in keeping with their position. Attitudes and behavior of this kind help to keep the Negro and the mulatto prisoner in the rural world from which they came. These attitudes and this behavior are not peculiar to Negroes and mulattoes since the same applies to white workers with a rural background. It so happens, however, that when these manifestations appear they are not alone but are associated with an image built up in the slave days. In other words, the idea recurs that "certain jobs are not for us," as if the white monopoly of strategic occupations still prevailed.

The compulsive effect of the "complex" [11] interferes in the occupational adjustment of the Negro in three different ways. First, it arouses a strong fear of rejection because of color. The results of the interviews suggest that this fear can be overcome with relative ease in the initial stages of a career and does not prevent him in any way from taking the opportunities that arise in occupations where acceptance of the Negro worker is traditionally safe. It arouses a fear of frustration from the moment a state of active competition with the white man for fairly good jobs appears. At this point, the dominant tendency is to look on the successes already obtained as a satisfactory reward. Feeling himself to be in a safe position (as a professional man or as assistant to a section or department head in a company, for example), he prefers to be satisfied with what he has and gives up the struggle for new promotions. The nature of this psychosocial effect seems to be quite clear. It spontaneously restricts his level of economic and professional competition with the white man. On the other hand the same complex leads to attitudes and behavior characterized by withdrawal in which people isolate themselves voluntarily or involuntarily from frequent contact with whites having higher social prestige. This factor also interferes in the level of career followed by the Negro and the mulatto. As a rule, at fairly high levels of economic and professional competition they fail to have social relationships which might help them carry out their occupational aspirations.

Second, there is a kind of folklore about the manifestations of race prejudice. News of rejections, actually or supposedly prompted by color, circulate and spread quite fast. If evidence accumulates that certain firms reject black candidates systematically, these firms get a reputation for being discriminatory and are less and less sought out by these candidates. The head of the personnel section of a factory which limited the hiring of black workers to Negro's work by order of the management confirmed this tendency. "Thus," he said," black persons seldom come here looking for a job."

The two effects described above help to make the occupational ambitions of the Negro highly vulnerable, seriously limiting both their levels of occupational aspiration and their career standards. A third effect is that rejections because of color, real or imagined, give rise to self-commiseration and compensating reactions which encourage complacency and unrealistic attitudes to defend the balance of the ego. These psychological reactions are useful to the Negro and the mulatto because they allow them to develop explanations for the causes of their failure in attempts to get a job or obtain the promotions they deserve. When they attribute their lack of success to racial prejudice, individuals carry on as before but to the detriment of their ability to improve themselves and therefore to compete professionally. A considerable portion of the black population has already discovered this fact and insists that, regardless of the apparent reason for rejection, a Negro should ask himself if he is competent or not and should take care to constantly improve his ability in his field of activity.

Finally, conformity appears in various forms. As part of the cultural heritage from a rural past, it still affects an important part of the black population. In this case it leads to unfavorable occupational adjustments and limits the average level of aspiration to what the whites define as "Negro's work" or to jobs which are "the best they can do." There is a second kind of conformity that is the result of being fooled and of studying in the school of disappointment. Judging by the results of our questionnaires, almost all Negro and mulatto workers are affected. They are those who despondently repeat variations of these typical replies: "I work because I have to, but one is certainly humiliated here"; "I have to stay in this job. There is nothing else I can do. But I hate my work." There is another, much more complex, manifestation of conformity which affects those who are relatively successful in carrying out their career plans. Quite often, having reached the occupational positions they wanted, instead of entering into the prevailing competitive spirit these people try to build up prestige by virtue of the exemplary nature of their capacity for professional achievement. As a result, they enjoy the great admiration of their employers, their supervisors, their subordinates, and their colleagues, that is, the type of prestige they wanted. Upon analysis, however, these cases reveal something in common—the achievement criteria being used are of an artisan nature and conflict in various ways with the requirements of a competitive society. The individual achieves his immediate objective but irremediably prejudices his long-term career. The impression is immediately created that "so-and-so is very good at the work he is now doing but unfortunately is no use for anything else." Alternatively, there is the more cruel and more generalized appraisal that "the Negro is only suitable for routine work." These observations, which we have limited to the strictly necessary, indicate how conformity, in any of its forms, becomes a source of limitations both in the establishment of levels of occupational aspiration and in the practical application of standards of occupational adjustment and professional achievement. Conformity, springing from different psychosocial and sociocultural causes, prevents the Negro and the mulatto from properly mobilizing the social techniques of occupational and professional competition that society requires.

Alongside these adverse factors and effects, there are other influences which help the Negro worker to adjust to the dynamic and structural requirements of the competitive social order. The rapid economic expansion that began in late 1939 profoundly affected the composition and the organization of the Brazilian labor system. Although the opportunities which arose did not benefit Negroes and whites to the same degree, large sections of the black population managed to greatly change their position in the labor market. Here we are principally interested in three basic changes brought about by the economic expansion. The general scarcity of manpower produced a strong quantitative pressure, which was particularly important for those strata of the population which were on the periphery of the capitalist labor system. Not only did numerous work opportunities and prospects of permanent employment arise, but there was also an economic and social reevaluation of the work which had formerly been classified as Negro's work. Owing to these circumstances there was a change in the prevailing evaluation of manual labor and its significance for personal dignity. Finally, a starting point was reached permitting the Negro to adjust himself to those occupations which would not wound important susceptibilities, but rather would increase his economic and social value. This quantitative explosion was significant in several respects. It permitted a rapid reabsorption of the Negro and the mulatto into work within the artisan labor system, from which they had been driven out by competition from immigrants. Thus, there were many more opportunities for work in the construction industry (particularly as bricklayers and bricklayers' helpers, but also as contractors, painters, carpenters, plumbers, electricians, etc.), in repair shops, in carpenter and cabinet-making shops, in upholstery stores, butcher shops, etc. At the same time, in addition to the availability of heavy work, there were opportunities which opened the doors of factories and offices to the Negro worker. Several heads of personnel sections have reported that these openings depended on the supply of and demand for employment. Where "there was no other way," with good or with ill will they resorted to employing Negroes. The overall effects of quantitative pressure were of special importance to the Negro woman. During the crisis in the former labor system she had been more protected than the man but, in compensation, she had been practically restricted to domestic services. Scarcity of manpower helped initiate her liberation from this invisible yoke. Gradually she found new opportunities in the artisan sector (in dressmaking, embroidery, bookbinding, etc.), and she reached new positions in factories, stores, and offices.

Corresponding to this quantitative expansion there was

qualitative pressure of exceptional importance. The great barrier caused by irrational interference with appraisal criteria had its origin in color. Economic growth obliged many firms in all economic categories to select, supervise, and promote personnel in a more strictly technical manner. Interviews with white administrators and with Negro and mulatto employees of various kinds show that this amounted to a veritable revolution in favor of the economic and occupational interests of the black population. Many firms only considered white candidates, and others had means of downgrading or neutralizing results which are favorable to black candidates. Nevertheless, progress was considerable. In large organizations, whether private or governmental, rational techniques of selection, supervision, and promotion of personnel stressed the candidates' qualifications and work productivity. Color was a secondary consideration or, for many purposes, purely and simply ignored. Owing to the effect of this qualitative pressure, the Negro and the mulatto found specific opportunities in work for which they had previously been avoided or rejected in offices, factories, banks, large commercial firms, etc.

These two effects are combined. The Negro worker admitted into the occupational structure of the production system gains new possibilities and incentives for reeducating himself for free labor. At first acceptance may be tentative, being conceded "despite the fact that he does not know the work well." Gradually the initial difficulties are overcome. The time comes when the Negro worker is recognized as a competent, respected tradesman. These changes embrace not only physical skills—the way energy is used and movements are trained—but also the Negro's mentality—the way he understands his position in society, his rights or duties as a worker, and the future of his children. New occupational aspirations are formed, new career standards, and a cultural outlook appropriate for one who is entering a profession. It is not simply a question of wanting a job as in the past, but rather one of wanting to arrive at the top, of competing for positions which used to be partially or totally inaccessible and of defining himself professionally on equal terms with the white man.

At this point we enter the area of incentives and social motivation. In reeducating himself for the free labor system, the Negro repudiates his rural cultural heritage and the burden which it represents. He overcomes precapitalist or anticapitalist habits, appraisals, and behavior and discovers the position that makes him the material and social equal of the white man—that which is offered by his occupation. Thus, not only does a new type of Negro legend arise—the legend of success—but one that pays dividends. Those who achieve their occupational ambitions serve as examples; others try to imitate them. An awareness grows that the Negro can equal the white man in work and in responsibility. Those who share this awareness have the opportunity to rid themselves of the dangerous protection provided by the use of race prejudice as a scapegoat. They stop explaining their disappointments and failures in this simple way and try to prepare themselves technically and morally for full competition with their white colleagues. At the same time entry into a real class places the Negro in the midst of class demands and the ideological struggles that divide society. Although he still resists proletarianization and values professional class symbols as instruments of social self-assertion, the experience broadens his understanding of equality with the white man and strengthens his competitive tendencies in the occupational area. Finally, he begins to have solid ground under his feet. His stable occupation not only assures him a position in society and a conception of the world but also develops the dynamic and structural basis the lack of which prevented him from participating normally in the competitive social order. Now he can think about bringing up his children, about the future of his family, about having a home and a better standard of living, and so on. Here we have a whole chain of links and motivations that create and generalize fairly substantial ideals of social improvement. He discovers that he is not the slave of his work, but that through work he can liberate and assert himself socially. When he establishes this view of reality, the Negro worker ceases to be a victim of his past and begins to use work as the only means at his disposal for carrying out his desire for social ascension and for making the white man accept him as an equal.

Few came to share this attitude. In fact the interviews revealed this kind of security only in a handful of intellectuals, members of liberal professions, technicians, and working-class leaders. The important thing, for the time being, is not the number of them but the trends that the small number enables us to observe. At this point we can close the historical circle that we opened in the first two chapters. The Negro as a free worker can be foreseen as a historical reality without distortions, as he probably will be in the near future. These conclusions lead us to a fundamental observation. The capitalist system was unfavorable to the Negro in his origins, not because of the insuperable limitations of the Negro worker but because he was treated, both before and after his liberation, as a sort of outcast. As the capitalist system itself expands and diversifies and the Negro worker finds really promising work opportunities within it, he is not only capable of seizing these opportunities, but does so in a way that is well known to be constructive. By so doing, he refutes those who, in the late nineteenth and early twentieth centuries, preached his "innate inferiority" and his "incapability of adapting himself to modern technology" and proves that the Second Abolition is under way. This Second Abolition really began when the Negro started to convert himself systematically into a free worker and it will end when he has overcome, through his efforts and the fruit of his own labor, the barriers that separate free men in a class society.

By fitting themselves into the nucleus of the occupational system of the larger society, the Negro and the mulatto gain social classification and begin to belong to the competitive social order. However, there are no data available on the degree to which this has taken place or is taking place among the black population. In a study published in 1938, Lowrie divided the society of the city of São Paulo into three strata:

the upper class, the working class, and the semidependent class.[12] This stratification is arbitrary, but it shows how difficult it is to define class position in a sector that remained more or less outside the competitive social order. Lowrie's discoveries suggest that the lower or semidependent class included, at the time, a considerable part of the black population. It is still not known, however, how recent alterations in the composition and organization of the labor system affected the socioeconomic stratification of the city. It is clear that they increased the number of Negroes and mulattoes having a class position.

Our observations disclosed two general trends. First, almost all those parts of the black population who managed to achieve social classification belong to the proletariat.[13] Second, the Negro and the mulatto tend to attain occupations or professions at an income level ensuring a standard of living and social prestige roughly characteristic of the middle classes of the larger society. Our evidence indicates that this trend affects a very small number of people. In addition, there are occasional cases where black individuals and Negro families really belong to the higher strata in the system.

Close examination of these two overall trends indicate that the absorption of the Negro into class society goes on at the same rate as his conversion into a free worker. For the time being it is impossible to describe the morphology of this process precisely. The Negro himself conceals the differences between the two strata. The importance of social classification in itself is so great that any sacrifice is justified as long as it provides social prestige, real or apparent. Thus the Negro woman who is a well-paid cook can display a standard of life equal to that of a Negro journalist or lawyer. In the eyes of the black population the external signs of status are what count. Individuals are considered as rich or having a prestigious position, which creates heterogeneous elites and a middle class with uncertain characteristics, characterized much less by real income and by position in the power structure of society than by style of life. This style of life is remarkable for its elaborate etiquette and refinements intentionally based on aristocratic, professional models.[14]

Since the attainment of social position is the real struggle of the black middle classes, there are obvious changes in their relationships with the whites and with the members of other Negro groups, changes corresponding to the social stratification mentioned above. For the first time they show certain tendencies to restrict racial interaction to the strata of the white population at the same social level. If these tendencies had taken root and grown stronger, it would seem that the occupational revolution now in progress was really contributing to a modification in the very structure of the system of race relations. However, it is not clear that this is occurring on a significant scale. Data on intermarriage in 1961, for example, indicate that the old standards for choosing marriage partners still prevail (see Table 9). Marriages usually take

TABLE 9

Marriages, by Color of Spouse, City of São Paulo, 1961

Men	Women				Total
	White	Mulatto	Negro	Mongoloid	
White	30,167	541	85	71	30,864
Mulatto	723	1,914	164	2	2,803
Negro	94	215	558	1	868
Mongoloid	87	2	—	877	966
Total	31,071	2,672	807	951	35,501

SOURCE: Situação Demográfica, Departamento de Estatística do Estado, Govêrno do Estado de São Paulo (separate of the Anuário, 1961) São Paulo, 1963, p. 10.

place between persons of the same color (97.74 per cent among whites, 68.28 per cent among mulattoes, 64.28 per cent among Negroes); the number of marriages between whites and mulattoes and Negroes is very small (1.75 per cent and 0.27 per cent respectively); and marriages between mulattoes and Negroes follow well-known lines of evaluation and color resistance (mulattoes with white women 25.79 per cent and with Negro women 5.85 per cent, Negroes with white women 10.82 per cent and with mulatto women 24.76 per cent). Data gathered by interviews and through direct observation complete this picture. Only occasionally do we stumble on situations of interracial intercourse of a permanent nature between families of the same social levels belonging to different color groups. Moreover, in the opinion of the black population, only a white man of low social position shows any tendency to accept close relationships with members of the black middle class. The latter, in turn, resist such relationships, principally when they have genuine middle-class status. In this case they do not evaluate the white man as an individual but according to his social level. All this indicates an incipient phase of transition during which the old forms of interracial relationships are becoming highly disorganized. However, the ambiguities and the lack of socioeconomic vitality shown by the higher strata emerging from the black population are disadvantageous to any expectations of social classification of the vertically mobile segments of this population among the other strata of society. In particular, in the eyes of white people (principally those belonging to the upper lower class, the middle class, and the upper class), these socioeconomic successes of the Negro and the mulatto are regarded and defined as simple indications that the Negro is improving his lot. This reaction reveals that there is still a strong reluctance in these circles to accept the aforementioned strata of the black population as an integral part of their own social levels.

Consequently the subjective criteria for social self-appraisal utilized by rising Negroes and mulattoes are openly recognized only by the black population and even then, as something legitimate and unquestioned, only by those who identify themselves as the elite or high society of this population. Owing to the relative isolation of these persons, to their tendency to capitalize on their real or apparent social prestige, and to their sociability, the various groups making up this elite have a peculiar style of life in comparison with other strata of the larger society. Their various recreational or cultural associations are relatively active, which brings the families of these circles into frequent contact and provides the rising generations with ample opportunity for interaction within their own social level. In his conclusions on a case study, one researcher made the following points: "Social life among Negroes is most noticeably intense at their dances. The middle class has its dancing clubs, where the chief preoccupation is to provide members with a 'decent' atmosphere, suitable for respectable young ladies. In addition, the middle class frequently pays visits and likes to offer lunches and dinners to relatives and friends. Among intellectuals this is somewhat marked." [15] Sometimes certain associations offer more ambitious programs (art exhibits or programs of a recreational and cultural nature). Rarely, however, do these programs bring together all elements in Negro high society, and they are hardly ever noticed by the remaining segments of society. As a result, outside their own circle their refined, conspicuous, and aristocratic style of life goes practically unnoticed. The benefits of social classification, so rich in dividends within the group, do very little (and in a fragmentary way) to modify the prevailing definition of the Negro and the mulatto, according to which color is associated with a dubious social standing— as a rule, low and dependent.

Vertical Mobility of the Negro and Mulatto

The foregoing analysis leads to the conclusion that gradual acquisition of and improvement in stable means of earning a living tend to create conditions favoring the absorption of the Negro and mulatto into the competitive social order. Gradually they cease to be left out of organized social life and manage to classify themselves within the prevailing system of social classes. This phenomenon might seem devoid of any sociological interest, since it apparently does not bring about any radical alteration in the social position of the Negro, who continues to be poor, to be concentrated in poorly paid occupations with little or no prestige, and to produce scanty elites which are more or less isolated and closed, as in the past.

Nevertheless, this phenomenon is a pure manifestation of vertical social mobility and is of enormous sociological importance. It not only shows how the black population is reacting to the competitive social order but also demonstrates that this social order tends to be open to social ascent by a racial category which had remained outside the bourgeois revolution. It would seem that certain barriers which were blocking or hindering the social classification of the Negro and the mulatto are tending to disappear, at least at the proletarian level. At last the Negro and the mulatto can enter the labor market and choose among several rewarding occupations. Though this may not seem to be very much, in sociological terms it represents a well-defined trend. As this trend becomes established the Negro overcomes, through his own efforts, his former pauperism and social anomie, and ceases to be marginal (in relation to the labor system) and dependent (in relation to the system of social classification). As in the case of other demographic sectors of Brazil which are being dragged out of hidden or systematic idleness by the pressure of economic growth, the Negro is beginning to achieve with some regularity the standard of living enjoyed by the urban industrial groups. The only important differences in this regard stem from color (with its socioeconomic and psychosocial implications) and from belonging to unemployed or underemployed groups which often huddle within urban centers.

The present study is based mainly on data gathered by field research in 1951, in some places supplemented, as an exception, by information gathered earlier, between 1940 and 1949, by Professor Roger Bastide and his former pupils or by the present author and his pupils, always at the request or suggestion of that distinguished French scholar.[16] At this stage we have focused the analysis on the following aspects of the phenomena observed: (1) stimuli and psychosocial requirements for the vertical mobility of the Negro and the mulatto; (2) obstacles to vertical mobility or to recognition of the status of the Negro and the mulatto; (3) techniques of vertical mobility or of status consolidation utilized by the Negro and the mulatto; and (4) psychosocial and sociocultural effects of the vertical mobility of the Negro and the mulatto.

With regard to the first topic we shall first consider stimuli and then the psychosocial requirements of vertical mobility for the Negro and the mulatto. The data gathered show that certain stimuli which functioned in the past are still present. Thus the two stimuli which regulated the mechanisms of mobility of the Negro and the mulatto in the traditional social order—the socializing influence of the white family and white paternalism continue to be effective. Temporary or prolonged inclusion in the bosom of white families explains why some black individuals clung tenaciously to personality-status ideas and to social aspirations that conflicted either with their socioeconomic possibilities or with the tendencies toward adjustment prevailing in their immediate social environment. As a result of fortuitous circumstances of birth, of the economic dependence of the mother or the grandmother (household maids to important families), to good feeling springing from his provision of small services, etc., a child could be included within the framework of those families and exposed for a rather prolonged period to the socializing influences of their style of life. Consequently he would begin to struggle valiantly for forms of self-realization atypical of his immediate social group. He would tend to evaluate the importance of education realistically and to definitely associate it with rewarding forms of professionalization. The cases observed suggest that, contrary to what is commonly thought, this tendency favors not only the mulatto or the light-skinned Negro. Both the light mulatto and the jet-black Negro have been benefited as a foster child, child of the household, family dependent, etc. The important thing in these cases was not the shade of color of the child but the connection that his mother or guardian had with the adoptive family. Moreover, the influence of the adoptive family went far beyond its direct obligations with regard to employment of the child. In some cases the child's education and initial placement in a career depended on what the family did. In other cases, however, the family did nothing practical but limited itself to aids which were symbolic, occasional, and merely encouraging. In every case the goals were the liberal professions and the positions that lay open to accountants, bookkeepers, dentists, lawyers, teachers, etc.

Nevertheless, at the time we made the principal survey these two types of stimuli had little practical importance. The very structure of the rich white family had changed in a way that made it no longer feasible to regularly absorb strangers and dependents. On the other hand paternalism was not well regarded by the whites or by the Negroes. The former saw in paternalism to the Negro a heavy and useless burden; in poor white circles it was regarded as an injustice. The following statement made spontaneously by someone interviewed under these conditions indicates what he thinks about it: "Negroes who succeed give themselves airs, because in this society when you get a good job it is not because of your real worth but because of protection and dirty politics."

The two stimuli in question are clearly related to the old behavioral patterns in race relations, which means that they occur sporadically and fail to meet present requirements. Four types of psychosocial stimuli stem naturally from the present living conditions of the Negro and the mulatto. First, there are those that result, as a condition or as an effect, from the modernization of the Negro's cultural outlook. Second, there are those which arise, structurally or dynamically, within the very mechanism of mass society. A time came when the market economy, with its complex network of factors and effects, began to embrace the entire population of the city. Thus, without any deliberate effort on the part of the whites or Negroes, there was a marked tendency toward a leveling in style of life, behavior, and social aspirations, with certain consequences to the social situation of the black population. To these two types of basic stimuli must be added two psychosocial reflex stimuli. Classification and social mobility create new reference points for the self-appraisal of black people. No longer is it essential to seek examples among the whites; rising Negroes and mulattoes provide better goals, goals which are not only easier to imitate and achieve but are even more appropriate and attractive. Furthermore, both goals provide the Negro with access to social roles that add a new dimension to his personal dignity. The Negro becomes more demanding of himself, of white people, and of other Negroes, and all this will reveal itself in his concept of the world, of himself, and of his position in society.

The modernization of the Negro's cultural outlook is linked to the psychosocial effects of his gradual absorption of models taken from society for the organization of behavior, personality, and social institutions. It must be understood from the outset that this process does not presuppose purely and simply the benefits of living in the city. Above all it concerns the successes achieved by the Negro through his interaction with the material and moral conditions of his social environment. In other words it shows how much the Negro has progressed in his efforts to become a man of his society and of his time.

This is a qualitative change of enormous dynamic significance. Although the tragedy of the Negro between 1890 and 1930 can be explained by his inability to adjust to an urban style of life, his present prospects of overcoming that situation and of integrating himself definitively with class society seem to find their explanation in his growing ability to think and act as a city dweller. Despite the discrepancies still existing between his attitudes, behavior, and values and those required by his situation, the numbers of black people suited for city life and capable of transforming this ability into a highly advantageous strategic factor are now much larger.

"A Negro is a person and has no reason to behave differently from others." This point of view embraces three basic psychological attitudes which are distinct and therefore discernible, although they manifest themselves in combination. First, there is resentment at receiving undignified treatment. As one of the interviewed persons said, "Today Negroes are acting with greater freedom. They no longer accept everything passively and many struggle for their right to be treated as men and not as Negroes." Second, they have an overwhelming desire "to have a better life" by securing stable sources of income and progressively improving them. "To be someone who counts" can only mean "to be equal to the white man" and for this reason one must "behave like a white man," throwing oneself actively into occupational competition. An excellent illustration of this tendency is the girl who worked as a maid during the day and studied at night. In her opinion, "girls should prepare themselves for life, leaving aside the idea that a Negro can never amount to anything." Her friends tell her that "her efforts are useless" and that "it's silly to work like she wants us to." She replies, "You have to be something in life." She thinks that "while you are young you can make your future. Sacrifices will be rewarded because I will be able to get new jobs and bring up my children better. When I get tired of working for others in domestic work, I will be able to change professions." At the time of the interview she had already completed high school, one course in homemaking and another in typing (not to mention an earlier one in dressmaking), and she was beginning an accounting course. This ability to do one thing while keeping one's eye on another and waiting at the same time for an opportunity to transfer to work that is better paid and more highly regarded, with firm decisiveness and high hopes, is characteristic of the psychosocial drive that motivates the "Negro who wants to get ahead." Third, it would be impossible to imitate the white man's success simply by obtaining a better job. The Negro shows that he has learned this lesson very well. He coolly accepts the world in which he lives for what it is, trying to assert himself through taking strategic advantage of existing opportunities and leaving for the distant future the transformation of the white man's mentality or of the social order. As we have seen above, other alternatives are arising. Certain strata of the black population intend to operate within the existing structures even before they are changed and whether or not they are changed at all. This demonstrates that desirable social opportunities exist despite prejudice and discrimination, and that many Negroes are willing to try to take advantage of them as quickly as possible.

Within such a psychosocial context, efforts toward social ascent developed which were, so to speak, specific to the black population. It naturally became very important to prevent irrational reactions to the manifestations of race prejudice from reducing the likelihood of social classification and mobility. Some examples will serve to illustrate this complex aspect of the Negro's adjustment to an urban style of life. One of the Negro women interviewed was particularly concerned with the complaints of friends and acquaintances about race prejudice. It seemed to her that they were quite often wrong. "They got the idea into their heads, and they don't try to find out if something happens to them because of prejudice or for some other reason." She gave two examples: "A friend took a competitive test. He failed. Then he began to say that he was a victim of prejudice. I argued with him. He had not prepared himself properly, and I myself had asked him not to take the test because he was not ready for it. He paid no attention to me and mixed up two different things." The other example concerned the informant herself: "I took a typing test in the Justice Department. I was rejected. The section head explained to me that I could not be accepted because I was not yet legally old enough. I agreed. I was actually sixteen years old and could not aspire to a job which required a minimum age of eighteen. If I had got it into my head that it was because of prejudice, it would have been worse for me and I would have suffered more because of it." As a hygienic measure she thinks that "Negroes should concern themselves less with the existence of prejudice, and less with trying to explain everything white people do and Negroes suffer in terms of prejudice. It's a disease. The more a person thinks about it the worse it is for him." Nevertheless, she is sensitive to manifestations of race prejudice, can identify them objectively whenever they arise, and knows which sectors of the black population are most affected.

Another of those interviewed also insisted on the importance of distinguishing specific evidence of race prejudice from aspirations or evaluations that are more or less unconscious. In his view, "prejudice is shown only when one is blocked under circumstances where a white man in the same position is not." He gave various examples illustrating in a concrete way how such events occur. In the light of this criterion he distinguishes between "prejudice" and "selection." Where he risks being rejected or insulted because of his color, he does not present himself; where rejection of the Negro springs from a mere lack of familiarity and experience on the part of the white man or from the latter's "fear of the Negro," he tries to press the matter, tactfully, prudently, and with proper behavior. "In certain places I don't present myself. I know that some people would treat me well, but I would be out of place among them. My circle is not made up of engineers and teachers." With such a grasp of reality and of conscious behavior new prospects are opened up for rational action toward goals. A person is not only able to choose better between alternative work opportunities or promotion on the job, but he is also able to face the various dilemmas that make a Negro's life a veritable drama.

For example with regard to choice of a marriage partner, a young, dark mulatto girl said that she definitively ruled the white man out of her marriage expectations: "It is not for reasons of the heart that I reject white men. I could feel the same affection for them as for Negroes." But she intends to avoid "the tragedy that arises after marriage. There are quarrels with the husband's relatives and friends, quarrels that become deeper because of differences in education and mentality. These become worse with the birth of children. Each one hopes that the child will have his own color or want him to be white. Disappointments may embitter the life of the couple." Then there is the question of ability to match up to their social roles. One woman who was interviewed went into the matter at some length. Since "she is in a good position," she thinks she understands what prejudice is and is not: "We people are very sensitive. Every disappointment, every failure, every conflict is attributed to race prejudice. The white man is blamed for everything. But the fact is that the same things take place between whites. One person does not manage to be promoted, another does not get a job, another has his request for a transfer or a raise turned down. It is often a question of pull, of personal favoritism, as much for the Negro as for the white man. One of them gets what the other one wanted because he is a favorite and not because he is black or white." With these ideas she tries to enlighten her husband and guide her children. The former had a friend with a college degree and had not got past the position of messenger, something he naturally put down to prejudice. The woman used to say to him: "Even if so-and-so were white he would not be any better off. He's stupid. It makes no difference whether he has a college degree or not." Her children (one girl and two boys) had their problems. The eldest was rebellious and she had a hard job persuading him to put up with the conflicts he suffered as a result of his color. She did what she could for him, helping him to overcome the barriers, which are well known and can be surmounted. Her daughter was upset at the behavior of a colleague which was overly offensive and humiliating. Nevertheless, thanks to her mother's help, she bore her trouble with dignity and even tried to put it in a good light so that her mother would not suffer on her account. She would say to her mother: "I don't care. I know that I have ability. They don't like me because I am a Negro, but they can't do anything about it because I do the work better than they do. I am capable and I pay no attention to what they do or what they think."

In short, to take strategic advantage of the social positions that were more or less accessible, the Negro had to change his way of reacting to race prejudice. He distinguishes it from rejection for other reasons. He makes choices and exercises options where different behavioral alternatives are clearly anticipated. Moreover, he does not go off into one corner to weep nor does he join collective protest. Generally speaking, he is more the master of his fate. He achieves greater awareness of the conditions and effects of his relations with white men, which enables him carefully to protect his vital interests, to shield himself from foreseeable setbacks, and to avoid disappointment and harmful conflicts. Instead of meeting the white man head on, he sizes him up and adapts himself by preparing to take advantage of what could be disastrous or even fatal.

In the same psychosocial context it becomes of the greatest importance that he conceive of his own vertical mobility as a pure, clear, and supreme objective. As a rule the desire for social ascent encompasses two conscious positions: the desire to overcome his dependent situation and his virtual isolation among Negro groups, and the corresponding desire to equal the white man in some particular activity. Both these desires were vigorously expressed in an interview granted to O Novo Horizonte [17] by the athlete Adhemar Ferreira da Silva: "The white man does not create social difference. It is the automatic result of the segregation to which the Negro submits, creating the worst kinds of environment and demonstrating that he has no desire to rise in the world or else he would find some way of doing it." He goes on to stress that sport "has the special purpose of not only eliminating barriers but also making men forget their possible social grudges, since each individual sees others as fellow sportsmen, without making any kind of discrimination. In sport we are equal." Such motivations are reflected in the behavior and the mentality of the rising Negro in an exclusive moral climate. He embarks on a crusade, the central feature of which is social ascent itself. Everything converges to this end and subordinates itself to it. This is illustrated by the campaign for the purchase of land and the construction of one's own home undertaken by O Clarim da Alvorada and expanded by the Frente Negra Brasileira. The leaders of this campaign had in mind not only comfort, economic security, or greater family stability. What stood out was the fact that the Negro was becoming a landowner, carrying out more fully his social roles as head of a family and bringing about in this way a social redefinition of the Negro personality.

Thus these actions were inserted into a broader process of cultural worldliness. Case studies made by Roger Bastide and our former students at the Casa Verde fully prove this connection. The Negro links together professional classification, the raising of his income level, and puritanical ostentation of the corresponding standard of living in such a way that it becomes clear that he is contributing to his own liberation from his Negro nature (as defined in the traditionalist sense) and to his social affirmation as someone who counts and as "an equal of the white man." Social ascent is not aimed at the accumulation of wealth or power but is directed toward acquisition of its own minimum material and moral content, which can assure the human beings involved in the process of sufficient social prestige for their genuine absorption by the prevailing social order. In other words, the Negro does not go so far as to make a springboard of social ascent by trying to use it to obtain surplus social benefits or compensations. He desires and uses it, avidly and ardently, as an end in itself conferring, at the same time as it is achieved, social dignity on those who participate in it. In this respect the Negro is different from the white man both Brazilian and of other extraction. Through social ascent he stubbornly expects to find in the end the way to economic, social, and political salvation. For this reason he struggles to achieve it with an ardor analogous to that which characterized the hopes raised by the rights movements. Social mobility is seen as an immense and absorbing achievement, worthy of any sacrifice, blinding people to the fact that a man is not an isolated entity in the world he lives in.

Two general effects of the inclusion of the Negro in mass society warrant closer attention. On the one hand there were tendencies to assimilate the career standards prevailing in the urban economy. Despite persistent dissatisfaction and frustration (for events did not move as fast as the black population would have liked them to) the Negro and the mulatto manage to assimilate the concepts and the behavioral patterns that make a free worker effective. In contrast to the past, they stop thinking that selling one's work is the same as selling one's self in a disguised fashion and that the work contract is a veiled substitute for slavery. At the same time they accept the discipline required for salaried work, both in the performance of routine tasks and in the control and supervision of the conditions under which services are rendered. As a result they overcome the limitations inherited from the precapitalist world and enter the economic world, where salaried work contributes to the accumulation of savings or is a mechanism of social ascent (through vertical occupational mobility). The foundation is laid for the purchase of land, construction of their own home, participation in higher standards of living, and in some isolated cases ownership of their own car and ostentation of the sybaritic expenditures characteristic of the middle and upper classes.

A similar process takes place in choosing a career. Not only the interviews but our questionnaires revealed the shaping of a new situation. Realistic choice and acceptance of accessible occupations have become an increasingly normal tendency. The corollary of this tendency is a propensity to take great strides, which result in vertical occupational mobility and more favorable participation in the distribution of income. In the whirlpool stirred up by the active desire to rise in the world we see such things as the cook who is studying to be a typist; the typist who is studying to be an accountant; the sleep-in housemaid who changes to a cleaning woman to earn more and thus to be able to educate her children and "have a decent life"; the laborer who is learning to be a bricklayer; the bricklayer who is learning to be a carpenter; and the touching examples: fathers who walk to work, go short on food, and dress plainly "to give their children a headstart." All these processes of occupational classification and mobility are focused on increasing or improving their own share of the black population's portion of the community's income.

Parallel with these processes certain tendencies toward permanent assimilation of the living standards of the white population are emerging and growing stronger. Inclusion of the Negro in the occupational structure not only enables him to participate regularly in the minimum necessary for a decent standard of life as a city dweller; it also, if he uses his income and credit strategically, enables him to differentiate and progressively enlarge his role as a consumer, and enter an area which was almost inaccessible to him in the past. This new position may cause him to express certain impulses toward luxury items, the result of long deprivation and an uncontrollable urge to display the status he has acquired (and with it the fact that he is a human being); it may also lead him to seek (although on a variable and uncertain scale) the refinements characteristic of the average standard of urban life. It is no longer reserved for the upper classes and even less "a white man's privilege" to have a radio, record player, refrigerator, washing machine, television set, one and even two or three houses, a car, a bank account, and a maid. Some families in the black middle class manage to achieve this standard fully; others partially attain it. Only one constant feature characterizes these trends among Negro groups. The desire still remains to have a plentiful supply of food, to express themselves through the shining appearance of their clothes and shoes and, principally, to achieve their ideal of imitating the style of life of the propertied elite at the turn of the century. This preoccupation is so overriding that one of the principal associations for Negroes who were vertically mobile received the revealing name of *Aristocrata Clube*. Many people do not understand this tendency toward luxury spending, refined social life, and an exclusive air that wounds poor Negroes. Its manifestations are viewed as a sort of false refinement and empty snobbishness, serving no useful purpose and deserving savage, damaging criticism.

A second commentary which we have chosen for its wide application clearly illustrates the nature of such criticism. Under a title in the form of a question, "Are There Negro Snobs?" Arnaldo de Camargo (1948) declares: "Yes sir, you bet there are! Plenty of them! You don't have to go looking for them. When you least expect it, you fall over them. Note that the impression is worse walking down the celebrated rua Direita. Those who frequent that street are lacking in education and manners, which would explain their attitude anywhere. But what are the snobs lacking? Don't you know? Well, what they need is goodwill toward other Negroes. They avoid speaking to a poorly dressed Negro because 'someone might catch them at it' and reproach them for this magnanimous gesture. But this snob is overlooking the fact that up to now he has done nothing to recommend his race. This even seems axiomatic because if he had he would not be swollen with pride. On the slightest pretext he explains['This race never progresses!' But of course, dear snobs. That way it never will. If all the Negroes who have the good fortune to see beyond their noses avoided this disease—which is only attractive in the white race (or in any other but ours)—the Negro Race would be further ahead today] At least we would avoid being called delinquents, idlers, loafers, and other fancy names that are often bestowed on us. And right now it would be undecided whether to go to the lecture of the Negro scholar Dr. N . . . or if we would prefer to go to the piano recital given by Miss Z . . . at the residence of the X family. That would be fine, don't you agree? But it will never happen while there are snobs among Negroes. And yet they say that the Negro Race is not like the White Race. Well, it has all the vices!"

Nevertheless the overall effects of such tendencies toward adjustment are constructive. Although the elite Negro may move away from his brothers in color and refuse to support the idealism of the rights movements, by his behavior, his social presentation, and his style of life he makes the white man form a new image of the Negro. In particular this helps to reduce, and sometimes even to eliminate, the cultural distance existing between the standards of living of the two racial strains. The white man is not less shocked—on the contrary he is inwardly enraged—when he sees his black neighbor, in a way that is notorious and is considered offensive, parade the standard of living in keeping with the social level to which he belongs. He never finds a reason for certain forms of ostentation and never manages to understand why the Negro needs a maid and prefers white maids. Thus the refined Negro carries out his historic task, despite his snobbishness and his cruel indifference to the problems of the poor Negro, the task of adding color to the racial composition of the various social strata of the larger society.

In short, in granting to the Negro certain opportunities to absorb new positions and social roles, the city gave him several possibilities for assimilating the white man's standards and style of life. This does not mean that an end was put to the old racial distinctions, nor that the traditional racial order collapsed from one moment to the next. It simply means a certain advance on the part of trends to democratize social guarantees assured by the competitive social order. Selection continues to be rigid and unsatisfactory, as we shall see in the following pages. However, various signs indicate the beginning of an orientation more compatible with the economic, social, and judicial-political foundations of class society. The resultant psychosocial stimuli acted constructively on Negroes. On the one hand they did so because the tendencies we have described permitted more effective and advantageous imitation of the examples provided by white people. The anxiety caused by the injustice inherent in the rapid rise of the Italian and the "Turk" was gradually replaced by psychosocial drives which forced the Negro to behave like those immigrants and their descendants. Although the fortune seekers belonged to the golden age of the past, some of their characteristics were still applicable—such as hard work, a sense of responsibility as head of a family, cooperation at home, willingness to accept any kind of economically rewarding work, and an earnest association of thrift and occupational mobility with social ascent.

It seems clear that the stimuli for vertical mobility, together with modernization of the Negro's cultural outlook and the structural or dynamic effects of the expansion of mass society, prompted important changes in his behavior, mentality, and concepts of status personality. Owing to these changes two developments took place which are of capital importance for a sociological grasp of the forms of ego involvement of rising individuals, both among Negroes and in society at large.

First, in the past black persons who were in any way eager to live better had only the white man as a point of reference for understanding the functioning of society. As Negroes and mulattoes managed to become classified in the competitive social order, new possibilities for self-reference were formed and consolidated among them. Their earlier judgment, based on the fascinating successes of the Italian and the "Turk," led to the belief "the poor man also has his turn." However, with the appearance of the black middle class other convictions were formed. Young people now preferred to say that "the Negro's turn has arrived" or "is arriving." A neighbor, an acquaintance, a friend, or a relative who became one of those who "had succeeded in spite of his color" constituted an excellent stimulus: "What one Negro can do, another can." The young man thirsty for success does not underestimate the example provided by his brothers in color; he feels neither belittled nor humiliated because another was lucky or was able to make a place for himself in life. In contrast with what had generally happened in the past—when the sour comment was "So-and-so says he has a college degree"; "His Negro lady friends think he has a college degree"; or "So-and-so says that he is an English teacher, but I don't know because I never saw him teaching"—a more constructive reaction tends to prevail, enabling the social differentiation of Negro groups to be of use to rising generations. Convinced that "they are no worse than the others," young people in particular are willing to tread the hard roads that seem to lead to social ascent.

Second, improvement in status and expectation that certain trends toward social ascent will continue are reflected in the concepts of human dignity prevailing among Negroes. Success arouses motivations that are too complex to be described in detail, but some general outlines can be given. It is no longer thought, as it was in the past, that personal dignity depends on observance of certain rigid standards of orderly life.

What must be emphasized here is not so much the pure and simple rejection of the passive submission of the Negro or of the white man's tendency to give him orders, but the very basis of a new outlook leading the Negro and the mulatto to a conscious conception of their rights and duties as partners within the social category to which they both belong. It is this identification that psychologically generates rejection of traditional types of adjustment and of the persistent manifestations of race prejudice. It therefore deserves special attention. Personal dignity becomes the axis around which revolve the social attitudes, behavior, and judgments of rising individuals as if they were veritable custodians of the prerogatives conferred by their social situation. The majority of Negroes therefore despise the passiveness of the ignorant Negro and blindly resent demeaning behavioral expectations on the part of prejudiced whites. They find no way of solving their moral dilemmas socially and drag around with them their frustrations, their dreams of perfect racial equality, and their puritanical zeal for respect of their personal rights. However, this does not arrest their drive for equality. They prompt forms of thinking and acting that are opposed to racial inequality and its consequences in the distribution of social opportunities.

Psychosocial stimuli for mobility were able to function dynamically because they found a suitable field. Changes that took place in the organization of the Negro's personality and, to an almost ridiculously small extent, in the outward situation of the Negro within society helped in various ways to advance or facilitate vertical social mobility among the black population. These psychosocial or sociocultural transformations of a conditioning nature served as prerequisites to the social ascent of the Negro and the mulatto. Limiting ourselves to the strictly essential, we must consider here: (1) rejection of the life style and the type of personality associated with the traditional pattern of racial adjustment; (2) the objective expression and occasional utilization of drives to rise in the world; (3) the formation of feelings and concepts of racial equality; (4) the formation of attitudes rejecting manifestations of race prejudice; (5) the appearance and universal adoption of rational techniques of selection and competition in society.

At bottom, all the psychosocial and sociocultural requirements for the black man's vertical social mobility are related to the breakdown of the traditional social order and to the reduction or the disappearance of its effects on the organization of the Negro's behavior and personality. From this angle, study of individuals who are rising socially permits us to select and analyze psychosocially what will happen in the long run to the whole black population if the trends we have indicated towards modernization of the Brazilian system of racial relations continue, and if no historical or social factors emerge to disturb or prevent the progressive integration of the Negro into the competitive social order.

The basic dynamic and structural component in the transformations that have taken place is rejection of the style of life and the type of personality associated with the traditional pattern of racial adjustment. The Negro and the mulatto cannot free themselves from their color or from the white man's appraisal of their racial character. Nevertheless, within certain limits they can modify their mode of interaction with their own people, with whites, and with the living conditions offered by society. With remarkable speed, as soon as they gained a foothold in the stratification of the prevailing social order, they made every possible effort to fill positions and perform roles analogous to those normally enjoyed by white people.

This brings out two points of the greatest importance. First, condemnation and rejection of their former way of life was not the result of pure and simple assimilation of the dominant race's standards of societal reaction at a time when psychosocial processes were in flux. The public consumption of *pinga* serves to disprove this interpretation. Upon adopting white values the Negro and the mulatto tended to abandon the habit of drinking *pinga* in bars and even in other public places. The very act of drinking *pinga*, even at home and in moderation, took on the appearance of something intolerable, as if it involved a kind of social degradation. However, the essential point is not connected with these aspects. The man who was afraid of being treated like a Negro because he was known or seen to drink *pinga* had already changed his view of things and his attitude toward his position in society (the same occurring, in the opposite direction, in the case of the rising Negro who openly flaunted his *pinga* drinking). Rather, this does mean that the patterns of societal reaction imitated from the white man are status symbols of limited structural and dynamic importance in the psychosocial processes in flux (that is, in the phase between abandoning the inherited social position and acquiring a new one).

Second, the rejection of their former way of life contains an element of decision and choice, but one with a view to the desired alternatives of social affirmation. "To be a person," to gain a position in a solid and respectable society, is what really counts. Between what one has and what one wants, it is the latter that gives rise to values orienting attitudes and behavior. The important thing is that in the transition phase the Negro created a fictitious status for himself, identifying himself with it and acting in accordance with his ideals. This mechanism permitted the elaboration of social values of an illusory nature that assumed a high degree of pretense (both toward his own consciousness and in relation with others, white, Negro, or mulatto). "To be upright," "to look well-dressed," "to behave correctly," "to do everything properly," "to leave others popeyed," "to command respect," and other aspirations of a similar nature oriented their intellectual outlook and led them to behave and assert themselves as if they had already acquired the status desired. Means were mistaken for ends, but this served a useful purpose for those who were actually rising socially. The moral demands of fictitious status, ingenuous and precarious as they may seem, permitted individuals to become that which they were not yet—and never would be unless they very boldly crossed the Rubicon.

These two points need to be carefully kept in mind. They serve as the very basis of the reference system that can be deduced from the way that the rising Negro is, thinks, and acts in taking advantage of the opportunities for classification in the competitive social order offered by existing race relations. Vertical mobility meant putting an end to an iniquitous state and taking on the style of life, the models of personality organization, and the social prestige of the white man. To be people and to feel, behave, and live like white people were one and the same thing. However, this was in no way an ideal consisting of false whitening, of breaking the line, or of passing as white. If we were to use figurative language, we would say that all that was intended was a sort of "social whitening," in the sense of a perfect democratization of the social prerogatives to which the Negro has a right in class society. Such whitening merely refers to social positions and roles and in no way implies an inclination to be or to seem white in racial terms.

The moral appraisal of the conformist Negro tends to spread, being shared by all those who want to rise in one way or another, as witnessed in the opinions of a young Negro student: "The white man does not hurt the Negroes. It is they who like to loaf around and have a good time. Instead of working to get on, they prefer to have an easy life. They don't want to study and they don't apply themselves at school like the whites. I have friends who prefer to shine shoes rather than look for a better job. When you talk to them about it they think it is nonsense. They say they are satisfied with what they have."

There is in addition the rather complex problem of a split among Negroes themselves. Under the conditions we have described, the Negro who is rising has to be prepared to withdraw and even to isolate himself from acquaintances, friends, and relatives. This distance seems to be natural and unavoidable—not like the price one is supposed to pay for the shame of being Negro. To the extent that he strives to succeed as a Negro, the black man nowadays does not avoid contact with his friends and relations for reasons of that kind. Some cases allow us to study such behavior objectively. It is the need to apply the new level of life, to find people with analogous social interests and similar aspirations, that lies at the bottom of avoidance motivations. Thus in repudiating the poor Negro it is not the Negro proper who is being avoided but a certain social class that he intends to keep away from at all costs. .Proof of this is the fact that he prefers to seek the company of other Negroes of a comparable social level instead of trying to associate exclusively with white people of a similar or lower social level. In one of the interviews one of the former leaders of the rights movements, a man very sensitive to loyalty to the fundamental interests of the Negro community, forthrightly declared: "My interests are not among ignorant Negroes; now I only want to look after my affairs and educate my children." Another fellow said that it was not through disaffection that he kept away from his former friends and companions but because he did not agree with their mode of life. He considered that it was not their color but their debauched or sloppy behavior, which "makes you ashamed" and "demoralizes Negroes in general," that he kept away from them. The fact is that the candidate to social ascent must be potentially ready to disconnect himself from his environment and should be materially and morally prepared to face the resulting human dramas.

Social ascent of the Negro depends on the manner in which his personality interacts with the psychosocial forces of the environment. To the extent that the open society closes the majority of its mechanisms for vertical social mobility to the Negro and the mulatto, they need to structure their behavior in order to achieve success within the opportunities available under difficult conditions. As a rule, a strong drive to rise is in the end the only support that individuals can depend on under any circumstances. Those who do not possess this armor have to settle for some form of failure and even those who have it sometimes go under to the buffetings of life, blaming society for the final outcome. What we must stress here is the unique importance of this psychosocial requisite. It becomes decisive in determining the probability of social ascent of persons taken as individuals, although it does not correct (and cannot correct) the sociohistoric factors of racial inequality.

The Negro is modifying his self-concepts of status and social roles. He is freeing himself from the moral pressures of the traditional world and consciously adopting the moral climate of the competitive social order. His rejection of manifestations of the effects of race prejudice takes on another hue. Negro protest was either silent or dramatic in the past. We find withdrawal as a first mechanism of nonconformity and then the collective explosions of the claims movements, of which the Frente Negra Brasileira was a typical manifestation. The two forms of protest were ignored by society. Upon equating himself psychologically, socially, and morally with the white, the Negro will be forced to face his racial dilemmas on an individual and concrete level. First he will have to face the manifestations and the effects of race prejudice as a challenge—a debasing thing that threatens his very position as a moral human being. Then he will try to face it while protecting his material and moral interests. The white man does not create open racial conflict; the Negro will do the same without resorting to the traditional techniques of submission or rebellion. He renews his attempts to get certain jobs; he takes advantage of the knowledge he has acquired of the maneuvers and the tricks of the white man; and he only accepts, at the very end, an isolation that is in many respects softened and gilded, because he participates at a social level higher than many poor white people.

The essential point in this repudiation of race prejudice is its nature. It involves hand-to-hand combat in which the last concession is deliberately ruled out. What the Negro forbids himself to do is to admit, directly or indirectly, his inferiority and consequently to complacently accept the old code of racial relations. Thus he rejects both passive adjustment with its collective isolation and active protest with its great promises for a remote future. He wants to live in the present and to have access to everything that he is entitled to. His social affirmation is tinged with attitudes of rejection that is militant though dissimulated and wise, of race prejudice and its socioeconomic or moral effects. Second, that which threatens the social aspirations of the rising Negro also endangers his representations of status and social roles. Manifestations of race prejudice have a painful effect both on the desire to live and be treated with dignity and on the desire for social equality on the part of the Negro and the mulatto. Even if worldly conditioning weighed more heavily than recent aspirations it would be difficult for the black man to stifle the demands of the world in which he lives and for which he is being socialized. It is consequently impossible to reconcile the mentality of the Negro who is rising socially with the traditional pressures of his environment. There is a psychological abyss separating the two things, as the results of our interviews conclusively proved. Even those who thought that "it's the Negro who has persecution mania," who maintained that "his complex is responsible for these ideas" [that prejudice exists], or who charge that "the Negro is to blame for his situation"—even these people reject in various ways any passive adjustment and the material or moral premises of the traditional pattern of asymmetric race relationships.

From this angle integration into the competitive social order depends on certain prerequisites. The Negro and the mulatto must stop conceiving of themselves, psychologically and socially, in the light of the image of the Negro built up in the recent past. Either they do this, and compete for the existing opportunities for classification and ascent, or they will continue outside the mainstream of organized social life and its economic, political, and moral benefits. Those who so heatedly debate the question whether race prejudice exists in Brazil should take this as their starting point. The Negro has to decide between the exclusion he consents to or the participation he insists on. On taking the second course he cannot tolerate an image of himself that is a distortion of any ideal of human personality and inevitably clashes with the types of personality status required by the competitive social order.

We must consider that the social order imposes certain standards that are sometimes in open competition above racial differences. This is especially true with large organizations, be they governmental, semigovernmental, or private. Selection of candidates for starting positions in several careers, and sometimes for promotion, is made through examinations. Under these conditions the Negro and the mulatto have access to opportunities that were closed to them in the recent past. Apparently these effects are received with some reluctance, and there are organizations (particularly private ones) that use subterfuges to facilitate the racial identification of candidates and their automatic exclusion. Nevertheless, standardization of selection and promotion techniques definitely favors those sectors of the black population that are qualified to enter the competition for skilled and better paid jobs. Moreover, traditional influence is still felt in two ways. On the one hand it is sometimes necessary to combine paternalism with the new practices. The following is an illustration: "With the creation of the department where I worked before I came here, there was a public announcement of a competition to fill twenty positions as clerk. Five hundred and eighteen candidates offered themselves, including me. I took part in the competition, but the result was not published. However, I later discovered that I had passed in second place. Logically, I had a right to the second opening. I was called, but I later learned that I was not to get it because at a meeting the managers of the department decided they did not want me to enter, since they considered that I would have a certain amount of difficulty in my dealings with some young ladies . . . who were also going to work there. Some managers considered that such young ladies would be uncomfortable working in the same room with a Negro. At this juncture one of the managers, whose brother I am by upbringing, stood up and said that I had been brought up in his father's house and had thus received the same training as he had, so he knew I could behave myself in any company, whatever it might be. Thus, not wishing to go against the opinion of the majority, he would not vote but wished to record his protest. He then left the room. In view of this they decided to hire me."

On the other hand tolerance is greater for employees beginning their career, and it diminishes later. Thus the candidate who is accepted with reservations marks time. To avoid this result, which is more or less perceived, some fall back on special influence. In this regard a white man, one of the directors of a large government organization, told us: "The competitions are public, and nobody can stop them from entering. Some have influential friends, like the two managers, and manage to get high positions." There is an obvious and well-founded consensus among the black population regarding the limitations inherent in opportunities obtained this way. However, they are not insignificant and being part of a general trend they warrant mention here. One should also realize that willingness to accept black clients falls into the same category.[18] Something analogous takes place with the growing acceptance of services provided by black professionals. The idea that what counts is competence seems to be behind these attitudes. When considered as a whole, manifestations of the same tendency that are apparently discrete and isolated take on special significance. They suggest that in several respects the replacement of traditional social techniques by rational social techniques promotes the gradual spread of criteria that reduce or eliminate the importance of color in actions and in human relations.

The foregoing data have already given an indication of the difficulties that the Negro and the mulatto face in trying to classify themselves socially and to compete with whites for wealth, power, and prestige. They have to overcome several kinds of resistance and obstacles to arrive at a position that, under analogous conditions, can be reached with the greatest of ease and speed by a white man starting at the same point. To the extent that the drive to rise finds less support in the outside world than in their subjective inclinations, rather active obstacles to the vertical mobility of the Negro and the mulatto, or to explicit recognition of their changes in status and social roles, crop up at all levels in the organization of behavior, personality, and society. Limiting ourselves to the essential, we shall examine here: (1) the direct or indirect effects of racial inequality; (2) the stabilizing functions of race prejudice; (3) the effects of reactive mechanisms to race prejudice; (4) the negative psychosocial drives of the Negro environment; (5) the interference of differential factors; (6) the neutral or negative nature of government action; (7) barriers to recognition of the status acquired by blacks; (8) the mechanisms for acceptance of the black man.

The principal barrier to vertical mobility for the Negro and the mulatto is of a structural nature. If entry into the competitive social order were rapid and uniform with regard to absorption of the racial strains present, the parallel between Negro and inferior social position, with monopoly of racial domination by the upper social strata of the white race, would have disappeared. Since this has not occurred, the difference between race relations in the 1950s and those between 1900 and 1930 is merely one of degree. In other words, expansion of the competitive social order became broad enough to be reflected at the level of race relations. The traditional pattern of unbalanced race relations began to enter an irreversible state of crisis and with it so did the aforementioned parallel between racial stratification and social hierarchy in the city of São Paulo. We should note, however, that it has only begun to enter a state of crisis. This means that we are still closer to the past than to the picture of an incipient and imperfect racial democracy. What will happen in the future depends on uncertain sociohistorical conditions and factors the continuance or effect of which cannot be foreseen at present.

In contrast with the situation from 1900 to 1930, the black population in Brazil is now entering an era of real hope. It seems that the "Negro's turn" has come, to use an expression of the informant in our investigation. It has come hesitantly, for the Negro is being carried along behind the sectors of the native white populations from the countryside and the cities, who are being shaken out of systematic or sporadic unemployment. But let us now analyze something that would have had little point in the discussion of the period from 1900 to 1930: the mechanisms mobilizing the Negro for organized social life within the larger society and consider what this represents sociologically as a phenomenon of vertical social mobility. Nevertheless, it must be clearly understood that we cannot endorse optimistic opinions. The distance already covered has been almost insignificant and corresponds neither to the requirements for a normal competitive social order nor to the collective aspirations of the black population as expressed through their social claims movements. In some respects Brazil has overcome part of the cultural lag that separated her racial order from her social order, but the imbalance between the two remains. It is true that the Negro and the mulatto advanced with the city, but they progressed blindly and in zigzags, as we shall see below, without creating solidarity of any kind among their fellow human beings. Everyone had so much to overcome in order to modify such deeply engrained attitudes and behavior that the painful and moving efforts of the Negro to be somebody failed to touch the heart or the reason or the imagination of other men. Alone and unprotected, the Negro continues to struggle in a world that is socially insensitive to his material and moral dilemmas—a world in which persons of another color are ashamed of acting as they do but do not have the courage to behave differently. As long as this is the case Brazil shall remain attached to the traditional pattern of racial domination which condemns the Negro and mulatto to inexorable social inequality.

It should be clearly understood that racial inequality is not merely an unfavorable circumstance. It rises up as a veritable wall against which the strongest, the most ambitious, and the most worthwhile hopes of the black population dash themselves and are crushed. It acts as a factor for inertia. As a group of young Negro intellectuals tried to explain to us, it is responsible for the ceaseless renewal of the vicious circle linking poverty, ignorance, disease, uncertain occupation, the lowest level of income, the lowest standards of living, and an inferior social position. Moreover, racial inequality nourishes and provides a basis for a defeatist and frustrated outlook that leads Negroes of all generations to the conviction that "it's no good making an effort." Conversation with persons holding these ideas soon reveals that statements of this kind are mere verbalizations to rationalize and hide personal frustrations or ambitions that are legitimate but socially infeasible.

Being a factor of sociocultural inertia, the effects of racial inequality have a certain generality and, in a broader sense, are associated with the perpetuation of the pattern of societal organization that engenders and maintains racial inequality itself. It is therefore here that one should seek the causes of limited competitive ability drastically reducing or blocking the desires of the black population for social integration. It is necessary to consider the aforementioned effects from two different aspects: those that result purely and simply from the black man's material situation and those that stem from the configuration of his moral world.

The stabilizing effects of racial inequality on the Negro's material situation appear in the form of a low level of employment and the correspondingly low level of income. The data gathered demonstrate abundantly that the Negro and the mulatto are still using the bulk of their efforts in the struggle to overcome the poverty and anomie described in Chapter 2. A white doctor who has vast experience with poor clientele in a crowded suburb of São Paulo volunteered the opinion that the Negro's great problem is poverty and disease: "They are discouraged about working but this is just a consequence of poor nutrition which in turn is a consequence of the low standard of living they have. Where there is no money there is no food and where there's no food there is disease. If the Negro is hungry and sick, he cannot take care of his cultural life and thus cannot compete with the white man. The white man has society on his side, whereas for the Negro everything is unfa-

vorable." Other information, and principally the impressive
account of Carolina Maria de Jesus, bear out this somber side
to the existence of the Negro in the 1950s.[19] The scenes described in the diary of a woman slum dweller dramatically
suggest that hunger, poverty, disease, and social disorganization, with their diverse and socially unfavorable consequences, continue to have a firm grip on a large part of the
black population. The basements and tenements have been
replaced by the shanties, "the filthiest junk lot in the world,"
"a branch of hell, or hell itself." [20] If the proportion of Negroes
in the socially unprotected and disorganized population is
reduced in compensation there is an increase in the gravity of
the social problems that this portion of the black population
must inevitably face. "We have only one way to be born and
many to die." With this sober statement Carolina Maria de
Jesus reveals the core of a gloomy and repugnant reality. To
be sure there are also Negroes who live in brick houses and
these are fortunately more numerous nowadays than those
who live in shanties, but the overall picture is more complicated than it was at the beginning of the century. Even in
poverty gradations appear—and sociologically very important
gradations because they make overcoming poverty an ideal for
many black families.

Against this backdrop the significance of racial inequality
as social concentration of wealth, power, and social prestige
becomes clear. Doubtless, the poor white shares equally in the
poverty, the degradation, and the corruption of this segment
of the black population, but starting from the same plateau
the white population manages to differentiate itself throughout all the levels of economic stratification and social hierarchy. This is not the case with the Negro who does not have a
class position or merely manages to classify himself in the
most precarious positions in the lower class and the middle
classes.

Even avoiding the ambiguities that would be introduced by
the concept of "structure of race relations," what is inherent in
racial inequality (as manifested today) can be seen: an eco-

nomic situation that tends to exclude the Negro from the opportunities assured by the competitive social order. In education, "the problem lies in the precariousness of the Negro's economic situation. . . . I presume that the greatest difficulty in the way of the Negro's school attendance lies solely and exclusively within the all-pervading economic factor. I don't believe that any father does not want his children to go to school. But it so happens that a father can never give a good education to his children because he is forced to resort to their work in order to support the home and this leads to the abandonment of the child." [21] Between "wanting an education" and "being able to go to school" there exists an almost unbridgeable chasm. Another informant was even more emphatic: "How can we send our children to high school if we don't have enough money to support ourselves? We have to send our children to the factories wherever they may be. Free education is a fiction. It does not exist." [22] Even those who see education as an avenue of social ascent rarely manage to use it for that purpose. A young Negro workman said: "Negroes in general have little urge or desire to rise. But even in the case of those who want to rise, their family's poverty makes them leave off studying and work even when they're not qualified for a better job."

Two illustrations will serve as examples of this tendency. A woman who worked as a cook indicated that "she was willing to make any sacrifice so that her children could go to school and become somebody." However, in practice she could not carry out this desire. Her son wanted to be a mechanic's apprentice "and was no problem." Her daughter, however, wanted to be a teacher. "It takes many years of study, we are poor and cannot afford to do without the girl's earnings during all that schooling." A boy of eighteen who delivered hot lunches wanted to study to get "better jobs" and "improve his life." Since he had to support himself and to help at home, his efforts were foiled. Similar cases could be described with regard to other opportunities assured by the competitive social order, but it is not necessary. It seems clear that the peristasis (total environment) [23] of the larger society is quite different from the part of this peristasis that can really be mobilized by the sociocultural participation of the black population. The environmental elements theoretically possible are drastically reduced when we go from the white to the Negro race. As a result the material situation of the black population severely restricts its possibilities of constructively utilizing its talents and other mature human capabilities.

As regards the second aspect, the moral plane, it is enough to point out that the disadvantages of starting almost entirely from nothing are reflected both in the quality of the individual's ambitions and in the extent to which it is possible to carry them out. Matters which do not begin to be problems for the majority of white people can be faced and settled by only a very small number of Negroes. The examples given above show that the father or mother may not assume their responsibilities, even when they are conscientious and try to give an education to their children. The examples also show that a youth may give up his studies prematurely even though he would like to continue. But the gradations of adversity go further. Sometimes adults struggle with what they think is "lack of goodwill on the part of the white bosses." Since they do not manage to solve the smallest questions, they project the consequences of their difficulties into the racial sphere. Nevertheless it is in the degree of social prestige and in the amount of power inherent in such prestige that the real explanation is found. What seems to be lack of appreciation, disdain, mistrust, or rancor against the Negro results from his inability to mobilize influences favorable to the achievement of his objectives through the social position he occupies. As a rule, a person's circle of social relations is too narrow to bring him the social prestige he desires, or else he is unable to effectively mobilize the social prestige inherent in his status. At bottom, the white social monopoly not only remains in full force but also has a disastrous effect on the state of mind of the Negro. He feels, and passes on, the uselessness of clinging to illusions. Thinking that the white man is better educated and that he is also more favored, the Negro becomes discouraged. He consequently acquires a defeatist philosophy that struggle is of no use because the best jobs are really for the whites. Thus we see how racial inequality acts dynamically as a factor toward inertia on the moral plane. The type of ego involvement in the competitive social order characteristic of the Negro and the mulatto does not protect them against mechanisms of self-identification inherited from the past. Not only are the potentialities of the larger social circle and the level of individual aspirations imbalanced, but the images by which these individuals judge themselves and build their career plans end up being confined to a very narrow area regarded as a sphere of proven or undeniable success.

According to the results of our survey, three influences acting together explain the adaptive and integrative weaknesses. First, there are certain institutional deficiencies among Negro groups. The degree of absorption and effective mastery of the environment's social techniques still continues to be the main source of the Negro's disadvantages in his competition with the white man. To the extent that the peristasis of the Negro does not coincide with the peristasis of the larger society, the former is irremediably lacking in the adaptive and integrative possibilities that culture provides. The best point of reference to study this problem is the functioning of the Negro family. The integrated Negro family manages to protect the child both materially and morally. Even under the disadvantage of a low and unstable income the desire "to give my child everything I didn't have" enables parents, through heavy sacrifices, to find ways to keep "my boy in school" until schooling is complete (usually primary, sometimes secondary, rarely through college). However, it would be a mistake to think that significant difficulties stem solely from their economic situation. Of course parents who do not even have enough money for food find it impracticable to educate their children. But the ability to face the problems associated, apparently or actually, with manifestations of race prejudice is as important and sometimes more important than limited income.

The anomalies so frequent in the organization of the Negro family aggravate the difficulties arising from a low income, establishing an atmosphere conducive to the neutralization of the constructive socializing influences of the adult generations. Consequently a child is prevented from going to school and, worse, he does not receive the protection and guidance necessary for adjustment to the way of life that is being socially imposed on him. He grows up neglected, subject to the pernicious influences of his immediate environment and to insecure personal criteria for judgment or for self-assertion. Furthermore, other social institutions in the Negro environment or in that of the larger society do not supplement the functions of the family. The Brazilian school is not equipped to correct the family's functional shortcomings, much less to handle the real or potential maladjustments of national, ethnic, and racial minorities; and the Negro environment does not possess the economic, social, and cultural vitality necessary to develop compensating reactive mechanisms. As in the past, for appearance's sake Negro associations include among their objectives aid to education and guidance for children and young people, but such objectives continue to be merely ideals. As a result, the rising generations are generally poorly cared for or totally uncared for, owing to chronic institutional deficiencies.

We face the same hard reality when we observe the functioning and the effect of the family as when we observe the functioning and the effect of other institutions of an economic, political, or recreational nature. Since the Negro and the mulatto are not systematically isolated, they have to achieve the same level as the whites through their sociocultural capacity for free competition. It would not be enough for them to reproduce in miniature among Negro groups what we might call white society. Under present historical conditions the situation requires them to achieve institutional equality through gradual integration into the prevailing social order. Matters thus become extremely difficult. Other national or ethnic minorities smoothed their way by means of institutionalized patterns of sociability, solidarity, and cooperation that were part of their sociocultural heritage. As we have seen, the black population could not count on this kind of thing and pays an excessively high price for the prospects of egalitarian integration. Several informants brought up the matter spontaneously, the majority to point out the initial advantages of systematic segregation. Although they do not desire it and condemn it morally, they see in this segregation the real cause of the Negro's progress in the United States. Others cited segregation repeatedly but not to the same extent, to explain the failure of the Negro in comparison with the Italian, the "Turk," and, especially, the Japanese. They stress the importance of mutual aid and cooperation as a source of the economic, social, and cultural vitality of these national and ethnic minorities. The fact is that the Negro himself perceives the drama surrounding him. Under pressure from the competitive situation itself and from the weaknesses of his social heritage, he does not enjoy conditions enabling him to mobilize the environment's institutional resources on a scale allowing him to meet the material and moral requirements of the prevailing social style of life. He consequently fails to exploit, though he may wish to do otherwise, the potentialities of culture in the solution of his human problems.

A second influence that helps to explain the adaptive and integrative weaknesses of the Negro lies in his lack of previous socialization. Each generation, in each of life's situations, faces the same basic difficulty: preparation that is deficient to varying degrees in adapting individuals for the psychodynamic and sociodynamic requirements of their social roles. The data indicate that opportunities for training are limited at two levels. First, lack of schooling or premature termination of schooling is an almost universal feature. Second, work at an early age is not, for its part, of a kind that would correct this tendency. As a rule, the accessible occupations contribute neither to the acquisition of specific skills for other types of professionalization nor to spontaneous learning of the techniques of reading, writing, and calculating. On the contrary, these occupations imprison young people in the activities of low economic and social value. These two tendencies act together to create a third that is especially pernicious: fixation in work habits and attitudes that are more or less incompatible with the rationale of the capitalist system of production. Consequently, even when the individual manages to break through the barriers to normal professionalization by virtue of his intelligence, tenacity, or vocational aptitude, he rarely possesses all the qualities necessary to reach the top of the career he has entered. In most cases individuals come up against the limitations inherent in a low starting point, and they often succumb to their lack of certain universal social techniques (ability to communicate, in speaking and in writing; aptitude for dealing with others, for exercising leadership and directing teams organized as groups; judgment in recognizing opportunities and skill in taking advantage of them at the right time).

These three tendencies are related to institutional deficiencies in the Negro environment and to their chronic effects on socialization. Because of them we speak of a drastic lack in the adaptive capacity and intelligence of the Negro (who is constantly sidetracked in occupations that are irrelevant or peripheral to the work system) and of the existence of a specific problem of socialization among the black population. Those who are not convinced pin the blame on the Negro himself, as if the father did not know how to bring up his children, as if the young man only thought of leading a good-for-nothing life, or as if the school of the streets was fatally dangerous. But the facts are more complicated. The type of adaptation and integration achieved by the Negro in the prevailing social order offers him no other chance of participating in its culture. He does not have full and regular access to education in manners, to ability to act, and to the social techniques that make a man lord of his will or master of his fate (to the extent that this is possible and necessary for drawing up and carrying out personal career plans). Consequently, even those who see that education is an avenue of vertical mobility and intend to use it as such for themselves or their children find their plans completely frustrated. For the black population such an effect has extremely negative repercussions. Through education the Negro not only acquires a way of becoming classified in the competitive social order but begins to gain a perspective that gives him the very ability to compete. Case studies and interviews have made it clear that formal education represents a genuine foundation for the development of social consciousness in the Negro and the mulatto.

The third influence limiting the upgrading of the adaptive and integrative potentialities of the black population concerns a sort of undeclared specialization that severely restricts the Negro's and the mulatto's chance of professional classification and economic competition. There is no longer any clear opinion on work that should be given to Negroes, but two forces spontaneously help to preserve the *status quo:* (1) the tendency for the Negro to accommodate himself to levels of employment where it is easy for him to be used and accepted; and (2) the usual tendency for the white man to exclude the Negro from occupations that require responsibility, organizational ability, and initiative. Our survey shows that the occupational progress of the Negro and the mulatto took place in a neutral area. An abundance of jobs requiring cheap and unskilled or semiskilled labor helped to incorporate a considerable portion of the black population into the economically active population. Nevertheless, changes in the level of employment were almost insignificant. As a result the drawbacks of a tendency to confuse professional aptitude with racial qualities when selecting employees continue to persist with remarkable obviousness. These views lead the Negro to declare resentfully that "the whites made them inferior," or to confide in a rather bitter tone that "because of my color they never gave me a chance nor even any hope." [24] They lead the white man to admit frankly that "it was not the Negro who specialized in the lower kinds of work and tended to find his vocation in cooking, football, boxing, police, and the Army; but it was the white man who made the Negro a specialist in these activities because, in refusing him access to others, he forced the Negro to look for a position in life."

What interests us here is the meaning of these unexpressed lines of racial specialization. In the autobiography of a Negro subject we find the following analysis of the situation of a car washer: "In this job we see the lack of foresight on the part of the Negro. Parking areas are not generally fixed. They are special concessions made by the owners of empty lots in exchange for cleaning and protection or for small rents. These lots are just waiting for one of those buildings that spring up so amazingly in São Paulo. When construction begins the parking lot disappears. In public squares and in certain streets parking spaces are always granted provisionally. There are places that pay well but when the boys earn, they spend. And when the rainy season comes they are forced to resort to other work to support themselves. The vast majority of car washers have no defined profession. Many use this occupation as a means of maintaining contact with political bosses and high officials in order to get a modest position as a janitor in some government office. Ninety per cent of the car washers in São Paulo are Negroes." [25] This example serves to illustrate the angle that concerns us. A good portion of the black population still has to live from hand to mouth, in search of marginal work that is badly paid and not steady. Thus the generations that follow are absorbed in a way that maintains the concentration of Negro workers in insignificant occupations and, what is worse, without any prospects for professional competition.

In a competitive system the adaptive and integrative prospects of any ethnic or racial category depend on the possibility of its keeping and continuously broadening certain opportunities for professional classification. The existence and persistence of certain lines of invisible specialization not only fail to meet this sociodynamic requirement but reverse what should happen normally if the Negro and mulatto are to be constantly assimilated into the competitive social order. Here lies the principal factor in the indefinite perpetuation of the Brazilian pattern of racial inequality. The tendencies toward racial distribution of jobs established by the organization of the larger society reproduce the past in the present and are far from offering any hope of radical modification in the near future. That is how the collective difficulties of the black population in obtaining a class situation among the economically active population can be objectively stated. This situation does not merely involve getting a salaried job. It also requires effective sharing in social privileges and opportunities for social mobility. In participating to a limited and marginal extent in the work opportunities and career prospects offered by the competitive social order, the black population finds itself condemned to limited participation in the other cultural spheres. One situation determines the other, since in a class society it is levels of employment that govern the form of participation in the flow of income and standards of living. Naturally, this largely explains why the Negro did not have greater access to the immense opportunities created by the expansion of the competitive social order that took place during and after the Second World War. He lacked the material base necessary to occupy positions that would enable him to take advantage of those opportunities. The same happened at the time of the commercialization of coffee and the first spread of urbanization: it was immigrants or their descendants and components of the native white racial stock that monopolized the really rewarding fruits of the recent intense economic growth.

The foregoing discussion leaves no doubt that racial inequality is the dynamic foundation of race relations today in São Paulo. The psychosocial and sociocultural factors having any definite importance to the liberation, the direction, and the smoothing of the processes reintegrating the system of race relations are connected with this inequality in one way or another. Not only do the whites resist, consciously or unconsciously, tendencies toward democratization in the standards of treatment of the Negro, but the Negro himself also contributes to the preservation of inequality by his attitudes or re-active behavior. In the final analysis, everything is related to sociohistoric processes that either further perpetuate the in-herited models of racial inequality or help to change them.

Race prejudice is particularly significant. Although it is expressed in a characteristically peripheral way, where it ap-pears, it acts as a stabilizing force reducing the impact of the competitive social order on traditional patterns of race rela-tions and preserving, to the greatest extent possible, the abil-ity of the white man to perpetuate indefinitely his monolithic racial hegemony.

We have already pointed out above that prejudice and dis-crimination do not create a social distance between the *socii* in the city of São Paulo. It seems clear that they function as mechanisms for the stabilization of prevailing patterns of race relations, which means that both contribute dynamically to maintain the relative positions of the racial strains present in the power structure of worldwide society. The results of the survey made in 1949 and especially in 1951 show conclu-sively that the city is still literally in the grip of images and judgments of a traditional nature. In a case study on a large mixed family, in which one branch went back four hundred years and another was made up of Italian immigrants, the researcher examined the reactions of upper-class whites to the potential innovations of the law against race prejudice. In the first branch the general opinion was that the law would strengthen the Negro's natural arrogance and aggressiveness. Thus it now became necessary to strengthen vigilantly those measures which formerly had permitted them to keep him in his place. In the second branch of the family the Negro was regarded "as if he were a strange object whose presence we must eventually get used to but whom we would never admit as really being one of us, participating in our life and belong-ing to our home." In their view there was "no place for him in their world," and he should be "put in his place." Random samples of opinion taken at various levels of racial contact show that there was in fact open and overt intransigence in some circles. One white informant who was personally opposed to the prevailing situation expressed himself as shown in the following exchange:

Researcher: So they [Negroes and mulattoes] can apply for any work? In the bank where you work, for example, would they be accepted without opposition?

Informant: Ah! That's something else again! Of course they are at a disadvantage. In the bank we have only two black employees. They are messengers and they're there because they're old employees. What's more, they'll never be anything else.

Similarly, the results of a case study involving a food factory show that there was no attempt to disguise the situation. The researcher [26] summed up the results of her observations, which were corroborated by questionnaires, as follows: "There is prejudice there and nobody tries to hide it. Black employees are only hired for cleaning or lifting the bags, in other words heavy work. Even so there is one section in the factory [the largest, making noodles, and occupying 200 employees out of 300] where Negroes are not employed at all, not even for such work." Less than 2 per cent of the total numbers of workers were Negroes, and there were no women among them. "As could hardly help being the case, all the Negroes that worked there (five in all) know perfectly well that they have a very limited range of possibilities before them. Outside of what they do there is not much to choose from and, most important, they know why there is not much to choose from, that is, they know about prejudice, that there is an order from the management that they should stay where they are" and should be kept out of the above-mentioned section. "So, formally or informally, consciously or otherwise, prejudice exists there, imposing various limitations on the social ascent of the Negro and on the change in standard of living that it would bring."

Rarely, however, is this situation transparently clear. Generally it is dissembled rejection that prevails. In a large organization that recruited the bulk of its personnel by means of standardized techniques, a very simple stratagem was used: only candidates with special recommendations were considered. When a candidate is presenting his credentials, recruiters "find a way to prevent Negroes from getting in. They may say that there are no openings or that they will call him when they need him. I know they don't let Negroes in." [27] In another organization, equally large and operating countrywide, where standardized selection was practiced, they demanded photographs and personal data on the candidate. Although they did not ask for data on racial characteristics, they were able to separate those who were unacceptable "because of their color" from the other candidates.[28] Finally, there is a great deal of information, amply corroborated, making it clear that interviews with heads of personnel sections served the same purpose almost universally and that recruitment for important or prominent positions is confined to whites.[29] There are no explicit reasons for such attitudes and behavior. Common-sense opinions provide rationalizations, the effectiveness of which depends on the degree of intolerance of the agents or of those responsible for discriminatory practices. Our survey made it clear that two types of judgment are often involved. First, there are judgments of a specifically prejudiced nature. There are whites who frankly hold intolerant views, as can be inferred from the following two quotations: "There is prejudice and there should be. With rare exceptions, when do we find Negroes occupying high positions? They belong to an inferior race." They are lacking in "ability, because in a thousand Negroes there is only one who stands out." Second, there are judgments that have some nuances: "The Negro would be equal to the white man if. . . ." Then "explanations of his inferiority" are sought in his economic, cultural, or social situation. "Cultural inferiority," "moral inferiority," and "lack of opportunity" are usually brought to the fore. Here are two typical comments showing how such rationalizations are strung together:

One informant writes: "If the Negro has a standard of living lower than that of the white, he owes it to various causes. The Negro came to Brazil as a slave and to this day, despite laws freeing him from slavery, he is a victim of the white man's contempt. Despite all the progress the white man never allowed the Negro sufficient liberty of action. There are always chains hampering his movements on behalf of his culture. The Golden Law gave them liberty, but the whites continue to humiliate the Negro with their prejudice, doing everything possible to place barriers in the way of his becoming "a person." If Negroes are backward today it is not only because some of them are lazy, delinquent, etc. They never had the same opportunities as the whites. First as slaves, then as farm laborers, then as the white man's servants, doing the worst kinds of work without any rights despite their liberty. This liberty hardly did them any good because they could not use it. Race prejudice, lack of background, ignorance all helped to keep them at a standstill in society. While the whites had everything, the Negroes served as a staircase helping the whites to reach the best positions. . . ." [30]

According to another informant "the white man is not more intelligent than the mulatto nor the mulatto than the Negro. . . . The white man is in better circumstances. Background and circumstances are the principal factors in the Negro's backwardness. They came as slaves from Africa, where they were already leading a miserable life, almost like animals brought by force to our farms where they found no better conditions. They never had a chance to learn, to use their intelligence, because they were always treated as working animals. How could they become equal to the white man, their enemy and Lord? This justifies their indolent attitude to their most important problems because they never had, nor do they have now, an awareness of their situation, because of their general ignorance. . . . The race prejudice that exists among the whites comes from colonial times, and we have already become accustomed to seeing the Negro as a lazy man without courage enough to face life and its struggles, and submitting to the whites and their demands. They have already accepted this state of affairs owing to lack of knowledge that would make them recognize that they are equal to the whites. If Negroes have a lower standard of living it is because they don't have the same opportunities, not because they don't work. . . ."[31]

Between these two extremes there are the odd or peculiar reactions of those who believe in natural aversion to the race or that "it is better for us not to mingle," and so on. It is interesting that the two most common types of judgment lead practically to the same conclusions. Theoretically we could separate those who discriminate for racial reasons and those who discriminate for social or cultural reasons. From the Negro's point of view, however, there is no point in such subtlety since either way he is rejected or accepted with reluctance. When he is looking for a job, there is doubt whether he has enough experience or competence to perform it before any evidence to this effect has been presented. If it is a question of giving him a supervisory job, similar doubts are cast on his ability to deal with others, "to deal with his subordinates," or "to behave himself with women." If it is a question of a job involving close contact with the public or carrying a certain prestige, they think "it would not look good to have a Negro in such a job." There are even restrictions to personal association with Negroes. The following statement is enlightening: "Whites and Negroes are equal, but the latter always have a complex that affects their attitudes. For example, the group where I play cards was joined by a mulatto married to a girl from a very well-known family. He played several times very properly, but one day, when he was losing, he accused his companions of cheating. Like they say, and it's true; 'when a Negro doesn't shit coming in, he shits going out.'" Even where he is accepted, acceptance is often limited to formal and specific contacts. In numerous interviews whites who accepted competition with mulatto or Negro colleagues stated that they did not invite them to visit their homes or to go out together socially. This set of restrictions severely wounds the more sensitive Negroes. Some even firmly believe that "it is a lie that the Negro can rise only by education and through his profession. . . . After he is educated and has become a competent professional, that is when the Negro's drama begins." Then, "he finds all doors closed by the white man."

These data clearly suggest that manifestations of race prejudice interfere with the mechanisms for integration of the Negro into normal social life. Being black and having an inferior social position are associated in a veritable iron circle, as if the traditional pattern of asymmetric race relations were still in full force. Intolerant whites seize on color and base their judgments on racially inherited attributes; tolerant whites reject these criteria, but yield in one way or another to traditional judgments. In the final analysis then, racial prejudice has the same effect, whether we view it as stemming from racial or social bases. It helps to maintain social distance between the two racial stocks, either by hindering social classification and mobility for the Negro and the mulatto or, finally, by reducing the impact of the modernizing influences of the competitive social order on the traditional system of race relations.

This analysis bears out the conclusions of Roger Bastide,[32] the distinguished sociologist who studied these aspects of race relations in São Paulo and reached some general conclusions which deserve close attention. First, "prejudice arises as a form of self-defense for the white man when he feels threatened by the rise of the black man. It is a question of maintaining the present occupational pyramid, with the white man in the leadership positions and the Negro at subordinate levels." Second, "the whites do not want to notice the black man's efforts to integrate himself into class society as a member of the proletariat; they preserve an image of the 'old Negro' in order to imprison him within certain sectors of society, so he will forego the better paid and more 'decent' positions." Third, the white man leaves the Negro to a harsh fate, abandoning the black masses "to their own fortune and letting them defend themselves as they can. . . . Control, here, is an absence of control. . . . There are no legal barriers: school, apprenticeship, and factories are by law open to all, so it is not the white man's fault if the Negro does not take advantage of his opportunities. One can't force him to seek a 'happiness' that does not correspond to his own concept of life, to his own ideal." Although the white man does not fear (nor does he have for the time being economic or professional reasons to fear) competition from the Negro, he preserves as best he can the old system of race relations. Hence the perpetuation of representations of personality status that exclude the Negro partially or totally from the social roles that would place him on an equal footing with the white man.

Besides this stabilizing function of a latent nature, race prejudice has other specific effects when it is expressed more or less openly. In the first place, it should be pointed out that racially intolerant persons have a warped view of the rising Negro, react with ill will toward him, and frankly reject him. Thus we frequently came across such reactions as: "No one can stand these people when they rise in the world. They become insufferable." "The behavior of the Negro who rises is generally unbearable. Feeling superior, he begins to take advantage of the situation and persecute his former colleagues as if they were inferior." In one instance the manager of a department took the Negro clerk who had won second place in a competition to a section head to ask "if he agreed to have this nigger work with him." To have appointed him without previous consultation might have seemed offensive. Another informant mentioned his school experience. His colleagues humiliated professors they considered Negroes. "They think that a Negro cannot occupy an important position; this is because of the prejudice that already exists in their family." [33]

Moreover, the data suggest that resistance to acceptance of a black colleague or supervisor never comes alone. In these cases people react as if they were being socially degraded by the simple fact of occupying a position equal or inferior to that of a Negro. They became furious and try in every possible way to undermine or prevent the success of their antagonist. They never spare him either in gossip or in personal contact. To them the situation seems disgraceful. In this position descendants of traditional families are most sensitive, but the interviews revealed that the descendants of immigrants are not far behind. They feel humiliated, principally when their black colleagues excel or are promoted. Then they begin to talk about "pull" and "low blows" to explain the success of these colleagues. Second, one must not lose sight of what it means to reject the Negro as an equal. Both the descendant of a traditional family who depreciates a colleague because of his color and is surprised that "a Negro can be this or that" and the descendant of some immigrants who "feels a gnawing pain inside" when "because of influence they promote an incompetent nigger," are yielding to sentiments and frustrations incompatible with the competitive social order. From this angle the social ascent of the Negro and the mulatto takes on the nature of a crucial test, on the one hand because it helps to reveal what lies behind apparently tolerant, open, and egalitarian racial adjustment and on the other because it defines the potential sphere of racial tension. For the time being the small number of rising Negroes coincides with a whole range of socioeconomic opportunities. If this situation changes, race relations are likely to be modified in an unpredictable fashion. Two facts are obvious. The limit of the white man's tolerance for strong competition from the black population has not yet been fully tested and, what is worse, resistance to "acceptance of the Negro as an equal" contains an element that is unmistakably and irreducibly sociopathic. This element could become a destructive agent if present conditions evolve toward a situation threatening (or seeming to threaten) the white monopoly of power.

The Negro's reaction to race relations and to what he himself refers to as "race prejudice" raises, in turn, a considerable barrier to his personal or collective desires for vertical social mobility. Here we have to distinguish two distinct psychosocial manifestations: (1) there is a rough and undifferentiated reaction springing from assimilation and passive observance of the Negro image constructed by the white man which fosters spontaneous adjustments that are profoundly apathetic; (2) there is also a more elaborate psychological reaction referred to among Negroes by the term "complex." In accordance with the forms of perception and explanation that have been culturally developed, it stands as a substantive reality and the real driving force behind the psychological duality of the Negro and the mulatto. The complex makes Dr. Jekyll transform himself into Mr. Hyde in the Negro's relations with the white man. In a desire to escape the painful moral climate projected around mulattoes' real or imagined expectations, the Negro anticipates attitudes, behavior, and values that undermine or destroy his best chances for normal integration into the competitive social order. We should therefore recognize certain nuances in the mechanisms of racial relationships. At the first level the individual accepts and tacitly recognizes his "inferiority." He does not dispute it or look on it as a moral affront. That is why he is not going to try to find out if racial prejudice "exists" or "does not exist." As in the moral world of the slave—or among the ruins of slavery, where permanent social disorganization was set up as a normal style of life—yielding was confused with resisting and surviving. At the second level the moral configuration of a person is set up as a standard. The Negro and the mulatto feel that "they are not inferior" to the white. Fear of insults, humiliation, and social degradation engenders tortuous and ingenious ways to defend the balance of the ego and personal dignity. The two types of reaction were unmasked and severely condemned through the racial counterideology worked out by the rights movements. Nevertheless, they persist and manifest themselves to varying degrees among Negroes today. The more the individual is in the grip of or identifies with the traditional social order, the more he resorts to passive capitulation. On the other hand the more the individual is attached to "ideals for an orderly life," without having the moral and material means of putting the white man's style of life into practice, the more he is a victim of the complex. Thus those who are able to bear in a balanced way the impact of the white man's presence and demands are rather few. According to rough and merely conjectural estimates based on limited experience, at the time of our research we established the following proportions: 30 per cent tended toward adjustments that were partially or wholly traditionalist; 50 per cent were under the effects of the complex in one way or another; 20 per cent leaned toward more complex, balanced, and autonomous models of personality organization and asserted themselves, psychologically and morally, in accordance with the competitive inclination and the egalitarian concepts of the "new Negro." These proportions indicate how powerful subjective barriers are and on what scale they operate as devastating forces, endangering or striking at the root of the black population's best desires for and efforts toward social ascent.

The complex produces similar effects, with the difference that enlightened persons are involved, that is, those who have benefited in one way or another from vertical mobility and the consequent widening of their cultural outlook. In the course of our inquiries we discovered that the white man himself is somewhat sensitive to the Negro complex. Moreover, his treatment of the humble Negro, whose adjustments are regulated by traditional concepts, reveals a distinct liking for the polite and respectful behavior that the complex prompts. He is charmed by the ceremonious manner and the spontaneous ability to "stay in his place" that separates the Negro with a complex from the "stupid" or "uncultivated" Negro without doing serious harm to the tradition of hierarchy. Nevertheless, being aware of subtleties, the white man does not attribute this type of conformity either to inherent characteristics or to a defect from slavery. He understands it objectively as the effect of the prevailing standards of race relationships. Thus, in one of the interviews, a white man of Italian descent explained that "there are intelligent Negroes" who "are trustworthy" and "reach important positions." He pointed out, however, that "the Negroes themselves feel inferior to the whites. They know they are not equal and accept the situation in which they live."

What interests us most, however, are the ways in which the

Negroes with a complex think, and act. The majority of them react to real or imagined manifestations of prejudice in a self-punishing way. Since they fear that their presence might be unpleasant to whites and that their hopes will be rejected, they try to avoid contact with them, especially with persons regarded as strangers or superiors. As a rule they also avoid open discussion of prejudice and the reasons for it, for fear of rejection, not only because of color but also because of something worse. As a result they are not inclined to compete unrestrictedly with the white man, thus seriously limiting their opportunities for professionalization and social ascent. For the same reason they rarely gather the knowledge and skills required by the careers they desire (or choose under pressure of circumstances). Their careers are characterized by a succession of failures, very rarely by success. However, the failures prompt characteristic self-defense reactions; they do not destroy hope. They are categorically attributed to prejudice, ill will, or the white man's fear. At one level the white man is alleged to monopolize the best jobs, at another level he is alleged to block the Negro's opportunities for promotion by withholding social recognition of his worth and his competence.

In their plans for vertical mobility the Negro and the mulatto also face negative psychosocial compulsions inherited through participation in the Negro subculture itself. For purposes of this analysis it will be enough to point out some of the more important aspects. First, there are certain compulsions revolving around a basic judgment that "it doesn't help the Negro much to want to rise because he will always remain black." This judgment has various meanings. It means not only that the Negro will not free himself from his complexes, resentments, or personal limitations but also that he will always be regarded and treated as black by the whites. The Negroes and mulattoes interviewed cited a series of attributes justifying that judgment: "lack of a strong will," "unreliability," "inability to lead," "lack of initiative," "inability to earn the confidence" of whites and Negroes themselves, and so on.

In the final analysis these attributes, put forward as negative features inherent in the Negro's character, are the dynamic products of the types of status personality socially attributed to the Negro and the mulatto. They do not involve, or seriously restrict, the acquisition of certain attitudes, behavior, and aptitudes essential for the performance of certain social roles in society.

Second, the ego-involvement in behavioral expectations and career prospects created by such an image leads, in turn, to adjustments that are irrational in different ways. Certain elementary convictions are formed leading individuals to believe that "Negroes have no brains" or at least that "Negroes in general are inferior to whites." We have now entered the very psychosociological basis of the complex, which consists in admitting a certain inferiority of the Negro in relation to the white to be innate and insurmountable. The grounds for this conviction are of little importance. It makes no difference whether people think that "the Negro will never be able to do these things" or whether they think in a more subtle way: "You can see that Negroes are inferior to whites, not because they are black—that's the color we are born with—but Negroes don't manage to rise like white people. I don't know if it's because they have no brains or because they need to work at an early age." The essential point is that such a conviction fosters undesirable and anachronistic adjustments. It is the dynamic source of decisions or actions that are irretrievably fatal to integration.

Third, making the initial personal effort to rise is very hard. After the individual has managed to overcome the psychological barriers within himself and in the environment, he still has to engage in a bitter and ceaseless battle with those who are reconciled to or satisfied with a Negro's life. Since the opportunities for ascent are limited, the majority openly resent their companion's efforts and literally regard them as an attempt to "cease being black." There is full awareness that success will bring the loss of their companion, that he will end up being ashamed of his relatives and friends, and—and this is what seems intolerable to them—that he will put on white airs. Thus, in addition to sabotaging his plans, they refuse him any material or moral support, however small it might be. Everything takes place as if there were a blind and invisible feeling of rancor against the one who wants to rise and therefore intends to cease to be Negro, socially speaking.

In interviews with Negroes and mulattoes who were struggling to change their lives and to become somebody we heard sad confidences that sounded like a condemnation of Negro by Negro: "They would rather help a white man than one of the same color"; "they hate to see another Negro rise"; "the trouble with Negroes is that they are generally enemies of their own race."

Fourth, one must consider the other side of the coin. As a rule the vertically mobile Negro saves up only for himself. Not only are the white man's favorable judgments restricted in their application, without benefiting the Negro race or Negroes in general, but individuals really separate themselves from Negro circles in accordance with the fruits of their success. At the most they regroup in exclusive social circles of elite Negroes who abominate the Negro masses, their socioeconomic situation, and their style of life. The reasons for this behavior have already been mentioned. The rich Negro must defend himself against parasites, who would altogether ruin him; and he faces a hard battle for moral acceptance by the whites and by Negroes themselves in his new social situation. This separation goes so far that one Negro subject declared in an interview that he knew "Negroes who had risen very high in the world," but he refused to name them "because they might not like me going around saying that they are Negroes and mulattoes." The important thing to note here is not so much the moral break brought about by social ascent, both for the rising individual and for the social circle to which he belonged, but rather the repercussion of such consequences on the Negro subculture. Thus there is no establishment of the tradition characteristic of social groups enjoying vertical mobility, with everything such tradition means in terms of identifying persons with certain collective goals above differences of personal achievement and social level. Absence of this tradition favors the extreme isolation of the Negro elite, who become more and more estranged from the human dramas of their former environment. Moreover, it helps to consolidate the general tendency to regard ascent itself as a sort of betrayal, threatening the integrity and continuity of Negro groups.

Fifth, in this moral context of resentment and contradictory judgments, tendencies arise toward retaliation that is extremely devastating. The elite Negro fastens onto an exclusivist view of the world that entitles him to ignore his past and to regard the Negro problem as a matter for the police. Nondescript and lazy Negroes are portrayed without any sympathy. The shamelessness that prevails among Negro groups is a difficult burden to bear; it is at the same time a public affront and a threat to the status acquired by the elite Negro. Thus the latter thinks that "the police should clean up Negro society. They should rid it of its bad elements, arrest them all, and send them to work in the interior." On the other hand the dependent or poor Negro shows no more good sense. He ridicules his fellow Negro who wants to rid himself of blackness by means of social prestige. He does not accept his parvenu's ethical code, he rejects his mania for sobriety and decency, makes fun of his "airs," and cruelly pays him back with deformed judgments. A female researcher came across a characteristic occurrence. The subject being interviewed, a mulatto woman, arrived "in a very angry state of mind." "Just now I saw a Negro woman all got up in a fur coat and rings! She looked like a monkey! It's ridiculous, they should prohibit such things. That sort of thing is not for Negroes!" When the researcher provocatively retorted that there was nothing wrong with that, quite the contrary, the woman exploded: "Ah! So you are for democracy, eh? In a democracy even Negroes are people, eh? Well I don't buy it; I hate those dirty stinking people!" Another investigator recorded the outburst of an informant who resented the "exhibitionism" of the women who frequented a certain place. "You can't go there anymore. It's always full of stuck-up little Negro women!" Many more examples could be given, but these are enough to suggest that reciprocal prejudice by Negro against Negro is taking shape and that this prejudice has a pernicious social effect on the equilibrium of Negro groups. It raises barriers to internal differentiation among black people and definitely makes social ascent an individual undertaking, as risky as it is unprotected.

We should also mention the influence of differential factors in limiting the vertical mobility of the Negro and the mulatto, and the nature of the effects of official machinery for intervention and control. For the first point, it is enough to mention the fact that, given the economic, social, and cultural conditions in Negro circles, the smallest differences in the degree of family integration, in economic situation, and in educational level are associated in the end with disproportionately large differences in effective utilization of existing opportunities.

The shade of skin color is rather important in determining the white man's degree of tolerance and inclination to cooperate. Although some whites are strongly hostile to mulattoes, the majority prefer to give a chance to the lighter Negroes. As a result the mulatto manages to assimilate more quickly and more easily the experiences required for adjustment to practical life on the levels at which these adjustments should develop. Regardless of shade of color, it is men who have the greatest difficulties. Although women find serious barriers when they try to adjust to occupations that are not regarded as Negro's work, men have to face the consequences of competition with white workers and professionals in a harder and more open manner. Thus negative judgments and stereotypes are much more destructive to men than to women.

The integrated Negro family represents an alternative for this differential influence. The more the Negro family approaches the models of organization of the white family, the greater its efficacy in socializing children and in helping young people achieve their ambitions. This process is reflected in the degree of stability of relations between parents and children and in the security of the wife and offspring; it also tends to have a beneficial effect on the stability and the level of income and on the abilities of the adult generations to fulfill their social roles normally. As a result the Negro family itself is able to carry out its social functions and to offer its members a minimum of material and moral support in their competitive relations with the whites. Naturally this situation is a specific differential factor among Negro groups. Children and young people belonging to disorganized families are at an obvious, often insurmountable disadvantage in comparison with children and young persons belonging to integrated families. This indicates indirectly that the social ascent of the Negro and the mulatto increases their capacity for developing the behavior and the adjustment demanded by the competitive social order.

As for the second point, the inconsistencies of official machinery for intervention and control are notorious. The shortcomings from which health and police services suffered in the period from 1900 to 1930, which we examined in Chapter 2, have become more serious. Lack of protection for children, abuses committed against young people and against Negro women, indifference to the unfavorable social effects of the disorganization of the Negro family and of Negro groups—all these are a constant source of indignation to politically sensitive elements of the black population. In the interviews these elements revealed violent anger and demonstrated unusual resentment of the government's disregard for the Negro. Not only do they consider that the Negro is abandoned and resent the lack of a policy for the use of our own resources, but they also point out that it is necessary to set up a kind of "National Negro Protection Service" capable of coordinating measures for effective health and for protection of the rural and urban sectors of the black population. They clearly perceive that they can expect nothing from private enterprise, either white or Negro. In the United States foundations of this kind have been established and are considered to be efficient. In Brazil, however, they say "the white sharks only look after their own interests" and "there are no Negro millionaires."

They also understand that is not enough to create free schools, protective services for children, homes for the sick and the aged, etc. As a rule the Negro is not in an economic or social position to use these institutions, either because he cannot bear the indirect costs of such services or because he has no access to them for lack of social relations and familiarity with the mechanisms of their utilization. One of those interviewed, reflecting the opinion of the majority, observed: "The opportunities granted in schools or elsewhere, either officially or by private parties, do not help the Negro except by chance. That is one of the difficulties. Those who occupy administrative positions avail themselves of these opportunities for their relatives, acquaintances, or white men's protégés. They should be forced to give such opportunities to Negroes. Since the whites dominate the legislature and the administration, they act in their own benefit. The Negroes get the crumbs." Others, less concerned with accusing the whites, are more insistent on the feasibility of using the services. One of those interviewed pointed out: "It's no good forcing schools to give X openings to Negroes or the children of Negroes. They will rarely be able to take advantage of the opportunities. What is needed is to give them a better economic situation. The Negro mother does not take care of her children because she can't. If she is married she must work to help support the home. If she's not married she must get money to keep herself and her children. Thus when Negro children have a mother —that is, when they are not abandoned or given to whoever will take them—they are left to their own devices most of the time. No one teaches them manners. They stay in the street, getting up to mischief. They don't learn what school is. They have no one to keep an eye on them, to guide them in life. School means nothing to them. If the child is a girl she goes to work at thirteen, fourteen, or fifteen years of age. She goes and looks after white children. And that is what happens with

Negroes. If we improved their economic situation, if we gave them an opportunity to live better, they could educate their children." In the light of such remarks it follows that what is wanted is government intervention that is radical in scope—in addition to schools, student maintenance, and social services, they want protective measures that result in improved opportunity for work and a higher level of income for the Negro worker of both sexes.

It is curious that the white man shares, to some extent, this view of the situation. He does not go so far as to imagine the need for a National Negro Protection Service, but he condemns the way official measures are taken and their inefficacy. For example, let us take the following statement. In closing a pessimistic description of the Negro's situation, the informant stressed: "It is mainly the government that is to blame for not encouraging the Negroes. Instead of giving money for samba groups and encouraging the Negro in soccer, the government should help the Negro to rise. What the government is doing is make the Negro believe that he's only good really for dancing and playing soccer." What counts, against the complex backdrop depicted by these accusations is an incontestable fact: the economic, social, and cultural situation generally limits the real utilization by the black population of the opportunities embodied in official health and control services. Furthermore, since these services do not take this fact into consideration, they end up being used predominantly by whites and sometimes clearly by social circles that could do without any direct or indirect help from the public authorities. These data are of interest to us because they suggest that some of the more accessible mechanisms of integration into the competitive social order do not benefit, or benefit only by chance, the great mass of the black population.

Even when the barriers to vertical mobility have been overcome, the way is not always entirely clear. Other obstacles arise to hinder full enjoyment of the social roles and privileges inherent in the social position occupied, from the viewpoint either of individual careers or of succeeding generations. The present discussion will only consider the main aspects of the situation: (1) white resistance to recognition of the Negro's social ascent; (2) resistance on the part of the Negro and the mulatto to recognize the ascent of the Negro himself; (3) the rising black man's difficulties in maintaining his acquired social status.

We should note at the outset that there is a vast range of evasive or restrictive racial attitudes, behavior, and judgments. Wherever and to the extent that the traditional code of race relations prevails, there may be manifestations of a certain irreducible exclusiveness or there may be veiled rejection. Either way, there is an attempt to "put the Negro in his place," that is, to maintain a close connection between color and the lowest social position. As a result, for purposes of association with whites of the same or higher social level, color partially or totally erases the benefits of social ascent. Wherever and to the extent that convention prevails, having its origins in class society and the corresponding urban civilization, either there is a definition of areas of tolerant acceptance of the competent Negro, the educated Negro, the important Negro, the wealthy Negro (through formal and impersonal contacts), or there are zones of genuine seclusion for the elite (where the whites regard social mingling as something undesirable in itself and consider racial mingling an aggravating factor that makes it intolerable and impossible to overlook). In approaching this matter we shall not attempt to consider all the possible adjustments throughout this wide range of evasive or restrictive racial attitudes, behavior, and judgments, but shall limit ourselves to the cases that are most frequent and which therefore appeared during our observations.

Prominent in white resistance to recognition of the Negro's acquired social status is a kind of linear reaction, a concept inherited from the traditional cultural outlook. Whites not only associate color with a very low social position but, what is much more serious, they presumed that "the Negro cannot be otherwise," as if slavery and disorganized social life had degraded the Negro's nature. This connection is clearly apparent in the following typical statement: "In Brazil the white man and the Negro are not separated, but the Negro is placed in a much lower position. . . . The Negro lives in tenements, in the company of people who are no good. Thus they drift into crime. Almost all robberies and crimes are committed by Negroes. . . . If white people came from the Negro's environment they would be no better themselves. That is why they avoid contact with Negroes. That is why they are not well regarded in our society. They think that Negroes are no good, that they make trouble and are dishonest." [34]

At a second level there is the effect of certain expectations and behaviors firmly established among whites. Regardless of whether they share that concept, a great number of persons tend spontaneously and unconsciously to associate color with very low social positions, without having any discriminatory or prejudiced intent. This is the inertia effect; being accustomed to deal with low-level Negroes, they build a social image of the Negro that resists disturbing redefinitions. These ambiguities are frequently repeated in associations between strangers. By immediately placing the Negro in an inferior social category, the white man may both address him in an unsuitable manner and hold unrealistic expectations of behavior. If the number of highly placed Negroes were larger and if their relations with whites were closer at different social levels, such confusion would probably have already disappeared. Nevertheless, it establishes the tone of interaction between the rising Negro and that part of the white population with which he must come in contact. This type of resistance—naïve, passive, and unwise—would be of little importance if it did not have a profound effect on the adaptive and integrative mechanisms of the Negro himself. Feeling in turn disrespected, offended, and humiliated, they either withdraw to avoid disagreeable experiences or insist on their rights. Some understand the roots of these ambiguities, take advantage of them, and develop compensatory attitudes by laughing at the white man's expense. The majority, however, react negatively. By withdrawing they condemn themselves to partial enjoyment of the social roles and privileges corresponding to their social position. In claiming their rights they show attitudes and behavior corresponding to the white man's negative stereotypes about the Negro. Although their lapses may be inadvertent and rectifiable, whites who are surprised by such a series of rude and violent recriminations inevitably tend to stick to ethnocentric judgments and begin consciously "to treat the Negro as he deserves."

Nevertheless, Negroes are better acquainted with the nature of the differential treatment that they find themselves subjected to in dealings with whites of the same or higher social level. In many testimonies they stressed in various ways that the latter tend to treat them "without any respect" and that "they think right away they should be giving orders." Some characteristic examples will perhaps best illustrate what often happens. Manner of dress served to distinguish the white from the Negro in the past. Certain clothes were only used by a Negro when he inherited them from his white protectors, already old and threadbare. The rising Negro manages to get a higher income and generally tries to dress very well. Not a small number of malevolent comments are made by whites and by Negroes themselves against this tendency. We have chosen, however, an illustration that is almost unique, since "white impertinence" was directed at a child's article of clothing: "For one reason or another [the female teacher] was always picking on him [the son of the woman being interviewed]. She even picked on his sweater making him take if off but not making the other children do the same. He complained at home but I backed up the teacher. I would say, 'You are right, but she gives the orders. She wants you to take off your sweater, so take it off. She runs the class and you have to obey.' 'But what if I'm cold?' 'It doesn't matter, son. Obey the teacher.'"

Another well-known sign of status is having a maid. Black women in the past, and even today, always formed the major part of the domestic servants in São Paulo. When she rises she, in turn, can have one or two maids. The white neighbors not only find fault with this but they let the woman know. Here is one account:

"I don't know why you want a maid."

"Why do I have a maid? Why, for the same reason you have."

"But there's more work to do in my house than in yours. You have no children and so-and-so [the couple's daughter] can already help you."

"I want a maid because I like to have a maid, because I don't want to do the housework. Also I can rest. Besides, I can afford to pay a maid. Everyone does the best they are able."

According to the informant, even the neighbor's little daughter, "repeating what she hears at home, also asked, 'Why do you want a maid? You don't have a little baby to look after!'" [35]

The expectation that a Negro woman should always be a household servant frequently obliges the middle-class black woman to face certain "irritations." This is how a husband describes the unpleasantness that his wife undergoes because of it: "She suffers a great deal from the rude remarks of people who call at the door to offer vegetables, household articles, etc. When she goes to the window or gets to the door they immediately ask something like: 'Is the lady of the house in? I want to speak to her!' or 'Go and get your mistress. I have something to talk to her about.' Some are even bolder and ruder. When she says, 'I am the lady of the house,' they reply, 'Stop joking. I don't have time to waste. Go and call your mistress!' They think that a Negro can't have a house that's a little better and live more decently." The following case suggests how the white man's "mania for giving orders" manifests itself. The headmistress of a school group went for the first time to a professional meeting of headmasters. "I didn't know anyone there. I was waiting at the entrance for a colleague who would introduce me to the others when an elderly and very pleasing lady came up to me and said, 'Go and call such and such a delegate. I want to speak to him.' I was puzzled by her attitude and was lucky enough to see my friend arrive, who introduced me to the other. She was somewhat taken aback and said to me, 'Please excuse me. I took you for an employee of the school. If I had known that you were my colleague, I would not have ordered you to go and get the education delegate.' "

The same suppositions create embarrassing situations in the treatment of members of the liberal professions. Of the numerous cases, the following are enough to give an idea of what usually happens. A white lady went to the outpatients' office of a health service. The doctor on duty was a Negro. When he opened the door she "went directly to him, taking him for a male nurse. She rudely ordered him to go and call the doctor because she wanted to speak to him. She shook like a leaf when he replied that he was the doctor." A farmer went to a laboratory to speak to a certain professor of chemistry who was a mulatto. "He rang the bell and when the door was opened he said that he wanted to speak to Professor So-and-so. The latter, who had answered the door personally, said, 'Certainly, come in.' The farmer then told him to notify the professor, to which the latter replied, 'I am the professor.' " Even in relations with company salesmen similar confusion arises. A mulatto dentist told us that sometimes he is waiting for a client or reading a newspaper in his waiting room. "A salesman arrives and sees me there. Some don't even pay any attention, they go straight away to look in the office to see if the dentist is there! Only then do they ask, 'Is the dentist out?' Then I say, 'I am the dentist!' The young men are embarrassed but I am amused. Others, as soon as they arrive and see me there in a white jacket, ask, 'Is the dentist in?' or 'May I speak to the doctor?' I avenge myself the same way, saying that I am the dentist or the doctor."

Noteworthy results were obtained by questioning 2,076 university students in the state of São Paulo, using Emory Borgardus's scale of social distance adapted to Brazilian conditions.[36] The mulatto and the Negro were identified as the racial groups with lowest acceptance as relatives: for marriage (14 per cent and 9.9 per cent of the replies respectively) and as friends (59.7 per cent and 55.5 per cent. In the case of the other questions the percentages of positive attitude were higher, but even so the mulatto and the Negro appear among the racial groups least preferred or most rejected: as a neighbor, 75.8 per cent and 71.9 per cent respectively; as a member of the same professional category, 74.9 per cent and 73.3 per cent; as a citizen, 77.4 per cent and 74.4 per cent. In closely matching results they appear among the groups that are strongly rejected, since, to the question whether "they would keep them out of the country," 5.2 per cent would exclude the mulatto and 7 per cent the Negro.[37]

The conclusions of Bastide and Van den Bergue are equally important. Analyzing the results of questioning 580 students from five different teachers' schools in São Paulo,[38] they were able to compare stereotypes, norms, behavior, and hypothetical relationships. "The relative tolerance of ideal norms of behavior contrasts with wide acceptance of stereotypes. Theoretical equality between whites and Negroes is accepted by 92 per cent, which is in accordance with the Brazilian democratic ethic. More than 60 per cent accept casual relations between whites and Negroes. The color line is found at the level of the closest emotional relationships. Sixty-two per cent are opposed to a degree of intimacy with Negroes going beyond simple friendliness. Seventy-seven per cent oppose miscegeneration with Negroes and 55 per cent miscegenation with mulattoes. . . . In actual behavior, according to the information given, and in hypothetical relationships, the sample was inclined toward segregation (although lack of real contact does not necessarily mean prejudice). Absence of contact with Negroes or mulattoes was reported by 104 persons. Of the sample, 95 per cent would not marry a Negro and 87 per cent would not marry a light mulatto. A paradox arises in the comparison of these four variables or dimensions of prejudice. On the one hand, we found broad adherence to democratic norms, and on the other a high degree of stereotyping, great segregation at the level of personal intimacy, and practically complete endogamy. This ambivalence establishes a real *Brazilian Di-*

lemma, though perhaps different from the *American Dilemma.*" [39] Both contributions show something that seems to us undeniable. Despite the pressure against open and systematic manifestation of race prejudice, a considerable portion of the white population makes choices or accepts stereotypes and behavior that go directly against professed norms of tolerance and racial equality.

It is still not known how this group of persons most given to discrimination and prejudice have reacted to recent tendencies toward classification and ascent for the Negro and the mulatto in the competitive social order. For this reason it is impossible to determine two things that would be extremely important for our purposes: first, whether this phenomenon helps to aggravate latent predispositions and, second, to what extent socioeconomic competition is connected with certain subterfuges that make discrimination and prejudice into mechanisms of status defense. Our supposition is that the Negro has not yet collectively threatened the economic, social, and cultural situation of the white man in Brazil to any marked extent. Where discrimination and prejudice in the forms they assume in Brazilian society are manifested most strongly we are not, strictly speaking, on the fringe of the competitive social order but at the limits of the effort to preserve our old system of race relations. This does not prevent the white man from mixing the two things here and there in concrete and limited situations involving competition with the Negro. Invalid, too, is the fundamental complaint of Negroes and mulattoes who condemn race prejudice as a mechanism for the white man's social defense. As for the first aspect, it is inevitable that the rising Negro will threaten whites of the same professional category and that these will take up the weapons most readily at hand to combat them, but such occurrences are far from assuming the proportions and the character of a social process. It might even be presumed (if certain conditions in the socioeconomic development of the city are preserved) that this may not even come to pass in the future. For the second aspect, the Negro's complaint is right, but what is being denied to him is much more than he thinks. To the extent that discrimination and prejudice produce the effect indicated, they do not merely favor the competitive advantages of the white man but, more importantly and before doing so, they block or hinder the very access of the Negro to the competitive social order. What is at stake is the structure of our system of race relations. Those who cling more or less intolerantly to the prerogatives of the white race are fundamentally opposed to the adaptation of the structure to the democratic social order. On the other hand those who simply resist the rising Negro for fear of losing status do not always go that far.

It is curious how this complex sociohistoric situation disorients the Negro and the mulatto. Confusing the three levels of resistance to their social classification and ascent, they fail to discern the relevant factor of greatest dynamic importance. Some cases are flagrant, where it is not difficult to point to discrimination and prejudice as they act very strongly. One grievous example was given in public debate. In a certain city in the interior of São Paulo the doctor on duty at a trade union health service went out on an urgent call. On seeing a Negro doctor the patient's husband did not permit the examination, saying, "Imagine if I were to let a Negro examine my wife!" As a result the woman died, and the doctor could only make out the death certificate, giving the reasons in his log to cover himself.[40]

Two other things are perceived, but projected in a limited context. First, there is the white man's ill will toward Negro candidates. The latter rarely get a chance to prove their professional competence, and when they do they are often rejected for reasons of color. It is striking how many of those interviewed repeat this explanation. Some believe that "the white man wants to protect his relatives and friends" or that "the bosses like to give the best jobs to those of their own race"; others suppose that "the white man is afraid of the Negro" (of his intelligence, his devotion to work, his will to succeed); finally, some think that "the white man is afraid to take a chance because of the Negro's bad reputation as a worker." However, they do not relate this behavior to its final result: exclusion of the Negro from the competitive social order and its direct results in the persistence of the old pattern of racial dominance. On the other hand they point out the intrigues of the white man, especially when he is in the process of being replaced by black colleagues, and the lack of protection that hinders or restricts recognition of the worth of the Negro professional and consequently limits his chances of promotion. Few manage to describe such intrigues coherently in such a way as to demonstrate that behind them there is really concealed a residual resistance to accepting the Negro as either equal or superior. To the extent that the competitive social order tends to absorb Negroes and whites as equals, the nature of racial tension is modified. The white man, who formerly was only engaged in an indirect and invisible defense of his superior position, must descend to undisguised individual combat. This aspect became very clear in some interviews, but the best illustration is provided by a dentist's experience. He made it clear that his white colleagues in the neighborhood attacked him "without pity or mercy." If one of his clients "falls into their hands," they immediately say: "What good work! Very good!" "Clients like to hear that, to know that their dentists are good, but when they say that I am the dentist, the other dentists begin to find fault. 'Well, this bridge here is not good. Here it's very wide, etc.' The next day the clients tell me: 'Yesterday I needed you, but you weren't in so I went to Dr. So-and-so. He told me that the work is not good for this and that reason.' Then I have to convince the client! I have a devil of a job to show them that it's all right." Nevertheless, in personal relations the same colleagues behave cordially and "pretend that they get on very well with me." Evidence of this kind shows that resistance to the Negro then becomes much more severe and drastic. Since it affects a small number of people at a time of full employment and rising average real income, its results are not very dramatic.

Insofar as the Negro is not fully socialized for the competitive social order, there are few who react intelligently and advantageously to such types of specific resistance. Disheartenment in the face of injustices or treachery gives way to withdrawal from competitive effort. The idea gains strength that "the higher the social category to which the Negro aspires, the greater the probability of resistance from whites in this social category." [41] This idea is a permanent feature of his cultural outlook and leads him to give up his ambitions. Moreover, since his participation in acquired social status is limited, he receives no encouragement to continue his career such as the white man gets. He manages to become a dentist, a doctor, a lawyer, or an engineer and later finds out that "money is not everything" or that "his color closes all social doors to him." He becomes isolated, loses courage, and perhaps begins to participate in middle-class Negro clubs. His incentives to rise undergo a crisis, since his career becomes pointless in view of the social demands of a style of life. In the autobiography of such a person, who tried to adjust himself to whites of the same economic, social, and moral level, we find the following passage: "When the Negro is permitted access to elite society, he is obliged to remain isolated and cannot remain there. When he does not suffer this isolation directly because he has friends who fit his situation into the environment, he does not find the same factor that might put his wife or children at their ease. The white woman is much more prejudiced than the man. White women, accustomed to seeing Negro women in their kitchens, do not become accustomed to seeing them in their living rooms. I think this is one of the reasons that lead cultivated and rich Negro men to marry white women, even if the latter are not in the same intellectual and economic situation. Wherever the Brazilian elite have their 'habitat' for social or sporting activities it is closed to Negroes." Thus, even when it seems that resistance owing to prejudice or to conscious forms of socioeconomic antagonism is harmless or secondary, one must consider its consequences. At the very least it undermines or destroys the moral bases of a person's security by hindering in various ways ego involvement in drives that give a meaning to life and encourage the individual to accept the hard alternatives of a competitive society. Since the Negro environment is unable to absorb and minimize this impact, the rising Negro is forced to suffer it under enormous tension, as if it were the beginning and the end of the world.

Barriers to recognition by the Negroes themselves of Negro social ascent are less elaborate and destructive. They spring from a feeling of loss, from fear that the friend, companion, or relative will come to be ashamed of his own kind and separate himself from them. On the other hand these barriers correspond psychologically to the Negro image built up by the white man. Just as the latter does not distinguish between color and social position in the case of a Negro, Negroes too tend to suppose that his racial condition makes him a social equal. In the first place, there is an elementary reaction that distorts and casts doubt on the socioeconomic position achieved by the rising Negro. If an acquaintance, friend, or relative obtains his diploma as a dentist or a lawyer after prolonged efforts, when speaking of him they say: "He says he's a doctor"; "He's a would-be doctor"; etc. In a life history the researcher, on comparing the subject's data with information from those around him, found the remark "he acts as if he had a degree, but I don't know where he got his diploma." In an interview the subject confided that he knew of a Negro who "said he was an English teacher . . . and liked to dress well and talk fancy, but I was never present at any class of the so-called teacher so I cannot say for sure whether he was telling the truth or not." Second, there naturally exists among Negroes a secular consensus that certain occupations "naturally belong to the white man." Other things being equal, a Negro client will seldom choose a businessman or a professional man of the same color. He has more confidence or enjoys it more when he uses the white man. A mulatto dentist explained to us: "Negroes in general are little inclined to seek out professionals of their own color. They think they are all the same as they are. Since they have no education and know nothing, they think all Negroes are in the same situation. As far as they're concerned, Negroes are no good for anything. The only good doctor is a white one. If the professional man does not live among Negroes, he gets no Negro clients. I never separated myself from my background. I spend a lot of time in Negro associations and participate in Negro movements. That is why a large part of my clientele is black."

Finally, there is a kind of tendency to blindly resist recognition of a relationship of inferiority toward another Negro. In a public statement we heard the following: "Speaking of barriers, I would like to make an aside here to say that also the Negro himself, when his fellow Negroes rise in a certain profession, in a different profession, the Negro himself sometimes does not admit that this fellow Negro has arrived at that point." [42] The meaning of this explanation may be made clear through a characteristic example. A gathering of Negro and mulatto intellectuals was held in the house of a French family. The maid did not like the event and remarked sourly: "Who do they think they are? They're no better than I am! In fact they're not as good. Aren't I lighter-skinned than they are?" In short, viewing himself with a social perspective constructed and guided by the white man, ill prepared to adjust himself to the competitive social order, and sometimes jealous of the successes that few as yet can achieve, the Negro himself raises various obstacles to recognition of social ascent on the part of members of his race.

These results suggest that vertical mobility creates a dramatic problem for the Negro. By observation of the white man he knows very well what his rights are and how he should enjoy them. However, in practice he sees the inevitable dilution of several social roles that he would like to play, often because of psychosocial attitudes on the part of those with whom he interacts socially. Sometimes it is the white housemaid who bursts into the living room and butts into the conversation. In this connection a government official, a light-skinned mulatto, complained: "No two days pass without the maid coming into the living room and even talking to visitors alongside us. We can't stop it."

This portrayal reveals that the Negro has great difficulty in

asserting his acquired status. On the one hand he needs practice in using the social skills that he is trying to exploit. He
wins an inner battle when he enters a fine restaurant, goes to
a good theater, or hires a white maid. But others do not
smooth his path and force him to resort to unusual and somewhat strange behavior. On the other hand whites need practice in accepting and dealing with the Negro as an equal or a
superior. Sometimes they force the issue, exceeding the limits
of equity and mutual respect. A Negro policeman gives us an
opportunity to see how this occurs. A patrolman told us that a
woman had brutally beaten two children, and he was sent to
arrest her. "I obeyed. I said, 'Let's go to the police station.' The
woman was furious: 'Look at yourself! . . . Who ever saw a
Negro arrest a white? Only yesterday you Negroes were in the
slave quarters! No Negro will arrest me!'" Another case occurred some time ago. It was described by a Negro soldier.
During Carnival he had just come off duty, fully uniformed
and equipped, and was inclined to celebrate. "I saw a very
pretty Negro girl and showed interest in her. I was going to
follow her when I felt a spit in my face and then another. I
wiped it off and hit the woman who had done that to me. She
was a white woman on the streetcar. I lost my head and took
her to the central police station, beating her with my sword on
the way. We went up Carmo Alley and I didn't stop beating
her. An Italian junior inspector was on duty. He heard the
case, then he said to me, 'O.K., you may go.' I left and hardly
twenty minutes had passed when I was spat on again. I turned
around. It was the same woman. I grabbed her again and took
her back to the central police station, beating her with my
sword. The inspector had already arrived. I told the whole
story again. The inspector ordered the woman to be put in jail.
I went back to where I had been. Suddenly, I saw the woman
coming down the Alley with two strong companions. I thought
to myself, 'This is it! There's going to be trouble!' The woman
came near me but didn't spit. I was on my guard. I began
hitting her and beating her with my sword. Her friends
wanted to intervene. I pulled out my revolver and we all went

again back to the central police station. I took two witnesses with me. At the police station I found out that as soon as the inspector had gone away to sleep the junior inspector let the woman go. I had the inspector called. He came and heard the whole case. The witnesses spoke up, saying that this was lack of respect for authority. The inspector had the woman and her two companions arrested and suspended the junior inspector." Naturally, situations of this kind are extreme and rare, but they indicate what difficulties the Negro may have in asserting his personality. Color serves as a point of reference, conferring on the white and, in other ways, on the Negro himself the right to lower the other person. As a result, a black person must resort to artifices or to violence, not only to defend his dignity but also to fulfill roles that he is socially obliged to discharge.

In the light of this ample description we can consider the barriers to acceptance of the black man that influence psychosocial conditions and effects. It has long been argued in Brazil that color does not interfere in the process of appraising the Negro and the mulatto. It has even been stated that wealth and prestigious social position "make the Negro white." Our discussion shows that, on the contrary, there is a persistent, devious, and complex interference. Although it does not prevent vertical social mobility, it obviously makes it more difficult and problematic. Indeed, this opinion prevails both in Negro circles and among various sectors of the white population in São Paulo and is frankly admitted. It is recognized that wealth and social position in themselves do not, for all practical purposes, remove the limitations resulting from race and, what is more important, the lines of resistance are known to become inevitably more marked as the black man tries to enjoy unrestrictedly all the prerogatives inherent in his social level.

We shall now complete our analysis by focusing on aspects that are crucial for an understanding of how acceptance of the rising Negro takes place and can be explained. It is clear that acceptance of the Negro and the mulatto is governed by images and appraisals constructed by whites. Although there is considerable conflict between these images and appraisals on the one hand and the probable form of real behavior on the other—the former are expressed as if they were open and the latter tend to be very limited— [43] taken together they define alternatives of personal and group behavior that in practice take a social form. Our inquiries revealed that the white man grants the existence of certain creative intellectual potentialities in the Negro. Even those who have an extreme and unshakable prejudice or those who believe "that there's something wrong with the Negro race" frequently share this opinion.

The conclusions of Bastide and Van den Bergue throw some light on this aspect of the intricate pattern of Brazilian race relations. "In contrast with stereotypes prevailing in the United States, 55 per cent of the sample consider the Negro intellectually equal to the white man (only 43 per cent consider Negroes less intelligent than whites)." [44] Since these conclusions concern individuals belonging to the middle class, a higher proportion of the total white population probably shares views allowing potential ability to rise in the social scale to be attributed to or recognized in Negroes and mulattoes. However, in explanations of real or apparent successes on the part of the Negro, whites show a certain perplexity. The majority prefer an ethnocentric type of evaluation, according to which a Negro's improvement results from his "good side." Owing to miscegenation the Negro is supposed to have inherited, to varying degrees depending on the extent to which his blood is mixed, intellectual and moral qualities derived in the final analysis from the white race itself.

Those who do not view the problem in this light adopt one of two basic attitudes. They may be undecided, and attribute the successes observed to the white man's constructive influences. This is what can be inferred from the opinions expressed in typical fashion by a member of a traditional family. She has an unshakable belief that Negroes are inferior to whites, but knows through experience that some Negroes escape this inferiority. "There's no explanation for this. . . . It's like a biological species that suddenly produces a redder flower." She spontaneously illustrated her views: "There was a jet-black Negro in my office who can be considered an exception. I consider him the only irreproachable Negro I have met in my whole life: morally very proper, perfect at his work, very stylish in his clean and well-cared-for clothes, extremely polite, more well-mannered than many a white. . . . His family was just as presentable." All this intrigued the person in question: "The only explanation I can find is that they must have been brought up in a refined white background. I never mentioned the subject, but the surname, B. L., also leads to this supposition because it could have only come from good people. Indeed, in the past it was a custom for slaves to adopt their master's name."

Then again, they may resort to an ambiguous construct that in one way or another amounts to the image of the "Negro with a white soul." In one personal document we come across the following characteristic formulation: "I have some uncles and aunts on my mother's side who hate Negroes (I should explain that my mother's family goes back four hundred years). These relatives absolutely refuse to have any close relationships with Negroes. When, by chance, one or another Negro goes to their house (even a Negro of social standing) he is treated with reserve, and my relatives try to avoid friendship with him at all costs. Only once do I recall having seen one of these relatives 'praise' a Negro: "What an intelligent Negro! He's not like a Negro at all!' " [45] One of the researchers, in a summary of the conclusions reached through the interviews, made clear this manifestation of white ethnocentrism: "When the question had been asked as to the basis for statements referring to the Negro's complex or to the defect with its origin in slavery, seeing there were (or are) Negroes who are great men, none of those I spoke to could attempt an explanation: they almost always limited themselves to saying that it was (or is) a case of exceptional individuals, something like 'they're only Negroes in color, otherwise they're white.' "

The documentation permits us to draw two more rather

important conclusions. In specific situations involving competition with the rising Negro, the white man openly identified with color prejudice does not share any of these alternative evaluations. He considers the Negro inferior and protects himself from contact with hostile exclusiveness. This behavior places insuperable obstacles in the way of the Negro who is rising socially. On the one hand it reduces the feasibility of his acceptance in circles of greater social prestige; on the other it closes off the most rewarding channels for social intercourse with influential whites and revives among the latter the tendency to respect the old standard, according to which systematic exclusion or exceptional acceptance of the rising Negro (and even of the great black man) is a matter for personal decision. We should, moreover, take into account the nature of the reaction of the Negro himself to appraisals that reduce him to the position of the example that proves the rule. In the past, integration into the periphery or into the nucleus of traditional families involved processes of socialization and identification with the social interests or values of the dominant race that made the appraisal "black man with a white soul" a desirable and ennobling symbol. At the present time, since a process is involved that is predominantly one of autonomous ascent by black men or families, appraisals of this kind are more likely to be regarded as "treacherous," "degrading," and "intolerable." Only Negroes putting on white airs and shameless mulattoes are pleased to be distinguished in this way from the rest of the mass of black people.

In his autobiography one middle-class Negro frankly describes his irritation: "I have had unpleasant experiences nearly every day because of my color. I don't know whether the frequency of these situations is the result of a wary attitude imposed by my state of mind that is perhaps transformed into resentment, that makes me prejudge white attitudes; but even so I must say that unpleasant experiences, that is, direct or indirect manifestations of prejudice, are quite frequently perceived in my contacts. One rather common manifestation of prejudice is that which involves a group of persons where only one is a Negro and the rest are white. Whenever in the course of the conversation some unfavorable comment is made on the behavior of a Negro or of Negroes in general the member of the group being attacked who is present is usually excluded by their saying 'you are not a Negro' or else 'you are black with a white soul.' I have often been in situations like that and protested vehemently because I never allowed attacks on my race in my presence. I don't allow praise either, because I don't believe my race deserves it after Abolition. I only yield to a conscientious and judicious analysis of the Brazilian Negro's real situation." [46] In this emotional, social, and moral context the Negro begins to regard exceptional treatment, with its symbolic standard, as a real insult, sometimes viewing it as an affront that cannot be withdrawn.

In view of racial appraisals of this kind it is understandable that the white man may consciously or unconsciously tend toward behavior of a very special discriminative nature. Given the material conditions and the external appearances required by the class situation in question, acceptance of the rising Negro varies as a function of three independent psychosocial variables. First, there is the aptitude shown by the subject himself (the Negro personality in social ascent) for identifying himself with social norms and values of different levels in society, as well as with the dominant race's ideal standards of personality organization. Owing to this aptitude, variable acceptance of the rising Negro is made conditional upon explicit recognition of something equivalent to a kind of social whitening.

A second variable is the direction taken by the white man's racial attitudes and expectations of behavior. The above-mentioned contradictions among stereotypes, norms, and actual behavior are not causes but results of a transitional situation involving true cultural ambivalence. At this level they reflect the existence of social forms of racial adjustment which are largely divergent, inconsistent, and even mutually exclusive. For purposes of our model the extreme poles, in terms of either detachment or approach, are of particular interest.

When the white man's behavior indicates strong stereotyping and is accompanied by simultaneous frustration (concealed or open) of ideal norms of reciprocal relations (in this case the Negro's), there is a tendency for more or less sharp manifestations of racial intolerance. When, on the contrary, the white man's actual behavior tends to be somewhat consistent with the ideal norms of reciprocal relations (in this case the Negro's), the negative effects of stereotyping may be either smoothed over or neutralized,[47] and there is tendency for rather clear-cut manifestations of racial tolerance. The basic fact is that interaction with the Negro does not in itself determine the direction of the white man's racial attitudes and behavioral expectations. As a result, this direction is related to psychological, cultural, and social processes inherent in the white man's character and the peculiarities of his national or ethnic tradition and in the implications of his class relationships. Consequently, acceptance of the rising Negro depends on the quality and the nature of subjective tendencies on the part of whites.

A third variable is the peripheral effect of particular factors that may exert social influence on specific adjustments. Certain duties or family obligations; moral or sentimental links explained in terms of liking or disliking, admiration or aversion; crudely material and rational interests—all of these may transform the white man's racial attitudes and behavioral expectations, making interaction with the Negro a dynamic factor in racial rapprochement or detachment. They can be explained as follows: tolerance, sometimes extreme and complex, on the part of prejudiced whites toward certain Negroes who are viewed as separate cases; intolerance, sometimes virulent and confusing, on the part of "good whites" [48] against certain Negroes or mulattoes who are regarded as "the kind who agree with those who run down Negroes." What must be emphasized here is the effect of contingent and peripheral factors on race relations. Acceptance of the rising Negro is also affected by circumstantial factors which particularize or personalize white relationships with certain black persons and lead to closer or more distant relations above and beyond conventional standards of adjustment.

The types of psychosocial behavior described above clearly reduce the rate and the impact of vertical social mobility for the Negro and the mulatto. They foster perpetuation of rigid forms of selection which are incompatible with the egalitarian foundations of a competitive society and which allow the white man to resist and in the final analysis manipulate the Negro's probability of social equalization. They also make the well-known mechanism of "the exception that proves the rule" continuous, up-to-date, and universal by adapting it to the integrative and functional conditions of class society.

Our interviews showed that whites, especially those who think that "there are a lot of good Negroes," are inclined to recognize that the Negro has to face a one-sided system of barriers. Here is a typical way in which this opinion was expressed: "When they [Negroes] rise in the world it is through their own worth. For a Negro to rise he really has to be something. The white man does some trifling thing and gets by but the Negro has to be first-rate, otherwise he doesn't get anything." Even an informant who argued against such an opinion made this mechanism clear: "The problem is rather one of education. The Negro is accepted even without being first-rate. Employers are afraid of hiring Negroes because they know they are ill mannered and fear they will be rude to customers and use bad language as Negroes do." Thus we see that the minimum expectation when hiring personnel is established by the level of white behavior. Even if the Negro is not required to exceed the standard, he is expected to do as well as the white man. The investigation showed that indifference or slack requirements exist only in connection with "Negro's work." One of those interviewed, who tried to prove that there is no race prejudice in São Paulo, replied as follows to the question whether Negro employees do the same work as whites: "Well, you're right there. The majority do manual work, but if one of them has merit he can be utilized better. The thing is that requirements for Negroes are higher than for whites." One of the researchers brought up an illustration. The headmistress of a private religious school had told him: "We require more from a Negro girl than a white girl before we accept her. The situation is very delicate and for a black girl to be respected she must be superior to a white girl under the same circumstances."

There are various ways in which the second mechanism, that of the exception that proves the rule, is preserved. Ideally this mechanism should not persist in the competitive social order, but should have disappeared with the master and slave system of which it was an indispensable part. Given the pecuniary basis of slavery, the several possibilities of gaining freedom, the need for using freed men in various occupations essential to the slave labor system, and the degree of miscegenation even at high social levels, this mechanism permitted certain black persons to be separated from their racial category without altering the position of this category as a whole in the prevailing social order. In the open society with a system of free labor the mechanism lost its function of regulating racial balance. Nevertheless, since modernization of the system of social relations did not immediately and profoundly affect traditional patterns of race relationships, the mechanism ended up impregnating and even perverting the integration and functioning of the competitive social order. To the effects of competition with the Negro the white man applies formulas analogous to those he used in the past, as if it were still necessary to safeguard the overlord's privileges and prevent the deterioration of inalienable prerogatives related to estate. Thus he distinguishes "the Negro with character," the "intelligent Negro," and the "well-mannered mulatto" from the Negro considered as a racial category. As a result the white man not only can apply a certain degree of liberty to his treatment of Negroes regarded as a sort of social equivalent of the white, but also can preserve obsolete racial judgments intact with a maximum of social efficacy, opening the way for strong negative stereotypes of the Negro and for actual behavior that is ethnocentric to varying degrees. In short he adjusts racially to the competitive social order without being prepared, materially or morally, to redefine the image of the Negro and judgments regarding the Negro race in the light of successes achieved by black men in free competition. Really outstanding successes are either ignored or used as a negative counterweight to accentuate the ridiculously tiny extent of the exceptions and the untouchable validity of the general rule.

Perpetuation of the mechanism in question is not merely a result of cultural lag. It seems that the extent of miscegenation in the city of São Paulo has excluded the Negro and the mulatto from certain social levels that were really benefited by the introduction of the competitive style of life. However, proletarization of the Negro and the formation of black middle classes are incipient phenomena. Neither phenomenon increases the visibility of the Negro and the mulatto at these social levels or brings on a crisis in anachronistic racial judgments. It is impossible to estimate the extent to which these conditions, allied to the effects of cultural lag, will corrupt the ideal bases of the competitive social order or, more important, whether they will subject this social order to distortions of a racially discriminatory nature. It is nevertheless clear that the low percentage represented by the black population, its relative sociocultural isolation, and its weak vertical social mobility impede any prompt or short-term correction of the distortions caused by traditional forms of racial adjustment in the integration and functioning of the competitive social order.

Our investigation showed that the mechanism palpably operates as in the past. The essential condition for a black person to count as an exception is still open identification with white interests, values, and models of personality organization. Even the Negro and mulatto who do not want to pass as white must apparently meet this requirement whenever and wherever they hope to be accepted and treated in accordance with the prerogatives of their social position. From this angle, where whites and Negroes are regarded as maintaining genuine association and friendly racial relations, social ascent for the Negro continues to be a process of infiltrating into the

white world and of depriving himself of his essential character. However, this condition does not in itself assure the Negro
of full social equivalence to the white man. This only tends to
come about when, in addition, the black person belongs to the
legal nucleus of a family group considered prominent. That
individual is not only an exception, but an isolated case. Some
may laugh at him behind his back and may even carefully
avoid him. Nevertheless, he will always be Mr. So-and-so to a
large number of whites in the same socioeconomic situation,
although white strangers and some of his more intolerant
relatives or acquaintances may consider him and treat him as
an ordinary Negro. The basic fact, however, is the extreme
degree of acceptance reached by this type of black person.

A typical illustration was provided by a lawyer belonging to
a traditional white family and markedly intransigent in matters of race relations. He spontaneously cited the P.'s [49] as an
example of "good people" with whom he maintains close relations, despite the fact that some of them are Negroes (in
reality they are light-skinned mulattoes). He pointed out that
they prove that "in Brazil everyone has a chance" since "they
are members of the Jockey Club and that is not something just
anyone can be." He further indicated that he would willingly
take orders from them: "You have the P.'s, J. and F.; they are
respectable people, they could be my superiors. But," he
stressed, "not the common run of Negroes, not at all." Our
research conclusively proves that only in this last circumstance does the Negro (or the mulatto often described as a
Negro) have a chance to mingle in white circles, living as if
he were white and suffering a minimum of unpleasantness
and discrimination because of his color.

As an exception, the individual ceases to be Negro or mulatto for many social purposes and is regarded as an important figure or a great man. The white man leaves color out of
the personal situation and uses this latter to justify his feelings, in both formal and friendly contacts. Home life, where
exclusivism is strongest, serves to illustrate this situation. He
does not merely welcome a Negro intellectual, a friend, or "a

wonderful fellow." He boasts: "A good husband like that is
what I would like you, my granddaughters, to have, even if he
is a Negro!" On the other hand when exclusivism can be
stretched without great damage the personal situation serves
as a basis for occasional tolerance. In a case study on interracial contact at dances [50] the researcher drew the following
conclusions: "In club dances of the social upper or the middle
class, Negroes are not admitted. It is true that one may find an
occasional light mulatto who has, so to speak 'crossed the
line.' Even so, unless he is a person who is well known and
easily identified by those present—a person, therefore, of undeniable social prestige—whites find his presence inconvenient; it's a sign that they are in a 'low-class' place. In this
respect the interview granted by a committee member of the X
Club in which he described the type of complaints caused by
the presence of light mulattoes is rather revealing. A Leoni-
das, a Cesarino Junior, or a Prado * are readily identifiable,
and anyone who does not know him and is disturbed by his
presence can receive an immediate explanation from anyone
else present."

Having examined this point we can take up the crucial
question of how color and social position enter into determina-
tion of the Negro's and mulatto's social prestige. Our inquiry
suggests that there is confusion regarding the social consequences of both these factors, not only among whites but also
among Negroes. First, certain standardizations encourage the
opinion that the black man's social prestige is a function of his
socioeconomic situation. To a large extent whites and Negroes
share the following traditional principle: "You are worth what
you have; if you have nothing you are worth nothing." Those
whites most identified with the ideology of racial democracy
go as far as those quoting the proverb above, declaring:
"Every time the Negro succeeds he becomes whiter, as Gilberto Freyre says." Analysis of this viewpoint reveals that it
presupposes neither belief in nor the existence of any equality

* *Editors note:* Important Brazilian family names.

between the two races. Here is a typical example, the case of a person remarkable for the zeal with which he attacked what many people think, namely that the Negro is inferior to the white. He thought that all races are equal and pointed to the United States as a sort of critical experiment, since there "a Negro can have his doctorate and be a medical doctor or even a capitalist," which "shows that Negroes are as capable as whites. Separation of the Negro and the white has favored the Negro; he was encouraged to get on in life." He was convinced that "within a century equality will be established throughout the world. We won't see it, but it's coming. It's inevitable. Then no one will separate Negro and white." As for Brazil, in his view "the Negro forms the lowest class." Beginning with social position, he explained the Negro's whole drama: "The Negro is in a greatly inferior position. He cannot progress. He is pushed into crime. Almost all robberies and crimes are committed by Negroes. If whites came from their environment they wouldn't be any better. That is why whites avoid contact with Negroes. It's because they're not well regarded in our society, because of that. They think that the Negro is no good, is not law-abiding nor honest." Despite this view of reality and future prospects of race relations he spontaneously declared: "It is right to consider the Negro inferior to the white. It's something that has come through the centuries. What good could come out of Africa? Nothing good could come from there. They don't have any doctors, nor engineers, nor lawyers. They are a lot of barbarians. People know that and think that the Negro is unable to do things that the white man can do."

Second, other rationalizations embody a diametrically opposed opinion. One section of the white population thinks that prejudice does and should exist. Sometimes this viewpoint indirectly involves the social consequences of racial stratification. It is expressed in reactions of this kind: "With rare exceptions, when are Negroes found in important positions? They belong to an inferior race." The number of Negroes and mulattoes holding this opinion is high. Among rural men, who are not yet well enough informed to be aware of the racial situation, this conviction takes on curious nuances. As an example there is the attitude of a mulatto contractor: "It's no good the Negro wanting to get on because he'll always be black." Among the so-called black middle class, however, appraisals are realistic and at the same time ambivalent and bitter. Since inclusion in the white world is a supreme ideal, tacit compromises with the existing racial order are established. They go as far as to blame the Negro himself, either because he cannot adjust to socially accepted behavioral expectations (accepted, that is, in various senses by whites) or because he is supposed to be too sensitive, whiny, or too rebellious. But actual experience leaves scars that cannot be concealed. The same people who put forward such viewpoints contradictorily admit that color is a barrier and that it excludes the Negro from rights he is entitled to through his economic and social situation. In this way the cultured, well-mannered, and rich Negro becomes the spokesman for explanations that take up again the unmasking themes of the rights movements. Feeling rejected and humiliated in his attempts to approach, he condemns white prejudice, calls it "maneuvers behind the scenes," and sees in it "fear of Negro intelligence." The contradictions inherent in such ambivalent attitudes and judgments do not prevent the painful certainty that "the Negro is left out because of his color" or that "it's no good his being intelligent, possessing character, or having social position."

This variety of viewpoints and judgments is the natural consequence of the extreme variety of situations in which racial contact takes place. There are certain circumstances under which the situation dilutes many of the social effects of color: black individuals are assimilated by important white relatives; they are accepted as exceptions; or conventional formalities take precedence.[51] Under other circumstances social position is undermined and even neutralized by color. A Negro lawyer may be taken for a janitor or even be prevented from entering a night club though he has money, is well-dressed, and is in the company of respectable whites. What matters, however, are the subtleties. Although adjustments resulting from social position benefit only a few isolated individuals and then often only in circumscribed areas of social interaction, limitations stemming from color are universally applicable. In reality the Negro and the mulatto are normally exposed to a real loss of social prestige, as if the levels of societal classification did not fully apply to them. Color serves, at one and the same time, as a racial mark and as a status symbol. Thus it inextricably identifies the Negro and the mulatto as a racial category (i.e., Negro) and as a social category (i.e., the lowest class). However, it so happens that the first category may or may not blot out the second, depending on the psychosocial and moral tendencies of the white agent. The rising Negro is a refutation of this equivalence of categories and the subterfuges that it sustains; but since the different social levels are not equally permeated with Negroes and mulattoes, the white man can ignore this fact and act according to the convention, which permits him a broad degree of arbitrariness in his treatment of the Negro. He may not treat as a Negro a black person belonging to a lower social category, just as he may treat as a Negro a black person of the same or higher social level. Structural changes in the racial stratification of society have not yet gone as far as to suppress the parallel between race and very low social position established in the past. This parallel not only persists in attenuated form in class society but continues to be arbitrarily manipulated by the white man in accordance with his feelings and his personal convenience as well as with his interests and social values.

These conclusions lead inevitably to recognition of two conspicuous facts. In the first place, color interferes negatively with the process of vertical mobility for the Negro and the mulatto. It is rare for them to enjoy equally with the white man all the social prestige inherent in the social positions they manage to achieve in the competitive social order. Second, usually unconsciously but sometimes consciously, the white man continues to defend a certain social disparity between the two races. Thus the old parallel between race and very low social position continues to hold for a large part of the black population. It is perpetuated as a means of preserving social distance between the two races because it has social value. The white man is reluctant to regard and receive the Negro as a partner and as an equal in the competitive social order, even when he reaches the same social level. Without there being any general fear of the real or potential risks of competition with Negroes,[52] there is a distinct resistance to including them in the social order en masse overnight. Although the social prestige to which rising black individuals are entitled is undermined and destroyed, gradual and necessarily slow absorption of the most capable among them is not prevented, but the establishment of perfect equality in relations between the two races is indefinitely postponed.

If these conclusions are valid, we may establish two essential points. In view of the white constellation of interests and social values—which, in turn, define the configuration and legitimacy of the prevailing social order—color (and not social position) takes on special significance in racial adjustments. If it were neutralized (or made socially inoperative for some reason), the parallel between Negro and inferior social condition would be inevitably doomed and with it the existing form of racial domination. But from the Negro's viewpoint, social position, on the contrary, has special significance as a criterion for enlarging his degree of participation in the interests and social values recognized by competitive society and as a means of progressively correcting and probably eventually suppressing limitations based on color and on its utilization as a racial mark and as an index of social classification.

An appreciation of these two points is absolutely crucial. Through them it can be clearly seen that the white man does not struggle against the Negro directly, personally, and consciously; that the white man does not manage to accept fully the principle that the open society presupposes social equality between different races; and that, in the broadest sense, his attitude is one of sociocultural conservatism. The Negro, in turn, does not struggle directly, personally, and consciously against the white man but regards the open society as being egalitarian, both socially and racially, and his attitude is, in the broadest sense, one of sociocultural innovation. He is inclined to accept white domination, but in accordance with the ideal standards of social relations of the competitive society. In short, we return to the sociological problems of social dynamics in a multiracial society. In denying equity to the rising Negro, the white man is really striving to preserve the existing social distance between the two races. Without desiring this historic role, he becomes a human factor contributing to cultural lag in race relations and encourages perversion of the competitive social order as far as race relations are concerned. The rising Negro, in struggling for maximum benefit from the social prestige he has acquired, is really involved in reducing and neutralizing the social distance existing between the two races. All unawares and without possessing the means to carry out this historic role, he becomes a human factor contributing to modernization of the competitive social order in the area of race relations and to the progressive elimination of sociocultural inconsistencies that threaten its normal pattern of integration and development.

These reasons make clear the importance to the Negro and mulatto of social techniques enabling them to enjoy, keep, or improve the social positions they have achieved. These techniques amount to veritable weapons of attack and defense for the thankless and obscure battles in which the rising Negro daily affirms his social self-assertion. Within the limits of this study we must consider only the most important aspects of these techniques at the different levels at which they can be invoked to rise in status, to make status recognized, and to show status.

The social techniques used by the Negro and the mulatto to improve their position (and therefore to rise in status) are usually imitated from the whites. They represent the psychological, cultural, and social progress made by the Negro in participating in the competitive social order. Our investigation indicates that this progress revolves around certain focal points. In view of the frequency of replies and the convergence of attitudes shown in our documentation based on interviews, life histories, and group discussions, the following presentation provides an idea of how these focal points were ranked at the time of the basic survey in 1951. First, there is the high value (one might almost say excessive value) of education as a factor in socioeconomic integration and competition with whites. Although a large proportion of the black population is indifferent to or confused about the practical importance of education, the groups moving upward (or eager to move upward) are characterized by a tendency to value school and school learning very highly as a supreme good and a kind of open sesame to modern society. In these circles there is striking agreement that lack of education is the real problem of Negroes. Avoidance or dropping out of school is condemned; lack of education is blamed for the Negro's failure in his struggle for better jobs and a persistence of restrictive appraisals by whites; and there is a strong tendency to regard an extremely low level of education as the real cause of the poor moral and material standards of existence among Negro groups. Successes in the area of education (and especially in higher education) are regarded and valued as indications of racial equality. They serve both to show the whites that the Negroes are equal in everything but color and to encourage the Negro to be proud of his color (or his race).

Second, consolidation of the Negro family leads certain mechanisms of domestic solidarity to produce positive effects on the possibility of vertical social mobility for rising generations. The father who has a profession and a guaranteed income turns with renewed courage to his children's problems. From this standpoint the increase in education is associated with changes in family organization and their effects on relationships between generations. Although these processes do not offer the black population a competitive shelter equivalent to that of immigrant families at the beginning of the century, it is clear that that portion of the population which is rising already manages to offer children and young people a starting point almost analogous to that of white children and young people in the same social category. In addition to education some have a small sum of money to begin life and may even receive a home of their own upon marriage. This situation is also reflected in the incomplete family. Because of such examples some unmarried mothers make unbelievable sacrifices to keep their child at school.[53] Negro families that are integrated but extremely poor try to share this tendency as best they can; either everyone makes a sacrifice so that a certain brother can study, or the father makes a great effort to educate his children. To sum up, tendencies toward integration on the part of the Negro family are gradually modifying the scene described in Chapter 2 by spreading awareness that solidarity at home is an essential factor in the struggle for a better life.

Third, in this setting the predatory individual holding the crude philosophy of "every man for himself and God for everyone" and of "as long as I'm all right, let others go hang" increasingly gives way to the complex pattern of individualism inherent in the competitive social order. The individual begins to see himself as part of a whole and at the same time as an autonomous unit. This attitude becomes an important social technique for two reasons: it frees the Negro from his tendency to wait his turn in the form of a gift from the white man and it shows that egoism requires a point of support and a relationship of a material and moral nature between the individual and his family. Hence the dynamic importance of this drive in adjusting the Negro to the associative climate that prevails in a mass society and to an understanding of both the negative and the positive aspects of individualism. As a result there is wider acceptance of a view of reality that leads the rising black man rationally to seek points of support and self-protection in the arduous competition for social position and prestige.

Fourth, in this context occupational mobility takes on the

appearance of a constructive and routine device. Invariably the final objective is achievement of a position that is better paid and therefore more secure. However, when specific options arise immediate gain sometimes comes second. Greater importance is attached to long-term opportunities offered by the job for the achievement of individuals' career ambitions. Security, acquired rights, duties, or friendship toward employers are disregarded or discretely placed in a secondary position. Thus the rising Negro takes on the typical mentality of a worker in a competitive economy. He defies his luck in order to have his turn since he knows that the only source of saving that he possesses is his capacity for work. He begins to have misgivings about getting a better job only when he is disillusioned or when he reaches the position he wanted. In any case, occupational mobility is consciously taken into account as a technique of social ascent.

To the above list should be added other techniques that are socially exploited in a more or less intentional way. One of them is realistic choice of occupation. Realization that work dignifies a man, independently of the income or prestige it provides, and that a capable man improves professionally has led to a wider tendency to accept very modest initial opportunities without bitterness. Life histories and interviews showed how highly qualified individuals (some having taken special courses) did not hesitate to begin with janitorial work. They know that "it's no good shouting against prejudice." Afterward at their work they tried to show their potential and later reached the better occupations to which they were entitled. Moreover, the first job tends to be viewed as the first step on a ladder, enabling the individual to reach other steps, depending on his ability (including ability to learn new skills), luck, and protection. It is curious how widespread these attitudes are. Answers to a questionnaire showed that choice of an ideal occupation (despite the wide range of preferences) was directed toward accessible occupations. To judge by the frequency distribution of replies, the ideal occupations preferred by men are those of driver and mechanic followed far behind by those of doctor, employee in commerce, and lawyer. In the case of women, it is those of clerk and dressmaker followed, at a level four times lower, by those of nurse, teacher, and artist. Interviews showed a similar pattern. Parents who could provide an education for their children were eager to encourage them to make realistic occupational choices. As a first job they encouraged choices that seemed to combine easy initial opportunities with promising prospects.

There are other techniques that deserve mention. (1) A positive attitude toward the value of work: The rising Negro rapidly assimilates the work images and judgments inherent in capitalist production, which give him new opportunities to compete with the white man and to take decisions that improve his life. (2) The formation and spread of arduous habits of thrift: Concern with having resources and applying them judiciously is not only growing but beginning to be regarded and used as a technique for socioeconomic ascent (roughly as immigrants did at the beginning of the century, although under more precarious and difficult conditions). (3) A tendency for the Negro to identify himself materially and morally with the white man as a citizen and a person: By assimilating the above-mentioned social techniques together with the corresponding attitudes, behavior, and social values, the Negro and the mulatto project themselves emotionally and logically into the competitive social order. Thus this tendency is reflected to some degree in all deliberate attempts at social ascent. (4) Cooperation with whites: In the case of certain goals, it would be impracticable or extremely difficult to be successful without help of representatives from the dominant race. Prior assimilation of the ways of being, thinking, and acting accepted by urban civilization permits the Negro to associate with the white man on an equal basis, allowing interracial cooperation (and not white protection) to take on the character of a means of social ascent.[54]

These social techniques reflect the modern aspect of the style of life emerging among Negroes. Nevertheless, there are still some rather close links with the past. For this reason we still come across black persons using obsolete devices to improve their life. In such cases a preoccupation with obtaining white protection in the old paternalistic style predominates. Apparently in this connection there is a sort of racial fear that is readily understandable in view of the Negro's economic, social, and cultural situation. In regarding whites as the dominant race, the Negro and the mulatto are forced to believe that vital decisions (even those concerning their own personal fate) are not in their own hands. The device of having a white protector, however, can be of great importance in two extreme cases. The somewhat rural Negro who is unable to establish himself in the city often depends on this device to obtain a steady job which is relatively advantageous. The educated Negro, whose career remains rather atypical in the light of the requirements of the competitive social order, is also dependent on this traffic in influence, whether he is employed in government or in business offices. Both tend to attach great importance to work opportunities in government service and direct their loyalty toward the white protector.

Finally we must examine other aspects of techniques to improve the Negro's life that do not fit into the alternatives described above. Since color is an unfailing symbol of social position, interracial marriage is a relatively popular way of supplementing prestige. To be sure, improvement in status takes place previously by other means but, by consensus of the two races, marriage of a Negro man with a white woman or of a Negro woman with a white man is irrefutable evidence of the improvement in question. The spouse benefited is considered to be the Negro, and he himself thinks that he is helping to "purify" the race and is participating in moral advantages (apparently related to estate) derived from the social situation of the white race.

In addition, consideration should be given to certain concepts peculiar to the Negro himself with regard to what improving one's life means. First, rising is equivalent to moving away physically, psychologically, socially, and morally from the Negro milieu. Since social differentiation among the black population is recent, the Negro milieu is still equated with economic dependency, social disorganization, and demoralization. Avoidance of contact with the Negro—especially with that Negro who is identified by the exterior image of the Negro that the white man has created—becomes an involved but indispensable technique to strengthen and safeguard a position that is in the process of being consolidated. Fear of losing prestige through real or imagined identification with the Negro thus creates a unique form of isolation that leads the rising black man to form social attachments according to estate concepts that no longer hold in society. He becomes more exclusivist than the white man of equal social category and staunchly defends the aristocratic features of his social position. Strange as this clearly compensatory behavior may be, subjectively it is important. By means of it a congeries of persons who scarcely know each other and are morally disunited and who, in addition, feel deprived of prestige because of their color identifies itself externally as part of a strict and relatively closed elite. From the viewpoint of the rising Negro, this means that avoidance of very poor Negroes, separation from his former environment, and aristocratic exclusivism help to point up certain incipient distinctions characteristic of an embryonic class.[55] This technique brings into play new social symbols of self-assertion on the part of the Negro, encouraging and providing a feeling of security for persons who are frustrated and yearning for prestige.

Second, in order to rise the black man also needs to be accepted in one way or another by the whites with whom he interacts socially (as colleague, employee, subordinate, supervisor, friend, acquaintance, or neighbor). Certain patterns of behavior take shape, patterns that are invisible to whites but which constitute the most bitter and depressing aspect of the rising Negro in the eyes of former leaders and followers of the claims movements. These are the endless tasks aimed at neutralizing the marks and effects of negative stereotyping on the person himself or his family. In order to improve his life the Negro has no alternative but to utilize social imitation, which is ambiguous, painful, and humiliating, but which pays off.

This behavior gives him the sensation that he is escaping a fate that seemed ineluctable and that the Negro can, after all, socially escape the downgrading effect of his color.

This analysis of the social techniques used by the rising Negro suggests how entangled and complex race relations still are in São Paulo. In practice the system of race relations denies the principles of integration of the prevailing social order (even from the standpoint of "black elites"). Consequently racial stratification, in comparison with the organization of the larger society, appears to be aberrant to varying degrees. It is evident that obsolete criteria for determining social prestige through color are persistent and still in force. Moreover, it is clear that the Negro meets serious and varied difficulties in his most legitimate attempts at ego-involvement and self-assertion in a social order that is only ostensibly racially open. These techniques make it very clear that the prevailing social order is still literally defined as the white world, and they demonstrate conclusively that the Negro must consciously and voluntarily impose a second human nature on himself in order to have access to this world and take a part in it. Notwithstanding the successive encroachments he makes on his own person, achievement of this second nature neither ends his drama nor furthers his material and moral equality with the white man. The Negro must then make strenuous efforts in several directions to defend and enjoy those portions of social prestige in which he should participate automatically. Despite these gloomy aspects, the same techniques reveal that a new reality is unfolding. The Negro is progressively absorbing the norms, behavior, and values of society. Consequently, the principal boundaries that converted this society into a world apart, fully enjoyed only by whites, are beginning to disappear. If these tendencies continue and if the number of Negroes and mulattoes effectively joining the system of social classes increases, in time these social techniques can be dispensed with, whereupon the Negro, in order to become integrated with society, will no longer have to prove socially that he is black only in color.

We can now take up the last topic to be covered in this part

of the chapter, the psychosocial and sociocultural effects of
the Negro's and mulatto's social mobility. We shall consider
only two aspects: (1) the direct effects of mobility on the
orientation of the Negro's and mulatto's behavior, on the degree of integration of the Negro milieu, and on the pattern of
race relations in the larger society; and (2) the secondary
effects on racial relations.

It would not be feasible to describe all the primary effects of
the Negro's and mulatto's social ascent that are of dynamic
significance. For this reason we have selected from the raw
material those aspects which throw the most light on the
process of reshaping the basis of racial adjustment and setting a new pattern for relations between Negroes and whites.
Insofar as we are dealing with personal documents pertaining
to rising black individuals, the data do not permit structural
analysis, nor do they enable us to say how and within what
limits these effects are helping to modify the system of race
relations within society by adapting it to the psychosocial and
sociocultural requirements of the competitive social order.
Nevertheless, they shed some light on the processes of change
that are affecting this system and will tend to affect it to a
greater extent in the future. Were it not for these processes
(viewed at this stage in the discussion in terms of their principal dynamic results), we could report no change in the Negro's material and moral situation or in his ability to interact
with the psychosocial and sociocultural forces that objectively
shape this situation. In presenting these results we shall follow the following schema:

I. Effects of vertical mobility that directly influence the orientation of the Negro's and mulatto's behavior
   1. Crisis in social relations
   2. Vertical mobility as the principal ideal
   3. Identification with the interests and values of the
      social position obtained or desired
   4. Rejection of the traditional Negro standard of living
   5. Awareness of race prejudice
   6. Nonconformity with and rejection of the traditional
      order

7. Ambiguity and ambivalence in defining loyalties
8. Emergence and spread of willingness to complete and undertake conflicting relationships with whites
9. Intensification of competition and conflict among Negroes
10. Satisfaction with the success of other Negroes in their plans for social mobility

II. Effects of social mobility that directly influence the degree of integration of the Negro milieu—emerging tendencies toward social differentiation and stratification in the colored population

III. Direct effects of social mobility on the rules governing racial relationships in the larger society
1. Forms of accepting the rising Negro
2. The reappearance of prejudiced and discriminatory attitudes and behavior

At the present stage of the change in racial relations the most significant dynamic effects from the sociological viewpoint are observed in the organization of the personality and the behavior of the Negro and the mulatto, so these aspects naturally stand out in our description. However, the order adopted does not reflect the degree of dynamic importance attributed to each topic by the agents themselves. We preferred to utilize an artificial arrangement that shows the connection between the different points and provides an overall view of the relationship between them.

The crisis in old friendships is a commonplace, though not fatal, occurrence. At first, when the rising individual is just beginning to advance, cordial appearances remain unchanged. Here and there small squabbles occur, caused by superficial misunderstandings. For example friends and relations do not get on well together because "so-and-so has suddenly become very proud" or "he pretends he doesn't know us" or because "from one moment to the next he started calling us parasites," "he slammed the door in our face," and so on.[56] As a rule it is in such an atmosphere that the person moves with his family to a better house. The physical separation from his former surroundings is full of manifestations of affection.

Relatives, friends, and the closest neighbors pay their last respects. The new house is shown to his intimates before and immediately after the move. But then, principally if there has been a real and substantial change in status, deterioration in relations enters its final stage. The person vanishes from circulation and cuts himself off from his former friends. He is afraid his new neighbors will confuse him with them and regard him as a Negro of lowly extraction. If it is necessary to avoid a scene there is a rapid handshake or a greeting at a distance. However, he avoids reestablishing the former intimacy. His attention is directed toward the new environment. Depending on the neighborhood and the social level of his neighbors, relations are cool, evasive, and sometimes forced. This aggravates even more his fear of being hurt by his recent past and greatly strengthens his attempts to dodge relatives and friends who are in a dubious situation. Then the shabby excuses come into play and are given and received coldly as irreparable and unforgettable insults. It is in this context, as we have mentioned above, that characteristic recriminations are made.

Naturally the most dramatic aspect emerges in relations among relatives. He makes every effort to avoid their visits in order to hide his humble origin. Although there may not be a complete break, he prefers to visit them in their homes. He takes with him persons they would like to see and sometimes one or another to help him if necessary. The relatives understand these tricks. They try to excuse those who use them to their friends, neighbors, and other relatives: "You know how it is. So-and-so now is a very important person. He's always busy. He's hardly ever home." Privately they confess their bitterness: "I'm ashamed to go to So-and-so's house because of the people he's friendly with"; "That gets me mad"; "I'm disappointed in So-and-so." Things become even worse and more dramatic when there are dependent elderly relatives who are darker. They are often condemned to a kind of social ostracism and suffer various kinds of humiliation.[57] In time the feverish desire to achieve social prestige weakens or is replaced by a feeling of security. Then again, he becomes nostalic. One or another link is reestablished, principally with relatives and intimate friends. However, this does not reestablish the balance of social relations as it was before. On the contrary, affairs are conducted as if they were grafted onto the social groups to which the rising individual belongs (or thinks he belongs). The sorrow of the break may be forgotten or sublimated, but it is rarely repaired.

Diffuse desires to improve one's life create and spread desires to rise. The conviction is formed that the Negro's problem is economic and that to solve it he must have everything the white man has. But only the success of many in achieving such objectives can convert vertical social mobility into the ultimate good and into a tradition. There is a marked difference between the two outlooks: when the Negro is in the first position he regards social ascent as an end in itself (something permitting him to be somebody and to have access to things that were always inaccessible to him); when he is in the second position, the Negro defines social ascent as a means of achieving other ends. Without any doubt, in terms of human drama and as a social problem, the Negro attracts more sympathy in the early stages of the process when his desires sound like a cry for social justice. However, it is at the last level that he begins to repeat the social history of other groups in the city (in particular immigrants) who also started from nothing. Our observations indicate that the number of those who lean toward the second type of judgment is still quite small. Even at gatherings at the most exclusive Negro clubs and at the big shows they put on, where the cream of the Negro elite can be seen, the number does not go beyond two or three dozen. Nevertheless, in practice this small number has enormous dynamic importance for a simple reason. Here we have new personality types who embody a new concept of the world. Here are people who have already succeeded in their efforts to become somebody and who frankly do not struggle on behalf of their race. They are aiming at the essential core of the values of a competitive society and really want power in all its forms. They undeniably suffer from incurable myopia, since they do not see the Negroes' collective problems or the constructive function that the rights movements could have if properly oriented. But it is also undeniable that they are performing pioneer roles of great importance. In the midst of a black elite that is so heterogeneous and debatable in nature,[58] this small group shows what real social ascent is. It ostentatiously shows that in competition with whites for wealth, culture, and power the real dilemma arises after (and not before) the achievement of the economic and sociocultural minimum that everyone should have in a democratic society. More important, this group creates new symbols and myths that express the moral climate of the competitive social order: Worthwhile effort should not be directed toward the slender rewards of a good job, which is almost always of a compensatory nature (and which therefore fosters manias for self-assertion that involve fictitious status). Rather, effort should be aimed at progressive elimination of the socioeconomic and political distance separating the Negro from the white man in the competition for power and social prestige. In short, new lines of action and thought are taking shape, opening the way for strong personalities and high ambitions. Consequently, for a small initial nucleus, rising ceases to be the equivalent of social redemption and takes on the same significance that it has for the rest of the community. Thus in one part of the black population there is being formed a state of mind that makes the accumulation of wealth, social prestige, and power the source of emotion and the controlling principle of human life in society. The dynamic influence of this state of mind in its fullest form is still limited. Among other things, it comes up against the limitations of a social heritage that subjects the greatest number of this population to the sway of immediate and hasty reward, and against obstacles that economically and socially restrict utilization of the competitive aptitudes of the Negro and the mulatto. One may presume, however, that in the long run this state of mind will have very important constructive effects. It is opening to the Negro a new historic level that fits some segments of the black middle class morally and materially into bourgeois ideals of life and adapts them to the means of socially achieving these ideals.

These results must be put in proper sociological perspective. Until now we have been dealing with the great mass of the black population and with the implications of their desire for social mobility. When we change our viewpoint and isolate a small number of those who have achieved greatest success, who are actually moving more quickly toward assimilation of the social values of society and are in continuous social ascent, we find a different situation. The struggle for ascent is no longer undertaken for the sake of sociocultural minima, and the compensation provided by fictitious or apparent status loses all its significance. However, this does not bring about disruptive or dramatic contradictions among Negroes. As we shall see below, purely bourgeois mobilization of a small sector of the Negro elite arouses noteworthy social tendencies, both in differentiation of the Negro milieu and in relations among Negroes. At present, however, this mobilization is an incipient phenomenon, and the aforementioned small number draws its strength from the links it establishes with the bulk of the black elite, within which it stands out and distinguishes itself through its leadership functions.

Whatever the central factor (social ascent as social redemption or as a spiral staircase), success in vertical mobility has resocializing effects that encourage the adjustment of individuals to the social position they have acquired. Owing to this resocialization—which varies in accordance with personal qualities, the families' socioeconomic situation, and the real opportunities to participate in the social roles inherent in the position achieved—social ascent channels and regulates identification of individuals with the status personality of the social levels to which they now belong or to which they hope to belong. Since social ascent benefits small sectors of the black population in an uneven and selective way, identification with the values of the dominant social order in the larger society does not find uniform social support throughout the different levels of the Negro's organized social life. At some levels, such as that of the organization of behavior, personality, and the family, the Negro may embark on full imitation of the white man and his style of life. At others, such as the organization of the family itself and especially of somewhat refined cliques and recreational associations, this imitation is subject to fortuitous influences arising from obsolete models of social self-protection, measurement of prestige, and racial self-appraisal.

Until now, the most constant feature of the rising Negro has been his rejection of the Negro's traditional style of life. Social ascent not only creates a mechanism for passing from one social position to another but also arouses an awareness that the Negro's social position is continuously and surreptitiously threatened by his color and that the image of the Negro constructed by the white man is the main threat to fruition of the social roles or rights conferred by the position achieved. Drinking, laziness, sloppy dress, unreliability at work, disorderly language or manners, appear as prohibitions that lead the majority of rising Negroes to behave themselves literally like anti-Negroes from the social viewpoint that the Negro himself attributes to whites. Nevertheless, it should be emphasized that social ascent brings about this reaction in constructive terms. For example, let us take the preoccupation with maintaining a strictly moral atmosphere at recreational gatherings of Negro associations. In a case study the researcher gathered ample material confirming this interpretation. Thus, at one of the most select clubs, he found the following reminder which had been distributed in printed form to those present:

IMPORTANT NOTICE!

Ladies and Gentlemen:

The *Progressive Club* is proud of being a family society and, this being the case, we consider it unnecessary to remind those present that they should conduct themselves with the utmost order, respect, good manners and composure, which necessarily should reign in an atmosphere where families are present. Therefore, be careful! because the committee of this club is closely observing all those who are disrespectful or who indulge excessively in alcoholic beverages in order to take energetic measures at future festivities of the *Progressive Club,* to wit: to categorically prohibit the admission of gentlemen and ladies who are regarded as inconvenient in this society.

BE CAREFUL! ORDERLINESS AND RESPECT!

In this way it was hoped to protect members and their families by offering them an atmosphere in which young ladies in particular would not be subject to the risks of "dangerous relationships." Nonmembers could only be invited when presented by a member; several individuals who had not been able to behave themselves became *personae non gratae,* and members who failed to meet expectations were excluded. Supervision went so far that even the wearing of stockings by young ladies was a minimum requirement, not to mention more serious rules that prohibited dancing the *quadradinho* [59] and prescribed how partners should address each other.

Simultaneous changes in social position and cultural outlook also provide the rising Negro with other opportunities to perceive and evaluate race prejudice. As he becomes materially and morally capable of making certain adjustments, he can discern in concrete cases where color constitutes a barrier to acceptance by whites. At the same time he learns to use the privileges of his social position to reach ends in opposition to their racial outlook. Within broad limits he comes to understand that acceptance by whites is secondary compared with the advantages to be derived from the full and normal fruition of certain social prerogatives that can be shared independently of any change in white character. In general the rising Negro becomes better equipped to perceive and defend his social interests in the context of existing race relations. Of course many tortuous forms of adjustment are sometimes countenanced and repeated, but it is not this aspect that is important at this point. Vertical mobility matures the Negro, preparing him for a prolonged game requiring patience. Through his own experience he learns that it is not within his power to modify the white man's nature and, what is of greater practical importance, that this is not indispensable for him to reach his immediate and selfish ends. Moreover, he builds an adaptive mechanism of considerable importance in that he begins to regard the Negro people's social ascent and its visible effects as having the manifest function of reeducating whites and offsetting their foolish prejudices. He thus achieves surprising moral liberty. The objective observation of the disastrous manifestations and consequences of race prejudice is separated from any notion of racial vengeance. Instead of piling up reactions and frustrations that could lead to a dead-end street, he prefers to force the doors open. Without doubt this behavioral orientation is explained by the ambiguity and the duality of Brazilian race relations. If all doors were closed, there would be no scope for such an alternative. Moreover, the large number of medium opportunities marking the present phase of socioeconomic expansion in São Paulo also helps to promote this kind of racial adjustment.

However, this adjustment holds two lessons which should not be underestimated. First, the adaptive and integrative powers of the Negro have been underestimated by the white man. As opportunities for vertical mobility arise he is showing himself to be a consummate master of the art of sociability, who forgets and pardons past bitterness for the sake of present or future benefits. Second, the virtues of a competitive society have an enormous power to attract and corrupt. When he assimilates the logic and feelings of competitive society the Negro forgets and pardons his former cruel master. However, he also becomes ignorant of his past and even of the drama of the Negro people. He concerns himself with manifestations of race prejudice in accordance with goals that are individualistic and self-serving in order to overcome this prejudice, neutralize it, or if possible take advantage of it. The techniques he employs can certainly be disseminated and without shadow of doubt this would ensure better mechanisms for the Negroes' collective defense and for alteration of the existing racial order. However, there is something else to consider. Until such a balance has been reached the great majority of the black population is condemned to unfair hardships. The individualistic ethic has taught the rising Negro neither the risks he is running while this situation lasts nor the advantages that he could enjoy if he were socially willing to condemn and proscribe it.

The social ascent of the Negro and the mulatto takes place in a climate that helps develop rebellious attitudes and leads to rejection of the traditional racial order. On the one hand the social disparities existing between the two races encourage a permanent state of potential frustration in black individuals. Even those who identify themselves with the official racial ideology often grant either the existence of outright favoritism in relations among whites or a policy of scandalous protection of foreigners and onesided use of the country's own resources. On the other hand social ascent itself exposes the Negro and the mulatto to critical situations. Even today the rural Negro thinks that "if Negroes were rich they could be the same as whites." It so happens that when the rising Negro becomes capable of distinguishing color and social position in his adjustments he quickly learns that wealth, admiration, and fine manners do not prevent him from being regarded and treated as a Negro under certain conditions and for various social purposes. This discovery is generally associated with disturbing and disconcerting experiences, as we have seen above. However, neither of these two modes of thought creates systematic rebellion in practice.

It is difficult for the Negro to turn his social dissatisfaction to constructive ends. Generally, whatever the white man's origin, there is a clear way for him to handle and correct his dissatisfaction, namely through the selfsame process of accumulation of wealth, social prestige, and power. The Negro normally finds himself subject to a destructive duality; at one level he carries out the requirements of his social position and at another he gains recognition of the validity and legitimacy of the social effects of these requirements. This duality will probably disappear in the future if there is a fair and complete integration of black people into the various social levels of the larger society. At the present moment it confronts us with two problems of prime sociological importance. First, it seems obvious that this duality shows that social ascent is helping to some extent to change the structure and the dynamics of the pattern of racial adjustment. The rising Negro, by accepting the prospects opened by ultraselective racial judgments, adapts himself psychologically and morally to the type of dissembled and latent nonconformity that has always permeated racial relations in Brazil. This type of racial nonconformity, by the way, may be extremely useful in the achievement of social goals by individuals or small groups. Second, this duality indicates how political and social neutralization of the black elites tends to take place at present. To the degree that the best of these elites cling to an obsolete social and ethical code, they are able to provide themselves with a constant supply of compensatory prestige through participation in conspicuous forms of social life and through the corresponding opportunities for leadership these forms offer. However, they become increasingly divorced from the great majority of black people and, what is worse, from the main stream of sociohistoric processes. Thus a very serious risk occurs. As in the United States,[60] they may surrender to complacent self-appraisals, to confused views of reality, and to treacherous moral compensations. Such an outcome would preserve the tradition of social peace in Brazilian racial relations, but at a high social cost—depriving a large proportion of the black population of the social rights and privileges enjoyed by whites and by somewhat favored sectors of the Negro elite.

These considerations also indicate that as long as there is some sort of parallel between color and social position the Negro and the mulatto will have to accept ambiguity and ambivalence in social definitions of their loyalties. In one highly significant interview we came across a typical statement to the effect that the rising Negro does not know which side he is on. It is true that as a citizen and a Brazilian he identifies himself with the prevailing social order and with the interests and values of the dominant race. However, in prac-

tice he is forced to make choices which sometimes lead him to
identify himself as a Negro and at other times to reject this
identification. Such ambiguity and ambivalence stem from
inconsistencies in the system governing racial relations. For
this reason the system does not arouse mechanisms characteristic of delinquent behavior or the corresponding forms of
societal utilization of techniques of racial nonconformity. Brazilian society has always been partially open, both under the
caste system and under the class system. Consequently, the
mechanisms of racial domination always ignored the fact that
the black population had leaders. Our investigation proves
that the impact of social change has not been strong enough
to change this unfortunate aspect of race relations. So far the
extent of the Negro's and mulatto's social ascent is such as to
affect only the lower levels and some intermediate levels of
the structure of class society. Moreover, racial relations in
terms of the power structure and its monopolization by the
dominant race have undergone no significant change. On the
contrary, the constant changing of the elites has had an adverse effect on the autonomy of the black population. During
the period of agitation the Negro elites were led by intellectuals who were somewhat aware of white tutelage and extremely independent of its direct or indirect pressures. For
this reason, despite great internal differences, they managed
to encourage and spread a racial counterideology possessing a
certain unity and remarkable moral autonomy.

In recent times the leadership of the intellectuals has been
undermined or eliminated. In their place men of action have
arisen, men shaped by struggle and drawn from various professions in small business and manufacturing—in short, men
who underestimated the usefulness of joint effort and gave
priority to forms of racial adjustment that seemed to favor the
fastest possible fruition of the social prestige inherent in the
position they had acquired. At the same time that they gave
their blessing to the most accessible channels for bringing the
rising Negro into the middle class, they adopted a social style
of living that separated the elites from the majority of the

black population. They were not altogether wrong: the course they followed favored more than any other their plans for social self-assertion, and their techniques of social action were fully compatible with the structure and operation of an open social system. Therefore, if the existing system of racial relations continued, in the long run nothing would theoretically prevent the changes going on from benefiting everyone in an equitable fashion. Nevertheless, they overlooked or forgot the sociohistoric, economic, and sociocultural factors that justify the egalitarian claims of integrationist racial minorities in an open society. From this viewpoint it seems clear that the dynamic influences directly set in motion by the social ascent of some portions of the black population are contained within the policy of assimilation embodied in the racial ideology of the dominant white social circles. Under these conditions it was inevitable that satisfaction of the selfish interests of the rising Negro would do little at this point to eliminate the ambiguities and ambivalence that make the prevailing pattern of racial adjustment so burdensome to the great majority of the black population.

The last three topics concern effects of vertical mobility that are undeniably constructive. They are related to the quality of the adaptive and integrative processes being utilized by emerging black elites. Insofar as the rising Negro aspires to a better position in society, he simultaneously changes his view of the world and his relationship with the white man. He wants something socially, although he seeks it at the limited level of private and selfish social interests. Consequently he makes strenuous efforts not to be excluded and, in particular, he identifies the white man as a kind of privileged competitor whom he must excel to reach his personal goals. Hence he abandons and steadily replaces the fearful attitudes and spontaneous submission to the white man in everything directly or indirectly related to his desire to rise and succeed. The data gathered show conclusively that these changes in outlook lead to the emergence and dissemination of standards involving competition and rivalry in relations with the white man. Success in social ascent largely depends on an ability to apply such standards. Although inclined to avoid extremes, the rising Negro tends naturally to accept and to place social value on racial competition in levels of income and employment and, if necessary or convenient, does not shrink from certain conflicts that involve the benefits he has achieved or place him in a strategic position to obtain increasingly greater benefits. Tendencies of this kind, which indicate a transformation of the character of the Negro and mulatto in social ascent, have become so widespread that they are readily observable. For example in an investigation made by means of questionnaires, the question "Do you think there are jobs in our society that are given only to whites?" was asked; 74 women and 238 men replied affirmatively, and 49 women and 123 men negatively. Furthermore, to the question "Do you think Negroes should try to get these jobs?" [61] 103 women and 328 men said yes and only 7 women and 19 men said no.

The same reasons have imperceptibly modified relations among Negroes who are vertically mobile. Not only are reciprocal judgments more realistic but the predatory tendencies characteristic of the phase in which human relations were linked to well-defined forms of parasitism have disappeared. In their place different attitudes have arisen, urging the individual to count on himself. Among the most popular formulas are: "He who trusts others is lost"; "I am my own best friend"; "The best friend is money in your pocket." These are in addition to more universal formulas, such as: "God willing, I must succeed"; "God helps him who helps himself"; "I must succeed." Given the situation in the Negro milieu, where success on the part of acquaintances, friends, and colleagues used to provoke depreciative and sometimes hostile remarks, one may wonder how such changes could take place in the patterns of social relationships without serious problems. The explanations seem to be obvious. Opportunities for classification in connection with proletarianization were made available to a relatively large portion of the black population. The best opportunities, which permitted real or imaginary classification in the middle classes, were in turn distributed through an ultraselective racial mechanism. The beneficiaries were diluted in the white milieu through a highly diversified number of situations in work and social intercourse. We obtain a complete frame of reference if we add to these two reasons the well-known fact that the Negro's ascent is slow and gradual, which favors resocialization and mobility on the part of isolated individuals or small groups of individuals. The black population is not becoming adjusted en masse to the requirements of regulated competition and of constructive conflict in personal relationships. The new patterns of social interaction tend to be implemented in the Negro milieu intermittently and by chance as the rising Negro is integrated into the social order of society. It is our opinion that such modifications may also be classified as changes that are affecting the character of the Negro and the mulatto. The conditions under which these changes are taking place socially indicate why the negative potentialities for rancor, hostility, and blind resentment did not explode suddenly when some of the opportunities dreamed of as a collective myth actually became available to very few of them. Since there is always the hope of being one of this fortunate group, the one-sided successes of others are felt by the great majority like small blows that are softened by the great illusion held by each individual that "his turn will come too."

Among the black middle class, particularly those who cannot be called elite, a different attitude prevails. The mobile Negro pins his greatest hopes on the reactive effects of social ascent. He hopes that these effects will reeducate the whites by making clear the Negro's real qualities and eliminating the objective or subjective basis for negative racial stereotypes. Although he rarely cooperates in the process (except when obliged to do so through family or inter-generation relationships), he is alert to success on the part of Negroes and mulattoes, recognizes it, makes it known, and is proud of it. Moreover, in some circles the advantages inherent in the infiltration of society's power structure by important Negroes are better understood and many are generously prepared to work

cooperatively toward greater infiltration. Herein probably lie
the ingredients of a new type of integration of the Negro
milieu, with the manifestation and spread of attitudes and
active behavior reflecting racial solidarity.

The direct effects of the Negro's and the mulatto's vertical
mobility on social differentiation and stratification of the
Negro milieu show some obvious tendencies. Greater participation in employment and income led to quantitative and
qualitative changes in the former Negro elites. Discriptions
that are valid for the period from 1910 to 1930 show that
these elites were composed of persons whose real status was
lower class, but who had steady jobs, could demonstrate certain aspects of the life of a white man of the salons, and
sometimes inherited their master's wardrobe. Observations
made by our researchers at special ceremonies such as wed-
dings, at parties in the home,[62] and at gatherings in important
clubs [63] showed that these elites are heterogeneous, but include many who are really middle class. The basic criterion
used by the Negro for appraisal and recognition of the status
acquired is standard of living. If this is regarded as high, even
if the occupational level of the person is low in the light of the
various criteria of society, a person may be regarded as rich
and belonging to the elite. This elite ranges from the cook and
the mechanic to the dentist, the accountant, the doctor, and
the layer and includes the driver, the clerk, the worker in
commerce, the real estate agent, the small businessman, and
finally the small industrialist. It is selected and expressed in
terms of estate, through an ability to exhibit a conspicuous
style of life and to keep it more or less closed both to the
"no-account" Negro and to the white man of "uncertain intentions" or "low moral standard."

Since the research was conducted, matters have changed
even more. The tendency toward internal differentiation is
quite distinct, and there are today Negro associations that are
ultraselective in choosing their members, taking into account
the candidates' occupational and economic level, social prestige, and moral standard. Consequently, differentiation of the

Negro milieu is beginning to reflect social level, although certain signs of compensatory status (related to a more or less conscious intention to dumbfound others with an aristocratic style of life) are still in evidence everywhere.

There are three consequences of great importance to our analysis. First, connection or association with whites is losing its former importance as a source of social prestige (or as a supplement to prestige). The former state of mind tended to attach excessive importance to such relationships.

Second, tendencies to fix and defend distinct social levels have two effects on differentiation of the Negro milieu. There are more or less conscious attempts to reproduce among Negroes white forms of sociability and social organization. Naturally such attempts involve the strengthening of attitudes and behaviors aimed at converting the black world into a miniature of the white world, which means that they noticeably help to accentuate social positions and roles according to a class regime. However, the idea is clearly established that the Negro should be a person without ceasing to be black. Therefore social distinctions must operate and hold through and despite color. The implications of this conviction are severe. It intensifies certain exclusivist and aristocratic tendencies on the part of old elites to the point of paroxysm, leading the rich Negro to despise, avoid, and show uncontrollable animosity toward the poor Negro and particularly toward the delinquent Negro.

Third, the upper levels (and thus those really belonging to the middle class in the eyes of society) adopt a double integrationist policy. In employment and income considerations within the larger society they force interaction with whites and egalitarian integration. In the intimate aspect of social life (the forms of sociability connected with the home, groups of friends, and recreative or cultural associations), they show great timidity and passively submit to the ethnocentric judgments and excessively rigid criteria of selection imposed by the whites. Hence the increase in social prestige and the resulting opportunities for social performance can only be used socially in the Negro milieu. Social ascent increases the extent of participation by black elites in the occupational and economic sphere, but at the same time it creates new ways for diffuse social isolation of the Negro and mulatto to persist and increase. Having no other social stage for his self-realization, the rising Negro closes himself within the more or less safe walls of such elites, compensating himself by strengthening the aristocratic exclusivism that characterizes them and by accentuating class lines within the Negro milieu and in his relations with whites.

The direct effects of the Negro's and the mulatto's vertical mobility on their relations with whites displays two general tendencies. First, to the extent that the mobile Negro has the special qualities necessary for identifying himself with or corresponding to white expectations of behavior, he can derive maximum benefit not only from the real or potential opportunities offered by egalitarian acceptance but also from the openly tolerant attitudes of persons sympathetic to the Negro or opposed to racial prejudice. In terms of the traditional mechanisms of racial adjustment, social ascent gives the black individual a good chance to be regarded and treated as the exception who proves the rule. In terms of the integrative and functional mechanisms of the competitive social order, social ascent gives the black individual a good chance to be accepted in formal and prescribed contacts which are regulated by social roles identified through his status personality. In practice the two chances for acceptance are largely combined, but in such a way that the traditional mechanisms absorb and weaken the competitive mechanisms of racial adjustment.

Second, there is the alternate and exclusive tendency characterized by the reappearance of attitudes, behavior, and judgments of an intolerant and discriminative nature. Just as within the traditional pattern there are those who refuse to compromise with the philosophy of the exception that proves the rule, within the competitive society there are those who refuse to make themselves the equal of a Negro through formal and prescribed contact. In this case resistance to the rising Negro is specific, since frequently the same persons accept humble Negroes or those who can be described as "poor devils." It seems that such extreme manifestations of racial intolerance can be explained sociologically as the conscious or unconscious opposition of these persons to a reduction in the social distance between the two races. They apparently fear that equality with the Negro brings about social degradation and an irreparable loss of security, social prestige, and power on the part of the white man.

Finally, we are able to make a tentative reply [64] to the controversial question of whether vertical social mobility on the part of the Negro and the mulatto is or is not an indication that color prejudice does not exist (or that there is at least social neutrality).[65] The evidence gathered, in addition to the two general conclusions previously reached, definitely suggests that social mobility on the part of the Negro and the mulatto has taken place, is taking place, and will take place in the future despite the existence and the inhibiting effects of color prejudice, which is reflected both in the restrictive appraisal of the Negro and in limitation of his economic, social, and political opportunities. There seems to be no doubt that the direction and effects of pressure for assimilation by society have had a strong but varied effect on racial relations. Comparison of the current sociohistoric situation with that in the recent or distant past shows that today São Paulo is closer to achieving that standard of racial democracy which is possible in a competitive social order governed by monopoly of power by the dominant race. Not only are racial judgments built up under the caste system beginning to enter a stage of definitive collapse but discriminatory measures arising from or justified by the master-and-servant code of racial relations are disappearing at a faster rate.

All this, however, does not mean that ethnocentric judgments and discriminatory behavior have been eliminated. They remain in forms that are sometimes attenuated or socially redefined, and they interfere with relations between

Negroes and whites. The white race, as a result of its power monopoly, controls the class situations fully shaped by the degree of development reached by the competitive social order in São Paulo, which means that action of an ethnocentric and discriminatory nature on the part of the whites is doing irremediable harm to the black population. In short, the data presented do not support the hypothesis that the vertical mobility of the Negro and the mulatto in recent years can be explained by an absence or a breakdown of color prejudice. On the contrary, they show that mobility exists despite the symptomatic presence of color prejudice. In addition they indicate that some of the manifestations of color prejudice are clearly associated with weakening of the tendencies toward vertical social mobility in the Negro milieu.

THE NEGRO PROBLEM IN A CLASS

SOCIETY

1951–1960

Introduction

There is an integrationist pressure in Brazil to compel the
Negro and mulatto to absorb the norms, patterns of behavior,
and social values of the competitive social order. But this
pressure does not draw on all the socializing forces of the
larger society. Basically, it is clearly associated with the need
to lessen the historiocultural distance between the sociocultural legacy of the black population and industrial civilization.
In sociological terms, this pressure is measured by the need to
absorb the Negro into the competitive social order, and as a
result to develop his loyalty to the economic, juridico-political,
and social foundations of this order. It does not cover other
areas of socialization and participation in economic interests,
social safeguards, or cultural riches. As a result, this integrationist pressure does not, strictly speaking, affect the prevailing patterns of the racial distribution of income, social prestige, and power. In the sphere of race relations, the class
society is becoming an open social system, but the patterns of
racial domination inherited from the past are not being up-
dated. Within this broad picture, what might be regarded as
the democratization of race relations is seen as a sociohistorical process that is heterogeneous, slow, and discontinuous.

These inferences are corroborated, empirically and theoretically, by the conclusions which may be drawn from the data
on the Negro's collective protests and on the mechanisms of
vertical social mobility inherent in the tendency toward classification of the black individual at the heart of the competitive
social order. Collective protests unleashed sociopsychological
tendencies among the Negro groups which corresponded in
content and meaning to the integrationist pressures of the
larger society. Nevertheless, they threatened the established
patterns of racial distribution of income, social prestige, and
power, for they aimed at the sudden universalization of those
economic interests, social safeguards, and cultural values
upon which rest the legitimacy and balance of the competitive
social order. Thus, the Negro problem was equated with the
ideal requisites for the integration and functioning of the
class system, and racial unrest was granted the character of
an organized and conscious struggle for racial equality. In
other words, while it was reacting to the integrationist pressures of the larger society, the Negro's collective protest
through the rights movements went too far. This explains why
the protest found no echoes among whites and spread only
through limited segments of the black population.

The mechanisms of vertical social mobility of the Negro
and mulatto, in turn, could be and were measured by the
quality and intensity of the integrationist pressure of the
larger society. Society opened, suddenly and on a social scale,
to the Negro and mulatto in the area of free labor and in the
heteronomous positions of the occupational pyramid associated with the capitalist system. The integrationist pressure
had direct structural and dynamic results on one level alone
—that of the differentiation of the occupational and professional roles of the black individual. Yet the historical hiatus
engendered by the conditions under which the bourgeois revolution and the consolidation of the competitive social order
occurred in the city was closed. The Negro finally found normal and permanent ways of becoming part of the class society. Nevertheless, other positions in the system, with their

corresponding social roles, were affected only indirectly, and in proportion to the socioeconomic vitality acquired by the developing strata of the black population. Not even the electoral roles associated with the national political power system were affected in any direct or immediate way. When the Negro is concerned with the obligations inherent in being a citizen of a republican national community, he does so haphazardly and strictly in terms of his material or moral interests. If the integrationist pressure of society were to be applied in this direction, we would have an objective and relevant index of the rise of sociohistorical forces which would tend to bring about with the greatest possible rapidity a socioeconomic and sociopolitical equalizing of the racial groups.

Given these external conditions, which would develop by stages the manner in which the competitive social order would be opened to the black population, the egalitarian impulses at work within this population would become subjected to a previous sociohistorical conditioning of a highly restrictive character and to a restricted, rigid, and unavoidable selection. It is not surprising, therefore, that the vertically mobile Negro should have cast his choice for a way of life as realistic as it is opportunistic, turning his back both on the rights movements and on the common interests of Negroes collectively. As some of them put it, "to think of collective movements brings bad luck," or "racial agitation takes a lot of work and is no use at all. It's like banging your head against the wall." They subscribed unconsciously to the rationale that "smart people don't ask for trouble," and they had grave reasons for doing so. To do otherwise would be to risk the security and the advantages of being part of the social order for the sake of mirages. Society has already shown the path to be followed, and with it the eventual solution to the Negro problem.

These results demand that we examine our subject matter from a broader perspective. First, it is necessary to discern whether racial tensions have repercussions of any sort on the pattern of integration of the competitive social order. We shall not deal with the broader picture of the manifestations of color prejudice, but merely determine how racial tensions are perceived and controlled socially. Second, we shall trace the actual configurations of what appears to be, in view of the contact situation, the *Brazilian racial dilemma*. In doing so, we shall come face to face with the central issue of our research and develop a stimulating perspective for the broadest conclusions we have reached.

Societal Reaction to Racial Tensions

The analysis carried out in the preceding chapter indicates that classification in the competitive social order is a structural and dynamic requisite for any change in the prevailing patterns of race relations. The reason for this is obvious. The relationship between color and dependent social position can only be broken if the Negro and mulatto attain a position of economic, social, and political equality with the white. Actually our analysis also suggests that such a position is not, in itself, sufficient to change the racial *status quo*. Whites ignore, consciously or unconsciously, the social effects of the Negro's classification on the social levels to which they themselves belong. Nevertheless, they cannot prevent socially rising Negroes from changing their conception of status, their mode of interaction with society, or their attitudes vis-à-vis the forms of racial adjustment inherited from the past. Gradually, imperceptibly, alongside the classification of Negroes and mulattoes in the competitive social order, patterns of race relations undergo sociologically significant changes. Over a long period of time, these changes (if the trends described are maintained) foster the slow but gradual adaptation of the system of race relations to the economic, juridico-political, and social requisites of that social order. We cannot say what would happen if the process were to gain intensive and constant momentum and were thus to become adapted to the pattern of integration of the class society and to the rhythm of its historical development in São Paulo. Under the circumstances of full employment and constantly rising actual average income at the moment, it would be probable that existing contradictions between norms, stereotypes, and actual behavior should cease. Because of the growing numbers of black individuals able to compete for and fulfill the social roles inherent in the positions they have achieved, the effective behavior of the whites ideally should be modified and channeled toward an accelerated democratization of the patterns of race relations.

So far, however, the sociological situation has been quite different. The absorption of Negroes and mulattoes into the structure of the class system has been so limited and hesitant that the old vicious circle remains relatively unbroken. Color continues to operate as a racial mark and as a symbol of social position, indicating simultaneously a dependent racial group and inferior social position. In addition, the majority of black individuals lack the means to break out of this confused state of affairs, which is both vexing and damaging. Even the vertically mobile Negro—a privileged person among the Negro groups—must struggle heroically, uninterruptedly, and ingloriously in order to enjoy minute quantities of the prerogatives associated with his social position. This egalitarian trend, itself timid and hesitant, is canceled by the social context. As we have seen, in 1940 the category of employer comprised only 133 Negroes and mulattoes to 15,261 whites—0.78 per cent to 97.04 per cent. Now, if we take as a point of reference the demographic color pattern, this ratio ought theoretically to be quite different under a system of socioeconomic equalization of whites and Negroes. The number of Negro employers ought to be approximately 13.5 times greater (or about 1,609 individuals), and the number of white employers ought to be approximately one-tenth smaller (or 13,804 individuals)— not to speak of individuals of Asian ancestry, who overshoot our hypothetical ratio by more than one-sixth.*

Thus, we must work in terms of a reality that does not fit

* Editor's note: The author is referring to the Japanese immigrants to Brazil. In the first part of 1967, 73 per cent of the Japanese colony in Brazil were proprietors (Intercambio Cultural Entre Brasil e Japão, Japanese Consulate, São Paulo, mimeo., n.d.).

the conventional rationalizations defended by those whites who identify with the Brazilian racial ideology. They misrepresent the racial reality as they view the Negro's position through the ideal norms of behavior and the egalitarian potential of the competitive social order. On the other hand they are deceived in their own social outlook as they cling to the notion that there are no racial distinctions among the lower classes. This does happen, but only in those contact situations peculiar to social milieus molded by folk culture. There, the Negro is equal to the white for nearly all social purposes, through a leveling downward. This is a sociodynamic consequence of absorption into the network of human relations created by a subsistence economy. In a metropolitan society, however, downward leveling implies at least membership in the working classes, and this would require the systematic proletarianization of those segments of the black population which are involved in the free labor system outside of the occupations pertaining to the middle and upper classes. This is the case only in part and in a fragmentary and hesitant way. This results, in actuality, in serious limitation of the Negro's integration into the class system. Only a few segments of the black population have managed to achieve *typical class positions* in organized fashion. Other segments of the same population—presumably more than half even now—remain on the periphery of the free labor system and the class system, victims of anomic conditions of social existence or of sporadic association in the metropolitan subproletariat. In short, in the contact situation described, downward leveling is not the same thing as equalizing with the white. To the contrary, it implies an indefinite perpetuation of the two polarities which have traditionally upheld the parallel between color and minimal social position in Brazilian society: social anomie and socioeconomic dependence.

Although this does not explain everything (since we must also take into account residual forms of intolerance in the cultural traditions of the various ethnic and national groups of *Paulistana* society), it provides us with a general background for determining sociologically *how* and *why* this parallel possesses both historical viability at the present time and the external requisites for sociocultural survival. From this standpoint it seems that Negroes as a group will be able to change their patterns of societal reaction to the expectations and behavior of whites only when they manage to become fully integrated into the class society, and when this integration occurs on an equal basis vis-à-vis other racial groups. Even though these two conditions are not sufficient to alter the general situation—since the racial behavior of whites is motivated and controlled by cultural factors alien to the structuring of the class system—they are decisive on two counts. First, they serve as material and moral foundation for a change in the status representations of the Negro and mulatto, as well as in the mechanisms of societal reaction of the black population to characteristic manifestations of racial prejudice and discrimination. Second, they provide a sociodynamic requisite for the organization of the conscious behavior of Negroes and mulattoes as a group, rendering it appropriate to the typical requirements of the class situation in the present sociohistorical setting. In the view of these two points, it seems obvious that the Negro requires material and moral foundations in order to use in a different way and for his own benefit the safeguards bestowed by social position. As long as color prejudice [1] operates predominantly under cover of clearly defined class situations, its victims ordinarily have to contend with insuperable difficulties, and it is often impossible for them to defend their social interests through the social techniques, forms of behavior, and controls consecrated and guaranteed by the competitive social order.

This posing of the problem immediately suggests that racial tensions arise above and beyond the social interests and values inherent in the class positions which are found in São Paulo. The motivation for the nonconformist behavior of the socially rising Negro (for, as we have seen, the desire to rise is in itself a choice containing an element of protest) is the yearning to be someone, to rise, to become part of the system and of the established social order. As a rule, the achievement of a position (that is to say, of a class position) is involved. Nevertheless, where the Negro and mulatto are concerned, this yearning can only rarely be fulfilled from within a class situation. As far as the white is concerned, in turn, actual competition with the Negro is almost nil. It occurs only sporadically, in isolated cases which have no repercussions on the prevailing patterns of race relations. None of the class positions which developed historically up to the present time is endangered by the presence of competition of the Negro and mulatto. As a result it is not class interests that interfere with the expression of color prejudice. Proof of this is easy to obtain: the development of the competitive social order did not contribute in any way either to the intensification of expressions of color prejudice, or to a change in its sociocultural patterns. Actually the Negro does not enter, as a Negro, in the sphere of systematic social awareness and understanding of the white. It would seem that this is so, to a large measure, because the Negro is not regarded socially as a real or potential competitor for the enjoyment of the limited and highly desired safeguards of the class system. For this reason, the importance of color is secondary. Systematically meaningful are the external symbols of wealth, social prestige, and power which characterize the socioeconomic levels of the social pyramid or the personal characteristics and aptitudes of individuals independent of their social position. Nevertheless this general condition of awareness and understanding of one man by another does not make for neutrality in the adjustments of whites with Negroes, nor is it to be regarded as proof of the absence of color prejudice. The latter is unleashed, in unilateral and limited fashion, wherever and whenever the Negro comes forth and his presence becomes obvious and inescapable. Then, independent of any social motivations or controls related to the organization of the class society, there automatically come into play specific mechanisms which place the Negro's person or interests and forms of behavior in the direct line of awareness, understanding, and reaction on the part of the white individuals.

However, the Negro has not (at least not so far) become an

inexorable reality which the white could not evade and had to face whether he liked it or not. To the contrary, the white can put the Negro in the background, ignore him, and plan the future as if society were racially homogeneous or if the powers of decision of the white racial group alone mattered within it. Now, it should be stressed in sociological terms that this factor, instead of arising as a positive requisite of racial integration along democratic lines, arose as a factor of inertia with profoundly negative results. Socially, it amounts to the general lack of interest of the white toward the Negro, which contributes to the indefinite perpetuation of certain archaic models of racial adjustment. The Negro is expected to adjust to the patterns of the prevailing civilization. But no need is paid to what this means, materially and morally, to society, or how it might or should affect the equality of Negroes and whites in terms of the enjoyment of the social safeguards ensured by the class system. Further, and this is clearly sociopathic, wherever the Negro breaks through on his own to relatively high social levels, such occurrences are regarded and explained as if the traditional criteria of racial demination, which excluded the exception to the general rule and manipulated it to strengthen the rule, were still in full force and as if the parallel between color and minimum social position were a normal ingredient of relations between Negroes and whites.

We shall deal in this part of the present chapter with the following themes: the forms of expression of color prejudice in *Paulistana* society, and the mechanisms of societal reaction to dissimulated and open manifestations of color prejudice. The discussion of these themes, with selected empirical data, will permit us to complete our analyses and will help us determine the degree of dissonance that persists between the patterns of race relations and the forms of the organization of social life prevailing in São Paulo in the industrial era.

Sociohistorical analysis sees color prejudice [2] as a sociopsychological and sociocultural form typical of Portuguese-Brazilian civilization. It combines prejudiced judgments and attitudes of an ethnocentric and utilitarian nature with discriminatory social motivations and controls, and offers the eidetic and ethologic bases necessary to such judgments and attitudes.[3] It also links them to standardized forms of behavior which grant it minimal effectiveness, cohesion, and continuity. In this regard both prejudiced judgments and discriminatory practices are universals, being endowed with a certain homogeneity and generality. It seems obvious (although this is not acknowledged openly) that the irreconciliable contradictions and inconsistencies engendered by the conflict between these judgments and attitudes and the ideal patterns of Portuguese-Brazilian civilization have not really been eliminated. To the contrary, a unique compound has been formed which conceals this conflict and reconciles individuals to its repercussions on the affective and cognitive levels of social behavior. To limit ourselves to fundamentals, there are two chief dynamic results of this conciliating compound of incompatible and ideally exclusive sociopsychological and sociocultural elements. First, color prejudice does not appear on the social scene in a systematic way, but as a surreptitious, ambiguous, and vague social reality. Second, color operates as a dual frame of reference: it inseparably links race and social position, socially stigmatizing an entire racial category. This factor may appear to be secondary; nevertheless, it is crucial. It compels members of the stigmatized racial group to accept the forms of racial adjustment which are enjoined upon them. They develop attitudes, judgments, and forms of behavior which are ambivalent, vague, and contradictory because of the duality of the frame of reference; they become unable to differentiate racial stigmatization from socioeconomic dependence and sociocultural isolation; and thus they are unable to oppose such attitudes, judgments, and forms of behavior. As a result they are compelled to face prejudice in a state of great psychological confusion and without the means to group themselves into integrated racial minorities. Regarding themselves *de jure* and *de facto* as active members of the established social order, they learn to deal with the noxious

effects of the racial contact situation only on the purely personal plane. Collective and organized recourse to radical techniques of exposure and protest are also closed to them, because racial tensions have been confined to the hidden level of
race relations and are regarded socially as an incontrovertible
threat to social peace. On the whole, everything contributes to
regulate, dissimulate, and contain expressions of prejudice,
subjecting them to the structural and dynamic requirements
of a civilization that has made social accommodation the ideal
goal of the societal integration of interacting racial groups.
Expressions of prejudice cannot be carried far enough to en-
danger the interests, ideals of life, and social values associated
with the historicocultural pattern of racial adjustment. On
the other hand, however, they cannot be abolished without
turning this complex automatically into a mere social equalizing of the racial groups involved.

   This takes us to the heart of the structure and dynamics of
the situation of racial contact prevailing in São Paulo. Expressions of prejudice prevent the differentiation, and consequently the aggravation of dissimulated color prejudice into
systematic forms of racial prejudice and discrimination. At the
same time, nevertheless, they tone down or cancel the repercussions in the sphere of race relations of the tendency to a
democratization of wealth, social prestige, and power. Thus
we uncover a very instructive aspect of our racial reality. It
suggests that those who point to Brazil as an extreme case of
racial tolerance have some justification. Yet, it also shows the
other side of the coin, which unfortunately has been neglected: racial tolerance is not at the service of racial equality,
and thus remains neutral to the human problems of the Negro
related to the racial distribution of income, social prestige,
and power. Indeed, this aspect is clearly linked to the protection and indefinite perpetuation of the racial status quo,
through effects which foster the indirect preservation of the
social disparities that condition the permanent subordination
of the Negro and mulatto. The victims of prejudice and discrimination are regarded and treated with relative decorum

and civility as human beings, but as if they were only half human. Their material and moral interests are not taken into account. What matters is social peace, with all it implies as an element of stability for the prevailing patterns of racial domination.

Those who consider racial relations superficially, without heeding the historicocultural pattern of social accommodation they involve or the implication of this pattern in terms of the racial distribution of income, social prestige, and power and the corresponding model of racial domination, do not really understand the existence, the deep complexities, and the persistent influence of the phenomenon. In the course of interviews and the experimental situations to which they lead, in the interaction of researcher and informant, obstinate and shocked denial was almost systematic. No one will accept the onus of being prejudiced. Only those who fall into the category of intolerant personalities and those who are typically neutral to color prejudice frankly admit its existence and its legitimacy or illegitimacy. Reality is uncovered gradually, through the accumulation of contradictions which do not affect the balance or behavioral tendencies of individuals. Questions such as "Would you bring a Negro to your home? Would you accept a Negro boss? Would you let your daughter (or sister) marry a Negro?" lead to a justification of inconsistencies, as a rule quickly perceived by the informant and accepted good-humoredly. "Yes, you're right. We *are* prejudiced. But what can we do?"

Not only has the opinion become widespread that color prejudice does not exist in Brazil, but this opinion has been enjoined on dissenters, white and Negro alike. Christian mores, in turn, have contributed to this tendency. The area of Portuguese-Brazilian civilization that suffers most from the sociocultural inconsistencies pointed out above is the religious one. Even though Catholicism prevented neither slavery nor color prejudice, it has spread a certain reluctance to face openly these dark aspects of human nature and of the organization of society. The other two influences are secondary, but not unimportant. Through the influence of Catholicism, and to a large measure through the longing to identify with (European) civilization, prejudice and discrimination are viewed as degrading, as though they were one with incivility and barbarism.

We shall now endeavor to determine the existing relationship between racial judgments, attitudes, and forms of behavior which are prejudiced and discriminating to varying degrees, and the types of contact involved in possible situations of racial coexistence. Knowledge of this relationship is of great importance. It provides immediate evidence of the boundaries within which judgments, attitudes, and forms of behavior of this type are socially approved or tolerated. It also gives indirect evidence of the degree to which such judgments, attitudes, and forms of behavior are governed, standardized, and regulated socially—in other words, through a common historicocultural pattern.

The data gathered show that four typical kinds of contact underlie the immense variety of possible relationships between Negroes and whites.[4] First, there is a sort of contact by proximity. The mere coexistence of different racial groups leads to a web of interdependence which makes the members of these groups members of "our group." Although the overall point of reference becomes the national community, everyone being regarded as a Brazilian, the basis of interaction is provided by what might be called mass sociability. As a result Negroes and whites are seen as pure entities, as though contact were strictly formal and defined in terms of the identification of individuals with the racial categories pertaining to "our group." On this level color prejudice is expressed in an impersonal and mild form, which is at the same time insidious and corrosive. Color is firmly asserted as a social mark that links the Negro and mulatto inescapably to an inferior racial group and a degrading social position. The best example of this can be found in certain sayings already quoted above: "Negroes are not human"; "There is no such thing as a good Negro"; and so on. To these we might add the alternative sayings used by the Negroes themselves: "Whites are no good"; "White trash"; "Deceitful white"; "If I liked whites I would carry a sack of lime on my back"; "White soul"; "Stingy white"; "I'm a Negro but I'm my own master." There are even more expressive sayings which seem to stress positive attitudes and judgments: "Poor thing, it's not his fault if he's a Negro"; "You wouldn't know he was a Negro"; "He's a Negro only on the outside"; "When a Negro is good, he's good all the way"; "Negro with a white soul"; etc.; and "Good white"; "Wow! A straight white!"; "You wouldn't know he was white"; "A white as good as white bread." Most of the negative stereotypes which stigmatize the Negro and mulatto racially and socially are expressed in verbalizations of this type which permeate our behavioral expectations. For this reason, not only are such verbalizations transmitted unconsciously, but they condition the formation of persistent images (of the Negro by the white and vice versa) and eventually cause ethnocentric judgments to take the place of reality judgments.

Second, there is contact governed by convention, in accordance with the premises of the traditional pattern of asymmetric race relations. The mask of civility places a wedge between personal feelings and deep-seated beliefs and the conveniences and decorum of life in society. In accordance with the ethical duality that prevails in a caste society, the white has enjoined upon himself—and thus upon the Negro as well—the general principle that each person must know his place and behave in accordance with the corresponding external requirements. The affective, logical, and moral context of this type of interaction leads men to regard the parallelism between racial and social stratification as natural, necessary, and unavoidable. Thus, even while he uses every available means to strengthen and retain the pattern of racial domination that engenders and maintains this parallelism, the white cultivates explicitly the prejudice that he is not prejudiced. Since the sole basic aim is to preserve a certain pattern of racial domination, it becomes easy to conceal this objective behind defense of the social order (or simply social peace).

Color is brought into play as a racial mark only insofar as it operates as a symbol of social status. We have two ways of uncovering this dissimulated form of racial prejudice and discrimination. There is that which arises when the conventions that govern racial adjustments are broken unilaterally by the "inferior" party; in other words, when the Negro or mulatto refuses "to be treated like a Negro" (even as a "Negro with a white soul"). In this case, the white endeavors mildly "to put the Negro in his place." (To recall an example already cited, he may have the visitor's meal served in the kitchen, even though the visitor is a mulatto, has a higher degree, and a white-collar profession.)

There is also that form which is disclosed when whites are compelled to reveal "what is going on inside." A small traffic incident, an innocent prodding of the informant's sensibilities, or a fight can contribute powerfully to a loosening of the tongue. We can list some representative examples: We came across a taxi driver drinking *pinga* with a Negro in a bar in Vila Nova Conceição. The scene appeared to be a friendly one. As soon as he was in his car, the driver said, "These Negroes, you give them a finger and they want your arm."

"Why?"

"That Negro wanted me to lend him a hundred milreis till tomorrow. He said it was to get him through the night."

"You didn't give it to him?"

"Of course not! He has some nerve."

"But isn't he your friend?"

"My foot! I don't even know him. I was having a drink and he asked me to treat him to one. I said OK. And next thing you know he was ordering a three-milreis *pinga*."

He confided further that he did not like Negroes because he found them impertinent and dishonest. We asked whether he considered them inferior to whites.

"That I can't say. I don't know enough about it. I only know that I've never seen Negroes in important positions. They're only in low positions." Then he recalled that he knew a "colored lawyer," but he added, "It's one in a thousand. All the others are illiterates. They don't know anything. You can't do anything with these people."

We pointed out the contradictions in his behavior. He had been drinking with a Negro, treating him in a friendly way, and yet these were the views he was expressing. He replied, "I don't like them. You have to accept them, or else they say you're stuck up. But I don't like them. What can you do? You have to live according to local custom. Here, this is our custom. I can't act differently from other people. People feel that you must accept Negroes—I don't accept them. I know they're not worth a damn."

In a group discussion among middle-class individuals of old Portuguese-Brazilian stock, we put up for discussion the opinion of one of the participants that "Negroes are inferior to whites." The person involved, who hires colored labor for his small industry, invites them for meals in his home, plays soccer with them, and associates on a friendly basis with those who appear to deserve his trust, did not hesitate to state without further ado: "Negroes are indeed inferior to whites. People who say they are not prejudiced are hypocrites. From the day I was in high school, I haven't come across a white person who wasn't prejudiced. But they hide it." He added upon further query, "As for the friendliness shown to Negroes by some people, especially in the upper classes, I think their behavior is comparable to their treatment of house pets. They treat Negroes as though they were pet puppies or kittens. They even give them their family names. Obviously they don't treat Negroes as equals. Then too, we can't confuse Negroes and whites. . . . Negroes know they are inferior and acknowledge that whites are more intelligent and must have authority over them. So they are meek and respectful and accept their place. They will never be able to attain the same position as whites, no matter what they may do." As he clarified his ideas, he emphasized spontaneously, "Prejudice is not due to color, but to the fact that Negroes are inferior to whites and have always served whites as slaves, servants, or laborers. Color serves to pinpoint people, and as a sort of frame of reference. It simplifies things by crystalizing the ideas that whites have about Negroes."

A barber of Italian-Brazilian descent told us about a brawl in which he had been involved and in which he had been hurt. (Circumstances led him to venture an "explanation" of his own accord.) "I was on my way home and Dito (a Negro who was a janitor at the school where they both worked) asked me to have a drink with him. We went into the Tabuleiro da Baiana and asked for two *pingas*. At this point a friend of Dito's came in. He was also a Negro, but a tall guy, a real giant of a man. He had hands *that* big, I'm not kidding. [He measured out a tremendous length.] He greeted Dito and said to him, 'What's up? You don't ask your friends for a drink?' Then we offered him a *pinga*. He accepted and talked for a while with Benedito. Then he turned to me and said, 'Look, give me five milreis. I want five milreis from you.' I answered, 'I haven't got five milreis. If you want, you can drink with us. But I can't give you money. All I have is the right change.' He answered, 'I already said I want five milreis from you!' He argued with me. He wanted me to give him the money. Dito stepped in. He tried to calm him down. But the friend didn't pay any attention and said, 'What's the matter? Are you turning against your own race?' Then I said, 'I don't give money to anybody. If you want to drink, drink. If not, get out! If you want five milreis, go and get some work!' The man didn't say a word. He gave me a hard blow on the nape of the neck which sent me face down on the bar and down to the floor. If there had been a glass there, I would have been killed. Instead of holding back his friend, Dito stepped away. At first I was dizzy. Then I came to, and I went half out of my mind. I was blind. I threw myself head first into his belly. He dived clear across the bar and hit his head on a marble corner. I was scared of him and kicked him in the shin. I wanted to kill the son of a whore. Then I kicked him twice in the face and I bent down and gave him a few more punches. If they hadn't torn me from him, I don't know where I would have stopped. He was bleeding from the mouth, the ears, and the nose." [5] "We ended up in the police station. But the officer knew me and let me go. I wasn't going to be arrested on account of a drunken nigger. I had hurt him, but I hadn't provoked him. . . . Later Benedito criticized me because I had hit his friend, who was drunk. I answered, 'You should talk. Your duty was to hold your friend back. Now you criticize me because I didn't get beaten up. That bugs you. You wanted him to beat me up because he belongs to your race. Well, let me tell you that as far as I'm concerned you no longer exist. I don't want to have anything more to do with you. This is it!' " The barber went on to make various comments about Negroes. "I have no sympathy for Negroes. I don't like those people. I say this to their faces. But they think it's a joke. . . . I don't take Negroes into my home. Do you think I'm going to take monkeys into my house?" He did not want them as friends because he regarded them as dishonest and immoral. "I have been going to Vila Matilde because my wife is ill and is staying with her mother. I've watched Negroes there. They're degenerates. They're not like other people. Whether they're married or single, they have no moral sense. If they have children they don't look after them. If they're married, it is as if they didn't have a wife. They live as if they were single. They have no notion of responsibility or decency like white people. Negro and mulatto women go with anyone who shows them cash. They'll go with anybody for any amount. It makes no difference whether he's married or single. I don't know if this is because they are very hot. It's a very different race, and it seems their women are hotter than others. Even married Negro women will have affairs with anyone who wants them. The washerwoman who works for us looks like she wants to eat me up with her eyes. It doesn't even matter if there are other people around."

Even in situations that demand caution, a breach of etiquette can cause a white person to lose his control. One of the women researchers described such an incident. A well-known physician was department head of a certain institute. On one occasion an informal party was organized in his honor. The social worker had the idea of entrusting a bookkeeper, de-

scribed as a light mulatto and the employee with the longest
tenure, with the words of greeting. "Dr. M.'s displeasure
clearly showed on his face, and half-way through the speech
he interrupted the speaker's praises and said drily, 'Dona
V. [the social worker] has some funny ideas.' The bookkeeper
was terribly upset. At the end of the party Dr. M. said to Dona
V., 'So, that clerk was all you could find to make the speech? A
mulatto!' "

To sum up, the two ways of uncovering prejudice permit us
to lift a curtain which is neither very thick nor very heavy.
There is a correct way of doing things in relations between
Negroes and whites. This way is strictly conventional. It does
not affect the deeper levels of sociability or the personality of
the individuals involved. It seems easy to understand why
whites should cling to such conventions. Even after the traditional patterns of racial domination had begun to break down,
the rule of the white race was still at stake for them. Yet large
numbers of Negroes and mulattoes—many of them partially
or totally free from the traditional conception of the world—
also prefer this model of racial adaptation. We shall cite as an
example the ideas of a mulatto girl who made subtle distinctions between color prejudice and other mechanisms of appraisal, selection, and rejection.[6] Before coming to São Paulo,
she had lived in Angra dos Reis and Rio de Janeiro. Here, she
settled in Santo André, an industrial suburb of São Paulo. She
was shocked by the attitudes of her neighbors, most of them
first-generation European immigrants. She noticed that "they
withdrew, in a way that might even be considered offensive, in
order to avoid relations with Negroes. They will not under any
circumstances make contact with colored people." Her "disappointment was such" that she "got to hate the city" and felt
that "São Paulo is the worst place for Negroes. In Rio there is
more tolerance than there is here. I noticed that some people
disliked Negroes and avoided relations with them. But I saw
more contact and more marriages between Negroes and
whites."

Third, there is the contact that is flagrantly divergent from

the traditional patterns of race relations, either on the white's
or the Negro's part, or both. Even where the traditional conception of the world is in full force, racially intolerant whites
stubbornly refuse to obey the rules governing race relations.
We have already indicated in various ways how such persons
"act in ornery fashion," expressing their deep-seated feelings
and refusing to treat Negroes "as if they were human." Their
golden rule is the well-known "like with like." Our research
showed that the number of whites of Brazilian descent who
still hold such attitudes is much larger than might be supposed.

Three facts may be inferred from the available evidence:
(1) Aside from occasional instances of racially intolerant
individuals, certain circumstances kept the "outbursts of
frankness" on the part of "pure-bred *Paulistas*" from breaking
the taboos governing race relations. (2) Such tendencies were
clearly aberrant—i.e., they marked the racial attitudes, opinions, and behavior patterns of a minority. (3) Although it is
impossible even to guess the size of this minority, our own
experiences and the results of our investigations show that it
included a considerable number of individuals. The sociological significance of such influences is clear. They show that the
traditional racial code also prevailed fully in São Paulo (as we
have already proved on other grounds in the first three chapters of this work). More important, they also prove that certain
aberrant ways of expressing racial intolerance existed prior to
and independent from the flow of immigration.

Nevertheless, immigration exercised a specific pull in the
same direction. Immigrants were the bearers of cultural traditions of their own which did not offer Brazilian solutions to
the problems posed by the mingling of races, but as they were
absorbed into the national mainstream and in turn took over
the local customs they reinterpreted the Brazilian cultural
tradition. This is the truly crucial feature as far as the Negro
is concerned. They never understood the two-faced game of an
acceptance that was at the same time a rejection, or of a
friendliness that was more apparent than real. They mistook

form for content, thoroughly upsetting the foundations of racial interaction. They would accept the friendship of black neighbors or colleagues only to find themselves later astonished by the liberties and impudence arising from a fellowship that was ill conceived and ill planned in terms of the Brazilian tradition. Thus, in order to "put the Negro in his place" they found themselves compelled to break relations with him or to avoid him in an offensive manner.

The vertically mobile Negro, in turn, becomes a source of problems. He wants to be accepted by whites of the same social level and demands the same treatment accorded by the latter to other colleagues and friends. Here is an example, taken from an interview with a young woman journalist and civil servant.[7] "At the office we had a Negro co-worker, educated, cultivated, well-mannered, who held an official position. He would go out with us, go to dances at the professional club, and ask the white girls to dance. We had to grin and bear it! Often, he and I would leave together and he would walk me part of the way home. I would go on talking, and put up with it. But inside I would be thinking: If anybody sees us they won't think that we are co-workers. Once a group from the office went to Pôrto Alegre,* where we went to several nightclubs. He felt he had the right to ask us to dance, and we couldn't refuse and then go and dance with someone else. You can just imagine the situation!" White people, especially in the upper segments of the lower classes and in the middle and upper classes, are puzzled by such situations. The ambiguities of color and inferior social position disappear. Either they accept and treat the Negro as an equal, or they cannot have any relations with him. Here again, deliberate and systematic avoidance is the easiest solution.

The following opinions of a white accountant are characteristic of those that prevail among the middle classes: Color prejudice was being discussed among a group of friends. This man disagreed with those who insisted that " 'the Negro is to

* *Translator's note:* The capital of the southernmost state of Rio Grande do Sul.

blame for his own situation and for color prejudice.' . . .
Color prejudice was created by the whites. It wasn't the Negro
who created this prejudice. A man isn't to blame for having
been a slave. It was the whites who tore them from Africa and
brought them to Brazil. But a man doesn't cease to be human
because he's a slave. I don't think it's fair to blame the Negro.
. . . The Negro's problem is one of education. If Negroes were
educated, they could show their worth. Sociologically speaking
[sic] there is no difference between races. They are all equal.
Whatever whites can do, Negroes can do too!" When pressed
with direct questions he frankly admitted, "Personally, I don't
want any contact with Negroes. I don't like to have anything
to do with them. . . . In my family no one likes Negroes. But
this has nothing to do with my opinions." An obvious inference can be drawn from these examples. In some segments of
the white population, the breakdown of the traditional patterns of race relations does not put an end to color prejudice.
On the contrary, it permits it to be expressed in stronger, more
obvious, and more offensive terms.

Fourth, we must discover the extent to which the development and differentiation of the competitive social order are
reflected in the structuring of race relations. On those levels
where this structuring followed normal integration patterns,
Negroes and whites meet as potential equals. We have already
noted the factors which undermine, limit, or neutralize this
sociohistorical process. Nevertheless, when Negroes actually
breaks through as competitors of the whites, they acquire
certain minimal requisites for differential participation in the
distribution of income, social prestige, and power. As we have
noted, this phenomenon is not sufficiently extensive to make
Negroes a collective threat to the security of whites. Depending on the shortcomings of the latter, the Negroes' reactions
may be either indirect and impersonal or individualized and
direct. The first category comprises those reactions induced by
the recent success of Negroes in certain occupational areas,
such as skilled labor. The thoughts of an elderly housepainter
are characteristic. "You can't trust Negroes. They're too dis-

honest and wicked. They think only of money. They want to
get it on Friday and to get a lot of it. They don't give a thought
to the work. . . . They're bad employees. They're often absent,
they're not careful in their work, and they're not conscious of
professional duties. They know perfectly well that they can
earn money painting, but they don't make the necessary effort. . . . They don't fulfill other obligations properly either. If
you trust them, you're sunk! You have to put up quite a fight to
make them do what they ought to do." His resentment was
focused on what he called "the invasion of the trade by black
people." Those concerned greet this news as disturbing, as
though Negroes dishonored the trade. In the second category
are the inevitable clashes engendered by interracial competition. As a rule the white treats his black colleague as though
he were a subordinate and a hanger-on. He takes on the duty
of protecting and guiding him. When he finds out that the
Negro can paint, and furthermore might outstrip him in free
competition, he resorts to various stratagems to secure permanent advantages. If these fail, there is no remedy but to accept
things as they are. Of course, as he plots his little schemes, the
white cannot always avoid an overt (and sometimes virulent)
display of color prejudice. Most significant, however, is the
fact that up to now such clashes and frictions have remained
limited and have not caused color prejudice to develop into a
conscious, sanctioned, and systematic social reality. We
should also consider that the competitive social order is not
yet sufficiently developed to do away with or to counterbalance
the irrational eruption of racial factors in various spheres of
human relations. If we consider both sides of the matter, it
appears evident that the competitive social order tends to
absorb the overt expressions as well as the concealed aspects
of color prejudice, in the best sense of the Brazilian cultural
tradition, thus dissociating them from typical sociohistorical
patterns of racial conflict.

The following trends were easily identified: (1) a widespread distaste for discussion of matters relating to color and
to the Negro situation, which made color prejudice a sort of

forbidden subject; (2) the tendency to identify with manifestations atypical in Brazil (particularly with the experiences of other groups, as in the United States, where racial prejudice and discrimination ordinarily take on an open and systematic character), which made it possible to deny its existence in Brazil; (3) the tendency to reduce the basic elements in the expression of color prejudice to purely personal matters and to cover up thoroughly those elements which might be said to be stubborn residues of prejudiced or discriminatory opinions and behavior. This of course permitted an expansion in the levels of treatment and appraisal of the Negro: external decorum coupled with partial or total exclusion of the Negro from any long-range contact with whites.

We shall proceed to an analysis of the foundations of color prejudice as it is found in São Paulo, limiting ourselves to basic facts and dealing only with three factors: (1) the social consciousness of the forms of color prejudice acquired by both Negroes and whites; (2) the interpretations each group has for such forms; (3) the ethical elements in the standardized behavior of whites and Negroes in social situations where color prejudice is expressed.

As for the first topic, Negroes and whites differ strikingly in their capacity for awareness of color prejudice. This difference can be crudely measured by the unequal numbers of answers obtained for each group in written statements. Whites do not perceive clearly the different expressions of color prejudice and do not properly recognize their sociopsychological and socioeconomic effects. Among both Negroes and whites there exist tentative interpretations for these differences in the awareness and understanding of the prevailing racial reality. It is all said to result from a sort of "prejudice on the part of the Negro," who is victimized more by his persecution complexes and his compensatory or self-punishing fantasies than by "actual prejudice on the part of whites." Explanations of this sort have a flagrantly ethnocentric flavor. Although the white can remain unaware of or indifferent to the negative consequences, direct or indirect, of color prejudice, the Negro cannot. These consequences compel him to break through his cultural horizon and to ask questions that clash with our current ideas of the race situation. It should be made clear that, first, such questions arise from ever-recurring experiences and, second, the understanding to which they lead can be tested and sifted through the selfsame experiences and incorporated into the sociocultural heritage of the black population. In other words, there are culturally determined alternatives in the awareness and understanding of the racial reality. In addition, these alternatives are shared unilaterally by Negroes and mulattoes, who thus launch some means to lessen or do away with those influences that block the cultural tradition. The differences evident in the black population do not invalidate this general hypothesis.

The varieties of awareness and understanding of color prejudice developed by whites have certain common features. Among them, the most important and decisive deal with the irremediable confusions resulting from the traditionalist culture. Such confusions are expressed in various ways. First, in a generalized unawareness of the existence of a Negro problem. In a characteristic statement written by a white woman informant from a traditional family, we find the following assertion, "I assume that the Negro has no problem. He does not feel ill at ease among whites, while the latter do among Negroes. Whites have a color problem although it involves the color of Negroes."

Then there is the debate over whether color prejudice does or does not exist. One of the women researchers held a discussion among ladies belonging to traditional São Paulo families and got a good example of this. One of the ladies defended with great feeling the notion that there is no color prejudice in São Paulo, giving as an example a black physician in Santos * who is married to a white woman from an excellent family and who has principally white patients. Another of the ladies disagreed, saying that "prejudice does exist and is expressed more or less strongly, depending on the situation, the people

* *Translator's note:* A port city near the city of São Paulo.

involved, and so on." She gave two examples in turn: that of an engineer described as "a very dark Negro" who replied in writing to an ad placed by a company in the capital, enclosing excellent references from his alma mater. The response was favorable. "When he came to take up his duties, they told him cruelly that they couldn't take him because he was black, that they wouldn't have considered hiring him if they had known about his color." [8] The other example referred to the experiences of a delegation of physicians from São Paulo who attended a medical congress in Bahia. The receiving party included a black woman physician. This impressed the São Paulo delegation most unfavorably, for they felt they were being "treated with little courtesy." Eventually, however, the caliber of that doctor caused them to change their minds.

Finally, such confusions are associated with characteristic inconsistencies. A person will attest that he is "unprejudiced" and is in favor of racial democracy, and at the same time express attitudes and opinions that run counter to such statements. Here is how a university student descended from a traditional and militantly socialistic family discusses the matter. "I believe that after all, in a democracy, everyone is equal, and we must treat the Negro decently. Of course, everyone has his place, and you can't be involved with them at all times —you can't trust them too far, for the Negro always lets you down in the long run. It's the old saying, 'The Negro who doesn't mess as he comes in, messes on the way out.' But they have their right to get ahead in life if they make an effort, and you can't act as people do in the United States, where they even lynch Negroes and where everything is segregated. After all, this is inhumanity—no matter how you look at it, it's not their fault if they are black. I believe that we shouldn't act as though there was any difference between us and them. . . . As for color prejudice among us, I don't believe there is any. There are none of those weighty restrictions which exist, for example, in the United States. No one forbids the Negro from moving, studying, or making his way in life wherever he wishes. There may be a few individuals who are prejudiced and who feel the Negro should be treated as he was in the days of slavery. But on the whole, among my closer relatives, everyone acknowledges that after all differences of color are no reason for us to place restrictions on Negroes, since no one chooses the circumstances of his birth and it's not their fault if they are born black."

Another widespread feature is the tendency to reduce color prejudice to an individual and thus to negligible pecularity. Hamilton de Oliveira asserted in a public statement, "I am white and I believe that color prejudice does exist in Brazil, as it exists everywhere. I have both colored and white friends, and I know that prejudice is a personal matter. There are people who are repelled by colored individuals and vice versa. And there are people who do scientific research in order to find out whether Negroes and whites can reach some under-standing." This tendency is apparent even in self-analyses. One of the women interviewers noted that a lady from a traditional family ". . . told me that she has no color preju-dice. To her, Negroes and whites are exactly the same. She doesn't believe that color is associated with moral or intellec-tual attributes. Nevertheless, she has a physical revulsion for black skin. She cannot say why, since as a child she had a Negro nurse of whom she was very fond. The feeling is quite strong and she is ashamed of it, so if she steps into a streetcar and sees an empty seat next to a Negro man or woman, she deliberately sits there to see if she can overcome her feelings. But the revulsion persists to this day."

A third feature that deserves special attention because of its widespread nature is the tendency to equate color prejudice with class prejudice. Even the Afonso Arinos Law, which includes among "legal offenses all practices resulting from race or color prejudice" stresses that it is aimed at "a change in the racist attitude that prevails among us, especially in the country's upper social and governmental spheres." [9] Now, manifestations of color prejudice are a threat "to future social peace," as stated in the legislative bill because they are not restricted to "upper social spheres." This was stressed even in the clear judgment delivered by Counselor Plinio Barreto, as though the only fact involved were the socioeconomic inequality of the two racial groups. "While all have access to public affairs, not all have access to certain social circles. To many, the Negro remains an inferior being, unworthy of associating with whites and of competing in society for the respect accorded to whites. . . . As long as whites retain the economic supremacy they inherited from the slaveowners of old, Negroes, for lack of adequate means, will continue to make up the poorer classes and prejudice will be maintained. No laws can do away with it. No law ever eradicated deep-seated feelings or changed the psychological attitudes of a people." [10] In spite of the truth contained in this truly complete description of the situation, decreasing the social and economic distance between Negroes and whites is not enough to recast the pattern of race relations. The insistence on confusing the external features of color prejudice with what is sometimes underestimated as a mere class prejudice thus leads to a real deadlock.

There is yet a fourth general factor which is found in extreme and dramatic cases, where reality loudly contradicts the dogmas of the prevailing racial ideology. We might take as an example the incidents associated with the turning away of Katherine Dunham and her group from the Esplanada Hotel.[11] In dealing with the matter, the *Correio Paulistano* pointed out that ". . . there is no color prejudice in our country. This truth is known and understood by all Brazilians and also by all those who visit our country. Hardly ever do we come across a situation where the behavior of a Brazilian leads to circumstances of this sort." [12] Another newspaper was more explicit, as shown in the following excerpt: "It would seem that the hateful problem is finally appearing among us. It will be a crime if it does, and for this very reason we must raise a loud clamor against it. The hand that dared to close that door surely was a foreign one." [13] Such an approach makes the foreigner a scapegoat and proclaims the Brazilian race tradition to be genuinely democratic. The Negroes themselves have partly yielded to this distortion, which has disseminated a superficial and one-sided view of reality, as though ethnocentric attitudes and prejudiced racial behavior were rooted exclusively in the influence of immigrants and the descendants of immigrants.

Wherever the specific demands of the patterns of equilibrium of the class society clash with established custom, the latter is radically altered. The management of the Worker Placement Department of the Regional Labor Office, for example, made public facts which in the past were aired only by leaders of the Negro movements: "Our Department has not managed, to this day, to place a single one of the black workers who have applied for office jobs. As a result individuals with excellent qualifications sometimes remain unemployed. This applies to persons who came to us recently and who had graduated from the technical course in high school as well as to an accountant." [14] Interviews with the heads of the personnel departments of some large private organizations similarly revealed that some companies have been compelled to choose between the suppression of systematic racial restrictions and a permanent shortage of manpower. Although these pressures do not affect all organizations and all levels of employment to the same extent, they point to the great difficulty involved in perpetuating certain customs and to the curtains that concealed them.

We shall endeavor to show with the aid of a few examples how color prejudice is understood and expressed in different social classes. In the lower class we find some fluctuation in the content and forms of awareness, which is probably due to differences in socialization. The closer the individual is to the rural Brazilian world, the harder he finds it to make basic differentiations; the greater the ego-involvement of the urban individual, the clearer his understanding of the Negro situation. Thus, according to a bricklayer who had recently arrived from the interior and whose grandfather was black (described as a "light mestizo"), "In Brazil there is no color prejudice. Troubles are family matters. It's quarrels that make people fight. They bring division." Nevertheless, he noted that in the city, as in the interior, "There are lots of people who'd never let their daughter or their sister marry a Negro. They think it's offensive if a white woman walks down the street with a sack of coal. This can only be explained through color. It's not that they think black people are inferior to whites, or that they hate them. It's just the difference in color." As he saw it, "Austrians, Germans, Polacks, Czechs, etc., don't want to have anything to do with Negroes. They only hire dark labor if they can't get anything else. . . . They don't want to have anything at all to do with Negroes. Italians too, but not so much anymore. This craze is just about over with them."

A tradesman of Italian-Brazilian descent, also from the interior but who had lived long in São Paulo, showed greater insight. According to what he had observed at the company where he worked, "They would never hire a Negro for any job. The boss not only doesn't like Negroes, he's also afraid of them." In the town where he had lived there was a strict separation of Negroes and whites in the park. For this reason, he was interested in the situation in São Paulo. He found that "Negroes are not well regarded in society. . . . People think that Negroes are no good, that they are disorganized and dishonest. . . . It's easy to find good jobs in São Paulo, as long as you're not colored. . . . The foreigners especially, who have everything in their hands, won't make any room for the blacks. They think that Negroes are thieves, that they can't be trusted." He confessed that before he married he had black friends, although none of them was an "intimate friend." After he married he neither visited nor was visited by any of those friends. "This often happens. As long as we're single we often get together for all kinds of purposes. Marriage and family life put an end to bachelor life. If a Negro visited me at home, I would receive him well. But I don't take the initiative to resume contact with my former Negro friends." As for intermarriage, he said, "No one likes to marry off daughters, sisters, or other relatives to Negroes. I don't think it's a good idea myself. As a rule, in São Paulo, people I know do all they can to prevent this. It's only in the interior that you have marriages like this, out of fear of those voodoo men. People think they're hexed, that it's dangerous not to let a girl marry the voodoo fellow." The situation in the United States aroused his interest. He believed it proved that Negroes and whites are equal and that separation has acted as a stimulus on the former.

In turn, a carpenter of French-Brazilian descent, born and bred in a section of São Paulo, showed considerable understanding of the dilemmas that confront the Negro. "Negroes have good reason to be aware of prejudice and to react to it. What goes on is no joke." He gave an example relating to the chemical laboratory where he worked: ". . . they had this obsession about not hiring Negroes. It's only a while ago that they began to take them for physical labor. There were no other openings." He also told of several cases of candidates being rejected from modest jobs because of their color. "Prejudice against the Negro is very strong, although people claim that Brazilians are not prejudiced. There is [prejudice] even among poor people, but far less than among the rich. The poor have less prejudice because they have to live close to Negroes at work and at home." He thought that there was more contact at work because many white people avoid "inviting Negro fellow workers to their homes. . . . Whites treat Negro colleagues as if they were not prejudiced." Yet he felt that prejudice is expressed indirectly in three ways: "(1) In bad jokes against Negro colleagues, whom they treat in a disparaging and malicious way—as though they were joking, but meaning to snub them. (2) In their attempts to avoid close contact with Negro colleagues. Those are the ones who are most prejudiced. They avoid all intimate contact and limit their relationships to the demands of the job. (3) In the comments they make. Even those who seem not to have any prejudice and lead you to think that color is irrelevant to them, make it plain that they're prejudiced against Negroes, the way they talk behind their backs. This is the rule. They discuss everything their Negro colleagues do with malicious intent. They scorn the Negro's personality and behavior. These comments are always disparaging and nasty."

On the whole, concrete experience not only directs but limits the awareness of the racial reality. Two points nevertheless deserve emphasis in this connection. First, informants make a distinction between color prejudice and other influences at work. The results of an interview with an upholsterer are significant in this connection. He acknowledged that "most people avoid any contact or relations with them" and he knew that in the company where he worked, "the bosses don't like Negroes." Nevertheless, he emphasized that Negroes missed good jobs by not applying for openings in that company. Second, we must note that whites from different national and ethnic groups engage in reciprocal retaliation. They try to "pass the buck" when it comes to the more unpleasant or vexing aspects of the situation. The following excerpt from an interview with an office boy shows this quite clearly. "My family is prejudiced, and very much so. My parents are Portuguese and my brothers Brazilian, but they're all prejudiced.[15] We live in Brás, in the midst of the commerical district. I don't know if it was because they always lived there, among Italians, that they got this prejudice. This may be part of it, because Italians are the most prejudiced people I know. They're not just prejudiced, they don't try to hide it. For example, in Rio the people are good. They treat everybody well. I don't know if they're prejudiced, but at least they don't show it. They treat white people well, and they treat black people well. In São Paulo people are quite different, and I think it's because of the Italians. Italians think that everybody else is inferior to them. If they praise someone from another country or of another color, or treat him well, it's sheer hypocrisy and usually for calculated reasons. They feel contempt not only for the Negro but for every other race and nation. In conversation they show a complete lack of consideration. They sing their own praises and when they discuss anything, they do it in such a way that they end up giving you an inferiority complex."

We cannot go here into all the various personal statements gathered among middle-class individuals. As a rule such people only give up the stereotyped traditional view of the racial situation when they are brought face to face with characteristic incidents. There was the housewife who tried to help a black servant with a toothache. They went to several dental offices, some of them with empty waiting rooms, and did not manage to get any help. The lady insisted and was told that nothing can be done since no appointment was made. "I said that in this case we would make an appointment. They said we couldn't, that they were all booked up." Finally, the wife of a dentist who was not in his office administered first aid and then saw to it that her husband looked after the patient. "She got treatment because we were lucky to come across the dentist's wife. Women have more heart." There is the clerk who notices the behavior of his department head, manager, or boss, and sees how he keeps from hiring or promoting colored employees. There is the personal director or manager who gets strict orders "not to hire Negroes," sometimes "without exceptions," sometimes "with such-and-such exceptions." As a result, their understanding of the racial reality is very limited. But it does give them staunch convictions and a special viewpoint. A bank manager wondered how anyone could doubt the existence of color prejudice in São Paulo. It seemed strong and obvious to him. The personnel director of a large industry with its headquarters in São Paulo said that color prejudice varied from north to south of the country (from minimal to maximal intensity). According to his own observations, it is more moderate in São Paulo than in the extreme south of the country.

Those who lack an external system of reference sometimes have more acute intellectual perceptions. Starting from self-analysis, they reach equally interesting conclusions. A woman lawyer and civil servant of Portuguese-Brazilian descent, for example, notes her "physical revulsion for her Negro servant" and says that her husband feels the same way. "I can't stand walking through Rua Direita on Saturday or Sunday night because of the numbers of black people. They're all Negroes! Whites and blacks are not equal. Because I studied sociology and psychology, I know that differences of behavior derive from social circumstances rather than color. But they are different. I could never have a Negro boyfriend, much less a Negro husband." Another example comes from a lady who was a college graduate and a language teacher. "Look, now that we're discussing prejudice in this intimate sense, I remember. About that couple who lived in Vila Nova Conceição (a Negro physician married to a German woman). . . . Once, as I was talking to a friend, she said to me, 'How could that woman take a Negro husband? Even if he is educated, refined, everything a man should be . . . I don't know! I don't think I'd have what it takes to be a woman . . . to sleep with a Negro!' I remember. At that moment I also thought of the intimacies of marriage and I felt a shudder going through me. It's funny! . . . We think we don't have any prejudice, and somewhere along the line we always do!" Even a small incident can lead to some understanding of reality, as suggested in a statement written by a teacher: "There should not be any prejudice against Negroes. I don't have any prejudice except against intermarriage. But it is very difficult to be completely 'exempt.' The other day (I know it wasn't right) I got mad at the landlady and said, 'She's acting like a nigger!' I was surprised at this myself, but I wanted to be offensive."

The data gathered show the frequency of three types of viewpoints. First, it reveals the combination of frank assessment of and indifferent complacency toward the racial problem. Thus, an educator stated that racial prejudice is very strong not only in São Paulo but in the rest of the country as well. But it is fated to disappear because of the gradual physical assimilation of Negroes into the white population. "This is the trend. Obviously it will take centuries. But in the future there will be no more prejudice among us."

In those segments of the middle classes that are most affected by the modernization of society, color prejudice tends to be expressed with nonconformist severity. A middle-aged woman teacher gave a characteristic answer: "I think that prejudice is a mark of ignorance. Color is not responsible for social position or the behavior of the individual. It's social conditions that act upon him and make for a certain position or form of behavior." Among the younger generation caught in this web of cause and effect, condemnation is often outspoken. A young woman university student wrote, "Personally I regard prejudice as a foul stain among us. I believe that prejudice is a stupid thing devoid of any logic. It is unseemly, especially among the civilized people that we claim to be. We know that scientifically nothing has been proved about the superiority of the white over the Negro—we know all this but we continue to regard the Negro as we would a leper. When shall a true 13th of May * dawn in our country?" Such attitudes have limited influence on the contact situation, because few segments of the middle classes are deeply affected by the intellectual revolution wrought by modernization.

Members of the upper classes find it harder to attain an understanding of the racial situation. Their area of informal and friendly contact with Negroes is so limited and so hedged in with restrictions that dramatic or shocking cases rarely become known. Even so, they offer glimpses of certain aspects of the situation independent of racial stereotypes or ethnocentric attitudes. The most hotly argued cases often refer to intermarriage. Painful experiences are remembered and used to prove that prejudice exists or that it is very strong. Unlike members of the lower classes, who describe everyday experiences, and members of the middle classes, who deal with key experiences, members of the upper classes have to rely on borderline experiences which place in jeopardy the very moral bases of the traditional conception of the world. A noted university professor from a wealthy and highly regarded family spontaneously told the interviewer, "There is no question that there is color prejudice in São Paulo. It may be that there is more harmony in other states. In São Paulo, however, prej-

* *Translator's note:* The date (May 13, 1888) when slavery was abolished in Brazil.

udice exists and is very strong. But it is expressed without violence. There is no need for research in order to understand this. We all know it. There are even frequent instances
of unpleasant contact between whites and Negroes. Even
though prejudice is not violent, as it is in the United States,
and takes a special form which permits contact with Negroes
in certain areas, it becomes obvious as soon as you touch on
certain intimate questions. Even in Bahia a white man would
rebel against the idea of giving his daughter in marriage to a
Negro."

The social outlook of a large portion of the upper classes is
clearly governed by a view of the traditional pattern of racial
interaction as being socially normal and necessary. This leads,
in some circles, not only to the typical reaction already mentioned above—"there is prejudice and it's right"—but to an
irrepressible tendency to distort the given data of concrete
experience.

As we have already stressed, the Negro is no less a product
of the sociocultural situation than the white. Nevertheless, he
has additional resources that permit him to break through and
even rebel against the limitations inherent in the prevalent
understanding of the racial reality. Concrete experiences are
not always interpreted in a strictly constructive way. But there
is a powerful force working for him: social interests and
ambitions conditioned or fed by his racial position broaden
and deepen his ability to perceive and understand this reality.
Suffering, shame, and rebellion, separately or together, lead
him to the bottom of the abyss.

Nevertheless, the Negro's awareness and understanding of
the manifestations and effects of color prejudice have certain
characteristic shortcomings. First, as happens among whites,
there are several chronic sources of partial or total blocking of
the Negro's cultural horizon. Like the white, he is often inconsistent, confused, and bewildered. There is the Negro who
shares the general, officially consecrated attitude, and who
writes in his answer to the mass questionnaire, "Yes, happily,
in Brazil there is indeed no color prejudice." [16] There is also

the undecided Negro. Interviews with an accountant provide a typical example. "I'm not sure whether what exists in São Paulo is prejudice or something with some other name. Whites don't trust Negroes—that's for sure. Negroes don't know how to do things. They haven't had time to get going like the whites. That's how the whites' attitudes against Negroes arose. But if Negroes got on the ball and reached the same level as whites, they would be accepted by them and treated differently. I don't know if there really is prejudice or if it's something else that comes from the white's distrust and the Negro's incapacity to behave as the white expects him to."

Finally, there is the Negro who adopts contradictory attitudes. In our analysis we reduced the contradictions to three basic formulas:

(1) Informants deny with wavering vehemence the existence of color prejudice. But they acknowledge openly that "it's no use fighting prejudice." In an interview with a dark mulatto woman dancer, for instance, the following typical attitudes were expressed immediately following a meeting devoted to a discussion of the matter: "They told a pack of lies. I don't know how anyone can lie so blatantly. There is no prejudice in São Paulo. Negroes are received everywhere and are treated well by whites. I've been everywhere. As a dancer, I've performed my folk numbers in places where many classy whites don't go, among elite families and among French families." Later, however, she stated unself-consciously, "It's no use trying to fight color prejudice and to improve the Negro's position. There is no unity among Negroes." [17]

(2) The informants deny, also with wavering intensity, the existence of color prejudice, but at the same time they preach the advantages of open and systematic segregation. On interviewing a young Negro stoker, for example, the woman interviewer got the following typical ideas, "I don't think any differences are made, as long as the person is skilled. I don't think that Negroes are harmed by individual whites, but rather by the economic circumstances in which most of them

live. I know something of the situation in the United States, of the struggles and prejudices. But I think that situation is better than the one here, because it leads Negroes to unite and to fight for better things."

(3) Informants do not deny the existence of color prejudice, but are afraid of raising the issue and compelling whites to become aware of the racial reality. In an interview with a mulatto accountant employed by a utilities company, for example, we find the following typical ideas: "The (Afonso Arinos) Law has its good points, because it gives Negroes and mulattoes a weapon with which to fight prejudice. But it's chief flaw is the fact that it emphasizes prejudice. It used to be like a needle in a haystack. No one had any clear awareness of its existence, especially whites. Now the law has accentuated it. And many whites won't like being compelled to accept the Negro."

Inconsistencies and nonconformities of this sort are, however, easily understood and explained. The Negro absorbs in various ways the prevailing racial ideology and sees himself, the whites, and the world in which he lives through the prism of this ideology. He achieves a victory when he manages to separate concrete experiences from this ideological context and to analyze them, with varying degrees of perceptiveness, without the direct or indirect pressures they exert upon him. In any case, the burden of socialization and cultural conditioning is quite clear. The blocking of any awareness or understanding of the situation follows a descending scale. It is intensive where the Negro is fully involved in the traditional cultural horizon. We shall recall at this point that two human types must be kept in mind simultaneously: the rural Negro who recoils with mistrust and caution from contact with the white, and the refined Negro who identifies fully with the interests, values, and world of the white. Both tend to deny the existence of color prejudice—the former out of inexperience, the latter because it would make his own acceptance an exception. However, while the former conforms inadvertently to the asymmetric pattern of racial relations because he was molded by the customs of rural culture, the latter plays a deliberate game aimed at social enlightening.

Beyond this, we must consider the cases of black persons who overcome the obstacles of color prejudice through the devious paths of marginal society. This applied on a large scale to Negro delinquents in the past, and is still often the case for the same. The delinquent is far from indifferent to external pressures, since the adaptive and integrative mechanisms he uses individually or communally are reactions to these pressures. It would be correct to state, however, that he does not face the psychological dilemmas which consciously or unconsciously torture those Negroes who accept the rules of the game of society and become victims of the "complex."

Finally, we cannot omit mention of the illusions of the middle-class Negro who is stubbornly oriented to the effects of social mobility and who asserts himself by means of compensatory or real mechanisms, through the external appearances of his social position. As we pointed out in the preceding chapter, he knows—from hard personal experience—what is and what is not color prejudice, and he is also familiar with all its ramifications. But he has no intention to redress them or to become involved in a crusade. The immediacy of his objectives alienates him consciously or unconsciously from racial problems. The fact is that out of sheer social calculation he attains a new form of passive capitulation. Flagrant contradictions expressed through polite rationalizations and which do not preclude the simultaneous disclosure of painful incidents or experiences serve as escape devices: "It exists, but I never experienced it"; "I watch my step—I never go where Negroes are not wanted"; "You must differentiate between prejudice and selectivity", "Our people are very sensitive, they see persecution everywhere." At this pole, we are very far from the mental blocks engendered by the traditional conception of the world. The individual "sees the situation with his own eyes." Nevertheless, his awareness and understanding of reality are filtered through social illusions and hopes which, if they do not blind him, may silence and disarm him.

There is a basic ambiguity in the characterization of the white as the source of color prejudice. Of course, in the various equations of color prejudice devised by the Negro, the white is always the active agent of ethnocentric appraisals and discriminating behavior (whatever the direct or indirect responsibility of the Negro for its origin). Certain gradations suggest the generalized character of color prejudice (it exists among the poor as well as among the rich) and show its varying intensity (it is stronger among the latter than among the former).

It seems clear that the old pattern of racial domination is on the wane. It is also clear, however, that this pattern (at least under the sociohistorical circumstances under consideration) is becoming adapted to an open-ended social order where income, social prestige, and power remain concentrated, from a racial standpoint, at strategic points and levels. The chief results of these changes were reflected at once in a negative way among Negro groups. On the one hand the social classification and vertical mobility of the Negro and mulatto were dissociated from the gradual formation of a racially identifiable, integrated, and autonomous Negro minority. On the other hand the elites were separated from the masses, fostering an insensitivity on the part of the Negro himself to the Negro problem which is without parallel in the cultural history of the city. To summarize, the attainment of typical class positions did not grant the black population any possibility of creating a social race situation compatible with the economic, social, and power structure of the class society. The Negro remains inarticulate and powerless before the white, without specific means of directly influencing the current reshaping of the patterns of racial domination. To confine ourselves to essentials, this leads to the following: (1) The nonexistence of a racial situation fashioned historically by the competitive social order deprives Negroes collectively of all sociopsychological sources of differentiation, reorganization, and unification of the perceptive and cognitive foundations of conscious social behavior. (2) The Negro attempts to fill the resulting vacuum by means of the perceptive and cognitive resources he has accumulated in the course of his struggle against slavery and against the patterns of racial domination inherent in the traditional social order, as though we were still in the first quarter of the nineteenth century. (3) These perceptive and cognitive resources have proved adequate for a much deeper, more realistic, and freer understanding of the racial reality than has been developed by whites, but it has not permitted understanding of this reality as a changing whole. Thus, basically, the yearning to belong to the system has restricted the cultural horizon of the Negro and mulatto and confined their social ambitions and aspirations—and with them their capacity for awareness of the surrounding racial reality—to the destruction of traditional patterns of racial domination. According to our hypothesis, this explains both the ambiguity of their conscious characterization of the white's active role in color prejudice, and their alienation from the meaning of this prejudice in terms of the collective destiny of the Negro group within society. Paradoxical as this may seem, the Negro unmasks the white, checking the rationalizations which conceal the sources and the visible results of color prejudice. Nevertheless, he submits spontaneously to the white man's game, confining his own awareness of racial reality to a historical context. Obviously the prospects would be different if the social perspectives of Negroes and mulattoes were any other than they are. If the starting point of their conscious social behavior granted basic significance to the sociopathic consequences of the racial distribution of income, social prestige, and power in the structuring of social relations, the yearning to belong to the system would be expressed socially in connection with the ideal goal of changing the system.[18]

This simple reversal of the social perspective makes it possible for the Negro to overcome the basic alienation that interferes with his awareness of color prejudice. Meanwhile, this awareness serves to compensate for the inconsistencies in the current racial thinking of the whites, as well as to give the Negro a realistic and pragmatic conception of the world which fulfills his need for social self-affirmation. If such a reversal of perspectives were to occur, however, the Negro would achieve the subjective requisites needed to regard his present and his future as those of an identifiable, integrated, and autonomous racial minority—i.e., he would gain the intellectual capacity to broaden his view of the world to the point required for a socially constructive role in the hesitant development of racial democracy in Brazil.

The Negro fought the manifestations and results of color prejudice on the level of his struggle for survival in the big city of the capitalistic era. Thanks to the breakdown of the seignorial and slaveholding order, to the establishment, expansion, and consolidation of the competitive social order, he was gradually able to alter his social goals. Nevertheless, color prejudice blocked his move from a peripheral, marginal position to the heart of the class structure. The social context thus compelled him to find out *why* he was rejected before he could succeed in his endeavors to belong to the system. Here we can see the positive influence of the social context which compelled the Negro to rise out of his lethargy, break into the white's world, and destroy his idols.

Our analysis of various types of written documentation showed that the Negro's awareness and understanding of color prejudice as a sociopsychological and historicocultural reality is surprisingly deep. Even though the intensity of concrete experiences, the maturity of the social outlook, and the firmness of the individual's basic convictions range from unabashed neutrality (among a small but significant minority) to racial fanaticism (in rare and isolated cases), if the evidence gathered covers practically every important aspect (such as motive, condition, and consequences) of the expression of color prejudice. It seems that on the level where the Negro responds dynamically to the demands of the situation, which is the level of the struggle for survival in the midst of the community and thus for the acquisition of those institutionalized social positions to which he has ready access, he has a clear-cut, distinct, and consistent idea of the racial reality. We must stress in particular what this means in sociological terms. The common-sense understanding amassed by the Negro in recent times, over less than two generations, involves a quite sensible conception of the prevailing patterns of color prejudice and makes it possible for him to do something about its effects, whether in the sphere of the organization of race relations or in that of voluntary controls which might direct those effects into socially desirable channels.

As for the first point, such common-sense understanding involves (*a*) criteria by which to recognize color prejudice, (*b*) awareness of the structural and dynamic links which connect color prejudice and patterns of racial adjustment, and (*c*) certain factors external to color prejudice which nevertheless exacerbate it. In recognizing prejudices the Negro has developed a deceptively simple technique: he draws the dividing line along the obvious (and thus irrefutable) differences between the treatment accorded to the Negro and that accorded to the white under similar circumstances. From this standpoint the basic factor is the social position and the prerogatives (rights and duties) this social position implies. Therefore, at the deepest level of his social awareness, the Negro sees color prejudice as a system of discriminatory practices used by whites in their social intercourse with black individuals. The subtlety of this awareness of reality does not reside here, however, but in the manner in which he solves concretely the problem of knowing what is and what is not color prejudice. The chief point of reference ceases to be the white. The victim is taken into account—rather than the executioner—and examined to see whether he might indeed qualify for the equality which he pleads for from the whites. There exists already a veritable folklore in connection with false prejudice, which recommends extreme prudence and moderation: "Not everything the Negro regards as prejudice really is"; "Our people are very sensitive"; "You would have to make sure whether it was prejudice or lack of ability"; "We have to differentiate between prejudice and selectivity," and so on. The Negro does not shun the use of color prejudice as a mechanism of self-defense, as a compensatory mechanism, or even as an outright scapegoat.

This complex of attitudes, expectations of behavior, and social techniques does not prevent him from attributing color prejudice to certain unchanging factors. Even if here too there is a certain amount of confusion, the chief trend is to regard color in a broader sense, as though it were a symbol both of the racial origins and of the social position of Negroes and mulattoes; and to feel that the white has categorically defined color as an index of overall inferiority (be it racial, economic, social, cultural, moral, or political). This demonstrates how much farther the Negro has traveled than the white in his understanding of racial reality. The white gets angry at the Negro and does not even want to hear of color prejudice because he is afraid that he is being accused of practicing some degrading form of racism. Not only is the Negro free of such designs, but he forges ahead, fusing the various factors which have always linked relations between whites and Negroes with the equation of racial and social stratification. With sharp and penetrating discernment, he places color in a sociohistorical category, thus linking what whites separate in theory but associate in actual behavior. For this reason the white claims that the Negro, when he attains a class position, finds that the social prestige he has gained does away with all limitations and restrictions associated with color. The Negro preaches the exact opposite: it is after gaining an education, skills, and a certain position that he meets the white face to face and finds all doors closed. It is easy to test this—all you need do is to subject the white person to certain contacts which might be called experimental. Nevertheless, the moral frame of reference is a complex one. Let us take one example. A young Negro told his mulatto friend that "the girls at the University probably are not prejudiced." He planned to invite

them to a cheap dive to see what happened. The friend retorted, "They won't go, and it won't have anything to do with
color prejudice. They wouldn't go to a cheap white dive either.
This is not their environment." When such a test is carried
out, the Negro sees to it that the frame of reference is adequate to the purpose at hand.

In understanding the structural and dynamic foundations
of color prejudice which permit the Negro to project his relations with whites onto the societal organization, nine items
are of special importance.[19]

(1) The Negro is fully aware of the importance of concealment in the white's behavior. His description of this propensity involves two harsh words—the two-faced or false quality
of the white. This is expressed with more neutrality and courtesy among the educated Negro groups, where it is said that
the white's friendliness is superficial—"a matter of polish." As
already indicated, however, no clear-cut rejection is associated
with this state of affairs. To the contrary, as stated by a
mulatto girl as she described her relations with her teachers,
"I don't know whether the courtesy and kindness of my teachers are real or put on. It may be that they're not sincere but
this doesn't bother me. The important thing is that they treat
me well and that I get consideration from them."

(2) Negative stereotypes in all their forms—whether ideas
of a folkloric and popular nature (as in the words set to
popular music), or white conceptions of the Negro's character
which restrict his acceptance—are understood in a formal
and concrete as well as a functional sense. Although awareness of concealment leads to hesitancy—but does not as a rule
interfere with the external course of social relations—an understanding of stereotypes is the very foundation of the Negro's self-defensive mechanisms and of what might be called
his "reactive prejudice." [20] In some cases, this understanding
even leads to stubborn mistrust which poison all relations
with whites.

(3) There is a clear awareness of the dual nature of the
white's ethical code, linked with an irrepressible reactive tend-

ency to regard the prevailing racial ideology as a false and misleading view of reality. Even though the data given from Chapter 4 onward do not require empirical support, the importance of this factor to the attitudes and patterns of behavior of the Negro and mulatto leads us to transcribe part of one of the typical statements we gathered. In a public discussion organized by a Negro lawyer who had been a leader of the rights movements, we heard the following thoughts: "The white could not, and still cannot, get used to the idea of regarding his lost property as a citizen on an equal footing. He had tried, through every possible means, to retain his lordly attitudes and to keep the Negro in his place, in the kitchen of the house, bettered by illiteracy, and feelings of inferiority, without providing him with a single opportunity. . . . There is a perfect technique, perhaps the fruit of tacit agreement, to conceal and subdue the collective guilt of the ruling group . . . a truly negative technique which even now, in the present day, is used successfully in Brazil's official international relations. This is the use of a tired cliché which has been discredited within our national boundaries. Actually, this method of publicity, of making unilateral history, is meant to create a sort of pressure, a certain psychological conditioning of our less wary and more susceptible foreign visitors, and deliberately leads them to view the problem of race relations through a distorting prism. Through this prism, everything is a bed of roses. The white is white, the black is white, the yellow is white. Everything conspires to an atmosphere or immaculate whiteness in which the various contacts of the various ethnic groups in the country—already assimilated or in the process of assimilation—have been and are being carried out beautifully, without clashes, mildly and placidly. . . . The matter was and is still disguised in such a way that the pressure is exercised even on certain learned sectors of the society, thus palming us off to the world as the most perfect example of racial democracy. This . . . is the version for foreign consumption. The prevailing atmosphere, our history books, our public media, our formal statements, all assert that we have

no color problems or color prejudice. This assertion, shared
naïvely even by outstanding citizens and personalities, is the
handsome cloak for foreign eyes, the sweet-sounding voice of
popular sayings. In fact, however, the Negro is a marginal
person and as such a discontented one."

(4) As a result of these forms of understanding, the Negro
tends to see the emergence and perpetuation of discriminatory
practices. He is prone to regard them as an inherent part of
the situation. One Negro accountant pointed out expressions of color prejudice in the business world, saying, "The
owners of stores and bars (there are no black waiters) are not
to blame for these barriers. It is the customers who compel
them to act as they do when they turn down a Negro. Obviously the Negro is prejudicial to business: a customer comes
in and there are two salesmen, one white and one Negro—if
the white one is busy, the customer waits until he is free. This,
besides making service difficult, also brings financial losses to
the owner."

(5) The Negro also becomes objectively aware of the
sources of the white's differential racial attitudes, judgments,
and behavior. He not only knows to what extent differences in
social level and cultural tradition (associated with the racial,
ethnic, or national origins of the various population groups)
are reflected in the intensity of color prejudice, as noted
above, but he also takes into account two other variables: the
relationship between tolerance or intolerance and the personality type of the white; and the variations due to the skin
shade, sex, age, etc., of the Negro or mulatto.

(6) Such understanding of the overall situation fosters in
the Negro a strong tendency to differentiate between individuals, values, and opportunities on the one hand, and his own
general opinions and judgments of the white, of the latter's
prejudice, and of its consequences (the concealed isolation of
black persons) on the other hand. This encourages the amass-
ing of valuable understandings in a society where selective
acceptance of the Negro hinges on the whims, sympathy, or
tolerance of the whites, and where the Negro can become with

relative ease the exception that confirms the rule. It also leads
to a certain maturity of judgment thanks to which men and
women, adults and young people try to separate the chaff
from the wheat—i.e., to pick out among their white acquaintances those who could be true friends or on whom you can
count. Incidentally, we heard in various interviews the same
statement that, in spite of color prejudice, there can be "a
deep, disinterested and true friendship" between whites and
Negroes. This belief, which is at the same time a hope, does
not baffle the Negro. On this point, he shows an acute awareness of the potentialities for racial coexistence in a society
where color prejudice is diffuse and unsystematic.

(7) The Negro is unable fully to catch all the variations in
the attitudes, hesitancies, and concealed forms of behavior of
the whites. Coexistence with whites has not yet gone far
enough to permit this. Nevertheless, he differentiates with
great insight between the two most frequent varieties of the
expression of color prejudice—the concealed and the obvious
—and he discloses that he knows something more—namely,
that the latter variety is alien and contrary to Brazilian tradition. So, whenever he can, he would rather use the evidence
provided by this variety in order to criticize and fight color
prejudice generally.

(8) Inevitably, the Negro is highly sensitive to the nuances
of the ingroup situation as they are reflected in the forms of
adjustment and awareness of the black individual himself.
The important thing here is his objective understanding, influenced by suffering and widespread disappointment because
of external conditions, his lack of participation in the larger
culture, or the white man's success. The degree of the Negro's
awareness, his moral autonomy, and loyalty to his own group
are regulated by these disappointments. As a result, substantial disagreements—even as to the existence or nonexistence
of color prejudice and the manner in which to fight it—acquire a suprapersonal frame of reference and can be placed on
levels which lessen the potential danger of misunderstanding
and conflict. The data gathered show that this frame of refer-

ence has been ineffective in the overcoming of differences. But it creates a modicum of respect and understanding for the other—if not for his motivations—in the never-ending frictions. In short, the Negro directs upon himself the formula he has used to understand the white and the overall situation, thus uncovering and adjusting intellectually to the various forms of differential sociocultural behavior, of personality, and of the orientation of his racial counterideology.

(9) There is one item which is not universal, but which is frequently linked to the most radical and intolerant interpretations of the Negro situation. This is the explicit role played by exploitation in the formation and retention of color prejudice. Understanding operates on three distinct levels: (1) the abolitionistic process as a historic despoliation and as the irremediable expulsion of the Negro to the periphery of organized society; (2) the material and psychological bases of the perpetuation of racial inequality, and thus of the connection between color prejudice and the defense of the privileges of the dominant race; (3) the different levels of the Negro's participation, rewards, and promotion in the free labor system, thus defining exploitation in terms of the retention of a reserve of manpower for undesirable jobs and of the lowering of Negro workers' levels of remuneration. This item, although it appears unsystematically and only in specifically nonconformist contexts, is of almost unique significance because it is the only factor in the revelation of racial attitudes which is not concerned with moral arguments and which points openly to an apparent link between color prejudice and the material interests of the dominant race.

As regards the factors external to color prejudice which contribute to its exacerbation, three points deserve special emphasis. It would seem that the Negro tends to stress his own ability to deal with the white. Those who lack experience in coexistence with the whites, and especially those who cling stubbornly to certain deleterious beliefs induced by the "complex," are said to aggravate the expressions of color prejudice and to convince whites that the best policy (not to say the only adequate policy) would be exclusion or ultra-exclusive acceptance.

Another point which is approached with relative insight relates to internal migrations.* Many of those interviewed broached the subject spontaneously, trying to hint at the difficulties inherent in the continuous turnover of the black population. Gradually the Negro learns to live in the city, to make use of its resources, and to shield himself from the concealed or obvious expressions of color prejudice. Nevertheless, the Negroes who come from rural areas without technical skills, financial resources, or experience cannot adjust to the city as a group. In short, the same problems are posed anew with each generation, as though the experience amassed collectively were useless. Finally, the Negro also becomes aware of the fact that the urban community has unforeseen drawbacks. Racial, ethnic, and national groups, as well as social classes, acquire new forms of autonomy and self-affirmation. As a result, they acquire the freedom to disobey socially consecrated rules and to enjoin their specific conceptions of the world. Thus, the Negro has become aware that concealed prejudice, bad as it may be, is preferable to obvious prejudice, and he has tried to understand the latter as part of the developing new situation.

As for the second point, the effects of color prejudice are seen, as we have pointed out, on two separate levels. Let us consider first those that rose to the social consciousness in the light of the organization of racial relations in *Paulistana* society. There, color prejudice is regarded as "the great problem of the Negro." Although it is clearly understood that prejudice does not operate in isolation and that the chief barrier to integration is economic inequality, the rights movements have spread the firm belief that eradicating color prejudice precludes rectification of the economic problems which lower the income and standard of living of the black population. On the

* *Editor's note:* The author is referring to the constant migration of poverty-stricken people, mostly Negro and mulatto, from northeast Brazil to São Paulo in search of employment.

other hand, it is emphasized that the distortion of racial consciousness fostered by the dominant race catches the Negroes themselves in its web, disarming them and impelling them to passivity. Here is a representative example of this attitude: "There is color prejudice . . . and it is quite severe, because aside from being prejudice it is hypocrisy. In the United States, where such prejudice is open, it has benefited the Negro, led him to have a look at himself and solve his own problems. In Brazil the very opposite occurred. The denial of color prejudice caused the Negro to fall ever lower. This is clear for all to see. The Negro has no opportunities. He has no opportunity to rise. This is a situation which, if it continues, the Negro race will be doomed to an inglorious disappearance from the racial scene." Such a logical, emotional, and moral context was naturally bound to give rise to a grim view of the effects of color prejudice. Whatever the limitations of its sociocultural legacy and its intellectual roots, in this area the exposure of old racial myths achieved its true aim. If things did not change, it was not the Negro who was to blame but the absence of effective communication and organized solidarity between the racial groups in social coexistence.

On this level, at least five basic opinions prevalent among Negroes require mention. First, there is one which is cultural and which boldly outlines the Negro's view of the open function of color prejudice. Through it, the white attempts to keep the Negro in his place, that is to say, to retain the social distance that prevails among the racial groups and to maintain racial inequality both in the relations between individuals and in succeeding generations. Second, there is the understanding that even selective acceptance involves a certain degree of isolation, that it does not arise from the black individual's restraint but from the attitude of his white friends. The third and fourth opinions are oriented toward those effects of color prejudice which make for psychological and moral drama. The third regards the inferiority complex as a reactive sociopsychological phenomenon. In this viewpoint, three factors are emphasized: its dynamic formation under pressure of ethnocentric judgments and discriminatory practices on the part of whites; the formative experiences of children and youths in their relations with whites of the same or of older generations; and the evidence that the complex is not an "atavism or something that might be transmitted from father to son . . . but something that arises from the various forms of behavior of the white toward the Negro." [21] This answers the argument, which enjoys some currency among whites, that the Negro "carries a servile attitude in his blood." The fourth opinion regards apathy and what might be called the passive capitulation of the Negro to the white. Both are ascribed without rancor to the root of subservient relations—the link between master and slave—and to those later circumstances which prevented the resocialization of the Negro into the order of liberty and equality. As a result a historical explanation is sought that would not be operative in those social configurations where the Negro can affirm himself. Apathy and passive capitulation are thus defined as anomalies that reflect not the Negro's will but an ineluctable destiny against which he intends (and hopes) to fight according to a nonconformist philosophy: "It is the Negro himself who must solve the Negro problem." [22] Fifth, the Negro makes a connection, although he does so in a somewhat confused way, between the expressions of color prejudice and the monopoly of power by the whites. Not only does he shrewdly point out that moral pressures indirectly engendered by such expressions of prejudice bring discord among black individuals and strengthen their tendency to flatter whites, but he understands that the rule of "divide and conquer" is part of an unstated code that makes color prejudice a portentous weapon of racial domination.

On another level, the Negro moved on to value judgments which had practical applications. The situation was not a simple one. As a group that was heir to a highly heteronomous racial condition and that did not have access to the mechanisms of solidarity of other ethnic or racial segments, even the path to self-enlightenment appeared difficult. Thus, it is not surprising that the great practical descriptions for the Second Abolition arose within the climate of racial turmoil engendered by the rights movements. Actually, no one went much beyond that in subsequent times. There was merely a change of attitude which is worthy of mention. As part of an authoritarian outlook, it was believed in some circles of the black population that the best course would be to "make the white swallow his color prejudice." This was the first expression of a simplistic answer to the white's own racial philosophy: What matters is not what you as a white person think or do, but what is possible for the Negro to achieve independently of the innermost preferences of the dominant racial group. Later this entire philosophy was toned down, but at the same time it acquired greater vitality and practical effectiveness. The Negro prefers to undermine the white's capacity for resistance by destroying those arguments that lend meaning to discriminatory practices. Thus he continues to deal with the same set of practical predescriptions: stabilization of the Negro family; elevation of women; education; acceptance of social controls that would compel obedience to the minimal standards of responsibility and solidarity that prevail among whites; fostering of a higher income and living standards; indirect reeducation of the white through the dissemination of the ideal personality types of the larger society among Negro groups; encouragement of collective action on the Negro's part toward the solution of his problems and toward the union of the Negro race. Nevertheless, the degree of maturity shown in the use of these social techniques, especially those that can be used on the personal level, has increased considerably. Even though he is not involved, or involved only slightly in collective disturbances or great collective debates, the Negro is beginning to face more effectively certain crucial and inevitable challenges. He perceives more objectively the connection between the quality of behavior and the type of adjustment to be developed. He faces with integrity (and sometimes also with shrewdness) the problem of adjusting his personality to the material and psychological demands of a class society. He tries to learn how to compete without too much personal stress and without provoking the white to open resistance, thus skillfully averting the danger of racial conflict.

We now shall turn to the other two aspects under consideration. It will suffice to present here the explanations offered for color prejudice by whites and Negroes, and for the ethical factors which govern the behavior patterns of whites and Negroes in those social situations where color prejudice is expressed.

We were able to single out sixteen explanations of color prejudice considered logical by whites, of which fifteen are typical and one is atypical. Among the typical explanations, seven give special consideration to the social images imputed directly to the Negro:[23] (1) "It's the fault of Negroes, because they act in a cringing way, as though they were still slaves"; (2) "They're not accepted because of their color"; (3) "They're a degenerate race"; (4) "Prejudice arises from the Negroes' lack of education"; (5) "Negroes are not inferior, but they feel that their color makes them inferior"; (6) "They are treated like this because of the conditions in which they live"; (7) "What they call prejudice is their own bias against the whites." The other eight typical explanations are based on qualities imputed directly to the white himself: (1) "Whites despise Negroes";[24] (2) "Negroes are held in low regard by whites and are therefore avoided"; (3) "Whites don't give opportunities to Negroes"; (4) "It's the white's rudeness"; (5) "It's a rich man's thing, copied by poor whites"; (6) "What matters is money"; (7) "This came from abroad. It's an immigrant's thing"; (8) "It's an imitation of the United States." None of the explanations cites qualities imputed to both Negroes and whites in terms of interdependence or reciprocal action. The one atypical explanation, in turn, was given by an intellectual. It regards color prejudice as the result of deeprooted feelings independent of social or cultural conditioning: "Color prejudice stems from positive and negative tendencies which lead individuals of the same race to come together and individuals of different races to reject one another."

We were able to single out fifteen explanations of color prejudice considered logical by Negroes, of which fourteen are typical and one is atypical. Among the typical explanations, six are based on qualities directly imputed to whites: [25] (1) "Color prejudice is a defensive weapon of the white"; (2) "Prejudice is explained by the pride of the former slave masters and by the hatred they had for Negroes"; (3) "It's an artificial prejudice born of the biases brought by immigrants"; (4) "An imitation of the United States, fostered by the hatred of Negroes that prevails among whites"; (5) "It arises from the white's hypocrisy"; (6) "It is the result of the white's backwardness and bad manners." Three other typical explanations are based on qualities directly imputed to the Negro: [26] (1) "It is the fault of the Negro, who doesn't know how to do things and how to behave properly"; (2) "The Negro is responsible because he doesn't rebel against white tactics"; (3) "Color prejudice is explained by the Negro's resentments (or 'complex')." Six typical explanations are based on qualities imputed both to whites and to Negroes, or to forms of social interaction between both groups.[27] (1) "It is a class prejudice, since color points to the economic and social inferiority of the Negro to the white"; (2) "The Negro was the white man's slave and never had resources comparable to those of immigrants. Abolition gave him liberty, but not economic or social freedom. He remained, as before, a helpless victim of the stereotypes that degraded him as an individual, as a person, and as a race"; (3) "The white race created for itself the concept of superiority, and for the Negro race the concept of inferiority. In accepting both concepts, the Negro sanctioned the use of color as a sign of the superiority of the white race and the inferiority of the Negro race"; (4) "Prejudice exists because the white never allowed the Negro to achieve true equality"; (5) "It's a mixed prejudice, of race and of class. It's not of race alone, because there are whites who accept Negroes. Nor is it of class alone, because certain limitations are applied to all Negroes, even wealthy ones. As a mixed prejudice, it's a prejudice of color"; (6) "The whites removed the

Negroes from their lives and got used to living apart from them. Now Negroes think that they're forbidden from going to certain places." The one atypical explanation is a development of an ultrapessimistic theme that characterizes "color prejudice as one of the miseries of human nature." It emphasizes that even after they become rich and integrated into respectable strata of society, Negroes may struggle under the restraints of prevailing avoidances and limitations.

What should be stressed in these data is the basic contrast in the use of awareness and understanding of color prejudice on the part of Negroes and of whites. Both work with the same conceptual tools. The Negro's understanding of the situation, however, is clearly governed by the direct or indirect assumption that color prejudice involves a sort of social exploitation practiced by one race against another. Thus, his conceptual tools are part of a social perspective that regards as equally important the endeavor to define prejudice and the attempt to correct it. As we see it, it is thanks to this social perspective that the Negro manages to lend a specific meaning, a generic meaning, and some historical insight to his conceptual tools, forging them so they will be at the same time a source of enlightenment and an instrument of individual or collective action.

The analysis of the ethical elements involved directly or indirectly in the expression of color prejudice yields results that are basic to a characterization of the dynamics of white and Negro racial behavior. The white's racial behavior is still largely (though unconsciously) governed by *ambiguous ethics*. This is made clear primarily by the very nature of the socially persistent expressions of the duality of the white's ethical code. Let us list eight typical aspects of these expressions, which reveal the sociopsychological context of the racial attitudes of whites: (1) The contrast between the overt and covert attitudes, judgments, and forms of behavior of the white toward the Negro continues to be characteristic and open, so that apparent outer friendliness exists alongside deep currents of aversion and avoidance. (2) The chief result of the dual ethical code is the partial or sometimes total clouding of the white's moral outlook, leaving the field wide open to ethnocentric judgments and discriminatory behavior. (3) To this result must be added the tacit distortion (prevailing among all prejudiced people) of the criteria of personal judgment of the Negro, thus fostering an influx of negative stereotypes about the Negro and the Negro race in general. (4) Similarly, the customary patterns of composure, thoughtfulness, and justice lose their meaning (usually in a partial and variable way) where the Negro is concerned. (5) Among whites there is a near-automatic combination of three related tendencies: applying exclusive or unilaterally demanding criteria of control to the Negro's accomplishments; recalling evidence concerning negative cases (or the negative aspects of specific cases), and generalizing from them to all black individuals, as though the resulting conclusions were proven, true, and indisputable. (6) In comparing whites and Negroes, criteria are taken from the patterns of the whites, without the consideration that Negroes do not enjoy the same material, intellectual, or moral advantages—in other words, proper perspective is often completely overlooked. (7) Even in positive cases of acceptance, in instances of contact with Negroes that fall within the category of the exception that confirms the rule, there remains the tendency to use controlling limits which are not universally applied to whites under similar circumstances. (8) There is a strong tendency to admit that irrational impulses ("a deep dislike," "an uncontrollable negative feeling," "an unrestrained revulsion") operate freely or under limited self-control in relations with "Negroes who don't know their place."

Ambiguity is also seen in the very nature of those moral influences that determine the social perspective of whites in race relations. Actually, whites use ambiguous ethics because they are still governed by the traditional pattern of asymmetric race relations. There is no other explanation for their attitudes and behavior. They are extremely insensitive, in the face of human dramas engendered by discriminatory practices, to the indisputable contradictions between negative stereotypes and the culture's conflicting ideal patterns, and to the obvious inconsistencies between the racial attitudes, judgments, and forms of behavior inherited from the past and the axiological, consciously shared bases of the competitive social order. They are extremely stubborn in the defense and perpetuation, on the ethological level, of the traditional patterns of race relations, through which they foster the Negro's psychological alienation (What lies behind statements such as "Negroes aren't human"; "The Negro must be put in his place"; "Negroes are not capable of self-discipline"; and so on, if not the white's moral autonomy and the Negro's total moral heteronomy?). They are extremely self-righteous, which is made clear in their endeavor to save face, that is to say, to channel criticism or anger not against prejudice òr discrimination in itself, but against its open expression. This leads to a sort of acute hypocrisy openly tolerant of color prejudice.

Such ethics explain the limited extent of the moral revolution. This revolution is now expanding, but it encounters a barrier in the lack of enthusiasm with which the standards of the competitive social order are applied to race relations. There are those who show violent disapproval, who define color prejudice as "a foul stain," "a stupid thing," "behavior unworthy of civilized people," etc. Yet in concrete situations such statements do not prevent those who utter them from making moral decisions that are ambiguous and sometimes shockingly contradictory. On the other hand, those who feel some responsibility for other people are not always sure of their own ground. One of the women researchers was confronted with a dilemma—to side with the Negro mother who would not let her daughter go to school, or to side with the daughter? And later, what could she offer her? Thus, many hesitations arise from the nature of the situation. Even when he wishes to be rid of the traditional patterns of morality, the white carries them with him and is compelled to take them into account. Society has not yet overcome them, for in this area it retains many archaic structures. The harmonious elements of the dynamics of the white's racial behavior are not altogether a product of the present time. There is a compromise with the recent past and even with the remote past, so that the moral universe of the white is strongly determined (and in view of the demands of the situation, clearly distorted) by the traditional patterns of asymmetric race relations.

Although the Negro does not altogether escape this inavoidable situation, we find quite a different picture when we turn to an analysis of his moral code as it relates to expressions of color prejudice. It would be impossible to deny that the Negro's racial behavior is governed by an ethic mirroring that of the white. He has assimilated the patterns of the white man's morality, and views himself, thinks, and acts in terms of a morality of the dominant race. Nevertheless, especially since the second decade of this century, he has not used this morality to hide behind. To the contrary, his interests and social goals led him to a complete change of perspective. Now that the socioeconomic structure that plunged him into a state of total and irremediable psychological alienation has broken down, he intends to follow those patterns of morality fully and without any reservations. He thus confronts the white with an impasse. He claims for Negroes, collectively and individually, the right to enjoy the white man's morality without any restrictions. As a result, besides being a reflection his ethics are egalitarian, holding as their supreme goal the endeavor to equal the white socially.

Like the white, the Negro is bound to the traditional conception of the world and its race relations. Nevertheless, the dynamics of his racial behavior are not determined by impulses in favor of the *status quo* and thus of stability in the prevailing system of race relations. It is caught up with and filtered through the complexities of the present to the point where moral responsibility turns to the present reality, and in a certain sense to the future as well.

The Negro builds up an entire ethical code that anticipates, qualifies, or forbids capitulation to the white. Passive surrender, with all the factors that governed and regulated it in accordance with the norms of the traditional pattern of asymmetric race relations, is decried as "despicable," "degrading," "revolting." This does not merely condemn the master-slave morality, but also dictates that the link for whites between the individual and his prerogatives as a human being be fully valid for Negroes as well. The white's standard and style of living, with its social interests and values gains importance, and not the white man himself. As a result, as the Negro identifies with the social order that prevails in the larger society, he severs himself from a racial stratification that originated neither through nor for this social order. He can thus loudly proclaim himself to be the herald and champion of racial equality. As he differentiates between white behavior and the white individual, the Negro elects to fight not the human practitioner of color prejudice, but the traditional asymmetric pattern of race relations, and the kind of domination of one man by another that derives from it. All this presupposes a characteristic zeal in most egalitarian ethics, at least during the period of their implantation and consolidation. The Negro endeavors to attain a strategic combination of objectivity and responsibility, both to disarm his opponent on the moral plane and to infuse social criticism with the relentless weight of moral indignation.[28]

From what may be inferred, the revolution in the Negro's ethical outlook has gone much farther than the evidence might suggest. There is actually a positive moral environment with potentials both for the unmasking of the opponent (or of the mere defender of the social order, in the case of those who still identify with the traditional pattern of asymmetric race relations) and for the exposure of ethnocentric judgments and discriminating practices to public censure (as sources of substantial and irreparable damage to the dignity of the individual and to the preservation of his psychological autonomy). No matter how much it may be stressed that such tendencies will remain ineffective as long as the moral patterns of the white's and the Negro's interracial behavior do not synchronize, one thing remains clear and indisputable. The moral pressures coming from the victims of color prejudice arise as dynamic forces that work toward the undermining of the functions of racial distinctions in the organization of the entire society.

The Brazilian Racial Dilemma

The preceding analysis completes our investigation of racial contact. It shows that the position of the black population still does not structurally or functionally match the class positions possible within the competitive social order of São Paulo. An explanation for this cultural lag was furnished in the process of a careful description and interpretation which combined a synchronic and a diachronic analysis of the present racial conditions. On the one hand, the breakdown of the caste and estate system associated with slavery had no direct repercussions on the forms of racial adjustments developed in the past. Not only did the traditional mechanisms of racial domination remain intact, but the reorganization of the society failed to affect in any significant way the preestablished patterns of racial distribution of income, social prestige, and power. As a result the freedom achieved by the Negro bore no economic, social, or cultural dividends. On the contrary, in view of certain specifically historical aspects of the city's economic development, this freedom met with the direct and indirect pressures of the population succession. The limited forms of sociability and integrated social life inherited by the black population from the slaveholding, seignorial days, met with destructive forces, and this population was faced with a long and intensive phase of social disorganization. These facts contributed decisively to the aggravation of unfavorable dynamic effects on the racial distribution of income, social prestige, and power. Anomalous as this may seem, a racial situation typical of the vanished social order remained unaltered, and the black population in its near totality became a substitute for the former rural and urban masses. On the other hand, the establishment and development of the class system did not follow a path beneficial to the gradual reabsorption of the former slave. The competitive social order arose and developed as an authentic and closed white world.

During the first period of the bourgeois revolution—which went on approximately from the breakdown of the slaveholding order to the beginning of World War II—it met the economic, social, and political demands of the large planters and the immigrants. During the second phase of this revolution, begun under the auspices of a new style of industrialization and the adoption of financial, technological, and organizational patterns characteristic of an integrated capitalist system, it was subordinated to the economic, social, and political interests of the bourgeoisie which arose during the previous phase—that is to say, in large measure, to the interests of the white upper and middle classes. The situation of the black population would have remained unchanged had it not been for the changes incurred by population succession. The gradual but drastic decline of immigration and the intensification of internal migrations engendered certain changes on the labor market and in the techniques of occupational selection. This phenomenon is recent, however, and as yet has had no significant repercussions on the patterns of racial distribution of income, social prestige, and power. Yet it is of enormous heuristic importance, because it shows that over the last twenty-five years the racial situation of the black population has undergone a clear change owing to the attainment of typical class positions by some segments of the population. This occurred, for the majority, through proletariatization; for a thin and heterogeneous minority, through incorporation into the middle classes; and in a few individual and sporadic cases, through incorporation into the upper classes.

The dynamic importance of this process derives from the sociopsychological relationship of the collective behavior of Negroes and mulattoes. As long as the competitive social order seemed totally closed to his longings for social classification and social ascent, the Negro either withdrew and isolated himself, thus aggravating the anomic effects of social disorganization prevailing among the Negro groups, or he joined racial associations and movements which provided an outlet for his unrest and collectively organized the Negro protest. As the pressures of the labor market gradually opened the competitive social order to Negroes and mulattoes, and as certain opportunities for social classification and vertical mobility arose, the Negro and the mulatto focused on the struggle to become part of the social order. They left the racial movements and threw themselves wholeheartedly into egoistic and individualistic competition. Both processes so far have had but meager repercussions on the situation of racial inequality. Nevertheless, they point to certain racial changes in the organization of the Negro's cultural outlook, behavior, and personality. The change in his cultural outlook caused him to become familiar with and react to the world in which he lived. It provided him with a racial counterideology which equipped him to expose the existence and the effects of color prejudice and which helped him to lessen effectively the cultural distance which separated his social longings from the demands of the situation. The change in his behavior gave continuity and effectiveness to the process of reeducation unleashed by the rights movements, and it reoriented his collective grievances, focusing them on viable and far-reaching goals. It offered the Negro the probability of entering the historical stage as a human being, with new societal supports, in order to compete on an individual basis with the white man and perhaps to fight collectively for the Second Abolition.

While all this is of considerable importance, the black population as a whole is merely on the threshold of a new era. In the past, out of sheer inertia, the distribution of income, social prestige, and power was sufficient to safeguard an absolute pattern of racial inequality. Now that this distribution begins to show signs of variety, other mechanisms come into play to safeguard and strengthen the economic, social, and cultural distance which always separated whites and Negroes in São Paulo. The worst is that the Negro has neither the economic, social, and cultural autonomy nor the political vitality to confront safely the disastrous repercussions of these mechanisms on his endeavors to become part of the social order. Powerless and bewildered, he witnesses the penetration of color prejudice into the byways of class relations, undermining his most constructive yearnings for social integration and adulterating the moral context of racial adjustments. In short he finds out that to become part of the social order, to become human, and to become equal to the white are different things with multiple gradations. Like a hydra, racial inequality is reborn after every blow. While common interests and bonds between social classes might unite individuals or groups above and beyond racial differences, the racial question divides and opposes them, condemning the Negro to a subtle isolation and undermining the foundations of the development of the competitive social order as a racial democracy.

The Brazilian racial dilemma is thus clearly outlined. Seen in terms of one of the industrial communities where the social class system developed most intensively and most homogeneously in all of Brazil, it is characterized by the fragmentary, unilateral, and incomplete manner in which it has managed to embrace, coordinate, and govern race relations. These relations have not been totally absorbed and neutralized, and have not vanished behind class relations. Instead, they have been superimposed upon the latter, even where they contradict them, as though the system of social adjustments and controls of the class society had no means at its command to regulate them socially.

Viewed from this standpoint, the Brazilian racial dilemma appears as a structural phenomenon of a dynamic character. It is expressed on the various levels of race relations. For this reason it would be easy to identify it in the behavioral lapses of individuals who believe they are not prejudiced; in the inconsistencies in the norms and patterns of interracial behavior; in the contrasts between negative stereotypes, ideal norms of behavior, and actual behavior in racial adjustments; in the conflicts between ideal culture patterns which are part of the axiological system of Brazilian civilization; in the contradictions between personality ideals and the basic personality types molded by this civilization. Yet it arose from a generalized and common cause: the structural and functional requisites of the class society apply only in a fragmentary, unilateral, and incomplete way to those situations of social contact where the social participants appear, regard themselves, and treat one another as whites and Negroes. In other words, the structures of the class society have not thus far succeeded in eliminating in a normal way preexisting structures in the area of race relations. The competitive social order has not been fully effective in motivating, coordinating, and controlling such reactions.

The descriptions given above permit us to understand and to explain genetically this cultural lag. It keeps recurring because the Negro undergoes persistent and far-reaching assimilationist pressures, and although he reacts to them with ever more reaching and persistent integrationist aspirations, he does not find adequate means of access to the social positions and roles of the social system. For the opposite to occur, it would be necessary for both pressures to be allied at least with a gradual social equalization of Negroes and whites. This teaches us something of great importance. The Brazilian racial dilemma is a phenomenon of a sociopathic character, and it will only be possible to rectify it through processes that will remove the obstacle introduced into the competitive social order by racial inequality.

This explanation permits us to place the Negro problem in a truly sociological perspective. It is a social problem not only because it shows irremediable contradictions in the racial behavior of the whites; because it manifests the indefinite persistence of unjust patterns of racial distribution of income, social prestige, and power; or because it proves that a considerable segment of the black population undergoes material and moral damage incompatible with the laws of the established social order. These are symptoms of chronic illness, which is more serious and more malignant: the minimal conditions of normal differentiation and integration in the

social system. The plasticity of the human social response and
of the functioning of social institutions permits a society to
operate satisfactorily even under conditions of chronic social
imbalance. However, as long as such conditions remain irremediable, such a society is condemned to abnormal or subnor-
mal forms of internal development. It can never expand to the
limits of normal differentiation and integration it might ideally achieve. In Durkheimian terms, we would say that it does
not fulfill the developmental potentialities guaranteed by the
corresponding type of civilization. Now, the Brazilian racial
dilemma faces us with a situation of this sort. The development of the competitive social order met with an obstacle, is
being impeded, and is undergoing structural distortions in the
area of race relations. From this standpoint, the rectification
of such an anomaly is not primarily and exclusively relevant
to the actors in the tragedy, including those who are affected
most directly and irremediably. It is basically relevant to the
very balance of the social order, that is to say, to its normal
functioning and development.

As we know, where human collectivities face social problems of this magnitude, they also show special difficulty in
finding and using appropriate techniques of social control. São
Paulo, of course, is no exception to this rule. The very situation that prevails arises in large measure from the fact that
racial inequality is socially understood, explained, and accepted as something natural, just, and inevitable, as though
the competitive social order had not altered the old patterns of
relationship between Negroes and whites. The sole unrestrained dynamic source of rectification is thus the development of the competitive social order. But this makes the homogenization of the social order dependent on spontaneous
impulses which are of their very nature too slow and too insta-
ble, not to speak of the obvious and thus foreseeable risk. The
tendencies uncovered do not exclude the possibility of a conciliation between the forms of inequality inherent in the class
society and the inherited patterns of racial inequality.

From this we may infer the importance of the practical

aspect of the problem. The mechanisms of societal reaction are innocuous or ineffective to varying degrees. Either they do not capture racial reality in the sense of a transformation of the competitive social order, or else they do—as with some of the social techniques used by Negroes—but they have no repercussions on the historical scene. Even so, two things become evident. First, the only truly creative and nonconformist influence which operates in accordance with the requisites for integration and development of the competitive social order arises from the collective endeavors of Negroes. In this sense, the reorganization of the rights movements and their updating is basic. Today, Negro groups are more highly differentiated. These movements should take into account the varieties of social, economic, and cultural interests which have grown among the Negro groups. Nevertheless, if greater heed were given to the need to involve whites in these movements, this variety of focuses of interest would be a positive fact, for it would accelerate understanding of democratic pluralism in a multiracial class society. Second, a large measure of the bewilderment of whites and Negroes alike arises from the lack of a democratic philosophy of race relations that would be socially acceptable and applicable by both groups. Within the moral context that prevails at the moment in racial adjustments, it is doubtful that anything of the sort might be attained. The white clings, consciously or unconsciously, to a distorted view of the racial contact situation. The Negro, in turn, when he breaks through this barrier, is not only heard but gives rise to irrational misunderstandings. Furthermore, through the very element of protest in his egalitarian longings, he struggles to rectify the inconsistencies and contradictions of race relations within a context of immediacy which is drawn by his impaired or unsatisfied economic, social, and cultural interests. For this reason, any broader constructive innovation would have to arise from rational techniques of control. Many countries have already faced similar problems, and show the way. It would be necessary to establish special services, on a national, regional, and local basis, to deal with the practical problems of absorbing varied population groups into a democratic society. Unfortunately the problem has been underestimated in Brazil, and there has prevailed the irrational approach of leaving such groups to a thankless fate which has almost always been unproductive to society as a whole. It seems obvious that we must think in terms of a radical change of approach that would also take into account population groups located in the big cities. In setting down a policy of racial integration along these lines, the various segments of the black population deserve special attention and strict priority. On the one hand it would be difficult otherwise to reclaim totally this important segment of the national population for the free labor market. On the other hand we cannot continue without serious injustice to keep the Negro at the margin of the development of a civilization he helped to create. As long as we do not achieve racial equality, we will not have a racial democracy, nor will we have a democracy. Through a historical paradox, the Negro today has become the test for our capacity to erect in the tropics the foundation for a modern civilization.

NOTES

Preface

1. An independent investigation which was carried out before the present study and before this book was published, and which has been used herein only partially and unsystematically, has revealed that the situation described above applies even in an area supposed to be one of "striking success" on the part of the Negro and the mulatto. See João Baptista Borges Pereira, *Cor, Profissão e Mobilidade: O Negro e o Radio de São Paulo* ("Color, Occupation and Mobility: The Negro and Radio in São Paulo") (São Paulo: Livraria Pioneira Editôra da Universidade de São Paulo, 1967), pp. 99–291.

2. C. Wright Mills, *The Sociological Imagination* (New York: Grove Press, 1961), pp. 143, 161–62.

1. The Negro and the Formation of the Class Society

1. Here is Ezekiel Freyre's description of the event: "One day eight years ago we were in Luiz Gama's office, to which a fugitive Negro slave had also come, his savings in hand, to request help in securing his freedom from this black man with a heart of gold who never denied such assistance. A short while later the slave's owner, who was a friend of Luiz Gama's, came at the latter's request.

Upon seeing his Negro slave he said, "How have I wronged you, boy? Don't you have a good bed, good food, clothing, and money? Why then should you want to leave a good master like me to be unhappy elsewhere? What do you lack in my home? Come on, speak up!"

The Negro, breathing hard, his head bowed, said nothing.

"He lacks," answered Luiz Gama teasingly as he gave the black man a friendly slap, "*the freedom to be unhappy* wherever and whenever he wishes."

2. By studying the newspapers *A Província de São Paulo* and the *Correio Paulistana* for 1887 and 1888, for example, it is possible to ascertain how deeply these matters—at first conditional liberty and later indemnities and assistance to agriculture—permeated the political debates and activities of the ruling classes. Ultimately the economic and political interests of the more prosperous plantation owners prevailed, and debates as well as the allocation of public funds were concentrated on intensifying immigration from Europe.

3. Bastide and Fernandes (1959, p. 41).

4. *Ibid.* These calculations are made from figures furnished by the 1886 census, which listed 12,290 foreigners in the city. Deducted from this total are the 205 Africans entered as foreigners.

5. Brazil, Ministério de Indústria e Obras Públicas (1898). (Data are listed according to the categories of the source.)

6. The newspapers, *A Província de São Paulo* and *O Correio Paulistano*, especially from 1887 on, show that indifference or solidarity in the face of mass escapes stemmed from the same motivation. Even the police, the army, and the law refused to intervene to protect slaveholding interests because it was clear that liberation of the slave and his children would abolish slavery without changing the existing reciprocal relations between the races or their positions in society.

7. The two poles of expectations (toward the white upper class and toward the immigrant) are expressed in the following statement credited to a slave: "You're a good master—you don't treat us badly—but since you've gotten fat and rich, you give land to foreigners, pay them for their work, and leave us just like before." (*A Província de São Paulo,* 11–9–1887.)

8. The letter of Paula Souza (1888) to César Zama reveals that the Brazilian laborer, to all extents and purposes, became a salaried worker as a substitute for the slave, in the transitional phase. He was even given the slave's quarters: "Many who lived off four bean plants and one acre of corn are now happily starting to work on the coffee groves and processing areas, and those I have employed fit into the former slave quarters just fine. It is true that mine are well built, but they are built in the form of a square—an offensive shape even here. [Slave quarters were often built around a quadrangle and the entranceway was locked at night.] They are still in the same shape, but without a lock, and today the workers actually prefer this shape because they can store their supplies inside without fearing damage from the livestock. My quadrangle is a large patio surrounded by clean, white houses whose entrances I will put on the outside now." Regarding the remuneration of workers, he states: "Your countrymen should also know that free labor isn't as expensive as it would seem at first. This was my greatest surprise in the changes we have undergone."

9. Alves (1888, p. 7) pointed out: "In various counties the landowners are startled at every step by armed masses of fleeing slaves who travel the roads to the urban centers where the support of sons, the tolerance of others, and the indifference of the majority give them the hope of impunity, without consideration for the dangers such illegal bands represent for all.

10. Letter to the editor from Campinas in *A Província de São Paulo* (3–23–1888).

11. It should be noted that the informant was the son of a Frenchman who had employed a Negro as a polisher in his workshop.

12. It was much worse in the interior because the treatment of the Negroes was crueler. *A Redempção,* in the vanguard of the opposition to such practices, denounced the behavior of a police chief in Itú: He arrested the Negro women who appeared in public well dressed and with their hair done, and took them to the jail to shave their heads and rap the palms of their hands with a stick. It also gives brief accounts of four

cases of lynching (cf. *A Redempção*, 5–13–1897). Newspapers occasionally related such occurrences. The following examples were related in *A Provincia de São Paulo:* In Piracicaba, "the government of Vila de São Pedro gave orders to policemen to prohibit the presence of Negroes on the streets of the village at night and to permit their presence in the village only until noon on Sundays. We call the attention of the respective authorities to this revolting abuse" (6–2–1888). A telegram from Casa Branca read: "Police chief Francisco Nogueira threatens to imprison Negroes who come to next Sunday's Abolition celebrations. I request strict measures be taken" (6–5–1888). News from Mogi Mirim: "We have been told that last week, on Coronel Guedes Street, several children—the daughters of freedmen—were running after their mothers in terror, fleeing persons who were trying to catch them and take them to someone who wanted to place them under guardianship. This must be stopped. We have been informed that a kindly shopkeeper on that street hid the fugitives" (7–7–1888). In Campinas: "Leandro, a freedman employed on Maria Doque's plantation, complained to police authorities that at the orders of his employers, he and two friends had gone that morning in a wagon to the plantation belonging to the Baron of Ibitinga in order to bring back from this plantation two families of freedmen who wished to be employed where he was. He had been called into a room and beaten. Because of his screams the door was opened and he fled, with his persecutors close behind. His two friends also fled upon seeing what had happened to him" (7–24–1888). Also from Campinas: "*O Correio* relates that the day before yesterday a brown-skinned man told the police that a plantation owner named Escobar was detaining the wife of the complainant, Escobar's ex-slave, on his plantation near Valinhos" (8–25–1888). These examples reveal the varied behavior of those who showed open resistance to the liberty and rights of freedmen.

13. Morse (1954, p. 191).

14. This is a very important point. In order to obtain the maximum resources for the solution of agrarian problems, that is, to intensify immigration, (those circles) had no qualms about sacrificing the interests of the ruling groups in terms of indemnifications they demanded. As a result the sole losers were plantation owners and farmers of less prosperous regions of São Paulo and the nation.

15. Public statement by Sofia Campos Teixeira. The authors of all the following statements became familiar with the conditions faced by freedmen in São Paulo during the transitional period through direct and close association with older persons.

16. Excerpt from a public statement by Francisco Lucrécio.

17. Public statement by Raul Joviano do Amaral. [*Translator's note:* Machado de Assis, Juliano Moreira, and Teodoro Sampaio were well-known Brazilian writers, statesmen, etc.]

18. Public statement by Nestor Borges.

19. This document was presumably written by Jorge Prado Teixeira,

a Negro teacher and promising young intellectual who died prematurely. He made a constructive contribution to our study.

20. Contrary to what happened in the United States, for example, where the caste system remains inbedded in the developing class system. It is clear that the perpetuation of the old order through *coronelismo* is not the same thing, for it merely involves the persistence of elements basic to paternalistic authority and to the landowning stratum of the Brazilian slaveholding society. Besides, whenever the process of change is rapid, it is more uncertain. [*Translator's note: Coronelismo* is the exercise of local authority by large landowners with the self-attributed or real military title of colonel.]

21. José Corrêa Leite; the passage quoted was taken from a case study made by Renato Jardim Moreira (n.d., p. 14, note 1), based on the information provided by Leite. Leite refers to the Negro newspaper, *O Clarim da Alvorada,* of which he was one of the chief sponsors.

2. Pauperism and Social Anomie

1. Unfortunately, Ellis limited himself to the data on the incidence of tuberculosis in 1929, and the relation of the disease to outside or biological factors is merely conjectural.

2. The record of diseases and physical defects, in particular, fails to suggest any kind of propensity or biological inherited incapacity of the Negro or mulatto population. On the other hand it should be observed that certain fluctuations in acceptance presumably relate to the possibilities for manipulation of the techniques of evading military service, which are not the same for the three groups.

3. Data taken from Table A–1, Boletin da Diretoria de Terras, Colonização e Imigraçio (1937, pp. 29–75).

4. Data taken from Table E–11, Boletin da Serviço de Imigraçao e Colonizaçao (1940, p. 145). See pp. 129ff.

5. As is known, a trend toward the redistribution of internal populations according to color is associated with these migrations (cf. Smith, 1954, pp. 280–81).

6. We would have the following conjectural table of the numerical proportion of Negroes and mulattoes in the *Paulistana* population based on Lowrie's estimates:

Years	8 Per cent	9 Per cent	12 Per cent
1910	19,185	21,583	28,778
1920	46,322	52,112	69,483
1934	84,809	95,410	127,214

7. In presenting these conjectures we must fulfill a professional obligation of indicating the manner in which we selected the percentages that were presumably legitimate at the time of each census. We have no

intention other than to formulate a system of reference that serves to indicate the approximate size of the Negro and mullato population of the capital during these years. Such conjectures therefore merit so little confidence that we have scrupulously avoided taking them into account in discussing the problems raised in this chapter.

8. We were surprised during our research that few light or dark mulattoes identified or classified themselves ostensibly as whites. Yet many identified and classified themselves as Negroes even though some would be considered white in the Brazilian racial consensus and at least one was phenotypically white.

9. This testimony was given in the course of a debate with five informants of the black middle class. Later on other aspects of the economic, cultural, and social situation of this strata of the *Paulistana* Negro population will be examined.

10. Cf. especially the following works by Giorgio Mortara: 1961 (pp. 198–206), 1950, 1951, 1948, 1952, 1956.

11. Mortara (1962, p. 25). The results of the 1950 census gave more weight to and confirmed the conclusions in this respect made on the basis of the 1940 census (cf. Mortara, 1952, p. 48).

12. Gilberto Freyre (1938, pp. 67, 229ff.) deals with the sexuality of the African, the Portuguese, and the Indian, revealing the lack of support for many current ideas about the matter and stressing the importance of slavery in the breakdown in the sexual behavior of Negroes and mulattoes. A good perspective on the significance, importance, and ordering of erotic activity in African tribal life can also be found in the extraordinary study by Schapera (1941). (Consult especially Chap. VII and pp. 50–63, 74–82 on sexual relations.)

3. Racial Heteronomy in a Class Society

1. The two periods alluded to refer to the time spans of the caste society and the class society.

2. Passage from a case study by Renato Jardim Moreira based upon data supplied by José Corrêa Leite (n.d.).

3. The concepts of ideology and utopia are used in accord with the sociological definitions proposed by Mannheim (1950).

4. The informant undoubtedly meant to say *menelique,* which is today still synonymous with "Negro" or "colored" among people of Italian descent in the city.

5. The informant's involvement in such situations is attributable to his status as *filho de criação* (foster son) of a rich and traditional family; he had access to social roles normally unattainable to Negroes. On the other hand, he himself stated that this family was very careful of the manner in which they treated him.

6. In this part of the work we shall also resort to data relating to 1941 and 1951, chiefly in order to define structurally and functionally the asymmetry that prevails in reciprocal behavior and in race relations generally, with its various sociodynamic results.

7. Maria Paes de Barros (1946, pp. 81–82).

8. There were two different mechanisms of vertical mobility for the Negro and mulatto. He could be incorporated into the nucleus of a traditional and important family (a very rare occurrence in São Paulo, both in the city and in the rural areas), or included in the periphery of such a family (a more or less frequent occurrence which was close to paternalism). Alternatively he could achieve vertical mobility on his own through the accumulation of wealth or the display of exceptional gifts (particularly intellectual ones), though this individuality did not exclude dependence on some important family or head of the *parentela* (kinship group). Even Luiz Gama was not exempt from this kind of dependence on important families. The second alternative occurred now and then in São Paulo, and a few individuals rose in this manner. Therefore we need not go into the matter any further and will discuss it merely in terms of the more general aspects of racial adjustments.

9. As a rule, such a statement was accompanied by a gesture: the speaker would reach behind his head and grasp his right ear with the fingers of his left hand.

10. Any gradations in the enjoyment of such rights and safeguards were of no or little import, for if the larger society had operated as an "openended system," the effects of vertical mobility would not have been impeded and undermined.

4. Social Movements in the Negro Milieu

1. If we adopted the classification of minorities proposed by Louis Wirth, Negroes and mulattoes would constitute an "assimilationist minority" in the light of the nature of these movements (see Wirth, 1956).

2. Quotations taken from the case study by Moreira and Leite (n.d., 3–4).

3. "It was Vicente Ferreira who introduced the term 'Negro' to substitute the term 'colored man.' The Mongoloid and the Indian are also colored men; this nonsense about the colored man—which says nothing—was ended." (Moreira and Leite, n.d., 9.)

4. This passage is taken from the *Manifesto à Gente Negra Brasileira* (Manifesto to the Brazilian Negro) (12–2–31, p. 8) by Arlindo Veiga dos Santos, General President of the *Frente Negra Brasileira*.

5. Quotations taken from statements by Dr. Arlindo Veiga dos Santos regarding the organization and objectives of the Frente Negra Brasileira.

6. We registered the Associação José do Patrocínio, the Associação dos Negros Brasileiros, the Centro Cívico Beneficente Senhoras Maes Pretas, the Centro Cívico Palmares, the Clube Negro de Cultura Social, the Federação dos Homens de Côr, the Frente Negra Brasileira, the Frente Negra Socialista, the Grêmio Recreativo e Cultural, the Grêmio Recreativo Kosmos, the Legião Negra Brasileira, the Movimento Afro-Brasileiro de Educação e Cultura, the Organização de Cultura e Beneficência Jabaquara, the Sociedade Beneficente 13 de Maio, and the União Negra Brasileira. This list, which is incomplete, should also include the

venerable Irmandade de Nossa Senhora do Rosário des Homens Prêtos and certain later initiatives such as the Associação Cultural do Negro, the Bandeira Cultural Negra Brasileira, and the Casa da Cultura Afro-Brasileira.

7. Public statement by Dr. Arlindo Veiga dos Santos.

8. This aspiration had existed since [the time of] the forerunners of the rights movements, as can be inferred from the following quotation: "May the date of July 14 run arms linked [sic] with that of May 13, the day that emancipated a race that with its sweat and blood made firm the foundation of the grandeur and wealth of this our immense country that is called Brazil" (A Liberdade, a critical, literary, and news organ dedicated to the colored population, São Paulo, 8–3–1919, Ano I, No. 2). The hymn of the Frente Negra repeated this theme in advocating: "Let the voice of prejudices cease, the formidable bastille fall," etc.

9. The Frente Negra Brasileira, like other "Negro associations," did what was within its possibilities to educate and to reeducate its members. The barrier, however, is much more complex because it involves unavailable economic, social, and cultural resources. In long-range terms, such problems have to be solved in the context of society, as we shall see later on.

10. The concepts of mechanical solidarity and organic solidarity are used with the connotations imputed to them by E. Durkheim (1902, chaps. 2 and 3).

5. The Egalitarian Forces of Social Integration

1. Unfortunately the data on the distribution of occupations in the city gathered during the 1950 and 1960 censuses were not released.

2. It should be kept in mind that many of those who qualify as employees are often engaged in heavy manual labor and, strictly speaking, are still not proletarian. They sell their labor and are part of the free labor system, but proletarianization is for them an incipient, and sometimes still distant, condition.

3. The sample is obviously a small one, and should not lead to more than provisional conclusions. However, it is noteworthy that domestic services accounted for 20.76% against 18.49% for the 1940 census. As for other activities, the rather large variations can be explained by the fact that we considered the occupations held by the informants, and not their position in a certain field of economic activity. Finally, there is an appreciable difference between our percentage for horticulture and gardening (2.33%) and that given in the 1940 census (4.35%). This difference is easily explained: The researchers presented their questionnaires in the center of the city and in suburbs where these activities are less common.

4. This may perhaps be explained by the way in which the questionnaires were used. The researchers were students who tended to approach black persons who belonged to their circle of friends or whom

they knew. In a systematic sample this percentage would very probably have been much larger.

5. The last two forms of reply were provided by the informants. Being relevant, they were retained.

6. Indeed, these results suggest that degree of literacy is irrelevant in the acquisition of experience leading to awareness of the situation. Data for the State of São Paulo (1940 census) show that the lowest proportions of those able to read and write and the largest proportions of illiterates are to be found among the black population. (The percentages of those who claimed to be able to read are: whites, 55%; Negroes, 34%; mulattoes, 38%; Mongoloids, 61%. The percentages of those who could not read were thus: whites, 45%; Negroes, 66%; mulattoes, 62%; Mongoloids, 39%.) Nevertheless, the Negro and the mulatto, despite this limitation, become aware of the requirements of occupational competition and of the effects of color prejudice at two different levels.

7. Incidentally, these two things are often intermingled in the Negro's and mulatto's sociohistorical situation, as we shall see in the second part of this chapter.

8. This attitude is fairly rare, but we observed it to some extent in both foreign and Brazilian firms, large, medium, and small.

9. Data gathered among employers and heads of personnel sections in large, medium, and small firms, all of whom were white, some being of Brazilian descent and others of foreign descent.

10. Of more than 1800 employees the head of the personnel section estimated that there were not more than 30 Negroes or mulattoes.

11. As we have already remarked, the "complex" is described, among Negroes, as the sum total of perceptive, cognitive, and ego-defense reactions to real or imagined manifestations of color prejudice.

12. Lowrie (1938, pp. 195–212).

13. Classification in the lowest stratum of class society is clearly a sign of vertical social mobility. Lowrie's system of reference stresses this fact, since it is a case of passing from the "semidependent class" to the "working class."

14. The dynamic aspects of this situation will be described later.

15. Taken from a case study by Renato Jardim Moreira.

16. The same observation applies to the data to be used in the next chapter.

17. Issues for April and May, 1951, under the heading "Cultura, Base Essencial para o Progresso"; quotations from a study on the Negro press in São Paulo by Cardoso, Fernando Henrique, MS 8–9.

18. One noteworthy case is that of the owner of a leading fashion store who sold a very expensive fancy-dress costume to a Negro woman. His saleswomen objected and he himself justified his action to his friends, saying that he could not choose the color of his clients and that since she could pay he had to sell.

19. Jesus, *Quarto de Despejo*, n.d. (The diary begins with entries dated July 15, 1955, and ends with an entry dated January 1, 1960.)

20. *Ibid.*, 133, 158.

21. Public statement by Mr. Jorge Prado Teixeira.

22. Public statement by Mr. Luiz Lobato.

23. For the concept of peristasis see Baldus and Willems.

24. Taken from the autobiography of a light mulatto with slightly Negroid features.

25. A literal quotation.

26. The researcher is white. At the time she was a stockholder in the factory and was well acquainted with the composition and operation of its administration.

27. Information provided by the chief accountant of the organization, a white man of Italian descent.

28. Our white informant, head of the personnel section, showed us the records in question, where photographs seemed to be part of the personal data required from each candidate.

29. We might add that some firms have nothing resembling a "racial policy." Heads of personnel sections, managers, and other officials follow such criteria on their own initiative.

30. Document in the handwriting of the informant, who goes on to describe how, in practice, his attempts at self-assertion are frustrated.

31. Document in the informant's handwriting. Literal transcription of some passages.

32. Bastide and Fernandes (*Brancos e Negros em São Paulo,* 1959, pp. 232, 234, 238).

33. Literal transcription from a document in the white informant's own handwriting.

34. Note that the informant disagrees with the opinion held "by many people" (as he says) that "the Negro is inferior to the white man."

35. The dialogue is given as presented by the informant.

36. Martuscelli (1950, pp. 53–73).

37. *Ibid.,* Table III, p. 61.

38. This investigation was made in 1951 by Lucilla Herrmann. The analysis of the results was made by Roger Bastide and Pierre Van den Bergue in their "Estereótipos, Normas e Comportamento Inter-racial em São Paulo" (in Bastide and Fernandes, *Brancos e Negros em São Paulo,* 1959, pp. 359–71).

39. *Ibid.,* 365–67. (We have omitted other references in order to confine ourselves to the essential.)

40. An episode described in public by Mr. Luiz Lobato. Personal and private data have been omitted to avoid distressing identification.

41. From a public statement by Mr. Luiz Lobato.

42. Public statement by Mr. José Pelegrini.

43. Bastide and Van den Bergue, *Brancos e Negros em São Paulo,* 1959, pp. 359–71.

44. *Ibid.*

45. This statement, being in a document drawn up by the informant,

has been quoted literally. It is well to observe that other documents fully bear out this statement.

46. We have quoted this personal, written statement in its entirety.

47. Naturally this occurs in extreme cases and is therefore rather rare. Nevertheless, our investigation showed that there are some whites who are neutral to color prejudice.

48. In the parlance of the Negro and the mulatto this term [*branco legal*] means a white man who is free from color prejudice.

49. This is a family that is considered to go back four hundred years and is very highly regarded.

50. A study carried out by Renato Jardim Moreira.

51. This happens in situations where people are treated according to their position. Even the white man who tries to avoid dealing with black persons feels obliged in these situations to treat them with the respect due to their positions and accepts such inconveniences philosophically, saying, "You take the rough with the smooth."

52. The opposite, therefore, to what rising Negroes themselves suppose.

53. It should be noted that many, for fear of "not being able to bring up their children," deliberately refrain from extramarital adventures or practice birth control.

54. This situation is so rare that we found only one case, which we have already mentioned above: the mulatto dentist who set up an office in partnership with a white doctor. However, we know of some analogous cases, mainly in retail business and in accounting offices.

55. See Bastide, *Sociologie du Brésil*, I, II, and *passim* for the results of our investigation.

56. This last expression, like the preceding one, involves rejection of any mutual aid obligations among members of a family or neighbors.

57. They do not always go out with the family. If they do go out, they may follow behind; for certain visitors they must be out of sight; to others they are not introduced; they do not always eat with the family when there are special visitors; etc. One of the documents, pertaining to a light mulatto lawyer, shows that one may go to extremely cruel lengths, even with one's own mother.

58. Judging by the economic, social, and cultural criteria of society as a whole, they do not always belong even to the middle classes.

59. A characteristic style of dancing in low-class Negro dance halls.

60. Frazier, *Bourgeoisie Noire*, 1955, *passim*.

61. This question was extended or redefined by many of the subjects as if it were: "Do you think that Negroes should aspire to jobs customarily held by whites in our society?"

62. Observations by Jorge Prado Teixeira.

63. Observations by Renato Jardim Moreira.

64. Tentative in the sense that it is only valid for the sociohistorical situation described.

65. The question of the social neutrality of color prejudice is raised

even by those personally involved, when they describe it as "a question of taste" or as being of "an esthetic nature."

6. *The Negro Problem in a Class Society*

1. We repeat here that we are using the concept as a sociohistorical category, that is to say, as it is found in the Negro's social consciousness and in the mind of more or less tolerant whites.

2. We have already indicated repeatedly that we use the term "color prejudice" as a sociohistorical category forged by the Negroes and shared to a large measure by the whites. As we have mentioned, this category is characterized by its comprehensive character. It merges the two technical concepts of racial prejudice and racial discrimination.

In view of the purposes of this chapter, we must stress how the two concepts are differentiated and how we have used them in our research. Racial prejudice may be defined as "a social attitude propagated by an exploiting class with the aim of stigmatizing a certain group as inferior, so that the exploitation of this group or its resources may be justified." (Cox, 1948, p. 393). In turn, "racial discrimination only appears when we deny individuals or groups the equality of treatment they may wish for" (Allport, 1954, p. 51). (Aside from the bibliography provided by these two works, important books will be found in the bibliography at the end of this work.)

The controversies surrounding the conceptualization of and approach to both phenomena cannot be discussed here. Nevertheless, we must stress that we do not regard racial prejudice as falling within the specific domain of personality, and racial discrimination as being exclusively pertinent to social structure, as do many American sociologists and social psychologists. Both may be viewed on the various levels of sociological analysis (of social action and relations; of collective behavior; of the socialization and organization of personality; of social norms, representations, and values; and of the differentiation and integration of social systems). In the course of our research we focused our analysis on the structural and dynamic aspects of the connections among racial prejudice, racial discrimination, and the patterns of integration of the social order. Thus, racial prejudice was viewed explicitly in terms of its functions, as a source of legitimation for social opinions, judgments, and representations which motivate, define, and govern social attitudes and forms of behavior. Racial discrimination, in turn, was explicitly regarded as part of the complex of processes which define, develop, and regulate the disparities resulting from the overlapping of social stratification and racial stratification within the larger social system.

3. On the concepts of *eidos* and *ethos* in sociopsychological and socioethnological analysis, see Bateson, 1958, pp. 29–30.

4. The documentation was obtained in various ways. Most of the data was gathered through interviews, mass observation (in the form of statements written by informants or given verbally in group situations),

and meetings or seminars with various types of individuals drawn from the Negro groups for the purpose of debating the topic of color prejudice as a social problem. These data were supplemented by questionnairs; life histories; case studies of dramatic, obvious, or irrefutable instances of discrimination; and some written statements excerpted chiefly from the daily press.

5. This account was confirmed by the other protagonist, Sr. Benedito.

6. At the time of the interviews the girl had finished high school and a typing course and was about to graduate as an accountant. She had worked to support herself through her studies.

7. This interview was given in mid-February, 1956.

8. The lady added that he committed suicide as a result.

9. *Diario do Congresso,* Rio, July 18, 1950.

10. *O Estado de São Paulo,* August 8, 1950.

11. The incident occurred in July, 1950, and gave rise to a big scandal. [*Editor's note:* Katherine Dunham, the American Negro dancer, was refused rooms in a luxury hotel in São Paulo presumably because of her skin color.] Renato Jardim Moreira made a case study of it from clippings taken out of 55 different newspapers in São Paulo and other parts of the country. We shall use only a few data from this manuscript study.

12. *Correio Paulistano,* July 13, 1950.

13. In view of the use to which we have put this excerpt, we shall not identify the newspaper.

14. Interview in *A Folha da Manhã,* São Paulo, May 22, 1959.

15. He would not bring home black friends or girlfriends (even light mulatto girls) for fear that his parents and brothers might mistreat or snub them.

16. In the personal statements, an average of three black persons out of ten expressed similar opinions or remained undecided.

17. We have similar statements made by men and women of various ages that we deemed unnecessary to give here.

18. It should be noted that to change the system, on the level of race relations and in the terms considered here, is tantamount to extending the principles that govern the integration of the competitive social order to the sphere of racial coexistence. We are thus dealing literally with "revolution within the order." If the expansion of the class system were more rapid and more homogeneous, and the absorption of the black population occurred at a constant rate, this process would be spontaneous—though of course governed by the interests and aspirations of the members of that population.

19. We could not find any order of importance for these items in the Negro's understanding of racial reality. The order used is thus arbitrary.

20. Here is a typical example taken from interviews with a mulatto woman teacher: "One day, after work, I went out with a white woman colleague. The following day she told me, 'My fiance liked you.' I answered, 'Don't worry, I might feel the same way about him, but I'm

not interested.' 'But he didn't say that to offend you!' 'Whenever he came around I would say, 'Look, here is your fiance,' and she would always say, 'He said he liked you.' " We can easily see the myriad hidden assumptions that motivated the mulatto teacher's reactions, and how they affected her normal relations with her colleague and the latter's fiance.

21. Excerpt from a statement by a Negro intellectual and civil servant.

22. This saying was disseminated by the first newspapers of the Negro press and by the rights movements. It appears in numerous personal statements.

23. The explanations will be given in order of frequency.

24. This explanation is given three times as frequently as those that follow.

25. Explanations (1) and (4) were given with the same frequency.

26. These explanations occur more frequently than the preceding ones (from one-and-a-half to three times as often). They are given in decreasing order of frequency.

27. These explanations are given in decreasing order of frequency. The first three occur two or three times as often as the others.

28. This will be fully appreciated if we bear in mind the force of such criticism when it is appropriately addressed to those inconsistencies in interracial behavior which bring into play the ideal culture patterns and the dynamic equilibrium of the prevailing social order.

GLOSSARY*

Afonso Arinos Law. Law making practices resulting from racial or color prejudices legally punishable misdemeanors.

Caboclo. An individual who is racially a white-Indian mixture. Socially, he is a poor farm laborer, usually illiterate, who may use a very small plot of land for subsistence farming but who often works as a tenant farmer or sharecropper.

Centro Cívico de Palmares. Negro organization founded in 1927 for educational purposes, but which soon became an active center of the rights movements.

Clarim da Alvorada (Clarion of Dawn). Leading publication of the Negro rights movement that first appeared in January, 1924, as a purely literary journal, but a year later became involved in the rights movement.

Dona. Term of respect for a woman, usually employed before her Christian name.

Estado Nôvo (New State). Name given to the regime of Getúlio Vargas after 1937.

Filho de criação. Child from lower class raised by upper-class family. Was both a member of the family and a servant for light chores.

Frente Negra Brasileira (Brazilian Negro Front). Leading Negro organization of the rights movement, founded September 16, 1931. It became a political party in 1936 and was outlawed by Getúlio Vargas in 1937.

Gremio Recreativo e Cultural (Recreation and Culture Club). One of the Negro organizations that was active in the beginning of the rights movements.

Macumba. Religious cult of African origin practiced in Brazil predominantly by Negroes and mulattoes. In some ways it is similar to the voodoo of the Caribbean area. The cults include "white magic" for healing, etc., and "black magic" to do harm to others. For further information see Wagley (1963, p. 241); Bastide (1946); R. Ribeiro (1952); Eduardo (1948, Chaps. V–VI); and Herskovits (1955, pp. 505–32).

Pardo. A designation of skin color literally meaning "brown."

Parentela. Entire kin group, including consanguineous and affinal relatives.

Paulista. A resident of the State of São Paulo.

* Organized by editors.

Paulistana. A resident of the City of São Paulo.

Pinga. A cheap alcoholic drink made from sugar-cane syrup; the drink of the masses.

Rua Direita. A street in the heart of the city of São Paulo famous in former times for the social promenades of the Negro and mulatto.

Sociedade Beneficiente 13 de Maio (Beneficient Society of the 13th of May). One of the Negro organizations that was active in the beginning of the rights movement.

A Voz de Raça (The Voice of Race). The newspaper of the Frente Negra Brasileira.

BIBLIOGRAPHY

Abranches, Dunshee de (1941). "O Captiveiro" (Memories), Rio de Janeiro.

Adorno, T. D., et al. (1950). The Authoritarian Personality, Harper and Brothers, New York.

Aguiar, Jaime de (1930). "Os Centenários e Nos," O Clarim da Alvorada, São Paulo, Ano VII, No. 31 (December).

Allport, G. A. (1950). "Prejudice: A Problem in Psychological and Social Causation," The Journal of Social Issues, supplement series No. 4 (Kurt Lewin Memorial Award Issues) (November).

Allport, G. W. (1954). The Nature of Prejudice, Addison-Wesley Publishing Co., Reading, Mass.

Almeida, Alberto de (1927). "Preconceito," O Patricínio, São Paulo, Ano 2, No. 21 (December).

Almeida, Vicente Unzer de, and Octavio Teixeira Mendes Sobrinho (1951). Migração Rural-Urbana, Secretaria de Agricultura, São Paulo.

Alves, Francisco de Paulo Rodrigues (1888). Relatório Apresentado á Assembleia Legislativa Provincial de São Paulo pelo Presidente da Provincia Exmo. Sr. Dr. Francisco de Paulo.

Alvorada, A. (1945). Commemorative Edition of the Proclamation of the Republic (November).

Amaral, Raul Joviano do (n.d.) Frente Negra Brasileira, Suas Finalidades e Obras Realizadas, pamphlet.

———— (1933). "O Negro e a Cultura," O Clarim da Alvorada, São Paulo, Ano X, No. 42 (May).

———— (1933). "Redenção," A Voz da Raça, Ano I, No. 14 (June).

———— (1935). "Sou Negro," O Clarim da Alvorada, São Paulo, Ano I, No. 4 (May).

———— (under pseudonym "Rajovia") (1936). "Novo Rumo," A Voz da Raça, São Paulo, Ano III, No. 54 (June).

———— (1945). "Basta de Explorações," Alvorada, São Paulo, issue commemorating the date of the discovery of America (October).

———— (1945). "O Negro Não Tem Problemas," Alvorada, São Paulo, commemorative issue (September).

———— (1947). "Tese Errada," Alvorada, São Paulo, Ano II, No. 18 (March).

———— (1948). "Designios . . . ," Alvorada, São Paulo, Ano III, No. 29 (February).

———— (1948) "Perspectivas," Alvorada, São Paulo, Ano III, No. 28.

Amaral, Raul Joviano do (1953). *Os Pretos do Rosário de São Paulo,* Edições Alarico, São Paulo.

—— (1961). *O Negro na População de São Paulo,* preface by Oracy Nogueira, unpublished manuscript, São Paulo.

Amaral, Rubens do (1941). "Aniquilamento dos Negros in Sao Paulo," *A Folha da Manhã* (November).

Andrade, Antonio Manuel Bueno de (1918). "A Abolição em São Paulo: Depoimento de uma Testemunha," *O Estado de São Paulo* (April).

Annaes da Camara dos Deputados de São Paulo (1928), Vol. I.

Araújo, J. R. "A População Paulistana," in Associação dos Geógrafos Brasileiros, *Abidade de São Paulo* (1958), Companhia Editôra Nacional, Vol. II, Cap. 4, São Paulo.

Araújo, Oscar Egidio (1941). "Latinos e Não Latinos no Município de São Paulo," *Revista do Arguiro Municipal,* Ano VII, Vol. LXXV, São Paulo.

Associação dos Geógrafos Brasileiros (1958). *A Cidade de São Paulo,* Companhia Editôra Nacional, São Paulo.

Azevedo, Fernando de (1944). *A Cultura Brasileira,* 2ª ed., Companhia Editôra Nacional, São Paulo.

Azevedo, Salvio de Almeida (1941). "Imigração e Colonização no Estado de São Paulo," *Revista do Arquivo Municipal,* Ano VII, Vol. LXXV, pp. 105–57.

Azevedo, Thales de (1953). *Les Elites de Coleur dans une Vile Bresilienne,* UNESCO, Paris.

Barbosa, Ruy (1945). *Obras Completas de Ruy Barbosa,* Vol. XI, 1884, Tomo I, Ministério de Educação e Cultura, Rio de Janeiro (Introdução de Astrogildo Pereira).

Barros, Maria Paes de (1946). *No Tempo de Dantes.* Prefácio de Monteiro Lobato, Editora Brasiliense Ltda., São Paulo.

Barros, Rafael de (1887). "O trabalho livre nas fazendas," *A Provincia de São Paulo* (October).

Bastide, Roger (n.d.). "A Criminalidade Negra no Estado de São Paulo," manuscript prepared for the Congresso do Negro Brasileira, based on data gathered by Mario Wagner.

—— (n.d.). "A Imprensa Negra do Estado de São Paulo," Estudos Africanos, 2ª Serie, Boletim No. 2, Cadeira de Sociologia I, Faculdade de Filosofia, Ciência e Letras, Universidade de São Paulo, São Paulo.

—— (n.d.). *Sociologie do Brasil,* 2 vols., Centre de Documentation, Universitaire de la Universite de Paris, Paris.

—— (1946). "A Macumba Paulista," in *Estudos Afro-Brasileiros.* 1ª serie, Boletim IIX of the Cadeira de Sociological I, Faculdade de Filosofia, Ciências e Letras da Universidade de São Paulo.

——, and Florestan Fernandes (1951). *O Preconceito Racial em São Paulo,* Instituto de Administração da U.S.P., São Paulo.

——, and Pierre Van den Bergue (1959). "Estereotipos, Normas e Comportamento Inter-racial em São Paulo," in Roger Bastide and Florestan Fernandes (1959). *Brancos e Negros em São Paulo,* Companhia Editôra Nacional, São Paulo.

Bateson, G. (1958). *Naven*. A survey of the problems suggested by a composite picture of the culture of a New Guinea Tribe drawn from *Three Points of View*, Second Edition, Stanford University Press, Palo Alto, California.

Beiguelman, Paula (1961). Teoria e Ação no Pensamento Abolicionista, 2 vols., mimeographed by the author, São Paulo.

Bergel, Egon Ernst (1962). *Social Stratification*, McGraw-Hill, N. Y.

Bertalanffy, L. Von (1952). *Problems of Life*, C. A. Watts & Co., London.

Bettelheim, B., and Janowitz, M. (1950). *Dynamics of Prejudice; A Psychological and Sociological Study of Veterans*, Harper & Bros., N. Y.

Bicudo, Virginia L. (1947). "Atitudes Raciais de Pretos e Mulatos em São Paulo," *Sociologia*, Vol. IX, No. 3, São Paulo, pp. 195–219.

————— (1955). "Atitudes dos Alunos dos Grupos Escolares em Relação com a Côr de seus Colegas" in *Relações Entre Negros e Brancos em São Paulo*, Editora Anhembi Ltda., São Paulo, pp. 227–310.

Boletim do Serviço de Imigração e Colonização (1940).

Boletim de Terras, Colônização e Imigração (1937).

Bouglé, C. (1935). *Essai sur le Regime des Castes*. 3rd ed. Librairie Felix Alcan, Paris.

Brasil, Congresso (1950). *Diario do Congresso*. Rio de Janeiro, 7–18–1950.

Brasil, Ministerio da Industria e Obras Publicas, Diretoria Geral de Estatistica (1898). *Sexo, Raça e Estado Civil, Nacionalidade, Filiação, Culto e Analfabetismo da População Recenseada em 31 de Dezembro de 1890*, Rio de Janeiro: Ministerio da Industria e Obras Publicas, Director Geral de Estatistica.

Brasil, Maria Cascaes (1956). "A Contribuição das Diversas Unidades da Federação e Regiões Fisiograficas para a População de São Paulo," *Estudos Demograficos, No. 246*, Laboratorio de Estatistica do Instituto Brasileiro de Geografia e Estatistica, Rio de Janeiro.

Brown, L. G. (1942). *Social Pathology, Personal and Social Disorganization*, F. S. Crofts & Co. N. Y.

Bruno, Ernani Silva (1954). *Historia e Tradições da Cidade de São Paulo*, 3rd vol. José Olympio, Rio.

Calmon, Pedro (1938). "A Abolição," *Revista do Arguivo Municipal*, São Paulo, Ano IV, Vol. XLVII (May).

Camargo, Arnaldo de (1946). "Explanação de Motivos," *O Novo Horizonte*, São Paulo, Ano I, No. 1 (May).

————— (1946). "Exortação," *O Novo Horizonte*, São Paulo, Ano I, No. 2 (June).

————— (1947). "Negro!!! Vôce é Importante," *O Novo Horizonte*, São Paulo, Ano II, No. 12 (July).

————— (1948). "Há Negro 'Snob'?" *O Novo Horizonte*, São Paulo, Ano II, No. 19 (March).

————— (1948). "Os Jovens Aconselham," *O Novo Horizonte*, São Paulo, Ano III, No. 25 (July).

Camargo, Arnaldo de (1949). *O Novo Horizonte*, São Paulo, Ano III, No. 36 (May).

Camargo, José Francisco (1952). *Crescimento da População no Estado de São Paulo e seus Aspectos Econômicos*, Faculdade de Filosofia, Ciências e Letras da Universidade de São Paulo.

Cambara, Joaquim (1918). "Deputado de Côr," *O Bandeirante*, São Paulo, Ano I, No. 2 (August).

Campos, Geraldo (1947). Interviewed in *O Novo Horizonte*, São Paulo, Ano II, No. 15 (October).

Campos, Sofia (1946). "Muito Pouco Para Nos," *O Novo Horizonte*, São Paulo, Ano I, No. 5 (September).

Cardoso, Fernando Henrique (1951). Study on the Negro Press in São Paulo, unpublished manuscript.

―――― (1960). "Condições Sociais da Industrialização de São Paulo," *Revista Brasiliense*, No. 28 (March–April).

―――― (1962). *Capitalismo a Escravidão no Brasil Meridional;* Difusao Europeia do Livro, São Paulo.

――――, and Octavio Ianni (1960). *Côr e Mobilidade Social em Florianópolis.*

Cenni, Franco (n.d.). *Italianos no Brasil*, Livraria Martins Editôra, São Paulo.

Chaves, Elias Antonia Pacheco e, et al. (1888). *Provincia de São Paulo, Relatório Apresentado as Exmo. Sr. Presidente de São Paulo pelos Senhores Dr. Elias Antonio Pacheco e Chaves (Presidente) Dr. Domingos José Nogueira Jaguaribe Filho, Dr. Joaquim José Vieira de Carvalho, Engenheiro Adolfo Augusto Pinto, Abilio da Silva Marques, Leroy King Book-Walter*, Tipografia King, São Paulo.

O Clarim da Alvorada (n.d.). "O Dia da Mae Preta," editorial, São Paulo, No. 8.

―――― (1931). Editorial about the Dia da Mae Preta, *O Clarim da Alvorada*, Ano VIII, No. 36 (September).

―――― (1931). "Frente Negra do Brasil," editorial, São Paulo, No. 37 (November).

―――― (1931). "O Nosso Dever é Enfileirarmos," São Paulo, Ano VIII, No. 36 (September).

―――― (1936). "A Legenda do Século," editorial, São Paulo, Ano VIII, No. 36 (September).

Cohen, A. K. (1956). *Delinquent Boys*, Routledge & Kegan Paul, Ltd., London.

Costa, Alcides da (1928). "Educação," *O Clarim da Alvorada*, São Paulo, Ano I, No. 8 (September).

Costa, Justiaiano (1936). Manuscript of speech before the Frente Negra Brasileira, p. 5 (September).

―――― (1936). "Saudação aos Homens Negros do Brasil," *A Voz da Raça*, São Paulo, Ano III, No. 58 (October).

―――― (1936). Unpublished manuscript of a speech delivered as president of the Frente Negra Brasileira at a ceremony on September 20.

Couty, Louis (1881). *L'Eslavage au Brésil*, Librairie de Guillaumin et

Cie., Paris; (1884) *Le Bresil em 1884*, Faro & Lino, Editeurs, Rio de Janeiro.

Cox, Oliver Cromwell (1948). *Caste, Class & Race: A Study in Social Dynamics*, Doubleday & Co., N. Y.

Davatz, Thomas (1941). *Memorias de um Colono no Brasil (1850)*, Livraria Martins Editôra, São Paulo. Introduction by Sergio Buarque de Holanda.

Davie, Maurice R. (1949). *Negroes in American Society*, McGraw-Hill, N. Y.

Denis, Pierre (1928). *Le Brésil du XXe Siècle*, 7th printing, Librairie Armand Colin, Paris.

Departamento de Estatística do Estado (1961). *Situação Demográfica* (Separata do Anuario, 1961), São Paulo.

Departamento de Estatística do Estado de São Paulo, Governo do Estado de São Paulo (1963). *Situação Demográfica*. Município de São Paulo, 1961, São Paulo.

Dias, Everardo (1955). "Lutas Operarias no Estado de Sao Paulo," *Revista Brasiliense*, São Paulo, No. 1 (September–October).

―――― (1962). *Historia das Lutas Sociais no Brasil*, Editora Edaglit, São Paulo.

Dobzhansky, Theodosius (1956). *The Biological Basis of Human Freedom*, Columbia University Press, N. Y.

――――, and Allen, G. (1956). "Does Natural Selection Continue to Operate in Modern Mankind?" *American Anthropologist*, Vol. 58, No. 4 (August).

Dollard, John (1957). *Caste and Class in a Southern Town*, 2nd ed., Doubleday Anchor Books, N. Y.

Doyle, Bertram Wilbur (1937). *The Etiquette of Race Relations in the South*, University of Chicago Press, Chicago. Preface by R. E. Park.

Durkheim, E. (1902). *De la Division du Travail Social*, 2nd ed., Felix Alcan, Editeur, Paris.

Eduardo, Octavio da Costa (1948). *The Negro in Northern Brazil*, Univ. of Washington Press, Washington.

Ellis, Jr., Alfredo (1933). *Pedras Lascadas*, 2nd ed., Editôra Piratininga, São Paulo.

―――― (1934). *Populações Paulistas*, Companhia Editôra Nacional, São Paulo.

Fernandes, Florestan (1959). *Fundamentos Empiricos da Explicação Sociologica*, Companhia Editôra Nacional, São Paulo.

―――― (1960). "Caracteres Rurais e Urbanos na Formação e Desenvolvimento da Cidade de São Paulo," Chap. VI of *Mudanças Sociais No Brasil*.

―――― (1960). *Ensaios de Sociologia Geral e Aplicada*, Livraria Pioneira Editôra, São Paulo.

―――― (1960). "Representações coletivas sobre o Negro: O Negro na Tradição Oral," in *Mudanças Socias no Brasil*, Chap. XIII, Difusão Europeia do Livro, São Paulo.

―――― (1961). *Folclore e Mudança Social na Cidade de São Paulo*,

Editôra Anhembi, S. A., São Paulo.

————, and Bastide, Roger (1959). *Brancos e Negros em São Paulo,* Companhia Editôra Nacional, São Paulo.

Fernandes, Francisco (1960). *Dicionário Brasileiro Contemporâneo,* Editôra Globo, Porto Alegré.

Ferreira, Hipatia Damasceno, Ernani Timotéo de Barros e José Etrog (1950). "A Composição da População Segundo a Côr, no Conjunto da Federação" *in Estudos sobre a Composição da População do Brasil Segundo a Côr,* I. B. G. E., Rio de Janeiro.

Ferreira, Vicente (1931). "O Dia de Fé da Raça Negra," *O Clarim da Alvorada,* São Paulo, Ano VIII, No. 32 (May).

———— (1931). "Raça Negra de Pé . . . ," *O Clarim da Alvorada,* São Paulo, Ano VIII, No. 35 (August).

Folha Da Manhã (1959). A Discriminação Racial Dificulta a Colocação de Empregados em São Paulo," *A Folha da Manhã,* São Paulo, 22-V (1959).

Frazier, E. Franklin (1949). *The Negro in the United States,* Macmillan Co., N. Y.

Frazier, F. (1955). *Bourgeoisie Noir,* Librairie Plon, Paris.

Freyer, Hans (1944). *La Sociologia, Ciencia de la Realidad.* Trans. by F. Ayala, Editorial Losada, S. A., Buenos Aires.

Freyre, Gilberto (1938). *Casa Grande e Senzala,* Schmidt—Editor, Rio de Janeiro.

———— (1936). *Sobrados e Mucambos,* Decadência do Patriarcado Rural no Brasil, Companhia Editôra Nacional, São Paulo.

Fromm, Eric (1956). *The Sane Society,* Routledge & Kegan Paul, Ltd., London.

Furtado, Celso (1959). *Formação Econômica do Brasil,* Editôra Fundo de Cultura, S. A., Rio de Janeiro.

Gerth, H., and Mills, C. Wright (1953). *Character and Social Structure,* Harcourt, Brace & Co., N. Y.

Ginsberg, Aniela Meyer (1955). "Pesquisas sôbre as Atitudes de um Grupo de Escolares de São Paulo em Relação com as Criancas de Côr," in *Relações Entre Negros e Brancos em São Paulo,* Editôra Anhembi Ltda., São Paulo, pp. 311–61.

Goldstein, K. (1951). *La Structure de l'Organisme,* trans. by E. Burkhardt and J. Kuntz, Gallimard, Paris.

Guimarães, Ruth (1948). "Nós, os Negros," *O Novo Horizonte,* São Paulo, Ano II, No. 19 (March).

Gunplowicz, Louis (1896). *Précis de Sociologie,* translated by Charles Baye, Leon Chailley, Editeur, Paris.

Harding, J., and B. Kutner (1954). "Prejudice and Ethnic Relations," in G. Lindzey, ed., *Handbook of Social Psychology,* Addison-Wesley Publishing Co., Reading, Massachusetts. Vol. II, Cap. 27.

Herskovits, Melville J. (1941). *The Myth of the Negro Past,* Harper & Bros., New York.

———— (1955). "The Social Organization of the Candomblé," *Anais do XXXI Congresso Internacional de Americanistas,* Editôra Anhembi, São Paulo, Vol. I, pp. 505–32.

Horney, Karen (1939). *New Ways in Psychoanalysis*, W. W. Norton & Co., N. Y.

Ianni, Octavio (1960). "Fatôres Humanos da Industrialização no Brasil," *Revista Brasiliense*, No. 30, São Paulo, pp. 50–66.

——— (1962). As Metamorfoses do Escravo, Difusão Europeia do Livro, São Paulo.

"L'Immigrazione Italiana dal 1886 all Oggi, Il Lavoro nelle 'Fazendas' e la Formazione della Piccola Proprieta" (1936). In *Cinquantani di Lavoro* degli Italiani in Brasile, Vol. I—Lo Stato di S. Paolo, Societa Editrice Italiana, São Paulo.

Instituto Brasilero de Geografia e Estatistica (1940). *Recenseamento de 1940*, Rio de Janeiro.

——— (1949). *Estudos sôbre a Fecundidade e Prolificidade da Mulher no Brasil, no conjunto da População e nos Diversos Grupos de Côr*, I.B.G.E., Rio de Janeiro.

Instituto Brasileiro de Geografia de Estado de São Paulo (1962). *Sinopse Preliminar do Censo Demografico*, Instituto Brasileiro de Geografia e Estatistica, Rio de Janeiro.

Jesus, Maria Carolina de. *Quarto de Despejo, Diário de uma Favelada*, edited by Audalio Dantas, 4ª ed., Livraria Francisco Alves (Editôra Paulo de Azevedo Ltda.), São Paulo. (The diary begins on July 15, 1955, and ends on January 1, 1960).

Johnson, Charles S. (1948). *Patterns of Negro Segregation*, Harper & Bros., N. Y.

Joviano, Raul (1947). "Marcha no Mesmo Sentido," *Alvorada*, São Paulo, Ano III, No. 22 (January).

Krech, D., and R. S. Crutchfield. *Theory and Problems of Social Psychology*.

Kuper, Leo, Hilstan Watts, and Ronald Davies (1958). *Durban: A Study in Racial Ecology*, Jonathan Cape, London.

Landtman, Gunnar (1938). *The Origin of the Inequality of the Social Classes*, Kegan Paul, Trench, Trubner & Co., Ltda., London.

Leal, Victor Nunes (1948). *Coronelismo, Enxada e Voto*, Edição da Revista Forense, Rio de Janeiro.

Leclerc, Max (1942). *Cartas do Brasil*, translated with preface and notes by Sergio Milliet, Companhia Editôra Nacional, São Paulo.

Leite, Dante Moreira (1950). "Preconceito Racial e Patriotismo em Seis Livros Didaticos Primarios Brasileiros," *Boletim de Psicologia*, No. 3, Faculdade de Filosofia, Ciências e Letras da Universidade de São Paulo, São Paulo, pp. 206–31.

Leite, Hercules de F. (1918). "Preconceitos de Raça," *O Alfinete*, São Paulo, Ano 1, No. 2 (3 de setembro).

Leite, José Correia. *O Alvorecer de Uma Ideologia*, manuscript to be published in the series "Cultura Negra" by the Associação Cultural do Negro.

——— (1929). "A Mocidade Negra," *O Clarim da Alvorada*, São Paulo, Ano VI, No. 15 (April).

——— (1929). "A Mocidade Negra," *O Clarim da Alvorada*, São Paulo, Ano VI, No. 16 (May).

Leite, José Correia (1930). "O Grande Problema Nacional," *O Clarim da Alvorada*, São Paulo, Ano VII, No. 31 (December).
—— (1930). "Sera o Inimigo do Negro o Proprio Negro?" *O Clarim da Alvorada*, São Paulo, Ano II, No. 28 (July).
—— (1933). "Um Ano de Silêncio," *O Clarim da Alvorada*, São Paulo, Ano X, No. 42 (May).
—— (1935). in *O Clarim da Alvorada*. São Paulo, Ano I, No. 4 (May).
—— (1946). "Atualidade do Negro Brasileiro," *Alvorada*, São Paulo, Ano II, No. 13 (October).
—— (1946). "Porque Lutamos," *Alvorada*, São Paulo (September).
—— (1947). "Preconceito, Casa Grande e Senzala," *Alvorada*, São Paulo, Ano II, No. 18 (June).
Liga Dos Amigos Da Luta (1931). "O que Necessitamos," *O Clarim da Alvorada*, São Paulo, Ano VIII, No. 37 (November).
—— (1932). "Ideias Contemporaneas," *O Clarim da Alvorada*, São Paulo, Ano IX, No. 39 (January).
Linton, Ralph (1940). Three essays in *Acculturation in Seven American Indian Tribes*, D. Appleton Century Co., N. Y. Editôra, São Paulo.
—— (1943). *O Homem*. Translated by L. Vilela. Livraria Martins
Linton, Ralph, ed. (1945). *The Science of Man in the World Crisis*, Columbia University Press, New York.
Lobato, Luis (1946). "Partidos Politicos da Raça Negra," *Senzala*, São Paulo, Ano I, No. 3, pp. 2–3 (April).
Lobo, Haddock, and Alois, Irene (1941). *O Negro na Vida Social Brasileira*, S.E. Panorama Ltda., São Paulo.
Lobo da Silva, Arthur (1928). "A Anthropologia no Exercito Brasileiro," *Archivos do Museu Nacional*, Vol. XXX, Rio de Janeiro.
Lowrie, Samuel Harman (1938). "Fontes Bibliograficas das Estatisticas de População no Estado de São Paulo," *Boletim Bibliográfico*, São Paulo, No. 1, pp. 76–77.
—— (1938). *Imigração e Crescimento da População no Estado de São Paulo*, Edição da Escola Livre de Sociologia e Politica, São Paulo.
—— (1937). "Ascendencia das Crianças dos Parques Infantis," *Revista do Arquivo Municipal*, Vols. XXXIX e XLI, São Paulo.
—— (1938). "O Elemento Negro a População de São Paulo," *Revista do Arquivo Municipal*, Ano IV, Vol. XLVIII, São Paulo (June).
—— (1938). *Imigração e Crescimento da População no Estado de São Paulo*.
—— (1938). "Origem da População da Cidade de São Paulo e Differenciação das Classes Sociais," *Revista do Arquivo Municipal*, Ano IV, Vol. XLIII, São Paulo.
Lucrecio, Francisco (1936). "A Constante Fundação de Nucleos Frentenegrinos . . . ," *A Voz da Raça*. São Paulo, Ano III, No. 57 (September).
—— (1936). "O Preto que Tem Alma Própria," *A Voz da Raça*, São Paulo, Ano III, No. 60 (December).

Machado, José de Alcantara (1905). *Suicidios na Capital de São Paulo (1876–1904)*, Gerke, São Paulo.

Madre de Deus, Frei Gaspar da (n.d.). *Memórias para a História da Capitania de São Vicente, Hoje Chamada de São Paulo*, etc., 3rd ed., Weizflog Irmãos, São Paulo e Rio de Janeiro.

Malheiros, Agostinho Marques Perdigão (1866). *A Escravidão no Brasil: Ensaio Historio-Juridico-Social*, Tipografia Nacional, Rio de Janeiro, Vol. I, pp. 32–33.

Malinowski, B. (1944). *A Scientific Theory of Culture and Other Essays*, University of North Carolina, Chapel Hill.

Mannheim, Karl (1950). *Ideologia e Utopia*, trans. by E. Willems, Editôra Globo, Porto Alegre.

Martuscelli, Carolina (1950). "Uma Pesquisa sobre Aceitação de Grupos Nacionais, Grupos "Raciais" e Grupos Regionais em São Paulo," *Boletim No. 3 da Cadeira de Psicología*, Faculdade de Filosofia, Ciências e Letras da Universidade de São Paulo, São Paulo.

Matos, Dirceu Lino de (1958). "O Parque Industrial Paulistano," in *A Cidade de São Paulo*, Associação dos Geografos Brasileiros, Companhia Editôra Nacional, São Paulo, Vol. III, Chap. I.

Matos, Odilon Nogueira de (1958). "São Paulo no Século XIX," in *A Cidade de São Paulo*, Associação dos Geografos Brasileiros, Companhia Editôra Nacional, São Paulo, Vol. II, Chap. II.

Mays, J. B. (1954). *Growing Up in the City*, The University Press of Liverpool, Liverpool, England.

Mello e Souza, Candido (1951). *A Familia Brasileira*, unpublished manuscript in Portuguese. Published in English in T. Lynn Smith and A. Marchant, *Brazil: Portrait of Half a Continent*, Dryden Press, New York.

Mennucci, Sud (1938). *O Precursor do Abolicionismo no Brasil: Luis Gama*, Companhia Editôra Nacional, São Paulo.

Merton, R. K. (1949). *Social Theory and Social Structure*, The Free Press of Glencoe, Ill.

Milliet, Sergio (1940). Three articles at beginning of year in *O Estado de São Paulo;* republished under general title "A Formula de Martius" in Roteiro do Café e Outros Ensaios.

—— (1941). *Roteiro do Café e Outros Ensaios*, 3a. ed. revista e aumentada. Vol. XXV da Coleção do Departamento de Cultura, São Paulo.

Monbeig, Pierre (1953). *La Croissance de la Ville de São Paulo*, Institut et Revue de Geographie Alpine, Grenoble.

Moraes, Evaristo de (1924). *A Campanha Abolicionista (1879–1888)* Livraria Leite Ribeiro, Rio de Janeiro.

Morais, Gervasio de (1930). "O Sacerdocio da Fé," *O Clarim da Alvorada*, São Paulo, Ano VII, No. 26 (13 de maio).

Moreira, Renato Jardim. "Brancos em Bailes de Negros," *Anhembi*, São Paulo, Ano VI, No. 71, Vol. XXIV, Outubro de 1956, pp. 274–288.

——, and José Corrêa Leite (n.d.). *Movimentos Socias no Meio Negro*, unpublished manuscript.

Morse, Richard M. (1954). *De Comunidade a Metropole: Biografia de São Paulo*, translation by M. A. Madeira Kerberg, *Comissão do IV Centenário da Cidade de São Paulo*. Ser de Comemorviçoasoes Culturais, São Paulo.

Mortara, Giorgio (1951). "Natalidade e Mortalidade no Municipio de São Paulo nos Anos de 1939 a 1949." *Estudos Demograficos*, No. 4, Laboratório de Estatistico do Instituto Brasileiro de Geografia e Estatistica, Rio de Janeiro.

————— (1952). *Estudos sobre a Natalidade e a Mortalidade no Brasil*, Rio de Janeiro.

————— (1948). *Estimativas das Taxas de Natalidade para o Brasil, as Unidades da Federaçaõ e as Principais Capitais*, I.B.G.E., Rio de Janeiro.

————— (1950). *Estudos sobre a Composição da População do Brasil Segundo a Côr*, I.B.G.E., Rio de Janeiro.

————— (1951). *Pesquisas sobre os Diversos Grupos de Côr nas Populações do Estado de São Paulo e do Distrito Federal*, I.B.G.E., Rio de Janeiro.

————— (1956). "A Fecundidade das Mulheres e a Sobrevivencia dos Filhos nos Diversos Grupos de Côr da População do Brasil," *Estudos Demograficos* No. 173 (mimeo) Laboratório de Estatistica do Instituto Brasileiro de Geografia e Estatistica, Rio de Janeiro (August).

————— (1956). *Pesquisas sobre a Mortalidade no Brasil.* 3a serie, I.B.G.E., Rio de Janeiro.

————— (1961). "O Desenvolvimento da População Preta e Parda no Brasil," *Contribuições para o Estudo da Demografia no Brasil*, Instituto Brasileiro de Geografia e Estatistica, Rio de Janeiro.

————— (1962). "A Fecundidade da Mulher nos Diversos Grupos de Côr, segundo as Unidades da Federação," *Estudos Demograficos* No. 268 (mimeo) Laboratório de Estatistica do Inst. Brasileiro de Geografia e Estatistica, Rio de Janeiro (May).

Mortara, Valerio (1951). "A População do Municipio de São Paulo Segundo a Côr," *Pesquisas sôbre os Diversos Grupos de Côr nas Populações do Estado de São Paulo e do Distrito Federal*, Estudos de Estatistica Teorica e Aplicado series No. 12, Instituto Brasileiro de Geografia e Estatistica.

Mourão, Edwald (1951). "A População do Estado de São Paulo segundo a Cor," *Pesquisas sobre os Diversos Grupos de Côr nas Populações do Estado de São Paulo e do Distrito Federal*, Estudos de Estatistica Teorica e Aplicada series, No. 12, Instituto Brasileiro de Geografia e Estatistica.

Mussolini, Gioconda, and Roger Bastide (n.d.) "Os Suicidios em São Paulo Segundo a Côr," *Estudos Afro-Brasileiros* 2ª serie, Boletim No. 2, Cadeira de Sociologia I, Faculdade de Filosofia, Ciências e Letras, Universidade de São Paulo, São Paulo.

Myrdal, Gunnar, Richard Sterner, and Arnold Rose (1944). *An American Dilemma: The Negro Problem and Modern Democracy*, 2 vols., 2nd ed., Harper & Bros., New York.

Nabuco, Joaquim (1883). *O Abolicionismo.* Typ. Abraham Kingdom & Co., London.

—— (1947). *Minha Formação,* Instituto Progresso Editorial, São Paulo.

Nogueira, Almeida (1888). Speech before the Provincial Assembly of São Paulo, *O Correio Paulistano* (8 de Abril).

Nogueira, Oracy (1942). "Atitude Desfavoravel de Alguns Anunciantes de São Paulo em Relação aos Empregados de Côr," *Sociologia,* Vol. IV, No. 4, São Paulo, pp. 328–58.

—— (1955). "Preconceito de Marca e Preconceito Racial de Origem. Sugestão de um Quadro de Referencia para a Interpretaçao do Material sobre Relações Racais no Brasil," *Anais do XXXI: Congresso de Americanistas,* August 23–28, 1954, São Paulo, Vol. 1, Herbert Baldus ed., Editôra Anhembi, São Paulo, pp. 409–34.

—— (1955). "Relacoes Raciais no Municipio de Itapetininga," in *Relaçoĕs Entre Negros e Brancos em São Paulo,* Editôra Anhembi Ltda., São Paulo, pp. 362–554.

Novicow, J. (1893). *Les Luttes entre Sociètés Humaines et Leurs Phases Successives,* Felix Alcan, Ed., Paris.

Novo Horizonte (1951). "Cultura, Base Essencial para o Progresso," (April and May).

Oliveira, A. (1918). "Aos Nossos Leitores," *O Alfinete,* São Paulo, Ano I, No. 2 (September 3).

Oliveira, Eusebio de (1932). "Escola!" *Progresso,* São Paulo, Ano IV, No. 48 (April 30).

Oliveira de Viana, F. J. (1952). *Populações Meridionais do Brasil,* 5ª ed. Livraria José Olympio Editôra, Rio de Janeiro (1st. ed. 1918).

Park, Robert Ezra (1950). *Race and Culture,* The Free Press, Glencoe, Illinois.

Parsons, Talcott (1952). *The Social System,* Tavistock Publications Ltd., New York.

Patrocínio, José do (1882). *Conferencia Publica do Jornalista José do Patrocínio Feita no Teatro Politeama em Sessão de Confederação Abolicionista de 17 de Maio de 1885,* Folheto No. 8, Tipografia Central, Rio de Janeiro.

Patterson, Sheila (1953). *Colour and Culture in South Africa: A Study of the Cape Coloured People within the Social Structure of the Union of South Africa,* Routledge and Kegan Paul Ltd., London.

Pierson, Donald (1945). *Brancos e Pretos na Bahia.* Companhia Editôra Nacional, São Paulo.

Pinto, L. A. da Costa (1953). *O Negro no Rio de Janeiro,* Relações de Raça numa Sociedade em Mudanca, Companhia Editôra Nacional, São Paulo.

Prado, Orlando de Almeida (1928). Speech published in Estado de São Paulo, *Annaes da Camara dos Deputados,* Vol. I.

Prado, Caio, Jr. (1942). *Historia Econômica do Brasil,* Editôra, Brasiliense Ltda., São Paulo. *Formação do Brasil Contemporâneo,* Colônia Livraria Martins Editôra, São Paulo.

Petrone, Pasquale (1953). "As Industrias Paulistanas e os Fatores de Sua Expansão," Boletim *Paulista de Geografia,* São Paulo, No. 114 (Julho), pp. 26–37.

Pipkin, C. W. "Poor Laws," *Encyclopaedia of Social Sciences,* Vol. XII, pp. 230–34.

Powdermaker, H. (1944). *Probing Our Prejudices,* Harper & Bros., N. Y.

Queiroz, Maria Izaura Pereira de (1957). "O Mandonismo Local na Vida Politica Brasileira," in *Estudos de Sociologia e Historia,* Instituto Nacional de Estudos Pedagogicos—Anhembi, Editôra Anhembi Ltda., São Paulo.

Radcliffe-Brown, A. R. (1952). *Structure and Function in Primitive Society,* Cohen & West Ltd., London.

Raide, Elias (1958). Articles in *Diário da Noite,* São Paulo, from January 21 to April 9.

Rajovia. See Amaral, Raul Joviano (1936).

Ramos, Arthur (1938). "O Espirito Associativo do Negro Brasileiro," *Revista do Arquivo Municipal,* Ano IV, Vol. XLVII, São Paulo, pp. 105–26.

Ribeiro, Darcy (1962). *A Politica Indigenista Brasileira,* Serviço de Informação Agricola do Ministério da Agricultura, Rio de Janeiro.

Ribeiro, René (1952). *Cultos Afro-Brasileiros do Recifé: Um Estudo de Ajustamento Social* Instituto Joaquim Nabuco, Recife.

Rodrigues, Pedro (1933). "A Frente Negra Brasileira," *A Voz da Raça,* São Paulo, Ano I, No. 11 (3 de Junho).

Rohrer, J. H., and Sherif, M. (1951), ed., *Social Psychology at the Crossroads,* Harper & Bros., N. Y.

Rose, A. M. (1951). *L'Origine de Prejuges,* UNESCO, Paris.

——— (1951). *Race Prejudice and Discrimination: Readings in Intergroup Relations in the United States,* Alfred A. Knopf, N. Y.

Ross, Edward Alsworth (1938). *Principles of Sociology,* 3rd ed., Appleton-Century-Crofts, Inc. N. Y.

Rugendas, Joao Mauricio (1940) (1835 1st ed.). *Viagem Pitoresca ataves do Brasil,* translated by Sergio Milliet, Livraria Martins Editôra, São Paulo.

Saenger, G. (1953). *The Social Psychology of Prejudice; Achieving Intercultural Understanding and Cooperation in a Democracy,* Harper & Bros., N. Y.

Saint-Hilaire, Auguste de (1851). *Voyage dans les Provinces de Saint-Paul et Sainte Catherine,* A. Bertrand, Libraire Editeur, Paris.

Santana, Edgard T. (1951). "Preconceito de Côr," in *Relações entre Pretos e Brancos em São Paulo,* Edgard T. Santana, São Paulo.

Santana, J. Guaraná de (1933). "Arregimentem-se Negros do Brasil: Na Republica e pela Republica," *Brasil Novo. Orgão Socialista,* São Paulo, Ano I, No. 1 (13 de abril).

Santos, A. J. Veiga dos (1927). "Palavras aos Pais Negros," *O Clarim da Alvorada,* special number in magazine format, São Paulo, Ano IV, No. 33 (May 13), p. 3.

Santos, Arlindo Veiga dos (1929). "Congresso da Mocidade Negra Brasileira: Mensagem aos Negroes Brasileiros," *O Clarim da Alvorada*, São Paulo, Ano VI, No. 17 (June 9).

—— (1931). *Manifesto á Gente Negra Brasileira*, pamphlet (February 3).

—— (1931). *Manifesto á Gente Negra Brasileira* (December 2, 1931).

Santos, Isaetino B. Veiga dos (1932). *Marieta a Heroina*, São Paulo.

—— (1932). "Patricios Negros!" *Progresso*, São Paulo, Ano IV, No. 45 (January 31).

—— (1933). "Liberdade Utopica," *A Voz da Raça*, São Paulo, Ano. 1, No. 9 (May 13).

Santos, J. Maria dos (1942). *Os Republicanos Paulistas e a Abolição*, Livraria Martins, São Paulo.

Santos, Manuel Antonio dos (1935). "Filantropia Escravocrata," *O Clarim da Alvorado*, São Paulo, Ano I, No. 3 (April).

—— (1935). "Trajetoria do Ideal," *Tribuna Negra*, São Paulo, Ano I, No. 1 (1st 2 weeks of September).

Santos, Ovidio P. dos (1946). "Eis aqui uma Concretização . . . ," *O Novo Horizonte*, São Paulo, Ano I, No. 1 (May).

—— (1948). "Eis a Politica a Ser Adotada," *O Novo Horizonte*, São Paulo, Ano II, No. 19 (March).

Schaden, E. (1962). *Aspectos Fundamentais da Cultura Guarani*, Difusão Europeia do Livro, São Paulo.

Schapera, I. (1941). *Married Life in an African Tribe*, Sheridan House, New York.

Schmidt, Afonso (1941). *A Marcha Romance da Abolição*, Editôra Anchieta, Ltda., São Paulo.

Secretaria de Agricultura, Indústria e Comércio (1937), "Movimento Migratório no Estado de São Paulo" D.C.T.I. *Boletim da Directória de Terras*, Colonização e Imigração, Ano 1, No. 1, October.

Secretaria de Agricultura, Indústria e Comércio (1940), "Movimento Imigratório do Estado de São Paulo: Quadros Estatísticos Básicos," *Boletim do Serviço de Imigração e Colonização*, No. 2 (October), São Paulo.

Sentinela Negra (1933). "Negros, Alerta!" *O Patricínio*, Campinas, Ano I, No. 2 (June 11).

Serra, Antonio de Campos (1887). Sections of a study that appeared in *A Provincia de São Paulo* (Nov. 13).

Serviço Sanitário (n.d.). *Anuario Demográfico*.

Simonsen, Roberto C. (1938). "As Consequencias Economicas da Abolição," *Revista do Arquivo Municipal*, Ano IV, Vol. XLVII, São Paulo. (1939) *Brazil's Industrial Evolution*. Escola Livre de Sociologia e Politica, São Paulo.

Smith, T. Lynn, and Alexander Marchant, eds. (1951). *Brazil: Portrait of Half a Continent*, Dryden Press, N. Y.

Smith, T. Lynn (1954). *Brazil: People and Institution*. Revised ed., Louisiana State University Press, Baton Rouge.

476 BIBLIOGRAPHY

Sociedade Brasileira Contra a Escravidão (n.d.). *Manifesto da Sociedade Brasileira contra a Escravidão*, Tipografia de G. Leuzinger & Filhos, Rio de Janeiro.

Sousa, G. G. (1933). "Com o Brasil Pela Raça," *O Clarim da Alvorado*, São Paulo, Ano X, No. 42 (May 13).

Sousa, Jose Egidio de (1931). "De Ontem a Hoje," *O Clarim da Alvorada*, São Paulo, Ano VIII, No. 35 (August).

Sousa, Luis de (1929). "O Momento," *O Clarim da Alvorada*, São Paulo, Ano VI, No. 15 (April 7).

—— (1933). "Como Pregar a Uniao," *O Clarim da Alvorada*, São Paulo, Ano X, No. 42 (May 13).

Souza, Everardo Vallim Perceira de (1946). "Reminiscencias—Em torno de Antonio Prado," in *Centenário do Conselheiro Antonio da Silva Prado*. Revista das Tribunais, Ltda., São Paulo.

Souza, Paula (1888). Carta do Conselheiro Paula Souza ao Dr. Cesar Zama escrito 19 de Marco, 1888, *Provincia de São Paulo* (April 3).

Souza, Rafael Paula (1936). "Biotipologia dos Universitarios Paulistas," *Revista de Biologia e Higiene*, Vol. 7, No. 1, pp. 25–40.

—— (1937). "Contribuição a *Etnologia* Paulista," *Revista do Arquivo Municipal*, Vol. XXXI, pp. 95–105.

Straten-Ponthoz, Le Comte Auguste von der (1854). *Le Budget du Bresil ou Recherches sur les Ressources de cet Empire dans les Rapports avec les Rapports avec les Interets Europeens du Commerce et de l'Emigration*, Librairie d'Amyot. Editeur, 3 vols., Paris.

Lo Stato Di S. Paolo (1936). "L'Immigrazione Italiana dal 1886 all Oggi: Il Lavoro nelle 'Fazendas e la Formazione della Piccola Proprieta," in *Cinquantani di Lavoro degli Italiani in Brasile*. Vol. I., Societa Editrice Italiana, São Paulo.

Taunay, Alfonso de (1939). *Historia do Café no Brasil*, Rio de Janeiro.

Thompson, Edgard T., ed. (1939). *Race Relations and the Race Problems*, Duke University Press, Durham, North Carolina.

Turner, R. H., and L. M. Killian (1957). *Collective Behavior*, Prentice-Hall, Inc., Englewood Cliffs, New Jersey.

Toledo Piza, Antonio de (1894). *Relatório Apresentado ao Cidadão. Dr. Cezario Motta Junior, Secretario dos Negocios do Interior do Estado de Sao Paulo pelo Direitor da Repartição da Estadistica e Arquivo Dr. Antonio de Toledo Piza em 31 de julho de 1894*. Rio de Janeiro: Tip. Leuzinger Secretaria dos Negocios do Interior do Estado de São Paulo.

Veiga, João Pedro (1896). *Estudo Econômico e Financeiro sobre o Estado de São Paulo*, Tipografia do Diario Oficial, São Paulo.

A Voz da Raça (1933). "A Frente Negra Brasileira e a Instrução," São Paulo, Ano I, No. 2 (March 25).

—— (1935). "Pela Liberdade da Raça," São Paulo, Ano III, No. 46 (June).

Wagley, Charles, ed. (n.d.). *Races et Classes dans le Brésil Rural*, UNESCO, Paris.

Wagley, Charles, ed. (1963). *An Introduction to Brazil,* Columbia University Press, New York and London.

Warner, W. Lloyd (1936). "American Caste and Class," *American Journal of Sociology,* XLII (September).

—— (1941). Preface to Allison Davis, Burleigh Gardner, and Mary R. Gardner, *Deep South,* University of Chicago Press, Chicago.

—— (1945). Methodological Note to St. Clair Drake and Horace R. Clayton, *Black Metropolis: A Study of Negro Life in a Northern City,* Harcourt, Brace & Co., N. Y.

—— (1952). *Structure of American Life,* University of Edinburgh Press, Edinburgh.

Werneck, Francisco Peixto de Lacerda (1878). *Memoria sobre a Fundação e o Custeio de uma Fazenda na Provincia do Rio de Janeiro,* 3rd ed., annotated by Dr. Luiz Peixoto de Lacerda Werneck, Eduardo & Henrique Laemmert, Rio de Janeiro.

Wilk, A. José da Costa (1888). Article in *A Provincia de São Paulo,* May 5.

Willems, Emilio (1949). "Race Attitudes in Brazil," *The American Journal of Sociology,* Vol. LIV, No. 5 (March), pp. 402–8.

—— (1950). *Dicionário de Sociologia,* Editôra Globo, Porto Alegre.

——, and Baldus H. *Dicionário de Etnologia e Sociologia.*

Williamson, Robert C. (1935). "Race Relations in South Africa," *Sociology and Social Research,* Vol. 39, No. 3 (January–February).

Wirth, Louis (1956). "The Problem of Minority Groups," in *Community Life and Social Policy, Selected Papers by Louis Wirth,* University of Chicago Press, pp. 237–60. Also in Linton (1945, pp. 347–72) and in Turner and Killian (1957, pp. 321 ff.).

INDEX